T5-BBB-280

THE GROWTH OF WORKING CLASS REFORMISM IN MID-VICTORIAN ENGLAND

THE WORKING CLASS IN EUROPEAN HISTORY

Editorial Advisers

Standish Meacham
Joan Scott
Reginald Zelnik

Books in the Series

The Logic of Solidarity: Artisans and Industrial Workers in Three French Towns, 1871–1914   *Michael P. Hanagan*

Ben Tillett: Portrait of a Labour Leader   *Jonathan Schneer*

Sweated Industries and Sweated Labor: The London Clothing Trades, 1860–1914   *James A. Schmiechen*

Divisions of Labour: Skilled Workers and Technological Change in Nineteenth-Century Britain   *edited by Royden Harrison and Jonathan Zeitlin*

The Growth of Working-Class Reformism in Mid-Victorian England   *Neville Kirk*

The Growth of Working Class Reformism in Mid-Victorian England

Neville Kirk

UNIVERSITY OF ILLINOIS PRESS
Urbana and Chicago

© 1985 Neville Kirk

First published in the United States of America by
University of Illinois Press, 54 East Gregory Drive,
Box 5081, Station A, Champaign, Illinois 61820

Manufactured in Great Britain

Library of Congress Cataloging in Publication Data

Kirk, Neville, 1947–
  The growth of working-class reformism in mid-Victorian England.

  (The Working class in European history)
  Includes index.
  1. Labor and laboring classes — England — Cheshire — Political
activity — History — 19th century.   2. Labor and laboring
classes — England — Lancashire — Political activity — History — 19th
century.   I. Title.   II. Series.
  HD8397.C47K57   1985   322'.2'094271   84–24147
  ISBN 0–252–01223–2

CONTENTS

TABLES

To Bob and Kate, and Norale and (the late) Frank Kirk

PREFACE

The general focus of this book rests upon changes and continuities in the direction and structure of the labour movement, workers' consciousness and social relations between the second and third quarters of the nineteenth century. More specifically, evidence concerning developments in the cotton districts of Lancashire and Cheshire is gathered together in an attempt to shed new light upon the easing of class tensions and the growth of reformism in England after the mid-1840s.

Attention is concentrated upon Lancashire and Cheshire for three major reasons. Firstly, notwithstanding internal complexities and variations of experience, the cotton districts provide dramatic, in some cases classic, examples of important shifts or 'breaks' in working-class attitudes and behaviour and class relations at mid-century. The precise nature and extent of such shifts will be examined in detail during the course of this study. For the moment it is sufficient to record that Chartism failed after the mid- and late-1840s to recapture much of its earlier dynamism and mass appeal in the cotton towns. By the 1860s Conservatism enjoyed a mass following; and the majority of labour leaders had moved into Liberalism. Class conflict did not suddenly disappear with the demise of Chartism, but root-and-branch criticisms of society did decline in frequency, intensity and appeal. Energies were increasingly channelled into the more limited and narrowed directions of the co-op, trade union and educational 'improvement' society. Industrial capitalism came, in practice, to be accepted as a fact of life, as a system to be lived with, or modified and reformed from within rather than frontally challenged.[1]

Questions concerning the significance of such developments (the 'decline of a revolutionary class consciousness'?[2], the emergence of a deferential factory proletariat?[3]) will be examined in due course. Of immediate importance is the suggestion offered in this study that, given their centrality to changes at mid-century, the cotton districts both merit investigation in their own right and furnish valuable insights into the overall stabilisation of British capitalism during the third quarter.

Secondly, in an attempt to advance our understanding of

developments in a range of local settings, the experiences of the cotton towns are compared to events and processes elsewhere — particularly to places such as Edinburgh and Kentish London where the 'break' was far less marked. As Gray and Crossick have respectively shown, Edinburgh and Kentish London witnessed enhanced social calm after the 1840s, but lacked the traditions of intense conflict between workers and manufacturing capitalists and militant independent working-class politics so evident in cotton during the 1830s and 1840s.[4] The provision of a satisfactory explanation for the diversity of local experience is surely crucial to the framing of an adequate explanation for trends at the national level.

Thirdly, the cotton towns constitute a useful testing ground for the general explanations of change at mid-century offered by historians. Such explanations range from traditional emphasis upon the key importance of economic improvement (Briggs, Read and many others[5]), to various usages of the notion of a 'labour aristocracy' (Hobsbawm, R. Harrison, Foster, Gray and Crossick[6]), to the recent theory of the debilitating effects of the consolidation of factory production upon the class combativity of workers (Joyce[7]).

The foregoing reasons and questions have shaped the organisation of the book. Chapter 1 sets the broad historiographical context — offering a critical review of the general explanations of change outlined above and indicating the main directions and arguments of the present work. Subsequent chapters situate general questions and issues against the specific framework of the cotton districts. Chapter 2 re-creates the regional picture — paying particular attention to the economic and social structures of the cotton towns, and tracing the rise and decline of independent working-class politics in a number of centres (special attention being paid to the Chartist strongholds of Ashton-under-Lyne, Stalybridge and Stockport). Chapter 3 brings new evidence to bear upon questions concerning the living standards of workers during the third quarter; considers the strengths and weaknesses of the 'improvement' thesis; and assesses the impact of trends in living standards upon the political and social attitudes and behaviour of the operative population. Chapter 4 concentrates specifically upon the material fortunes of the labour leadership and their institutions (co-ops, friendly societies and the like): a collective biography of the leadership is compiled; and conclusions offered as to the extent to which personal success, collective and institutional advancement, and newfound concessions and overtures to labour from the state, employers and the established political parties underpinned the marked, if partly unconscious, drift into reformism on the part of the leadership. Chapter 5 concerns itself with the nature and significance of working-class culture — mainly providing a critique of the claims that 'respectability' was essentially either a socially soothing device which bound together 'respectables' from various layers of society (thus preventing a resurgence of widespread class conflict during the mid-Victorian period) or, as practised by the working-class, the sole or main preserve of a collaborationist 'labour aristocracy'. Chapter 6 turns to consider industrial questions — asking whether the key to changes in class attitudes and behaviour are to be found in patterns of trade union development and industrial relations. Did, for example, the mid-Victorian years conform to the Webbs' picture of a 'watershed' in trade unionism? Did the cotton industry witness the growth of (mainly semi-skilled) unions which adopted some of the cautious and moderate features of the skilled 'new model' unions? Did industrial conflict decline in intensity and frequency to provide, as claimed by Joyce, a new 'institutionalised calm' in which employer paternalism and worker deference flourished? Or did established patterns of conflict and suspicion survive even the 'golden years'? A detailed examination of areas of conflict and reconciliation between labour and capital provides the empirical base upon which largely 'pessimistic' conclusions are erected. The final chapter examines the much neglected themes of ethnic allegiance, ethnic conflict and the interactions between class and ethnic feeling. It is claimed that, in the wake of a massive increase in Irish Catholic immigration into Lancashire and Cheshire in the immediate post-Famine years, ethnic conflict escalated sharply, and was partially responsible for the decline of the impressive labour solidarity of the Chartist period. The Conclusion summarises some of the wider issues and debates raised by this study, paying particular attention to a consideration of the ways in which the various aspects of workers' 'experience' (which embraced aspects of both social being and social consciousness) interacted *as a whole*.

A materialist explanation of the onset of mid-Victorian stability and reformism is propounded. Central importance is attributed to the emergence of a restabilised and dynamic capitalism — which greatly enhanced the scope for class manoeuvre, for concessions and initiatives towards labour 'from above', and the advancement of sections of the working class within the system; and the marked growth of (particularly cultural and ethnic) divisions within the working class of the cotton districts — which greatly diminished the potential for class solidarity and the appeal of independent political action. To argue in this manner is to take issue with those views which attach key explanatory importance to either the appearance of a 'labour aristocracy' or a deferential cotton proletariat. Workers in Lancashire and Cheshire at mid-century were not, for the most part, cowed, deferential, collaborationist or incorporated (at least not to anything like the extent claimed by various historians); and a 'labour aristocracy' — however defined and characterised — was neither a novel nor singularly key feature of working-class life in the majority of cotton towns. However, the frequency and, at times, intensity of industrial and class conflict and the continued importance of the theme of independence in working-class life in the post-1850 cotton districts could not conceal the fact that the broad contours of the social system increasingly came to be seen as permanent features, and that workers sought their 'emancipation' not in a 'revolving of the whole system' but in gradual, limited, piecemeal reformism. In advancing these conclusions, and in both opening up new and relatively neglected areas of investigation and subjecting the more well-trodden areas to the test of fresh evidence, it is hoped that this book will make a useful contribution to nineteenth-century labour history.

In researching and writing this book I have accumulated many debts of gratitude: to numerous librarians and archivists (especially at Manchester Central Reference Library) for their invaluable assistance; to Wyn Morris for help with the typing; to Terry Wyke for compiling the index; and to countless friends who have endured my ramblings on labour history and offered useful advice. Special thanks to Dorothy Thompson, David Montgomery, Edward Thompson, Joe White, Alan Fowler, Andrew Bullen, Terry Wyke, John Mason, Ron Noon, Sam Davies, Gareth Stedman Jones, Patrick Joyce, John Rex, Gabriel Tortella, David Sabean, Julius Rubin, Leon Fink, Steve Sapolsky, Fred Segal, Steve Jones, Ron Schatz and Eric Taplin — all of whom have made constructive criticisms of various aspects of my work. I am particularly grateful to Dorothy Thompson and David Montgomery who have been a constant source of inspiration and guidance over the past 15 years. To the late Pam Robinson I am indebted for her boundless enthusiasm for a subject which, in comparison with the arts, must have appeared somewhat arid. Kate Dyer has provided much love and support, kept my feet firmly on the ground, and fully alerted me to the dangers of insularity and élitism which are all too prevalent in English academic institutions. Finally, I must defer to the fells of Bleaklow, Kinder and Chinley Churn and the sport of fell running — they have given me the freedom to air my thoughts.

New Mills, 1984

Notes

1. G.S. Jones, 'Class Struggle and the Industrial Revolution', *New Left Review*, 90 (March–April 1975), esp. pp. 66–7.
2. See J. Foster, *Class Struggle and the Industrial Revolution: Early Industrial Capitalism in Three English Towns* (1974), esp. Chs 4 and 5. The 'central theme' of Foster's study is (p. 1), 'the development and decline of a revolutionary class consciousness in the second quarter of the century'.
3. For the emergence of a deferential proletariat see, P. Joyce, *Work, Society and Politics: The Culture of the Factory in Later Victorian England* (Brighton, 1980). For a review of Joyce's book see my 'Cotton Workers and Deference', *Society for the Study of Labour History Bulletin,* 42 (Spring 1981), pp. 41–3; and pp. 14–24 below.
4. R.Q. Gray, *The Labour Aristocracy in Victorian Edinburgh* (Oxford, 1976), pp. 155–64; G. Crossick, *An Artisan Elite in Victorian Society* (1978), Ch. 10, esp. pp. 201–10.
5. A. Briggs, 'National Bearings', and D. Read, 'Chartism in Manchester' in A. Briggs (ed.), *Chartist Studies* (1959), pp. 56, 291.
6. E.J. Hobsbawm, 'The Labour Aristocracy in Nineteenth-century Britain', *Labouring Men* (1964), pp. 272–315; R. Harrison, *Before the Socialists* (1965), Ch. 1; J. Foster, op. cit.; R.Q. Gray, op. cit.; G. Crossick, op. cit.; H. F. Moorhouse, 'The Marxist Theory of the Labour Aristocracy', *Social History*, 3, no. 1 (1978), pp. 61–81.
7. P. Joyce, op. cit., esp. pp. 54–5, 96–103.

The Textile Districts of North-West England

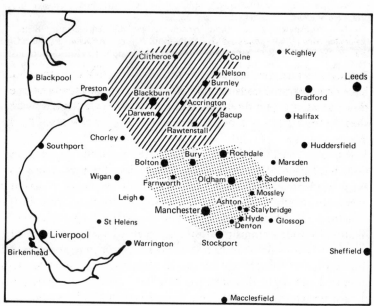

cotton weaving area   cotton spinning area

1 THE GROWTH OF REFORMISM: DEBATES AND ISSUES

The purpose of this opening chapter is to establish the general theoretical and historiographical context in which this specific study of
the cotton districts of Lancashire and Cheshire is situated. The
establishment of such a context is necessary for the following reasons: to make clear to the reader from the outset the main areas of
interest, and the key assumptions, questions and explanations which
inform this study; to set the framework of reference in which the
dialogues between fact and theory, local and national developments
will take place; and, as such, to provide a safeguard against drifts
into empiricism and parochialism. The main body of the chapter is
devoted to a critical review of the various explanations of mid-
Victorian reformism and stability offered by past and present historians and others. The chapter will, in conclusion, outline the major
thrusts and arguments of this study.

The History and Nature of the Debate

During the past two decades historians of mid-Victorian labour
have demonstrated considerable interest in two longstanding questions: to what extent did the years around 1850 constitute a 'watershed' in the history of labour? (the question originally posed by the
Webbs[1]); and wherein lay the key (s) to change and continuity? As is
well known, various and conflicting interpretations and explanations have been offered. In terms of the first question, there now
exists widespread agreement that, in view of its exaggerations and
oversimplifications, the Webbs' belief in a complete break in the
structure and ideology of the labour movement (particularly in
relation to trade unionism) cannot be accepted *in toto*. Conversely,
there exists considerable disagreement as to whether the notion of
'discontinuity' should be scrapped altogether or retained in a
modified and sophisticated form. Musson, the leading advocate of
the former viewpoint, highlights the various continuities evident in
the trade union movement between the second and third quarters of
the nineteenth century, and contends that those changes which did

occur (both in relation to trade unionism and other aspects of the labour movement) were extremely limited and gradual in character.[2] By way of contrast, Hobsbawm, Harrison and many other historians have argued that not only were major discontinuities in evidence, but also that discontinuities greatly outweighed elements of continuity.[3]

My purpose here is not to rehearse the finer points of detail of this disagreement — these have been thoroughly documented and assessed elsewhere[4] — but to make clear to the reader from the outset the 'position' which will emerge during the course of this book.

A comprehensive reading of the secondary literature concerning the national picture and detailed research into developments in the cotton towns had led me to the conclusion that Hobsbawm and Harrison make a sound case in favour of 'discontinuity'; and that Musson, despite his sharp eye for detail, and his astute criticisms of some of the views of the more 'extreme' advocates of change (especially those of the Webbs and Foster[5]), nevertheless underestimates the *overall process* of change at mid-century. Musson's partiality and empiricism — his tendency to select and highlight those facts and instances which support his case at the expense of counter instances; and his frequent failure to assess the typicality of such instances in relation to the wider social processes and structures of which they form a part[6] — underpin this underestimation. Thus there surely exists overwhelming evidence to suggest that, despite the persistence of class tensions and industrial conflict during the post-1850 period, class relations overall mellowed somewhat in comparison with the second quarter.[7] In terms of trade unionism, Musson is right to claim that the 'new models' were neither so novel nor so pacifistic and capitalist-minded as suggested by the Webbs. However, is it not also the case that most post-1850 unions, whether of the skilled or semi-skilled, came to terms with the new order of industrial capitalism and sought to come to agreement with employers as to the 'rules of the game' far more readily and widely than in earlier decades;[8] and that, as emphasised by Harrison, the national trade union movement was increasingly dominated by the generally cautious, moderate and exclusive unions of the craft and skilled? Certainly, as we will see in Chapter 6 of this study, the leaders of the post-1850 cotton unions prided themselves upon their moderation, and were anxious to arrest rank-and-file 'adventurism'. Independent working-class politics did not suddenly die in 1848, and

Musson is once again right to remind us that Chartism continued to make its presence felt throughout the 1850s. However, these facts must surely not be allowed to obscure three central aspects of the process of political 'discontinuity': that by the mid-late 1850s Chartism had become a pale shadow, both in members and wider appeal, of its former self; that, as Harrison observes, independent working-class politics increasingly came into being in relation to much more limited aims (to enable workers to 'rise in the social scale' rather than to 'knock property on the head'[9]); and that erstwhile Chartist activists and supporters were, by the end of the 1860s, to be found as supporters of Liberalism or Conservatism. Political fragmentation was, in all probability, one aspect of an overall sharpening of divisions within the post-1850 working class;[10] and narrowed, more limited goals and tactics were characteristic not only of working-class politics but also of the whole range of labour's institutions. In sum, as the pages of this book will confirm, central explanatory importance lies with 'discontinuity' rather than 'continuity'.

In relation to the second question — the underpinnings of change — many explanations have been proposed. Varying degrees of emphasis have been placed upon the following factors: the re-stabilisation and expansion of the economy on the basis of railway development and the growth of the capital goods industries; the absence (with the significant exception of the Cotton Famine) of major, protracted depressions, and the modest but nevertheless significant improvements in the standard of living and regularity of employment of large numbers of workers;[11] the virtual disappearance of certain occupational groups, most notably handloom weavers, which had provided Chartism with much of its radical, even revolutionary, impetus; the rise to dominance within the labour movement of a new, relatively privileged and politically moderate 'labour aristocracy' which detached itself from the mass of workers;[12] the very real gains made by sections of the labour movement (the remarkable progress achieved by the co-op movement, increased trade union recognition, etc.) which involved sections of the working class far more deeply, if ambiguously, in the *status quo* than previously;[13] and the concessions afforded to workers and organised labour by, mainly large, employers.[14] All these factors went some way towards enhancing class toleration, sometimes co-operation, and in reducing the level of working-class anger at the unfairness of the system as a whole.

It is, however, at this point that problems of explanation become more complex. For, whilst it is relatively easy to compile a long list of contributory factors, it is far more difficult to arrange these factors in a tight order of priority. Attempts to do so have been productive of major debates and disagreements. Traditionally, for example, explanatory primacy has been attached, often in a straightforward (sometimes extremely simplistic) fashion to economic and social improvement.[15] Chartism was seen by many as the creed of hard times and its demise as the more or less inevitable result of the onset of mid-Victorian prosperity. Echoes of this viewpoint are still with us today but its overall appeal, as the *key* explanation of change, has greatly diminished. The researches of various historians have demonstrated that Chartism was not simply or solely the product of 'distress'; that post-1850 real wage gains for the mass of workers were at worst non-existent or, at best, neither so great nor so sudden as often assumed; and that, on a general level there exists no simple or necessarily direct correlation between 'improvement' and political and social moderation.[16] Most striking, perhaps, has been the popularity of a generalisation based upon inadequate empirical support and sometimes expressed in the manner and language of a narrow economic reductionism.[17]

Dissatisfaction with the overall explanatory power of the notion of 'improvement' has led, since the 1960s, to a growing, indeed increasingly dominant, interest in the labour aristocracy thesis. Of all the explanations of changes in working-class behaviour at mid-century it is this latter thesis which has commanded most attention and which, until recently, effectively restricted the opening up of other, wider lines of investigation and explanation. It is to a consideration of the notion of labour aristocracy that we must now turn.

Interest in the labour aristocracy has been particularly marked among Marxist historians — some, but by no means all, of whom maintain that the growth of a labour aristocracy constitutes the key to change. Hobsbawm, the most distinguished exponent of the thesis, maintains that the years after 1840 saw the emergence of a distinctive stratum of workers (approximately the top 10–15 per cent of the working class), better paid, more privileged, separate from, and generally more respectable than the rest of the working class.[18] Moderate in its politics and trade unionism (although prepared to strike as a last resort) this labour aristocracy was 'inclined to accept the views of its employers' and, most crucially, was successful in imposing its moderate viewpoint upon the labour movement.

According to Hobsbawm, the labour aristocracy thus played a decisive role in reducing class tensions, and steering the labour movement away from class conscious independent politics and into the path of liberal-radicalism.[19]

Foster, too, sees a labour-aristocratic explanation as crucial. For Foster, the emergence of a labour aristocracy was the 'key component' in the decline of a revolutionary working-class consciousness and the reassertion of bourgeois control in Oldham in the late 1840s.[20] Foster's aristocrats are not to be confused with a traditional craft élite: and their privileged position issued primarily not from high wages (in contrast to Hobsbawm), but from authority at work. In Foster's opinion, it was the breaking down of craft controls mainly in the 1830s and 1840s,[21] the undermining of the craftman's autonomy at work which paved the way for the creation by employers of an aristocracy of labour — a segment of *production* workers, stripped of craft control, and involved in the process of management. Acting as pacemakers and supervisors of the semi- and unskilled mass in cotton, engineering and coalmining, these labour aristocrats thus acted, according to Foster, not to enforce discipline against the management (as had allegedly been the case with the earlier craft élite), but to act on management's behalf to speed up the labour of others and counteract the newfound bargaining strength of the semi-skilled operatives.

Foster further contends that divisions at work were accompanied by cultural fragmentation in the outside community, and that the labour aristocrats ritualistically assimilated bourgeois values.[22] Openly collaborationist at work, the checkweighmen in coal, and the pacemaking cotton minders and skilled engineering pieceworkers acted, according to Foster, as the system's 'messenger boys and interpreters in the labour community'. In their co-ops, temperance societies and adult education institutes, these aristocrats came within the 'cultural orbit' of the local bourgeoisie and consciously divorced themselves from the public-house culture of the mass of workers. And:

> While the self-educators spoke the language of their betters, the mass took pride in an aggressively opaque dialect. And while the social life of the smaller group was spent almost entirely within an intimidating complex of formal institutions, the free-and-easy friendly society remained the only — and exceptional — organising element for the majority.[23]

In short, Oldham's bourgeoisie came to hold all the trump cards. Not only had they survived the upsurges in working-class militancy in the 1830s and 1840s, albeit at the price of some concessions to labour[24], but they had also created a collaborationist labour aristocracy which could serve to contain working-class radicalism.

Both Hobsbawm and Foster thus emphasise the central role played by the labour aristocracy in the growth of mid-Victorian stability. Gray and Crossick, while critical of this central emphasis and calling for a wider framework of explanation,[25] nevertheless usefully employ the notion of a labour aristocracy to explain the development of fragmented and generally moderate workforces in the specific contexts of mid-Victorian Edinburgh and Kentish London. Gray and Crossick point to the existence in these urban areas of an élite of skilled, well-paid and relatively secure workers who, while far less collaborationist and individualistic than Foster alleges was the case with Oldham's aristocrats (class pride, independence and a faith in collective action were of continued importance to skilled workers in Edinburgh and Kentish London[26]), nevertheless 'demonstrated an acceptance of the broad contours of the political economy in which they lived', and formed 'an exclusive group with aspirations and values distinct from others' — particularly the mass of unskilled workers.[27] Of final importance is the fact that Gray's and Crossick's aristocrats are not, for the most part, to be found among Foster's production workers stripped of control, but in industries (metal, shipbuilding, printing, building and engineering[28]) in which 'craft control' remained of key significance.

The studies of Hobsbawm, Foster, Gray and Crossick are illustrative of the major ways in which the notion of a labour aristocracy has been employed by historians. There is no doubt that such studies have greatly advanced our understanding of the values and behaviour of an important section(s?) of the mid-Victorian working class. However, considerable doubts concerning the explanatory adequacy of the labour aristocracy thesis remain. Gray himself has recently noted that it is 'probably true that the labour aristocracy pointed to a series of problems, rather than offered an explanation'[29] — a view shared by Stedman Jones, Moorhouse and others. Such problems will now be examined.

Firstly, would it not be more accurate to refer to theories rather than *the* theory of the labour aristocracy? We have already seen that the labour aristocracy has been variously defined and characterised by historians. There surely exists, in the interests of clarity and rigour, a pressing need for greater precision in relation to both the aristocracy's primary mark of identification (whether wage levels, authority at work, or some other characteristic) and its attitudes and behaviour.

Secondly, we require a more precise account of the changes which the emergence of a labour aristocracy is held to explain. This criticism might appear somewhat redundant in terms of the national picture. Concern at this level rests, as noted, with the increasingly narrowed, more moderate aims of the labour movement and overall stabilisation. However, against this national framework must be set considerable regional diversity. And such diversity demands not the abandonment but the refinement of existing generalisations.

The examples of, on the one hand, Foster's Oldham and, on the other, Gray's Edinburgh and Crossick's Kentish London illustrate both regional variations of experience and the ways in which the labour aristocracy has been employed to explain widely varying degrees of change. In *Class Struggle and the Industrial Revolution* (1974), John Foster used the notion of a labour aristocracy to explain a major rupture in Oldham's working-class history, the decline of a 'revolutionary class consciousness' from the mid-late 1840s onwards. Foster has since denied that his main intention in *Class Struggle and the Industrial Revolution* was to portray working-class radicalism in the Oldham of the 1830s and 1840s as 'some early variant of revolutionary class consciousness'.[30] Despite this revision, Foster does, however, continue to argue that for much of the Chartist period workers in Oldham did unite against the capitalist system and were receptive to their leaders' pleas for the creation of an 'alternative social system', a 'non-capitalist society'.[31] The central point to note here is that, despite the problematical nature of the content of working-class consciousness in Oldham,[32] there is little doubt that Oldham, as with many towns in south Lancashire, did experience a decline of class-conscious Chartism, enhanced class toleration and the emergence of a more moderate and reformist labour movement during the third quarter of the century.[33]

By way of contrast, neither Edinburgh nor Kentish London experienced such dramatic changes: indeed, it is questionable as to whether we can locate a marked break at all in class relations and the consciousness of workers in these places. Chartism was much stronger in Edinburgh than Kentish London — but in neither place were class conflict, mass class solidarity and opposition to manufacturing capitalists and their allies (in contrast to the cotton districts) especially strong. The radicalism which prevailed in Edinburgh and Kentish London in the 1840s was predominantly anti-aristocratic rather than anti-capitalist in character, tended to be of the 'rational', 'improving' type, and often served to unite (again in marked contrast to much of Lancashire) middle-class liberals and working-class radicals.[34] As Crossick notes of Kentish London, 'the most important influence of all was the absence of any continuing sense of class hostility'.[35] The movement into Liberalism in Edinburgh and Kentish London during the third quarter did not, unlike the experiences of towns such as Stockport, Ashton-under-Lyne and Stalybridge, signify a sharp break in consciousness (radicalism in Kentish London was, 'of a traditional kind that could inform mid-Victorian popular Liberalism as easily as Chartism'[36]) and the dilution, even abandonment, of the social criticism and implicit social programme of Chartism.[37]

Given such continuities, or at best limited and gradual changes in Edinburgh and Kentish London, what do Gray and Crossick's specific applications of the notion of a labour aristocracy seek to explain? If these two authors wish to depict the values and life-styles of élites of skilled workers at a particular period in time, then they have done so with great sensitivity and sophistication. But surely there are very severe limits to which the labour aristocracy constitutes an explanation of a major break in Edinburgh and Kentish London when such a break was conspicuous by its absence.

Furthermore, may it not be the case that the generally moderate character of working-class politics in Edinburgh and Kentish London during both the second and third quarters resulted from the continuous dominance in the local economies of skilled workers who were, for the most part, threatened neither by serious technological change nor by the growth of 'dishonourable' sectors of trades? Crossick, for example, notes that the dominant trades of Kentish London were 'not those of the old skilled artisan élite, whose economic and status problems underlie the history of London radicalism in the first half of the century'. 'Aristocratic' occupations in engineering, shipbuilding and the metal and building trades were of particular importance in Kentish London.[38] In Edinburgh, printing, building, engineering and a host of small-scale consumer crafts provided a solid base for the growth of a skilled élite.[39] In both urban areas many of the skilled were, despite the recurrent problem of economic insecurity, sharply differentiated, in terms of wage levels, conditions of work and general status, from the (mainly) unskilled mass. The occupational structures of Edinburgh and Kentish London did not, in themselves, guarantee the emergence of a group consciousness on the part of the skilled élites, but they did stand in sharp contrast to many of the cotton towns which were dominated by a single industry carried on by a mass of semi-skilled operative families.[40]

What the above suggests is that the existence of an articulate group of relatively privileged and moderate workers in Edinburgh and Kentish London was probably not a new feature of the third quarter. Of considerable, indeed novel, importance during the latter was the rapid expansion of the capital goods sector which, with its heavy demand for skilled men, substantially reinforced the labour aristocracy — new aristocrats in the metal trades joining older aristocrats in building and printing in the capitals of England and Scotland.[41]

This brings us to the third and most damaging criticism. Gareth Stedman Jones and A.E. Musson, historians holding antagonistic ideological positions, nevertheless agree, and convincingly demonstrate, that a labour aristocracy (whether defined in terms of wage levels, pacemaking and subcontracting, or exclusive group consciousness allied to wages and authority at work) was *not* a new creation of the mid-Victorian period.[42] At both national and local levels there is abundant evidence to suggest that subcontracting and pacemaking existed prior to 1850, as undoubtedly did 'a social hierarchy of labour, with an "aristocracy" at its summit'. And Musson, albeit in exaggerated fashion, has long pointed to the sectionalism and exclusiveness of skilled workers during the first half of the century. As Stedman Jones suggests, such criticisms amount to a denial of any direct or general correlation between the restabilisation of the post-1850 period and the emergence of a labour aristocracy. The implications of this line of reasoning for the works of Gray and Crossick have been discussed above. In terms of Foster's book, the results are extremely damaging. Foster's 'key component', the labour aristocracy, is shown to rest upon very weak empirical foundations. As Stedman Jones points out in relation to côtton spinning, 'there existed a sub-contracting stratum of the labour force before, during and after the heroic period of Oldham's class struggle' — a view endorsed by Lazonick who, in an impressive and well-substantiated article, maintains that the introduction of the self-acting mule did not involve the creation of a *new* pacemaking grade; rather, both the old hand-mule spinners and the new self-actor spinners performed the same managerial functions of recruiting and supervising their assistants.[43] In coal mining, notes Stedman Jones, 'no local labour aristocracy in the material sense is demonstrable at all'. Only in the case of engineering do subcontracting and reformism 'convincingly coincide' — but even in this case 'evidence of previous political militancy . . . is not very ample'. Finally, it should be remembered that the development of piecework in engineering was opposed by the unions, and that the whittling away of craft skills and autonomy was probably a far more protracted process than suggested by Foster.[44]

Patrick Joyce has also offered some telling criticisms of Foster's work. Joyce adds his support to Stedman Jones's view that it was not the spinner's privileged position at work, his strong bargaining position, which underlay his increasingly conservative and accommodative attitudes during the third quarter but, on the contrary, his greatly enhanced vulnerability and dependence upon the employer following the introduction of the self-actor mule (which adversely affected wage, status and skill levels), and the transference of 'real' control of the labour process from worker to employer. By 1850 the self-actor spinner possessed no special skills and his privileged position in cotton was largely dependent upon the goodwill of the employer who used the spinners to recruit, supervise and intensify the labour of the piecers.[45] Furthermore, notes Joyce, the degree of control exercised by the self-actor spinner was not great, and the section of the adult male labour force which he confronted directly was limited. More critically, perhaps, Joyce contends that the piecer was often the son of the spinner, and that the deployment of the spinner's family across the whole range of mill occupations subverts Foster's notion of 'working-class status fragmentation'. Finally, evidence based mainly upon Blackburn, suggests to Joyce that the voting and political allegiances of cotton operatives were shaped far less by occupational and status considerations than by the powerful influences of factory and employer upon the local community.[46]

Finally, a serious question mark must be set against Foster's belief that there developed in Oldham a sharp cultural division between the labour aristocracy and the rest of the working class. Nowhere in *Class Struggle and the Industrial Revolution* does Foster adequately substantiate his claim that the labour aristocrats dominated the co-ops, temperance societies and adult education institutes to the exclusion of the mass of workers.[47] As will be shown later in the study,[48] whilst the 'authority-wielding' and better-off sections of the

working class in Lancashire and Cheshire were often heavily represented at the leadership levels of Foster's 'aristocratic' institutions,
nevertheless the membership, indeed leadership, of these institutions was far from being the sole preserve of any labour aristocracy;
'respectability' thus had a much longer occupational tail in the cotton towns than suggested by Foster.[49]

To summarise and conclude this discussion of the labour aristocracy. As Gray has recently noted, 'the labour aristocracy thesis has
helped historians to get beyond a view of the working class as a
homogeneous entity, and encouraged them to investigate the experience and activity of different groups'.[50] Special tribute must be paid
to the pioneering endeavours of Hobsbawm and the provocative
thesis offered by Foster. These two historians have provided many
of the questions and conclusions around which the widespread
debate has revolved. Nevertheless, the various criticisms outlined
above suggest that an emphasis upon the emergence of a labour
aristocracy as the *key* to mid-Victorian stability and reformism is
unconvincing: an aristocracy of labour existed prior to the 1840s
and its presence and influence varied greatly from place to place.

To support such a conclusion is not, however, to deny that privileged skilled male workers often did act exclusively and hold moderate political and social views. I agree with Royden Harrison's view
that the moderation of the mid-Victorian labour (especially trade
union) movement was in large measure a reflection of the increasingly dominant position of such skilled males within that movement.[51] Unlike its predecessor, the post-1850 labour movement was
not heavily influenced by fiercely dissatisfied groups of depressed
outworkers, craftsmen faced with a severe decline in economic independence and status, and a newly-fledged factory proletariat
experiencing the full traumas of the new system. By the 1860s
such groups had either disappeared, become less common, or had
become more accustomed to the routines of the factory. And, in
terms of trade unionism, the dominance of coal and cotton lay
in the future. The labour movement lay in the hands of moderate
and 'responsible' men who, whilst laying strong claims to the
rights of male citizenship, wished to achieve a stake in
society.

The various weaknesses of the labour aristocracy thesis have
recently resulted in mounting appeals for the development of a
wider framework of explanation. Moorhouse, for example, has suggested that:

> . . . if quiescent attitudes and behaviour are *not* directly linked to some particular stratum in the working class then the search for the roots of reformism can evolve into the much wider, and infinitely more difficult, question of the development, negotiation, and constant renegotiation of culture, of the myriad processes of social control and so on . . .[52]

And similar, if less ambitious calls have issued from labour history conferences.[53] Given such a development, it is appropriate at this point to turn to a consideration of the two most important attempts so far made — by G.S. Jones and P. Joyce — to cast our explanatory net wider and deeper.

In his excellent (1975) review of Foster's book, Stedman Jones offered an exciting and subsequently influential framework of analysis. The key to reformism is to be sought, according to Stedman Jones, not primarily in special cases (such as the labour aristocracy) but in overall changes in the nature of English capitalism between the second and third quarters of the century.[54] Stedman Jones attached special importance to two developments. Firstly, a 'new stage of industrialisation' considerably reduced imbalances within the economy between the industrialised sector and the rest, and ended the capitalist crises of the 1830s and 1840s. Railway building, the 'most obvious feature' of this new stage, played a crucial role in this process:

> It lessened the impact of cyclical crisis, stimulated coal, iron, steel and machine production and resolved the crisis of profitability. More than any other single factor, it assured the successful transition to a modern industrial economy.[55]

With the restabilisation of the economy, the fate of industrial capitalism no longer hung in the balance. Earlier widespread fears of deterioration towards a 'stationary state' diminished and the system as a whole assumed an air of permanence and inevitability hitherto lacking. Secondly, with the consolidation of modern mechanised industry (a trend most marked in cotton), effective or 'real' control over the labour process passed, often in the wake of bitter struggles, from workers to employers. The autonomy of the craftsman was undermined and, while formal divisions of status were left intact, all sections of the labour force were forced to adapt to effective capitalist control of production.[56]

Stedman Jones contends that it is against this new, determining context that the ideology and direction of the labour movement during the third quarter must be set. New conditions and structures led to the adoption of changed tactics and perspectives. Desires to create an alternative social order and to retain control over production — which had underpinned much of the appeal of Chartism and the struggles of spinners and weavers — increasingly lost their relevance to a proletariat bereft of control at work and faced with the seemingly 'irremovable horizon' of industrial capitalism. The system could not be wished away. It had to be either negotiated or overthrown. And, given the defeats of Chartism and the general political and socio-economic context of the mid-Victorian period, gradual, patient and piecemeal reform became the order of the day. The earlier class combativity was not forgotten but channelled into 'a narrower form of labourism'. Lacking independence, and vulnerable in the labour market, workers turned towards a narrow concern with wage bargaining and accepted the wider structures of the system as given.

In such a manner does Stedman Jones offer important insights into the general structural underpinnings of reformism, and a specific connection between changes in the labour process and worker consciousness. His conceptual framework does, however, contain two weaknesses. Firstly, the specific history of the control issue in cotton provides the basis for what is possibly an excessively wide generalisation. As Gray notes:

> . . . Stedman Jones may be working with an over-general, once-for-all view of the transition to industrial capitalism. The impact of capitalist development, especially in the nineteenth century, was not simply to destroy skills, but to create the basis for new forms of skilled labour, within which craft methods and traditions could assert themselves.[57]

In short, worker experiences in relation to the control issue were less uniform and more varied than possibly suggested by Stedman Jones. Secondly, in his search for underlying (especially economic) structures, Stedman-Jones perhaps pays insufficient attention to the issues of worker consciousness and the complex interactions between agency and conditioning. What part did cultural and other structures and traditions play in the formation of consciousness? What was the content of the latter? And how did workers experience and handle changes in structure? These are questions which are touched upon but which merit further investigation. To offer such criticisms is not to belittle the vast explanatory potential of Stedman Jones's framework of analysis which should act as an important stimulus to research into changes in control and consciousness. When set against a range of local experiences Stedman Jones's structural explanation may well be refined and qualified but not invalidated.

An interesting feature of Patrick Joyce's *Work, Society and Politics* (1980) is the utilisation of Stedman Jones's explanatory framework to support novel conclusions. For Joyce claims that the cotton proletariat's vulnerability in mid-Victorian Lancashire (after being defeated on the control issue) was productive not only of defensive, reformist behaviour and a narrowed social vision but also, and more significantly, dependence (particularly upon the employer as provider of work) which in turn was the seedbed of deference.[58] Joyce's central focus rests, therefore, not upon reformism — the labour historian's traditional area of study — but upon the emergence of a deferential cotton proletariat. And we are informed by the author that the 'internalization of the paternalist ethos' by modern factory workers is 'of the first importance'. In challenging a deepseated association between the nineteenth-century factory system and class conflict, Joyce is taking to task those labour historians who have failed to explore 'the reverse of the coin of independence'.[59]

Before looking at the steps by which Joyce builds his structure of deference, it is worth noting that the term deference is employed 'advisedly'.[60] Joyce is aware of the pitfalls of loose, ahistorical and idyllic usage, and of the considerable difficulties involved in interpreting often ambiguous evidence. Deference is used to refer to both attitudes and behaviour: it constituted, within the specific context of the cotton towns, 'an aspect of the class relationship of employer and workpeople'. Deference is claimed to take greatest effect when, 'a totality of influence and direction over people's lives is most clearly achieved'. Accordingly, it was at work and in the factory neighbourhood, where the employer's influence could 'hardly be exaggerated', that deference flourished best.[61]

Deference had at its core inequality and subordination, but, according to Joyce, its success derived primarily neither from coercion nor ideological penetration from above; rather, the experiences of work and community bound employer and worker together in a tie of emotional identification, and ensured the 'real inwardness' of deference. Joyce attempts to demonstrate the strength of this tie in a number of ways: employer cultural and social sway over the factory locale; undifferentiated worker political and religious allegiance to the master; and, perhaps most significantly, in the ebbing of class conflict.[62] We are informed that deference operated, 'with sufficient power . . . greatly to erode the consciousness of conflict but never to displace it, to change the form in which conflict was perceived but not to obliterate its perception'. Class conflict became more limited and institutionalised in character, increasingly confined to a minority of workers who were employed in non-factory occupations.[63]

According to Joyce, Chartism, with its 'artisanate' view of the world, spoke with force to those workers whose craft status was in the process of being destroyed, but failed to address itself to the situation of the fully-fledged factory proletariat bereft of independence and control. Essentially a 'pre-mechanical' movement, Chartism failed to develop an economic 'rhetoric and theory' of the new mechanised order of modern industry. Joyce writes:

> The goal of a non-capitalist economy of free producers did not encompass the changed social relations modern industry was ushering in. The employer's rights of direction in industry were not attacked, merely his role as middleman. Industrial capitalism was equated with a politically based system of unequal exchange . . . the causes of poverty were political and not economic . . . The relationship between radical theory and the work situation and social assumptions of the craft sector will be apparent: to the craft worker the employer was a nebulous figure, for it was only in his role as capitalist and not employer that he could compose a class.[64]

Thus, with the completion of mechanisation, 'the factory worker was increasingly bereft of a radical critique capable of comprehending the changed class relations of his position as a factory proletarian'. Little wonder, claims Joyce, that the development of a fully-fledged proletariat in Lancashire in the 1840s was accompanied by a marked decline in the influence of Chartism.[65] Joyce also contends that trade unions and co-operative societies, whilst perpetuating the traditions of working-class independence and cultural autonomy in the post-1850 period, became increasingly limited in their appeal and failed, for the most part, to offset the overwhelming influence of factory and neighbourhood.[66]

Why did such profound changes occur? As noted above, Joyce fully accepts and builds upon Stedman Jones's explanatory framework. We are informed that the cotton operatives' vulnerability and dependence (the central foundations of Joyce's structure) produced a search for stability and security in an uncertain world and the more or less total subordination of labour to capital. Joyce quotes Marx to the effect that the consolidation of modern industry breaks down all resistance to the sway of capital, and draws an interesting contrast between the experiences of cotton operatives in Lancashire and workers in the West Riding of Yorkshire. Joyce maintains that in Yorkshire, where fully mechanised industry developed later, workers retained a measure of control over the labour process and were accordingly far more class conscious and independent-minded than the factory proletarians of Lancashire.[67]

Having pointed to the central importance of dependence, Joyce then proceeds to demonstrate the ways in which the need for security was met. Firstly, he claims that the reconstitution of the cotton operatives' family unit and paternal authority in the workplace (following the disruptions of earlier decades) did much to restore the equilibrium of, and the 'traditional' division of labour within the family and promoted acceptance of the authority structures of the new system. The restoration of paternal authority within the operative family buttressed the paternalism of the employer, and was part of the newfound symmetry between family and work.[68] Secondly, Joyce claims that there was a consolidation of community feeling at mid-century which gave cotton operatives a sense of place, of belonging, and linked them, via a network of institutions, to the local employer. In part the result of a lessening of population flux. communal sociability signalled, as often as not, deference and subordination rather than 'class selfhood'.[69] Thirdly, it was, however, the paternalistic and, most often, large employers of labour who did most to ease cotton workers' uncertainties and to transform dependence into deference. Joyce is at his best when charting the 'mighty reassertion' of employer paternalism after 1850. He vividly reconstructs the ways in which paternalism operated in the factory and local community (works dinners and 'treats', various trips, all manner of cultural and social provision, and increased recognition for trade unions), and the successful response which paternalism evoked (as reflected in the growing number of worker testimonials to their employers).[70]

Paternalism could thrive best in a stable environment. Once again, notes Joyce, Lancashire was favourably placed. The expansion of cotton provided the profits which made paternalism possible. And, crucially, the attainment of a new level of 'institutionalised calm' in labour relations in cotton during the second half of the century contributed greatly to the success of paternalism. Joyce attributes much of this calm and stability to the growth and recognition of moderate, bureaucratic cotton unions.[71] He contends that the institutionalisation of labour relations removed 'the prime source of class antagonism' — workplace relations between workers and employers — substantially from the fields of conflict and facilitated the growth of deference.[72]

In such a manner does Joyce build his structure of deference. Immediate tribute must be paid to the ingenious and often novel nature of the arguments presented and the clever way in which the various parts of the structural whole are fitted together. There is little doubt that in documenting the softening of attitudes and behaviour on the part of some large employers Joyce has filled an important gap in our understanding of the easing of class tensions at mid-century. Conversely, major doubts and questions concerning both method and content remain. I believe that Joyce's structure of deference is erected upon somewhat questionable assumptions and shaky empirical foundations. As I hope to demonstrate in some detail later in this study, there exists plentiful evidence of continued class conflict and worker independence in cotton after 1850 which fits uneasily into a framework of stability and harmony.

For our present purposes, it is sufficient to outline some of the problematical areas in Joyce's work and the nature and direction of the criticisms offered. In terms of questions, the following are perhaps worthy of further investigation. Do not the various parts of Joyce's structure fit together too snugly in order to promote the smooth functioning of the whole? Where are the tensions and contradictions in this structure? Is it not the case that some of the author's key arguments (such as the integrating, socially soothing effects of the reconstitution of the operative family and the marked growth of communal sociability) rest more on assertion than adequate empirical support? Does not *Work, Society and Politics* reveal the weakness of a particular kind of structuralism in which worker consciousness (dependence and deference) tends to be 'read off' in unduly hasty and overly deterministic fashion from economic structure (the onset of modern industry)? How solid does the overall structure become if one of its props is shown to be defective? Is not Marx's notion of the subordination of labour to capital employed in an unbalanced way — with excessive emphasis placed upon worker vulnerability and insufficient attention given to the reverse of the coin of dependence, class conflict? Indeed, would not a more detailed examination of worker consciousness and the influence of the labour movement (which are treated far too briefly) reveal a cotton workforce which, while on necessary occasions deferential,[73] was far more independent that claimed by Joyce? Finally, in his underestimation of the influence of independence among workers and in his very close attention to the thoughts and actions of paternalistic employers, has not Joyce tended to accept, too uncritically, a view of social reality as presented from the big house?

Concentration upon two areas of study — Chartism and the pattern of industrial relations — can hopefully throw some light upon the questions posed above. In terms of Chartism, it will be remembered that Joyce makes three central claims: that Chartism was an essentially artisante movement; that it was incapable of addressing itself to the situation of the cotton worker bereft of control; and that it failed to develop an economic 'rhetoric and theory' of the new industrial order. I believe that all three claims are questionable.

Firstly, the undisputed fact that craft workers faced with threats to their control and independence often played a prominent part in Chartism surely does not necessarily mean that the latter was *essentially* the creed of the artisans. In offering such a conclusion, Joyce tends to view Chartism mainly through the eyes of the London or Birmingham artisan and to underestimate the extremely broad appeal of the movement to labourers, colliers, factory workers, schoolteachers and many other occupational groupings.[74] Moreover, workers exercised widely varying degrees of control both within and across these occupations. For example, Chartism in south Lancashire and northeast Cheshire enjoyed strong support not simply among spinners in control struggles, but also among weavers whose control battles had been lost between the mid-1820s and early 1830s, and other groups, both inside and outside cotton (cardroom hands; labourers, etc.) for whom control was of little importance.[75] Richard Pilling constituted the classic example of a former handloom weaver who had been forced into the factory by economic necessity, who continued to 'detest the factory to the bottom of his heart'; and yet who, as a proletarian powerloom weaver stripped of control at work, had passionate commitments to Chartism, trade unionism and the short-time movement.[76]

Secondly, there does exist strong evidence that Chartism did offer proletarian workers an impressive and forceful critique of the new order of mechanised factory production. Desires for continued control and independence were undoubtedly part of this critique (Pilling, for example, did greatly lament his former independence and high status as a handloom weaver). Crucially, however, Chartism's indictment of a factory system run along capitalist lines went wider and deeper than the control issues. Pilling's speech at his trial at Lancaster in 1843 is a good example of the depth and force of this indictment. Pilling detailed, on the basis of personal experience, the evils of the system: overproduction; intolerably long hours of labour; competition and the beating down of wages; unemployment and poverty in the midst of plenty; the employment of child and juvenile labour and the break-up of the family; lack of independence and control; the reification of human beings under commodity production; the many tyrannical and hypocritical actions of the cotton manufacturers — their insensitivity to the sufferings of the operatives, blind adherence to the tenets of orthodox political economy, opposition to combination among workers and their frequent victimisation of labour activists (Pilling had been blacklisted in Stockport) and their abhorrence of Chartism.[77] Perhaps the most important point to note is that these were not the grievances of an isolated individual. At Lancaster, O'Connor, Leach and other Chartist defendants pinpointed similar evils.[78] And as Foster, Tholfsen and Dorothy Thompson have demonstrated, the grievances articulated by Pilling lay at the heart of Chartism's appeal to the factory population of the North.[79]

Given the general success of this appeal, it is thus surely somewhat misleading to closely relate (as does Joyce) the decline of Chartism in Lancashire to the emergence of a factory proletariat lacking control over production. It is true that the influence of Chartism declined somewhat in many cotton towns from the mid-1840s onwards — at a time when the spinners had largely lost their control struggle. However, against this possible relationship, we must set the different chronology of the control issue in weaving (the fight had been lost by the late twenties in many towns), and Chartism's partial recovery in the cotton districts in 1847 and 1848.[80]

Chartism's decline, both nationally and in Lancashire, was in all probability due less to the consolidation of factory production than to greater efforts to accommodate the interests of working people by the state, the established political parties, and, to a lesser extent, employers, than had been the case during the long reign of 'Old

Corruption' and the decade of blatant 'class legislation' after 1832;
to the various setbacks and defeats suffered by Chartism; and to
the opening up of opportunities for gradual and piecemeal advancement within the system which were eagerly seized by the co-
operative societies and other working-class institutions. As
Stedman Jones has recently claimed:

> The programme of Chartism remained believeable so long as
> unemployment, low wages, economic insecurity and other
> material afflictions could convincingly be assigned political
> causes. If, for instance, lack of political representation and a
> corrupt system of power rather than economic phenomena were
> responsible for the misery of the working classes, then it followed
> from this that partial reforms like the ten hours bill or the repeal
> of the Corn Law, could not bring real improvement, indeed were
> more likely to hasten deterioration, since they left the system
> intact . . . Once, however, the evidence suggested that real
> reform was possible within the unreformed system . . . then radi-
> cal ideology could be expected to lose purchase over large parts of
> its mass following . . .[81]

Thirdly, despite his underestimation of the ability of Chartism to
mount a critique of factory production, Joyce does raise — along
with Foster and Stedman Jones — extremely important and difficult questions concerning the *precise nature* of the kind of critique
offered. What, in fact, was the content of working-class radicalism
in the late 1830s and 1840s? What were the ultimate goals of
Chartism? Did the movement fail to develop, as claimed by
Stedman Jones and Joyce, a Marxist theory of exploitation *within
production*; or is Foster correct in his belief that workers, at least
in Oldham, exhibited a 'revolutionary class consciousness', as
expressed in demands for 'a total change of the social system' and
the creation of 'a non-capitalist society'?[82] I will attempt to come to
grips with such questions in Chapter 2 of this study. The reader
should, however, be immediately aware that, whilst in agreement
with Foster's belief that workers in Oldham (and I would add, much
of south Lancashire and northeast Cheshire) did develop an impressive anti-aristocratic and anti-capitalist critique, I am extremely
doubtful as to whether this critique was accompanied by a mass
revolutionary consciousness of a (presumably) *socialist* character.
The features of the 'alternative social system' allegedly desired by
Oldham's workers remain vague in *Class Struggle and the Industrial
Revolution* (a reflection of the lack of clarity and unanimity among

Oldham's Chartists as to ultimate goals?) and Foster does not adequately document his particular notion of 'class consciousness'. In all probability Stedman-Jones is correct to suggest that the programme offered by Oldham's radical workers was ('even if the aims of the Oldham workers could be wholly summed up in the demands of the Short Time movement in the 1830s') *de facto* anti-capitalist, not consciously socialist.[83] We will observe in Chapter 2 that much the same was true for the remainder of south Lancashire. It was, of course, only in the post-1848 period that part of the Chartist movement adopted a formal socialist programme.

Despite earlier disagreements, I do, therefore, support Joyce's claim (which is, in turn, based upon Stedman Jones's conclusion) that Chartism did not, for the most part, develop a *socialist* 'theory and rhetoric' which involved the (Marxist) notion of *necessary* exploitation within production. By way of contrast, despite their strong condemnations of acts of capitalist oppression within production, and the deep and persistent class conflict which such condemnations reflected, Chartist leaders such as Leach and McDouall could simultaneously exhort the mass of 'unfair' masters to mend their ways and follow the example of the minority of 'fair' masters. Such leaders did not wish to 'take over the mills and expropriate their owners'.[84] In sum, the Chartist theory of exploitation in production was essentially *experiential* and *conditional* rather than *necessary*.

This weakness of an organised socialist presence and theory within Chartism should not, however, blind us to the fact that, as noted in the case of Pilling above, Chartism was pervaded by deep and powerful feelings of opposition to the general unfairness of existing society and by equally powerful desires for the creation of a radically different society in which workers would be afforded their due reward and recognition. Chartism thus developed out of experience, out of 'felt' grievances; and articulated the daily hopes and demands of workers. And, as Hobsbawm has astutely observed,[85] such 'commonsensical' or 'spontaneous' (these terms are employed in a non-pejorative sense) grievances and aspirations constitute a source both of strength and weakness in working-class movements. They provide the moral dynamism and inspiration essential to mass movements, but tend, by their very nature, to be somewhat vague and imprecise. Such was arguably the case with Chartism. As Stedman Jones has suggested,[86] the Charter meant 'working-class power to determine its own destiny', but 'how it would do so was not always clear'. As is well known, there existed considerable disagreements and confusion within Chartism concerning tactics and final goals. Chartism was an essentially umbrella movement; and beyond a common commitment to the six points there existed several ideological tendencies, some more carefully formulated than others, which often competed for popular support.[87] This lack of precision and agreement in terms of tactics and goals meant that, in the event of changed conditions, there existed no firm safeguard against a drift into reformism. Even during the 1830s and early 1840s when class conflict and opposition to Chartist demands were most marked, some Chartists combined a fervent desire for 'The Great Change' with the hope that employers and the authorities would experience a change of heart towards the 'reasonable' and 'just' claims of workers. In short, elbow room for manoeuvre and reform was thus not often completely ruled out of court. And, given the increased recognition of the labour movement and the softening of attitudes and policies in the post-1850 period, it is perhaps not surprising that reformism took root.

This discussion of the nature of working-class radicalism has taken us well beyond the question of deference. We must now return to *Work, Society and Politics* and the area of industrial relations. As we will observe in Chapter 6, plentiful evidence suggests that industrial relations in Lancashire during the third quarter were far less harmonious and workers less dependent than Joyce maintains.[88] Despite the emergence of a mainly moderate trade union leadership in cotton and concessions by employers to organised labour, advances in union recognition were patchy with many employers still extremely reluctant to deal with unions. Bureaucratisation and centralisation in union affairs were often insufficiently advanced to remove control from the rank and file. And, as demonstrated in numerous local disputes and the wider unrest of 1853–4, 1861 and 1867, industrial conflict persisted, sometimes at a high level of intensity, throughout the 'Golden Years'. With the more complete institutionalisation of collective bargaining in cotton after 1875, we might expect to witness Joyce's 'institutionalised calm'. It is, however, debatable as to whether such a state of affairs came into being. The historian of cotton trade unionism informs us that, ' . . . the uncertain years from 1872 lead into a major slump . . . and initiate a generation's extensive conflict'.[89] The important stoppages at Oldham in 1875, Bolton in 1877, the Great Strike of 1878 and the lock-out of 1891 — bore witness to this conflict.

Joyce does make three exceptions to his general Lancashire

picture of stability and harmony: Ashton and Stalybridge with their 'recalcitrant populism'; Oldham with its poor labour relations; and the Burnley area with its worker militancy and early appeal of socialism. Joyce does, however, view all three cases as deviations from the norm. Ashton and Stalybridge are, for example, portrayed as 'rather exceptional' towns, with peculiar local circumstances (the pressure of a large, volatile and non-unionised sector; the continued mass following of 'quixotic' local leaders such as J.R. Stephens; and the overwhelmingly Liberal-Nonconformist composition of the local millocracy) productive of class conflict. In Oldham 'anonymous limited companies' predominated and there was subsequently a marked lack of employer paternalism. Finally, the Burnley experience is held to indicate 'the validity of the Lancashire rule', late mechanisation being accompanied by continued worker independence and radicalism.[90]

These ingenious explanations of the 'exceptional' nature of industrial and class conflict and worker independence are, however, far from convincing. There is, for example, surely a limit to the number of exceptions which any general rule can stand. The widespread nature of industrial conflict suggests that the experiences of Ashton, Stalybridge and Oldham were far from being 'exceptional'. For example, Stockport (which is barely mentioned by Joyce), with its mixture of Conservative and Liberal employers and its early mechanisation, experienced considerable industrial conflict in the post-1850 period. And this conflict was most pronounced in weaving where (sometimes paternalistic) employers were reluctant to have any dealings with trade unions.[91] The Burnley experience also presents problems for Joyce's model — the consolidation of factory production, mechanisation and capitalist ownership and control resulting *not* (as a consistent usage of the mechanisation thesis would maintain) in increased worker dependence and deference but, as Joyce himself points out, in continued industrial conflict and strong worker support for socialism.

In sum, variations of experience within the cotton districts and the continued and widespread existence of industrial conflict cast serious doubts upon Joyce's notions of 'institutionalised calm' and a cowed, deferential proletariat. Joyce has done us a great service in widening the terms of debate beyond the narrow confines of the labour aristocracy thesis and in drawing our attention to the role played by employers in the onset of mid-Victorian stability. The notion of a deferential cotton proletariat can, however, probably be added to Stedman Jones' list of ambitious but largely unnecessary sociological explanations of the decline of working-class independence and radicalism.

Conclusion

This chapter has examined the strengths and weaknesses of the key explanations of mid-Victorian reformism and stability offered by past and present historians. The main conclusion to emerge from this examination is that, whilst such explanations have greatly advanced our knowledge and understanding of the mid-Victorian years, there nevertheless remain many unresolved questions and areas of debate, and relatively untapped areas of potentially fruitful investigation. More specifically, recent heavy emphasis upon 'labour aristocratic' explanations has tended unduly to restrict our lines of approach and field of explanation. Taking its cue from Stedman Jones and Joyce, this study aims to widen our explanatory framework. And in its explorations of a number of interrelated areas and themes — the interactions between (especially economic) structure and consciousness,[92] the nature and content of reformism, the sociological and institutional roots of reformism, the role of ethnicity and the like — this study aims to make a modest contribution towards filling some of the gaps in our knowledge and understanding.

Before setting out on this voyage of exploration, it might first of all be advisable briefly to remind the reader as to the main arguments of this study, especially in their relation to the explanations reviewed above. As at the national level, one is immediately struck by the increasingly narrowed goals and gradualistic practice of workers and their institutions in the cotton districts during the third quarter. Ernest Jones and others could still, at least in the 1850s, denounce the tyranny of capitalists *as a class* and demand fundamental social change. Such denunciations and demands were, however, increasingly out of step with mainstream labour movement thinking; and during the 1860s Jones himself was far less outspoken in his criticisms of capitalism, standing in the 1868 elections as a Liberal Party candidate in Manchester alongside many of his erstwhile political opponents.[93] Equally striking was the stabilisation, as opposed to harmonisation, of overall class relations in the post-1850 period.

Such 'discontinuities' arose for a variey of reasons. As will by now be evident, little importance is attached to 'labour aristocratic', 'deferential' or 'incorporationist' explanations. Of undoubted importance were changes, concessions and initiatives 'from above'. The spread of employer paternalism; the rise of the 'new model' employers;[94] the patchy but more widespread recognition of trade unions by employers; accelerated Conservative and Liberal attempts to accommodate some of the interests of the working class;[95] and a softening in the attitudes and policies of the state towards working-class demands as reflected, for example, in the Ten Hours Act, the Second Reform Act and the trade union legislation of the 1870s[96]. All these factors exerted varying, but significant, degrees of influence upon the ebbing of class conflict.

Changes 'from above', were, however, of extremely limited effect unless accompanied by developments in working-class 'experience'[97] which promoted moderation and reformism. Indeed, it can plausibly be argued that concessions 'from above' often came about more *as a response* to the newfound 'moderation and restraint' of the working class rather than as the direct consequence of working-class militancy[98] and struggle. In terms of working-class 'experience', the defeats suffered by Chartism in 1848 and the falling away of mass support; the successes increasingly attendant upon other forms of organised working-class endeavour; the substantial improvements in the material conditions and status of labour leaders, and the less substantial, but nevertheless real and 'felt' material gains made by the mass of operatives in a highly successful industry operating within a generally dynamic economy — were of major importance in initiating and/or reinforcing the drift into reformism and in convincing workers of the newfound viability of the capitalist system. The increasingly dominant belief within the institutions of organised labour was that the system was in the process of being prised open, of being compelled, mainly as a result of unremitting pressure from the organised working class, to pay greater recognition to the interests of workers. In short, many workers no longer saw themselves as complete 'outsiders': they had gained a stake, however tenuous and ambiguous, in the system. To claim this is not, however, to suggest that the labour movement and the working class were in the process of becoming fully 'incorporated' into capitalism. Industrial and cultural conflict between classes persisted during the third quarter of the century, and many workers retained a strong sense of class pride and independence.

Such evidence hardly lends itself to the notion of 'incorporation'. Nevertheless, we must remember that conflict and class pride operated within the context of an overall acceptance of the system. Finally, ethnic and cultural divisions within the post-1850 working class worked against attempts to build labour solidarity and the appeal of independent working-class politics. By the last 1860s the majority of 'respectable' labour leaders had moved into Liberalism; and Conservatism had developed a mass base around the issue of 'No Popery'.

Notes

1. S. and B. Webb, *History of Trade Unionism* (1920), Chs 3, 4.

2. A.E. Musson, *British Trade Unions, 1800-1875* (1972); and his *Trade Union and Social History* (1974).

3. R. Harrison, *Before the Socialists* (Ch. 1), provides a fine, comprehensive account of the issues involved.

4. Ibid., H.F. Moorhouse, 'The Marxist Theory'; . . ., op. cit.

5. A.E. Musson, 'Class Struggle and the Labour Aristocracy 1830-1860', *Social History*, 3 (1976); and Musson's, *British Trade Unions*.

6. In this context, Musson is rightly taken to task by Foster. See J. Foster, "Some Comments on 'Class Struggle and the Labour Aristocracy' "; *Social History*, III (October 1976), esp. pp. 359-60, 363-75.

7. See, for example, H. Perkin, *The Origins of Modern English Society, 1780-1880* (1969), Ch. IX.

8. E.J. Hobsbawm, 'Custom, Wages and Work-load' in *Labouring Men*, p. 350.

9. R. Harrison, *Before The Socialists*, p. 21.

10. See below, Chs 4, 5 and 7.

11. E.J. Hobsbawm, *Industry and Empire* (1969), Ch. 6; G.S. Jones, 'Class Struggle and the Industrial Revolution', pp. 66-7.

12. For debates concerning the labour aristocracy see H.F. Moorhouse, 'The Marxist Theory'; A. Reid, 'Politics and Economics in the Formation of the British Working Class: A Response to H.F. Moorhouse', *Social History*, 3, no. 3 (1978); J. Field, 'British Historians and the Concept of the Labour Aristocracy', *Radical History Review*, 19 (Winter 1978-9), pp. 61-85; R. Gray, *The Aristocracy of Labour in Nineteenth-century Britain c 1850-1914* (1981), p. 63.

13. E.P. Thompson, 'The Peculiarities of the English', *Socialist Register* (1965), pp. 343-4.

14. For political and industrial concessions see J. Foster, *Class Struggle and the Industrial Revolution*, pp. 207-11. For the growth of employer paternalism see P. Joyce, *Work, Society and Politics*, Chs 4, 5.

15. A. Briggs, *The Age of Improvement* (1962), pp. 394, 402-4.

16. For continued worker hardship see J. Foster, *Class Struggle*, pp. 95-9; G.J. Barnsby, 'The Standard of Living in the Black Country during the Nineteenth Century', *Economic History Review*, 2nd series, vol. XXIV, no. 2 (1971), pp. 220-39; M. Anderson, *Family Structure in Nineteenth Century Lancashire* (Cambridge, 1971), pp. 31-2; A.T. McCabe, 'The Standard of Living on Merseyside 1850-1875', in S.P. Bell (ed.), *Victorian Lancashire* (Newton Abbot, 1974); R.A. Church, *The Great Victorian Boom* (1975), pp. 71-5. For a detailed discussion of living standards in Lancashire see Ch. 3 below.

17. See W.W. Rostow, *The British Economy in the Nineteenth Century* (Oxford, 1948), esp. pp. 122–5. For an incisive critique of the economic reductionism of Rostow-inspired 'growth historians' see E.P. Thompson, 'The Moral, Economy of the English Crowd in the Eighteenth Century', *Past and Present*, no. 5. (February 1971), esp. p. 78.

18. E.J. Hobsbawm, 'The Labour Aristocracy' p. 272. See also Hobsbawm's comments in *Soc. Stud. Lab. Hist. Bull.*, no. 40 (Spring 1980).

19. E.J. Hobsbawm, 'The Labour Aristocracy', p. 274.

20. J. Foster, *Class Struggle and the Industrial Revolution*, pp. 224–38.

21. The weavers had lost their struggle by 1830. Control struggles in engineering were protracted, lasting throughout the nineteenth century. See. J. B. Jeffreys, *The Story of the Engineers 1800–1945* (1970 reprint); J. Hinton, *The First Shop Stewards Movement* (1973).

22. For reference to the 'ritualistic assimilation of bourgeois values' see J. Foster, 'Capitalism and Class Consciousness in Earlier Nineteenth Century Oldham', PhD Cantab. (1967), pp. 272ff.

23. J. Foster, *Class Struggle and the Industrial Revolution*, p. 223.

24. Ibid., pp. 207–11.

25. Gray has noted that the emergence of labour-aristocratic tendencies was 'just one aspect of a wider process of stabilization of capitalist rule', *Soc. Stud. Lab. Hist. Bull.*, no. 40 (Spring 1980), p. 7. In Crossick's opinion, 'the development of the whole of the working class, as well as of class relationships outside the working class, must be analysed if the overall stabilization of the period is to be understood. If the existence of a fragmented working class, with a labour aristocratic elite, is one component of that explanation . . . it must remain only that'. G. Crossick, *An Artisan Elite*, p. 16.

26. G. Crossick, op. cit., pp. 305, 306ff., 320–1; R. Gray, op. cit., pp. 139–43; T.R. Tholfsen, *Working Class Radicalism in Mid-Victorian England* (1976), pp. 12, 17, 102ff.

27. G. Crossick, op. cit., p. 19.

28. Ibid., p. 44; R.Q. Gray, *The Labour Aristocracy in Victorian Edinburgh*, op. cit., pp. 21–8.

29. R.Q. Gray, *Soc. Stud. Lab. Hist. Bull.*, op. cit., p. 7.

30. J. Foster, 'Some comments on "Class Struggle and the Labour Aristocracy",' *Social History*, III (October 1976). In this article, Foster writes (p. 357): 'First, on the nature of working-class radicalism in Oldham. Was the intention to prove that this amounted to some early variant of revolutionary class consciousness? In a limited sense, yes — because the vindication of the argument about liberalization, that the ruling class did change its politico-economic perspective in the 1840s and 1850s, must depend on demonstrating some prior challenge to the capitalist nature of British society. But this was not the main intention and, if it had been, it would have been a very unsatisfactory and superficial one. For while it is easy enough to perform a yes-no duet around some abstract concept of socialist consciousness, the key problem for the historian is rather to specify the forms of class action and consciousness that did emerge — indeed doubly so for these uniquely early concentration of factory workers, 'the eldest children of the industrial revolution' as Engels called them, who had to make their own way with precious little previous experience to guide them.'

31. J. Foster, *Class Struggle and the Industrial Revolution*, op. cit. On page 73 Foster refers to a 'mass consciousness' in Oldham; and on page 74 to a 'mass realization of demands for a total change of the social system'. Oldham's working-class leaders felt able to 'put forward demands for an alternative social system', p. 107. Finally, on page 148 Foster notes in Oldham 'the struggle for a non-capitalist society'.

32. G.S. Jones maintains that if the class consciousness of Oldham's workers was revolutionary, 'it was in a democratic not a socialist sense'. G.S. Jones, op. cit.,

p. 59. D.S. Gadian contends, in marked contrast to Foster, that Oldham was characterised in the 1830s and 1840s more by class collaboration than class conflict. D.S. Gadian, 'Class Consciousness in Oldham and other North-West Industrial Towns, 1830–1850', *Historical Journal*, 21, 1 (1978), pp. 161–72. I believe that Gadian underestimates the extent of industrial and class conflict in Oldham and the strong tradition of independent working-class radicalism. An excellent development of such views is to be found in R. Sykes, 'Some Aspects of Working-class Consciousness in Oldham, 1830–1842', *Historical Journal*, 23, 1 (1980), pp. 167–79. For further discussion of the nature of working-class radicalism see, pp. 20–1, 61–6 below.

33. For the decline of Chartism in south Lancashire see Ch. 2 below, pp. 67–70.

34. R.Q. Gray, *The Labour Aristocracy in Victorian Edinburgh*, op. cit., pp. 155–64; G. Crossick, op. cit., Ch. 10.

35. G. Crossick, op. cit., p. 199.

36. Ibid., p. 204.

37. See Dorothy Thompson's comments in *Soc. Stud. Lab. Hist. Bull.*, no. 15 (Autumn 1967), p. 28. Also, *The Early Chartists* (1971), p. 15.

38. G. Crossick, op. cit., p. 44.

39. R.Q. Gray, op. cit., pp. 21—7.

40. See Ch. 2 below, pp. 32–9. It is important to note not only the greater industrial diversity characteristic of Kentish London and Edinburgh, but also the nature of local élite structure. The social élites of Kentish London and Edinburgh were, unlike their counterparts in cotton, not directly involved in relations of production with the local workforce, and were mainly non-industrial in character (financial, commercial and professional occupations were of central importance). Gray and Crossick maintain that the absence of an aggressive industrially-based bourgeoisie was an important contributory factor to the low levels of class conflict prevalent in Edinburgh and Kentish London. G. Crossick, op. cit., pp. 90–103; R.Q. Gray, op. cit., pp. 19–21.

41. R.Q. Gray. Ch. 3, pp. 24–7; G. Crossick, Ch. 3.

42. G.S. Jones, op. cit., esp. pp. 62–3; A.E. Musson, 'Class Struggle', op. cit.

43. W. Lazonick, 'Industrial Relations and Technical Change: the Case of the Self-acting Mule', *Cambridge Journal of Economics* 3 (1979), pp. 244–5.

44. G.S. Jones, op, cit., p. 63.

45. Questions concerning the spinners' skills, independence and job security are of central importance. It should firstly be noted that, although not traditional handicraft workers, the hand-mule spinners did see themselves as 'skilled', and, as has often been observed (Stedman-Jones, op. cit., p. 51; W. Lazonick, op. cit., pp. 234–5; R. Sykes. 'Early Chartism and Trade Unionism in South-East Lancashire' in J. Epstein and D. Thompson (eds), *The Chartist Experience: Studies in Working-Class Radicalism and Culture, 1830–1860* (1982), p. 182), hand-mule spinning did require manual skill, strength and mechanical ability. As noted by Stedman-Jones (loc. cit.): 'Almost from the start, the cotton spinners described their occupation as a 'trade', were strongly organized, successfully imposed a wage level comparable to that of the artisan, and achieved limitation of entry into the trade and a degree of control over hours of work — in other words, a form of craft control comparable to that within manufacture.'

Secondly, technological change in the 1830s posed a 'formidable threat' to the mule-spinners' 'craft' control and status. The new long mules and the coupling together of pairs of mules increased the number of spindles worked by a single spinner. This, 'resulted in substantial unemployment and increased workload for those who retained their jobs' (R. Sykes, op. cit., pp. 181–2). It was, however, the introduction of the self-acting mules during the 1830s which posed the greatest problem, threatening to, 'transform the operative from a specialised worker into a machine-minder and to allow the replacement of the male artisan by female or juvenile labour' (G. Stedman Jones, op. cit., p. 51). The magnitude of these threats underlay the industrial militancy of the spinners between 1830 and 1842 and their heavy involvement in Chartism. (R. Sykes, op. cit., pp. 181–5; J. Foster, *Class Struggle and the Industrial Revolution*, op. cit., pp. 100–1, 107–18). In practice, the threats were never *fully* realised: male spinners were not widely replaced by females; but the spinners' wages (estimated to be an average between 12s 6d and 15s per week for self-actor minders in 1841: R. Sykes, op. cit., p. 182), status, skill, independence and control over the productive process were greatly eroded by the mid-1840s. The 'control' struggles had been lost and the self-actor spinners were the possessors of no special skills — hence their vulnerability, and dependence upon the employers in the 1840s to protect their 'skilled' status. And the employers accepted this arrangement on the grounds that (as had been the case with the hand-mule spinners), it 'enabled them to use the spinners as a supervisory élite with a vested interest (because they were paid by the piece) in intensifying the labour of the low-paid and unorganised piecers'. J. Hinton, *Labour and Socialism: A History of the British Labour Movement, 1867–1974* (Brighton, 1983), p. 5; W. Lazonick, op. cit., p. 245.

46. P. Joyce, 'The Factory Politics of Lancashire in the later Nineteenth Century', *Historical Journal*, 18, no. 3 (1975), pp. 531–40; P. Joyce, *Work, Society and Politics*, op. cit., pp. 51–2, 96–7.

47. Foster notes that a small group of 'aristocratic' workers occupied prominent leadership positions in the co-ops, temperance societies and adult education institutes, but nowhere is an attempt made to examine the occupations of the wider membership of such organisations.

48. See below, Ch. 5.

49. Ibid., P. Joyce. op. cit., p. 289; H.F. Moorhouse, op. cit.

50. R. Q. Gray, The *Aristocracy of Labour in Nineteenth--century Britain*, op. cit., p. 63.

51. R. Harrison, *Before the Socialists*, op. cit., pp. 13–15, 25–32.

52. H.F. Moorhouse, op. cit., p. 73.

53. *Soc. Stud. Lab. Hist. Bull.*, no. 40 (Spring 1980), pp. 6–11.

54. G.S. Jones, op. cit., esp. pp. 65–7.

55. Ibid., p. 66.

56. Ibid., pp. 63–5.

57. R. Q. Gray, *The Aristocracy of Labour*, op. cit., p. 32.

58. P. Joyce, *Work Society and Politics.*, op. cit., esp. pp. xiv–xxiv, Ch. 3.

59. Ibid., p. xvii. Joyce has subsequently noted (*Social History*, January 1984, p. 74) that *Work, Society and Politics* overemphasized 'the degree of the textile operatives' internalization of the paternalist ethos.' This represents a modification rather than a substantial change to Joyce's original position.

60. Ibid., pp. 90–5.

61. Ibid., p. 94.

62. Ibid., Chs. 2, 5, 6, 7.

63. Ibid., p. xvi.

64. Ibid., p. 313.

65. Ibid., pp. 63–4.

66. Ibid., Ch. 9.

67. Ibid., pp. 59–60, 63–4, 73–9.

68. Ibid., pp. 53–7, 93–4, 111–17, 125.

69. Ibid., pp. 103–10, 125–6.

70. Ibid., Ch. 4.

71. Ibid., pp. 60, 64–82.

72. Ibid., pp. 60, 82.

73. Ibid., p. 95, Joyce employs the term 'subjugatory deference' to refer to 'acquiescence born chiefly of calculation'.

74. For the wide appeal of Chartism see, D. Thompson, *The Early Chartists*,

op. cit., pp. 12–13; J. Foster, *Class Struggle and the Industrial Revolution*, op. cit., p. 132; A. Briggs, *Chartist Studies*, op. cit., pp. 4–10; D. Jones, *Chartism and the Chartists* (1975), pp. 24–32.

75. For Chartism's base in cotton see, T.D.W. Reid and N. Reid, 'The 1842 "Plug Plot" in Stockport', *Int. Rev. Soc. Hist.*, vol. XXIV (1979), p. 67; J. Foster, op. cit., pp. 131–60.

76. For Pilling see, M. Jenkins, *The General Strike of 1842* (1980), Ch. 4.

77. *The Trial of Feargus O'Connor and Fifty-eight Others at Lancaster* (1843), pp. 248–55.

78. Ibid., pp. v–ix (O'Connor), pp. 277–84 (Leach).

79. J. Foster, op. cit., Chs 4, 5; D. Thompson, op. cit., intro.; T.R. Tholfsen, op. cit., Ch. 3.

80. See Ch. 2 below, pp. 58–9.

81. G.S. Jones, 'The Language of Chartism' in J. Epstein and D. Thompson (eds.), *The Chartist Experience: Studies in Working-Class Radicalism and Culture 1830–60* (1982), p. 15. For the gains made by co-operative societies and other working-class institutions from the mid-1840s onwards see Ch. 4 below, esp. pp. 148–54.

82. J. Foster, op. cit., pp. 74, 107, 148; G.S. Jones, 'Class Struggle and the Industrial Revolution', op. cit., pp. 57–8; P. Joyce, op. cit., p. 313.

83. G.S. Jones, 'Class Struggle' op. cit., p. 46.

84. 'The Language of Chartism', op. cit., esp. pp. 29–34.

85. E.J. Hobsbawm, 'Trends in the British Labour Movement', *Labouring*, op. cit., pp. 334–7.

86. G.S. Jones, 'Class Struggle', op. cit., p. 58.

87. For divisions within Chartism see, J.T. Ward, *Chartism* (1973), pp. 220–34, Ch. 6.

88. Ch. 6 below, esp. pp. 267–72.

89. H.A. Turner, *Trade Union Growth, Structure and Policy* (1962), pp. 123–4.

90. P. Joyce, op. cit., pp. 60–1, 68–9, 72–3, 103–4, 151, 320–1.

91. See Ch. 6 below, pp. 247–53.

92. For recent debates concerning structure and consciousness see R. Johnson, 'Socialist-Humanist History', *Hist. Workshop Journal*, 6(1978); R. Samuel (ed.), *People's History and Socialist Theory* (1981), pp. 375–408; E.P. Thompson, *The Poverty of Theory and Other Essays* (1978), pp. 193–397; S. Hall, 'Theory and Experience', *New Statesman*, vol. 99 (30 May 1980).

93. See Ch. 2 below, p. 87.

94. R. Harrison, *Before the Socialists*, op. cit., pp. 34–9.

95. For popular Liberalism see Ch. 4 below, pp. 161–6. For Conservatism see Ch. 7 below; also my thesis, 'Class and Fragmentation: Some Aspects of Working-Class Life in South-east Lancashire and North-east Cheshire, 1850–1870' (unpublished PhD Pittsburgh, 1974), V; P. Joyce, *Work, Society and Politics*, op. cit., pp. 201–21.

96. See Ch. 4 below, esp. pp. 69–70.

97. I adopt Edward Thompson's usage of the term 'experience'. According to Thompson, '. . . experience is exactly what makes the junction between culture and non-culture, lying half within social being, half within social consciousness. We might perhaps call these experiences: I — lived experience; and II — perceived experience . . . What we see are repeated events within 'social being' — such events being . . . often consequent upon material causes which go on behind the back of consciousness or intention — which inevitably do and must give rise to lived experience, experience I, which do not instantly break through as 'reflection' into experience II, but whose pressure upon the whole field of consciousness cannot be indefinitely diverted, postponed, falsified or suppressed by ideology.' E.P. Thompson, 'The Politics of Theory' in R. Samuel (ed.) op. cit., pp. 405–6. For a critique of Thompson's position see, S. Hall, 'In defence of theory', Ibid., pp. 383–5.

98. It is, however, exceedingly difficult to provide a satisfactory answer which has general application. Matters were often complex and far from uniform. For example, John Foster contends that sections of the bourgeoisie in Oldham deliberately attempted from the mid-1840s onwards to 'win back mass allegiance' by offering concessions (support for the Ten Hours Bill, household suffrage, etc.). Such concessions constituted, according to Foster, a direct response to the strength and militancy of workers' struggles. (*Class Struggle and the Industrial Revolution*, op. cit., pp. 207–9.) In terms of the passing of the Second Reform Bill, both the enhanced moderation and capacity for organisation and 'revolutionary potentialities' of the organised working class were factors of major importance. According to R. Harrison, 'it (the working class) had attained precisely that level of development at which it was safe to concede its enfranchisement and dangerous to withhold it' (*Before the Socialists*, op. cit., p. 133).

In respect to employer concessions to organised labour, Harrison maintains that it was the dangerously exposed social position of the large employers of labour and the generally moderate attitudes (as opposed to their capacity for militant action) of craft and skilled trade unionism which brought about a greater willingness to recognise trade unions (ibid., p. 37). In cotton it was, arguably, the increased moderation and caution of the post-1850 union leadership which was partially responsible for the *slow* mellowing of employer attitudes. It must, however, be emphasised that (as Harrison suggests) many employers remained extremely hostile to the recognition of new unions, especially of the semi- and unskilled (see Ch. 6 below). In terms of employer paternalism, it would appear to be the case throughout the cotton districts that whilst not unknown during the second quarter of the nineteenty century, paternalism became a widespread phenomenon only from the mid-1850s onwards — precisely at that point in time when Chartism had lost its mass following and when, industrially, workers and their unions were generally in a weak position, having (despite the adoption of the Blackburn Standard List in 1853) suffered a major defeat over the 10 per cent issue. (See Ch. 6 below; also H.I. Dutton and J.E. King 'The Limits of Paternalism: The Cotton Tyrants of North Lancashire, 1836–1854', *Social History* vol. 7, no. 1 (January 1982.) It is, finally, significant that in terms of middle-class cultural initiatives and approaches to the working class, the hand of friendship and guidance was readily offered to the mid-Victorian Co-operative Movement which was viewed as a splendid example of self-help, but far less readily to trade unions which, despite their moderate noises, were viewed as dangerously 'wrongheaded,' independent and collectivist in character (see Chs. 5 and 6 below). In sum, both the strengths and weaknesses, the revolutionary potential and the enhanced moderation of the labour movement were responsible for the granting of concessions. (A further factor to be included must surely be the greatly stabilised and secure economic and financial position of, especially large, capitalists during the third quarter — paternalism could, literally, be afforded.) On balance, it would, however, seem that the decline of mass Chartism and the growing moderation and reformism of the labour movement were of key importance in terms of a mellowing of attitudes and policies 'from above' (see, for example, Ch. 4, esp. pp. 152–4, Ch. 6, esp. pp. 284–300).

2 THE COTTON DISTRICTS

The purpose of this chapter is to reconstruct some of the main socio-economic and political features of the regional and local contexts in which the general debates and explanations concerning the onset of reformism are to be situated. Attention is accordingly devoted both to the cotton districts of Lancashire and Cheshire as a whole and to selected towns within these districts in which Chartism had enjoyed mass appeal. Given their heavy dependence upon cotton, their aggressive (and largely Nonconformist and Liberal) cotton manufacturers employing large numbers of operatives in their huge combined firms, and, most significantly, their tradition of acute class conflict and their strong support for militant, class conscious Chartism, Ashton-under-Lyne, Stalybridge and their surrounding districts constitute an obvious point of study.[1] Stockport, with its more diversified industrial structure, its larger share of small and medium-sized cotton factories, but with its impressive tradition of working-class radicalism (in which support for industrial and political action often went hand-in-hand) and strong Chartist movement also receives special attention.[2] Discontinuities or 'breaks' were clearly in evidence in all these towns at mid-century: by the 1860s Chartism had almost disintegrated; militant Toryism was building up a mass base; and labour activists were generally being drawn into the Liberal camp. Industrial conflict was still much in evidence, but the former unity between working-class industrial and political action had been ruptured and the wider system was no longer seriously called into question. In short, Ashton, Stalybridge and Stockport (alongside Oldham and other towns in southeast Lancashire and northeast Cheshire) provide important testing grounds for the various explanations of discontinuity.

Before focusing attention upon these towns it is, however, first of all advisable to consider the socio-economic profile of the cotton districts as a whole. And the major economic feature to emerge is the continued domination of cotton over people's lives. In comparison with its 'heroic age' between 1780 and 1840, the mature cotton industry of the third quarter of the nineteenth century experienced far less spectacular rates of growth (between 1840 and 1872 cotton's average annual rate of expansion of output was more than halved), but overseas markets expanded, prices stabilised, and earlier crises of a declining rate of profit were largely overcome. In short, the cotton industry was an eager participant in the Great Victorian Boom.[3] In terms of its employment function, cotton continued to occupy pride of place in Lancashire. As Table 2.1 demonstrates, whilst the percentage of the total population of Lancashire employed in cotton did not reach the 33 per cent mark characteristic of the years between 1800 and 1830, it did, during the third quarter, remain very high, as reflected in percentages of 18.66, 18.36 and 15.96 for, respectively, 1851, 1861 and 1871. In 1861, 34 per cent of the total population of Blackburn was employed in cotton.[4] The corresponding percentages for Preston, Oldham, Bolton, Stockport, Ashton and Stalybridge were, respectively, 30, 29, 24, 34, 31 and 41.[5] And in the United Kingdom the number of cotton employees increased from 374,000 in 1841 to 450,000 in 1871.

Table 2.1:   The Cotton Industry as an Employer of Labour

	Number of employees	Percentage of population of Lancashire	Percentage of UK labour force
1801	242,000	35.96	5.04
1811	306,000	36.96	5.56
1821	369,000	35.04	5.95
1831	427,000	31.94	5.93
1841	374,000	22.44	4.45
1851	379,000	18.66	3.91
1861	446,000	18.36	4.13
1871	450,000	15.96	3.75
1881	520,000	15.06	3.97
1891	526,000	13.39	3.58
1901	544,000	12.44	3.26

Source: D.A. Farnie, *The English Cotton Industry and the World Market 1815–1896* (Oxford, 1979), p. 24.

In terms of the sexual composition of its workforce, cotton was, of course, predominantly a female industry. By 1851 some 15 per cent of Lancashire's adult men and almost 38 per cent of the adult women in paid employment were in cotton.[6] And, as shown in Table 2.2, the percentage of females employed in cotton throughout the United Kingdom increased steadily during the nineteenth century, from 54.3 per cent in 1835 to 59.6 per cent in 1862, and to 62.3 per cent by 1907. The vast majority of female cotton operatives were, by the end of the third quarter, mainly single and in their teens or early twenties. For example, in the three major weaving towns of Blackburn, Burnley and Preston, three-quarters of the unmarried women worked (mainly in cotton), and in the spinning towns of Bolton and Oldham more than two-thirds of unmarried women did likewise.[7] Married women continued to make up a significant proportion of the paid workforce in the north Lancashire weaving towns, but in the spinning belt in the south of the county, where employment opportunities for men at comparatively high rates of remuneration were more varied and plentiful and where women's wages in cotton were generally lower than in the north, married women's employment was far less common. Thus, whilst approximately one-third of the married women in Blackburn, Burnley and Preston had paid employment (in Burnley approximately 38 per cent of married women went out to work), the corresponding figure for Bolton and Oldham was less than one-fifth.[8] The growing popularity of the Victorian cult of domesticity also acted as a powerful drag upon married women's paid employment, especially in the southern part of Lancashire where skilled spinners or engineers were increasingly reluctant to 'lose face' by their wives' acceptance of paid work. Nevertheless, by 1900 some quarter of a million Lancashire women were employed in the cotton mills, and, as two authorities on the subject declare, 'It became the common expectation for a girl from a working-class family in one of the cotton towns to work in a mill until she was married, and quite possibly afterwards as well'.[9]

In 1851 almost 17 per cent of men aged 20 and over in Lancashire were employed in cotton. And, as demonstrated in Table 2.2, the percentage of men employed in the UK cotton industry actually rose slightly over the century, from 26.4 per cent in 1835 and 1862 to 28.3

Table 2.2:   The Sexual Composition of the UK Cotton Labour Force, 1835–1907

	1835 %	1862 %	1907 %
Men	26.4	26.4	28.3
Lads and boys	12.4	9.1	7.9
Lads: Half-timers	6.9	4.9	1.5
Total males	45.7	40.4	37.7
Women	30.8	39.0	45.7
Girls	17.3	16.7	14.9
Girls: Half-timers	6.2	3.9	1.7
Total females	54.3	59.6	62.3

Source: G.H. Wood, *The History of Wages in the Cotton Trade During the Past Hundred Years* (Manchester, 1910, p. 136 (Table 46).

per cent in 1907. Against this, the percentage of all males (men, lads and boys, and half-timers) in UK cotton did, however, show a significant decline: from 45.7 per cent in 1835, to 40.4 per cent in 1862, to 37.7 per cent in 1907. This decline was caused primarily by the introduction of legislation which sought to reduce the employment of children and juveniles. Thus by mid-century it had become illegal to employ children under eight years of age at all and children under 13 full-time: in 1850 only 5 per cent of the Lancashire cotton labour force was under the age of 13.[10]

In relation to the various jobs performed within the cotton industry, there existed a clear and hierarchical division of labour between males and females. The latter were usually excluded from the spinning process itself (the preserve of 'skilled' males), and concentrated their efforts into preparing the loose cotton for the spinners and weaving the spun yarn into cloth.[11] A more detailed breakdown of these broad areas of work reveals females as card-frame tenters (occasionally), as piecers and winders, and as weavers. Female weavers constituted, by 1900, almost one-third of all cotton operatives and two-thirds of the total female cotton workforce.[12] Males were to be found as strippers and. grinders, piecers, winders, beamers, spinners, overlookers and weavers.[13]

The jobs performed by male cotton operatives were usually better paid and of higher status than those carried out by females. For example, in 1871 the male strippers' and grinders' average weekly earnings were 21/-, whilst blowing and cardroom women averaged only 12/-, and drawing-frame tenters 12/9d. In the same year the male self-actor spinners in Manchester and district averaged 30/- weekly; female ring and throstle spinners received a meagre 12/-.[14] Differential wage rates and earnings were, in part, a reflection of the levels of skill, physical strength and danger involved in the performance of the various jobs in cotton. Mule-spinners, for example, were generally regarded as 'skilled' workers and the work of strippers and grinders was hard and sometimes dangerous.[15] This was, however, by no means the whole story. Certain tasks performed by female operatives involved skill, physical effort, and the ability to cope with monotony and repetition. Threats of physical danger and illness were present for many male and female workers, cardroom operatives, for example, being highly susceptible to byssinosis.[16] Furthermore, the level of skill demanded in the male preserve of self-actor spinning was, in comparison with the skilled trades in building and printing, minimal. The self-actors were, to coin Joseph

White's excellent phrase, 'contrived aristocrats', whose high earnings and status from the 1850s onwards derived not from the enforcement of a formal system of apprenticeship, but from effective control over the supply of labour into spinning and the wages paid to their assistants, the piecers.[17]

Underlying the wage and occupational hierarchies in cotton was the increasingly widespread assumption that men, as the primary breadwinners, were 'naturally' deserving of more remunerative jobs than women. It is true that this assumption became less marked in the predominantly female weaving districts of north Lancashire, and that by the late 1880s the Northern Counties Amalgamated Association of Cotton Weavers strongly supported the payment of equal rates of pay to both male and female weavers who operated the same number and width of looms. But, as Liddington and Norris observe, actual practice in north Lancashire was complex, and 'there was considerable controversy over whether equal pay really existed . . .' Generally speaking, it appears to have been the case that male weavers in the north did tend to monopolise the large, wide looms which brought them a weekly advantage of some 4/- over the three- or four-loom female weavers. Completely equal pay in weaving was, therefore, a myth.[18]

Occupational, financial and status gradations also existed *within* the spheres of male and female labour in cotton. For example, the relatively well-paid female weavers were often said to consider themselves a 'cut above' the lowly-paid 'force' (i.e. cheeky) and 'un-ladylike' cardroom women. And it was generally agreed that the women in the winding room formed a rather distinct, select group (perhaps as a result of being able actually to talk to each other during work, a bonus denied to workers in the extremely noisy weaving sheds).[19] Similarly, male card- and blowing-room hands came low in the occupational and status hierarchies of male operatives; and, as is well documented, the spinners, especially from mid-century onwards, were increasingly characterised by an indifference to the plight of many other grades of operatives and by sectional patterns of trade-union organisation.[20]

It is important to note at this stage that differentiation within cotton did not preclude the development of labour solidarity both within and across occupational grades. The high degree of support offered to Chartism by all manner of cotton workers provided concrete evidence of this contention. Differentiation did not lead automatically or necessarily to internal conflict and fragmentation:

differences and distinctions are to be clearly distinguished from divisions and strife. Poor pay and long hours, demands for trade union recognition and political representation, an end to employer 'tyranny' and state hostility — these have, historically, constituted some of a veritable multitude of issues around which impressive demonstrations of labour solidarity have been built, and which have overshadowed differences in income and skill among participating groups. Surely the extent to which, and the conditions under which, internal class divisions and conflicts or sources of unity predominate is a matter for *historical* investigation. To argue in this manner is to suggest that a purely structural (i.e. sociological) investigation of the cotton workforce's, indeed the entire working class's, patterns of internal differentiation is inadequate to the task at hand. A strong grasp of structure must be combined with a sound grasp of historical context and of process, of changes over time, both in structure and consciousness.[21] We will return to a more detailed consideration of such matters in our examination of Lancashire Chartism later in this chapter.

Cotton operatives worked in an industry which was increasingly characterised by geographical specialisation. Certainly by the end of the 1880s weaving was concentrated mainly in north Lancashire and spinning in south Lancashire and northeast Cheshire. This geographical division was in only its early stages at mid-century. Thus in 1850 the representative unit of production in cotton was the combined weaving and spinning firm, which, in total, accounted for 31 per cent of the firms, 52.5 per cent of the spindles. 82.6 per cent of the looms and, most significantly, 60.8 per cent of the labour force employed in the English cotton industry.[22] The 1850s did witness the rise of specialist spinning firms in south Lancashire, and the 1870s and 1880s were to see the spectacular expansion of weaving firms in the north. But against such developments we must set the expansionary peak achieved by spinning in north Lancashire during the 1870s, and the successful adaptation to the new division of labour by south Lancashire's substantial weaving industry. Nevertheless, by 1890 geographical division and specialisation were facts of life: the combined firm was no longer the representative unit of production; the northeast weaving districts around Burnley had experienced rapid growth; and, just as three-fifths of the looms were centred upon north Lancashire, so three-quarters of the spindles were in operation in south Lancashire.[23]

Both within and between Lancashire's weaving and spinning

districts there existed important variations in the size of cotton factories. In the north, for example, there emerged differences between the older centres, such as Blackburn and Preston, and the newer weaving centres around Burnley. Blackburn and Preston were, at least by the latter part of the third quarter of the century, characterised by well-established, generally large units of production, and wealthy employers who prided themselves upon their strong local connections and their paternalism.[24] By way of contrast Burnley, Nelson, Colne and Darwen — the 'centres of greatest expansion in population and industrial production from the 1870s onwards — were areas in which the small-scale *parvenu* employer flourished (low capital requirements in these centres — with manufacturers frequently hiring both looms and power[25] — facilitated ease of access to weaving). And, forced to operate in a highly competitive market, the small-scale weaving capitalist constantly sought to reduce costs, especially in relation to labour. Attempts to increase the number of looms per worker and cut the standard piece-rate per unit of output were common, as was opposition to trade unionism and evasion of the established Lists; the upshot was 'a primitive system of . . . labour relations' in which employer paternalism and worker deference were generally conspicuous by their absence.[26]

South Lancashire and northeast Cheshire were the bastions of the large combined firms, complete with their old-established market connections and ease of access to abundant supplies of capital and yarn (Manchester being the commercial and financial centre of the southern districts). These southern districts were the home of 'the leading industrial clans of the county' (the Masons of Ashton, the Whittakers of Hurst, the Birleys and Callenders of Manchester, the Kershaws of Stockport, the Cheethams of Stalybridge, and the Heskeths and Eckersleys of Bolton — to name but a few[27]), who, during the third quarter, consolidated their wealth and power and mellowed many of their attitudes and polices towards labour. In addition to the dynasties of Blackburn and Preston, it is thus among the large, wealthy employers of the south that Joyce finds the language and practice of paternalism most common.[28] Ashton, Glossop, Hyde, Stalybridge and Mossley were the veritable homes of the giant combined firms[29]: but Stockport, Manchester and Bolton also contained some extremely large units of production in cotton.[30] Oldham, by way of contrast, was a centre of small and medium-sized cotton factories, at least until the arrival of the Limiteds during the 1870s.[31]

In relation to the cotton industry as a whole, the large units of south Lancashire were untypical. As Farnie notes, 'The representative unit of enterprise in the cotton industry was the small rather than the large firm and the representative employer was a yeoman of industry rather than a captain of industry'.[32] However, despite the continued importance of the small employer, we should take careful note of Joyce's observation that, from mid-century onwards, market forces 'increasingly favoured the larger employer' who was better equipped both to weather the storms of the Cotton Famine and cyclical depression, and to take full advantage of mid-Victorian expansion.[33] Between 1850 and 1890 there occurred increases in the numbers employed in the average spinning, weaving and combined firms from, respectively, 108 to 165 operatives, 100 to 188, and from 310 to 429.[34] Furthermore, once the distribution of a town's workforce by size is considered, then the full significance of the large and medium-sized firm is revealed. In the 1880s, for example, the largest 13 of Preston's 80 cotton firms employed 47 per cent of the cotton workforce; in Bolton 10 firms out of a total 101 employed 45 per cent; in Blackburn 16 out of 96 employed 50 per cent; and in Ashton 4 out of 40 had 40 per cent.[35] The persistence of the small firm as the representative unit of production should not, therefore, be allowed to obscure both the large size of many firms and the high concentration of ownership in the main centres of the industry.

Beyond the confines of cotton various artisan and skilled occupations constituted the major sources of employment. Thus Gadian's examination of the 1841 Occupational Abstracts reveals that, in addition to the 40 per cent or so employed directly or indirectly in cotton, some 30 per cent of the adult male populations of Bolton, Stockport, Burnley, Ashton, Bury, Oldham and Preston were engaged in the building and metal trades, shoemaking, tailoring and other crafts.[36] And Anderson has calculated that artisans made up some 33 per cent of the waged population of Lancashire in 1851.[37]

Usage of the terms 'artisan' and 'skilled worker' merits some brief, cautionary comment. It must constantly be borne in mind that nineteenth-century artisans and skilled workers did *not* constitute a homogeneous, uniformly privileged group, and that, as Thompson, Prothero and Hobsbawm have admirably and conclusively demonstrated, there existed significant variations of experience among such workers.[38] As is well known, shoemakers, tailors, handloom weavers and mule spinners were examples of artisans and skilled workers adversely, if unevenly, affected during the first half of the nineteenth century by employer attempts to reduce costs and expand production. The displacement of men by machinery, the beating down of prices and wages, the employment of 'illegal' men and additional apprentices, the introduction of piecework and subcontracting, the promotion of 'sweating' and the attacks upon trade unionism and custom and practice — these were some of the methods used by employers in an attempt to achieve greater profits.[39] This was, however, an uneven process. Groups such as glassblowers, coachbuilders, printers, and to a lesser extent skilled engineers and building trades operatives, whilst not completely free from employer attacks, were, nevertheless, more successful in preserving their independence, status and wage levesl.[40] And it is surely significant that, whilst the higher, more privileged and secure trades tended to remain aloof from involvement in radical working-class political and industrial action, the 'lower', more threatened and beleaguered trades provided impressive support for the Chartist movement.[41]

The above comments act as a safeguard against the adoption of an exaggerated picture of uniformly privileged artisans and skilled workers in Lancashire and Cheshire. It is true that the rapid mid-century expansion of the engineering and metal trades, and the textile machinery industry (which, in total, accounted for 3 per cent of Lancashire's paid labour force in 1851) did much to boost the numbers and self-awareness of the skilled working class. This was particularly the case in Manchester, Oldham, Bolton and, to a lesser extent, Blackburn — the centres of such industries.[42] But against this development, we must set the virtual destruction of handloom weaving and the growing insecurity, poverty and despair suffered by countless tailors, shoemakers and other once-proud artisans.

A further 15 per cent of Gadian's adult males in selected cotton towns were miners or labourers. And Anderson estimates that by 1851 approximately 7 per cent of Lancashire's paid labour force were labourers, the majority eking out a meagre existence in casual employment.[43] For those females employed outside of cotton, domestic service (which, although cleaner and less dangerous than employment in cotton, remained, nevertheless, unattractive in the cotton districts on account of its low rates of pay, long hours and severe restrictions upon individual freedom[44]), millinery, dressmaking and seamstressing constituted important sources of income. It should also be noted that charwomen and washerwomen, groups much neglected by historians, made up a sizeable 7 per cent of the paid female population of Lancashire in 1851.[45]

Beyond the ranks of the manual working class, some 10 per cent of Gadian's 1841 selection and 17 per cent of Anderson's Lancashire survey for 1851 were tradesmen and shopkeepers; and a small professional and white collar élite (5 per cent of Gadian's adult males) sat atop the social pyramid.[46] As was the case with artisans and skilled workers, the bourgeoisie was far from being a unified whole, in terms of both structure and consciousness. Thus shopkeepers and sections of the petty bourgeoisie (which consisted of tradesmen, small employers, 'little masters' and the like) were often closer to the manual working class in income and life-style than they were to the rich merchants and large employers — a fact recognised by O'Connor and other Chartist leaders in their appeals for support to shopkeepers and other sections of the 'middle classes'.[47] Thus Foster has convincingly shown that, far from forming 'a massive social tail to the bourgeoisie proper' (as was the case in Northampton and South Shields), small farmers, shopkeepers and other 'borderline' occupations in Oldham had a very close political and cultural identification with the working class during the 1830s and early mid-1840s.[48] As Anderson writes of Lancashire's tradesmen and shopkeepers:

> Some high class specialists, in the town centres, had customers of the higher social groups and were reasonably affluent. More typical, however, . . . were the little provision shops, pawnbrokers, beershops, and public houses scattered here and there in the working class districts of the towns. From these little shops the family scraped a living little better, at best, than that of the families round about. Below even this group, came the mass of itinerant salesmen of all types and of both sexes, many of whom were almost totally destitute.[49]

In addition to its social isolation in many cotton towns during the Chartist period, the bourgeoisie proper (that is, excluding non-bourgeois, but also non-manual occupations such as shopkeeping and clerking) may well have conformed to the Oldham pattern of a pronounced division between 'big' and 'petty' groupings.[50] Certainly, many of the towns in the southern areas of the cotton districts had much in common with Oldham, as did centres such as Blackburn in the north. Large, sometimes huge mills (being, in several towns, far more substantial than those in Oldham), and extremely wealthy cotton families, tightly interlocked by marriage, religion and politics, were highly visible in Ashton, Stalybridge,

Stockport and elsewhere.[51] These 'upper class' dynasties were clearly distinct, both materially and culturally, from the vast mass of tradesmen, small employers and others who made up the 'middle classes'.[52] However, of utmost significance in Oldham, and in all probability throughout south Lancashire from the mid-late 1840s onwards, were the growth in support for the bourgeoisie from among those borderline occupations which had previously sided with the working-class movement; the successful bourgeois challenge mounted to the working class; and the negotiated, often troubled but unmistakable consolidation of bourgeois hegemony.[53]

In turning to a consideration of the main economic and social features of the Chartist strongholds of Ashton, Stalybridge and Stockport, we can sharpen our focus somewhat, and variously develop, reinforce and modify the Lancashire- and Cheshire-based observations offered above.

As in the cotton districts as a whole, all three centres experienced rapid population growth during the first half of the nineteenth century. For example, as shown in Table 2.3, Ashton's population more than doubled between 1801 and 1831, and increased more than fourfold between 1801 and 1851. This expansion resulted almost

Table 2.3: Population Changes in Ashton, Stalybridge and Stockport, 1801–71[a]

	1801	1811	1821	1831	1841	1851	1861	1871
Stockport	14,830	17,545	21,726	25,469	50,154	53,835	54,681	53,001
Ashton	6,391	7,959	9,222	14,035	22,678	29,791	34,886	32,030
	1794		1823					
Stalybridge	1,100		5,500	14,216	18,141	20,760	24,921	21,043

Sources: *1851 Census. Number of Inhabitants, 1801–51*. Vol. I. See, especially, Appendix to the Report, *Comparative Populations of Principal Towns in 1801 and 1851*; Vol. LXXXV, pp. cxxvi–ii; *1851 Census. Ages, Civil Conditions, Occupations and Birth-Places of the People*, Vol. II, pp. 622ff; *1871 Census, England and Wales*, Sessions 1871–2, Preliminary Report with Tables, Vol. 1, pp. 9–15.

Notes a. The figures are for the municipalities of Stalybridge, Ashton and Stockport.

b. The presentation of accurate figures for the municipality of Stalybridge in the decade prior to the 1851 Census presents considerable difficulties. The town of Stalybridge was situated partly in the Township of Dukinfield, Cheshire, and partly in Ashton-under-Lyne Parish, Lancashire. According to the 1851 Census (see above, *No. of Inhabitants*, Appendix, p. cxxvi), 'no correct statement of the population (of Stalybridge) can be made for the years prior to 1851'. It is, however, possible to arrive at approximations by extracting the relevant information from the 1841 Census (i.e. that part of the town of Stalybridge in the Parish of Ashton-under-Lyne is listed as consisting of 5,747 inhabitants; that part of Stalybridge in the Township of Dukinfield consisted of approximately 12,394 people (Town of Dukinfield = 10,000, to be deducted from the figure (22, 394) given for the Chapelry, unfortunately not the Township, of Dukinfield: total = 12,394 + 5,747 = 18,141), and by consulting the calculations made by contemporaries and historians. See, especially, N. Cotton, 'Popular Movements in Ashton-under-Lyne and Stalybridge before 1832', M. Litt. (Birmingham Univ., 1977) pp.20–1; E.A. Rose, *Methodism in Dukinfield* (1978); *1841 Census*, Enumerators Abstract, pp. 31, 145.

entirely from the emergence and growth of Ashton as a spinning and weaving town which was increasingly geared towards the spinning of medium counts from American cotton.[54] Ashton's neighbours in the Tame valley, Stalybridge, Mossley, Dukinfield and Glossop, were, likewise, extremely heavily dependent upon cotton, and developed rapidly as 'new' towns during the early decades of the nineteenth century. Stalybridge, for example, grew from a nucleus of 'a few houses straggling along the road' during the latter part of the eighteenth century (with a population of just over 1,000 in 1794) to become a bustling cotton town of some 20,000 inhabitants by mid-century (with a reputation for its 'frontier' mentality of toughness, turbulence and acute class conflict).[55] To the southwest the larger cotton town of Stockport experienced an increase from a total of almost 15,000 inhabitants in 1801 to over 50,000 inhabitants by 1851.

Population increase was at its most rapid during the years between 1821 and 1841, showing astounding advances of 158 per cent in Stalybridge during the 1820s, and 90 per cent in Stockport during the decade 1831–41. As Table 2.4 demonstrates, Ashton also experienced extremely heady growth (52 per cent in the 1820s being followed by 61 per cent during the 1830s). Table 2.4 further shows that (as was generally the case in the cotton districts[56]) the rate of population increase slackened considerably from the early 1840s onwards. Stockport provided an extreme example of this process, the rate of growth falling from 90 per cent to 7 per cent to 1 per cent in the respective decades of 1831–41, 1841–51 and 1851–61. Ashton and Stalybridge also witnessed a declining rate of growth, but in a far less extreme form. Thus rates of increase of 31 per cent and 17 per cent for Ashton during the decades 1841–51 and 1851–61 and 27 per cent and 14 per cent for Stalybridge during the same period hardly constitute instances of demographic stability. Finally, given their extremely heavy dependence upon supplies of American cotton, Ashton and Stalybridge were severely affected by the Cotton

Table 2.4: Rates of Population Change in Ashton, Stockport and Stalybridge, 1821–71

	1821–31 %	1831–41 %	1841–51 %	1851–61 %	1861–71 %
Ashton	+ 52	+ 61	+ 31	+ 17	− 8
Stockport	+ 17	+ 90.6	+ 7	+ 1	− 3
Stalybridge	+ 158	+ 27	+ 14	+ 20	− 15

Famine, as reflected in absolute declines in their respective populations between 1861 and 1871 of 8 per cent and 15 per cent (see Table
2.4).[57] Stockport suffered less acutely during the Cotton Famine,
but even so its population fell by 3 per cent during the same period.
After 1871 rates of increase picked up again, but for the remainder
of the century were well below pre-1851 levels for Stockport and
pre-1861 levels for Ashton and Stalybridge.

What conclusions, if any, can be drawn from the population
trends and statistics presented above? More specifically, what light
do the experiences of Ashton, Stockport and Stalybridge shed upon
Joyce's contention that there existed a 'close connection' between
declining rates of population growth and the onset of 'social calm'
in various towns throughout the cotton districts from the early 1840s
onwards? (Joyce's thesis being that the growth in neighbourhood
feeling and sense of belonging, consequent upon population stability, bound together workers and employers in a shared culture based
upon paternalism and deference[58]). And what of the corollary that
high degrees of class conflict and working-class radicalism and
population growth went hand-in-hand? Before answering such
questions, two relevant methodological cautions must be struck.
Firstly, it should be noted that Joyce does *not* present a thesis which
posits an exclusive, invariable and one-to-one causal relationship
between rates of population growth and degrees of class conflict
(such a thesis would be simplistic, extremely narrow and, in many
instances, erroneous[59]). Rather — and this brings us to our second
caution — Joyce does recognise the complexity of factors involved
in the onset of mid-Victorian stability (rates of population growth
being 'only one item on a long agenda'), and therefore places population stability within a wider explanatory framework: the conclusion offered being that a 'link' or 'close connection' did exist
between stability and 'a general decrease in the rate of population
growth' during the two decades after 1841.[60]

Beyond these cautions we can suggest, on the basis of the demographic evidence for our three towns, that there possibly did exist a
connection between the two developments; but whether this connection was as close as suggested by Joyce, and whether an enhanced
sense of neighbourhood and community spirit united workers and
employers to anything like the extent claimed by Joyce, are far more
open to question. In support of Joyce, Stockport did provide a case
of a town whose rate of population increase fell away dramatically
during the 1840s, and slowed to a trickle during the following

decade. Significantly, Chartism lost much of its impetus in Stockport from 1842 onwards, and was more or less defunct by the mid-late 1850s.[61] The somewhat different pictures of Ashton and Stalybridge also conform to Joyce's thesis, a far higher degree of population expansion at mid-century being accompanied by the continuation of a high degree of class conflict.[62] It is, however, at this point that our support becomes far more qualified. There are, for example, exceptions to Joyce's rule (in the 1860s Bolton enjoyed a high rate of population growth and yet was characterised by relative social stability and a generally moderate labour movement[63]); post-1841 rates of population growth in many cotton towns, although lower than during the heady expansion of the pre-1841 era, were nevertheless far from negligible (both in 'calm' and less 'calm' towns)[64]; and, as noted above, demographic trends constituted but one part, and in all probability a relatively minor part, in the overall explanation of stability. Furthermore, Chapters 5, 6 and 7 of this book will demonstrate that, whilst neighbourhood feeling undoubtedly existed, it is highly questionable as to whether it provided the secure foundation for inter-class cultural unity as suggested by Joyce. In their cultural activities, as at work, cotton operatives tended to be far more independent and class conscious (whilst paying ritual deference to their employers on the necessary occasions) than a thesis of the deferential proletariat would have us believe. For these various reasons, the links between population stability and class harmony are probably far less solid than claimed by Joyce.

More solid was the link between growing neighbourhood consciousness and stability and the sharp increase in hostility to Irish Catholic immigrants which occurred in many northern towns from the late 1840s onwards. Chapter 7 will offer a detailed investigation of this theme, but it is worth noting at this point that during major outbreaks of anti-Irish rioting, such as at Stockport in 1852 and Ashton and Stalybridge in 1868, the encroachment of Irish immigrants into what many locals had come to define as 'English' streets and neighbourhoods constituted a major source of resentment on the part of large sections of the 'host' community. The Irish Catholics were increasingly seen not as welcome victims of the Potato Famines of the 1840s, but, unlike the pre-1850 Irish immigrants, as a single, unwelcome outgroup intent upon inflicting 'alien' patterns of thought and behaviour upon their country of settlement.[65] In these ways the rapid influx of a 'new' population into increasingly settled neighbourhoods was productive not of working-class solidarity and radicalism but intra-class conflict.

The populations, both 'immigrant' and 'local', of our three towns were heavily concentrated in the cotton industry, and, especially in Ashton and Stalybridge, industrial diversification was very limited. Thus the factory inspector reported that in 1861, 41, 34 and 31 per cent of the respective populations of Stalybridge, Stockport and Ashton were employed in cotton manufacture.[66] Ashton's 36 spinning and weaving mills housed 10,856 operatives (4,957 males and 5,899 females) out of the borough's total population of 34,886 inhabitants. In addition to cotton, Ashton and its immediate vicinity accommodated a total of 14 machine, hatting, turning, colliery and silk works — but the number of workers employed in these works was only 1,150. In truth could the factory inspector thus describe Ashton as a town 'almost entirely' dependent upon cotton.[67] Ten years later cotton still ruled the roost. As shown in Table 2.5, a House of Commons Return of 1871 estimated that of the 10,051 persons engaged in 'manufactures' (as opposed to all areas of employment) in the parliamentary borough of Ashton no less than 9,080 (3,739 males and 5,341 females), or 90 per cent, were to be found in cotton. And, as late as 1911, 40 per cent of the paid workforce of Ashton and neigbouring Hurst were cotton workers.[68]

Table 2.5: Parliamentary Borough of Ashton-under-Lyne, Manufactures 1871

| | Number of works | Total number persons employed | | |
		Male	Female	Male & Female
Textile fabrics and wearing: apparel				
Cotton factories	40	3,739	5,341	9,080
Boot and shoe making	12	13	1	14
Millinery, mantle, stay, Corset and dressmaking	14	0	35	35
Tailors and clothiers	17	13	91	104
Hatters and cap makers	6	10	32	42
Not named above	5	8	42	50
Metal manufactures:				
Manufacture of machinery	14	226	0	226
Nails and rivets	1	1	0	1
Brass finishing	9	58	0	58
Clocks and watches	1	1	0	1
Misc. articles of metal	32	93	0	93
Leather manufacturers:				
Tanners and curriers	1	1	0	1
Manufactures connected with food:				
Bakehouses, biscuits, con-				

fectionery	4	6	0	6
Not named above	1	1	0	1
Manufactures connected with building, etc.:				
Builders	3	7	0	7
Marble and stone masons	2	2	0	2
Carpenters, joiners, etc.	10	17	8	25
Painters	12	19	0	19
Cabinet and furniture makers	7	14	0	14
Not named above	1	1	0	1
Miscellaneous manufactures:				
Ropemakers	1	9	0	9
Healdknitting, etc.	4	25	51	76
Earthenware	1	2	2	4
Letterpress printing	8	56	0	56
Coachbuilding	1	3	0	3
Coopers	5	6	0	6
Not named above	13	79	38	117
Total	225	4,410	5,641	10,051

Source: *Ashton-under-Lyne Corporation Manual, 1873–4*, p. 58.

Cotton was of even greater importance in Stalybridge. Thus in 1861 Stalybridge's 39 cotton mills employed a staggering 10,404 (4,586 males and 5,818 females) of the total borough population of 24,921; there also existed 27 bobbin turners and machinists which employed 1,110 hands.[69]

Stockport did have a more varied industrial structure than Ashton and Stalybridge, but, as an examination of the 1851 Census reveals, cotton still reigned supreme. Thus, as compared with the respective Lancashire percentages of 17 and 15, 38 per cent of Stockport's adult males (aged 20 and over) and 33 per cent of Stockport's adult females were to be found in cotton manufacture in 1851.[70] And in terms of the *paid* working population of the borough[71], cotton accounted for 55 per cent. As Table 2.6 demonstrates, approximately 45 per cent of Stockport's waged males (8,107 out of an estimated waged male workforce of 17,762) were cotton operatives in 1851. Labourers (10 per cent), traditional craft wòrkers (10 per cent), shopkeepers and traders (7 per cent), skilled workers in the building industry (5 per cent) and engineering workers (2 per cent) constituted the other occupational groups of any significance — but all were greatly inferior to cotton. Among females this picture was even more marked. Thus some 68 per cent (8,982 out of an estimated waged female workforce of 13,058) of Stockport's paid female workers were cotton operatives. Domestic servants (6.9 per cent), milliners (5.7 per cent), and washerwomen and charwomen (4 per cent) were the other principal occupational groups. We should also note that approximately 25 per cent (7,216 out of 28,546) of the *total* female population of Stockport worked at unpaid tasks in the home.[72]

Between the censuses of 1851 and 1871 Stockport's hatting industry underwent considerable expansion (employing 3.7 per cent of the males and females aged 20 and upwards in 1871), but in other respects the occupational structure of the town changed little. Engineering, for example, failed to expand and cotton retained its 'traditional' dominance, employing in 1871 some 32 per cent of Stockport's adult population.[73]

The dominance exercised by cotton and — especially in Ashton and Stalybridge — the general lack of industrial diversification had extremely important effects upon the social structures of our three towns. For — to return to our earlier remarks concerning class and

Table 2.6:   Principal Occupations, Stockport Borough, 1851

	Males	Females	% waged male workforce (17,762)	% waged female workforce (13,058)
Cotton manufacture[a]	8107	8982	45	68
Labourers[b]	1825	–	10	–
Traditional crafts (Coachmakers, hatters, tailors, shoemakers, etc.)	1804	–	10	–
Shopkeepers and traders	1320	–	7	–
Woodworkers, cabinet makers, builders and building trades workers	900	–	5	–
Engineering and machine works	429	–	2.4	–
Domestic servants	–	897	–	6.9
Milliners	–	756	–	5.7
Washerwomen, manglers, charwomen	–	549	–	4

Notes: a. 5,091 males aged 20 and over, 3,016 under 20; 5,368 females aged 20 and over; 3,614 under 20.
b. Includes agricultural labourers and gardeners.
c. Excluding labourers.
Source: *1851 Census, Ages, Civil Conditions, Occupations and Birth-Place of the People*, Vol. II (1854), pp. 648ff.

differentiation — what clearly existed in these towns was, at least in structural terms, a relatively homogeneous cotton proletariat which derived its livelihood from the sale of its labour power to capitalist employers. Internal differentiation was, as already noted, by no means absent, but unlike, for example, Kentish London and Edinburgh, the working population was not characterised by the presence of a large and exclusive craft and skilled élite, which was increasingly anxious to divorce itself from the mass of unskilled workers.[74] And, even in comparison with Oldham and Bolton — where Foster's 'labour aristocrats' were far more prominent, especially in engineering — and cosmopolitan and diversified Manchester, Ashton, Stalybridge and Stockport possessed relatively homogeneous industrial and social structures. It is also worth noting that the latter three towns also had very *large* working-class populations. For example, in the early 1840s two reliable contemporary sources estimated the size of the working class to be 60-odd per cent , 81 per cent, 90 per cent, 94 per cent, 85 per cent and 84 per cent of, respectively, the total populations of Manchester, Ashton, Stalybridge, Dukinfield, Stockport and Oldham.[75] It was, thus, within the context of single-industry dominance that Chartism developed its mass following in Ashton, Stalybridge and Stockport.

In contrast to the overall picture in the industry, the majority of cotton operatives in the three towns were employed in relatively large units of production which were dominated by wealthy employer families. Thus as early as the 1830s the Stockport and Ashton districts had developed a reputation for 'bigness'. As Table 2.7 demonstrates,

Table 2.7: The Average Size of the Workforce in Cotton Mills in Northwest Towns, 1838

Town	No. of mills	No. of workers	Workers per mill
Stockport	86	23,772	276.4
Blackburn	44	10,460	237.7
Manchester	182	39,363	216.3
Middleton	12	2,537	211.5
Wigan	37	6,137	165.9
Ashton	82	12,143	148.1
Bolton	69	9,918	143.7
Bury	114	13,652	119.8
Rochdale	117	10,520	89.9
Whalley (includes Burnley)	113	9,960	88.1
Oldham	220	15,291	76.5

Source: D.S. Gadian, 'Class Consciousness in Oldham and Other North-West Industrial Towns' *Hist. Jnl.*, I, 1 (1978), p. 168.

Stockport topped the league table of workers per mill in the northern cotton towns in 1838, and Ashton occupied a respectable mid-table position.

In terms of the size distribution of cotton firms, the parish of Ashton was especially well endowed with large and huge (mainly combined) establishments, having in 1841 six firms of 1,000 + and eight of 500 + as compared with the respective figures of five and six for its closest rival, Manchester (see Table 2.8). Within the parish of Ashton there also existed a substantial number of small and medium-sized cotton factories, 38 (40 per cent) of a total of 93 firms employing under 100 operatives, and a further 29 (31 per cent) finding work for between 100 and 199 operatives. Twelve of the parish's cotton firms (almost 13 per cent) housed between 200 and 499 workers; and the very large (500 +) and huge establishments (1,000 +) together accounted for 15 per cent. Thus some 28 per cent of the parish's cotton firms employed 200 workers and upwards — a percentage which was higher in Ashton borough, the area of the heaviest concentration of the large and massive mills.

Table 2.8:   Size Distribution of Lancashire Cotton Firms — by Workforce Employed, 1841.

| Town | Total firms | Firms employing the following labour force | | | | | |
		0 +	20 +	50 +	100 +	200 +	500 +	1,000 +
Blackburn	49	1	3	15	13	9	5	3
Manchester	115	3	13	10	35	43	6	5
Ashton (parish)	93	2	13	23	29	12	8	6
Bolton	55	1	7	13	11	19	2	2
Bury	87	15	17	14	19	16	5	1
Whalley	127	25	31	23	7	16	5	0
Rochdale	77	10	17	20	16	14	0	0
Oldham	201	67	50	31	33	17	3	0

Source: D.S. Gadian, 'Class Consciousness in Oldham and Other North-West Industrial Towns'. *Hist. Jnl.*, I. 1 (1978), p. 169.

In 1854 Stockport borough's 56 cotton firms employed 17,025 operatives, a crude average of 304 operatives per firm.[76] However, as in the case of Ashton, we would be wrong to suggest that Stockport's firms were uniformly large. Indeed, as Table 2.9 reveals, 13 (23 per cent) of Stockport's 56 firms employed less than 100 workers, and a further 16 (28 per cent) employed between 100 and 199 operatives. In sum, therefore, 51 per cent of Stockport's firms accomodated, in each case, less than 200 operatives.[77]

Table 2.9:   Size Distribution of Cotton Firms in the Borough of Stockport, 1854

	Firms employing the following labour force				
Total firms	1–99	100–199	200–499	500–999	1,000 +
56	13 (23%)	16 (28%)	18 (32%)	5 (8.9%)	4 (7%)

Source: Calculated on basis of information in *Stockport Advertiser*, 1 April 1854.

The importance of the above qualification does not, however, invalidate our earlier emphasis upon the crucial significance of large units of cotton production in Stockport's economic life. To refer, once again, to Table 2.9: no less than 60 per cent of Stockport's cotton firms employed between 100 and 499 operatives. A further 32 per cent employed between 200 and 499; and 16 per cent employed upwards of 500. Final confirmation of the crucial importance of 'bigness' in Stockport, Ashton and Stalybridge was provided by the factory inspector in 1863. Ashton was listed as having an average per cotton mill of 300 operatives, Stockport of 274 and Stalybridge of 266. By way of contrast, Salford had an average of 242, and Oldham of 167.[78]

In all three towns there existed a marked concentration of economic (and other kinds of) power in the hands of a relatively small number of families. The latter constituted Joyce's 'cotton dynasties', the leading influences among Foster's 'big bourgeoisie'. Thus at Stockport in 1854 the four largest cotton manufacturers, the Kershaws, the Marshalls, Robert McClure and Lingard and Cruttenden, employed a staggering combined total of 5,600 operatives, some 31 per cent of the borough's total cotton workforce. James Kershaw, Liberal MP for Stockport from 1847 to his death in 1864, employed 2,000 cotton operatives (11 per cent of the borough's total cotton workforce) in his immense Mersey and India Mills[79] (See Table 2.10). A Congregationalist and civic improver, Kershaw regarded himself as a firm but generous employer and was, in the opinion of the Conservative *Stockport Advertiser*, the 'greatest and best employer of labour' in the locality.[80] Robert McClure, another key figure in Stockport Liberalism and mayor of the borough in 1861, employed 1,200 operatives in his Travis Brook Mill.[81] Lingard and Cruttenden had a cotton workforce of 1,000, and the Marshall family employed a total workforce of 1,400 at their Heaton Lane and Portwood Mills (see Table 2.10). Unlike Kershaw, McClure and several other millowners in Stockport (the Eskrigges, Waterhouses, and Peter and Henry Marsland, to name

but a few), James Marshall and his family were active Conservatives. James Marshall himself was Mayor of Stockport during the
late 1840s, and, along with Samuel Christy (of the hat manufacturing firm), James Heald, the Conservative candidate for Stockport,
and Cephas Howard and the Fernleys (both extensive manufacturers of cotton), made strenuous efforts to extend the popular
appeal of Stockport Conservatism during the mid-Victorian
period.[82]

Table 2.10:   Stockport Borough's Cotton Firms, 1854

	Owner(s) and location of firms	Numbers employed
	Greenwood and Wilkinson, Newbridge Lane	25
	Taylor, Churchgate	40
	Whalley, Newbridge Lane	45
	Arden, Park	50
	Moorhouse, Portwood Bridge	50
	Taylor and Burton, Newbridge Lane	50
	Stewart, Throstle Grove	50
L	Pendlebury, Lancashire Hill	60
	Williamson and Sadler	60
	Cheetham, Carrs	60
	Nicholls, Bridgefield	65
	Hulme, Brinksway	65
	Newton and Scattergood, St Petersgate	65
		13 employed between 1 and 99
	Cummings, Wharf Street	100
	H. Barlow, Portwood	100
L	Edward Walmsley, Sandy Lane	100
	M. Newton, Lancashire Hill	100
	S.W. Wilkinson, Heaton Lane	118
	T. Coussens, Newbridge Lane	120
	Hope Hill Mill	125
	W. and J. Leigh	130
	Hallam, Higher Hillgate	134
	Hardy and Andrew, Park	147
	F.S. Clayton, Park	150
	J. Marsland, Sandy Lane	150
C	Walmsley, Heaton Lane	150
	White, St. Peter's Square	150
	Ashe, Carrs	160
	Read, Sandy Lane	170
		16 employed between 100 and 199
	Gabriel, Hempshaw Lane	200
	Heaword, Brinksway	220
	Newton and Scattergood, Carrs	250
	Hulme, Victoria Mill	250
	C. and T. Bailey, Mottram Street	250
	Twyford, Old Road	250

Owner(s) and location of firms		Numbers employed
	Thornley, Newbridge Lane	250
	B.G. Cooper, Portwood	260
L	Eskrigge and Carver, Park	270
	S. Barratt, Lancashire Hill	285
	Coussens, Newbridge Lane	300
L	H. Marsland, Mill Lane, Park	336
	T. Stewart, Park	350
	Lucas and Co., Kingston Mills	380
C	Fernley and Bradley, Higher Hillgate	400
	Wright, Heaton Lane	415
C	Wilkinson, Portwood	450
L	Waterhouse and Hampson, Edgeley	450
		18 employed between 200 and 499
	John Lees, Heap Riding Mill	500
C	Fernley, Chestergate	560
	Robinson, Spring Bank	560
	Whitelegg, Great Underbank	600
C	C. Howard, Portwood	850
		5 employed between 500 and 999
	Lingard and Cruttenden (3 mills)	1,000
L	R. McClure, Travis Brook Mill	1,200
C	J. Marshall, Heaton Lane and Portwood	1,400
L	J. Kershaw, Mersey and India Mills, Heaton Lane	2,000
		4 employed 1000 +
	Total firms = 56	

Source: *Stockport Advertiser*, 1 April 1854.
L = prominent Liberal.
C = prominent Conservative.

Unlike Stockport, with its mixture of Conservative and Liberal employers, Ashton and Stalybridge were both heavily dominated by Liberal and predominantly Nonconformist employers.[83] As P.F. Clarke observes, 'Ashton and Stalybridge . . . probably came as near as anywhere to exhibiting that conflict between bourgeois Liberalism and working-class Conservatism which was the staple of the myth of Tory Democracy'.[84] T.H. Sidebottom, the victorious Conservative candidate at Stalybridge in the 1868 general election, was himself a millowner, as was 'Tommy' Mellor, similarly triumphant at Ashton. But both these men were unrepresentative of the political complexion of the local millocracy, and traded heavily, as did Conservative millowners at Stockport, upon popular antagonism towards the Manchester School manufacturers.[85]

As at Stockport, economic and political power was concentrated in a few hands. At Ashton, Hugh Mason, owner of the-massive Oxford Mills and founder of the 'model' Oxford community, dominated the West End. An active Congregationalist and the leading Liberal of the borough, Mason was both an implacable enemy of trade unionism and, at least after 1850, a leading exponent of paternalism.[86] The Whittaker family employed virtually the entire waged labour force at the neighbouring village of Hurst, and were strong Liberals.[87] The Buckleys, Reyners Kenworthys, were likewise large, wealthy cotton manufacturers active in Liberal politics in Ashton.[88] At Stalybridge the Cheethams, Leechs and Platts were the major employers, all, once again, being active Liberals and newfound converts to paternalism.[89]

The character and attitudes of the employer élite were, of course, of fundamental importance in moulding the behaviour and values of the working class. Unlike, for example, Edinburgh with its heterogeneous industrial structure and its professional, commercial and financial élite largely removed from immediate, day-to-day contact with manual workers,[90] much of Lancashire, and certainly the three towns highlighted above, possessed highly visible, wealthy and relatively unified industrial bourgeois élites directly involved in relations of production with the cotton proletariat. And given the commitment of large sections of the Lancashire élite to the 'truths' of orthodox political economy, their support for the introduction of the New Poor Law, their membership of the Anti-Corn Law League, and their opposition to trade unionism and universal manhood suffrage, it was hardly accidental that large numbers of 'their' workpeople turned to independent class action as a means of remedying their multifarious grievances. Whether the more widespread adoption of paternalism and the general mellowing of employer attitudes and practices from the late 1840s onwards exerted a significant influence upon the decline of working-class radicalism will be treated in due course. For the moment we must turn our attentions to an examination of the main manifestation of working-class radicalism during the 1830s and 1840s: Chartism.

The researches of a number of scholars[91] have firmly demonstrated that Chartism had a mass presence in the manufacturing districts of northern England. Barnsley, Bradford, parts of the northeast, and cotton towns such as Ashton, Stalybridge, Oldham, Stockport and many others, were centres of special prominence, where class conflict and the politics of 'physical force' were very much to the fore.[92] The northwest had made an important contribution to the national struggle for reform in 1831 and 1832, and during the 1830s was to witness the growth of radical trade unionism, chronic industrial 'unrest', mass opposition to the introduction of the New Poor Law, strong support for factory regulation, widespread condemnation of the claims of orthodox political economy, and, finally, the coming together of these various movements and grievances under the broad banner of Chartism. So strong had the radical working-class presence become by the late 1830s that the northwest fully deserved Gadian's description as, 'the foremost stronghold of popular political organisation in the country'.[93]

The experiences of Ashton, Stockport and Stalybridge — which, in turn, were illustrative of developments in several other towns in south Lancashire and northeast Cheshire[94] — can briefly be traced in order to add substance to the general comments made above. In Stockport — a town with a strong tradition of radicalism and working-class activity — the local Chartist movement dated its origins to a visit to the borough by Feargus O'Connor in December 1835.[95] Towards the end of August 1838 Richard Pilling and several other radicals formed a Stockport Radical Association, which was effectively the first Chartist organisation in the town. At that point in time relations between the Chartists and middle-class reformers were becoming strained, and, as a result of disagreements concerning economic and social issues, the extent of political reform to be attempted and the questions of arming and violence, finally snapped by the spring of 1839. What had emerged in Stockport by 1839 was a mass, independent, militant, and extremely class conscious working-class movement, of which Chartism was the central pulse. Indeed, between the latter part of the 1830s and the conclusion to the strikes of 1842, Chartism was to enjoy hegemony over the local working class, having particular appeal to spinners, weavers and many other sections of the factory population.[96]

Similar developments were in evidence in Oldham where, as Foster and Sykes have established, instances of 'class collaboration' were greatly overshadowed by the development of a powerful, insurgent and independent working-class movement which, at least in Foster's opinion, made a successful, if temporary, bid for control of the local state machinery.[97] Class conflict was, in all probability, even more intense in the Ashton, Stalybridge and Glossop districts. As Dorothy Thompson notes, alongside Barnsley and Bradford, Ashton was one of the three towns in the north of England 'which had the highest levels of Chartist activity throughout the whole period of the movement'.[98] In 1837 working- and middle-class reformers in the Ashton district were to be found as supporters of the local Reform Association, but this proved to be a tenuous unity which, as at Stockport, failed to survive the growth of militant Chartism in 1838 and 1839. The stamping grounds of the fiery Tory radical Joseph Rayner Stephens, and those impressive Chartist leaders, Peter Murray McDouall, Timothy Higgins and John Deegan, the Ashton district witnessed massive torchlight meetings, frequent recommendations to arm (Stephens's language of 'war to the knife', McDouall's support for 'ulterior measures'), the widespread manufacture of arms and pikes, and plans for insurrection during these two years.[99] The Whig authorities and the more radical elements within local Whiggery would have no truck with this 'physical force' Chartism: in December 1838 Stephens was arrested; McDouall's arrest followed the Bull Ring Riot in July 1839; and mass arrests took place during the latter part of 1839. Thus by the end of the decade the split between Chartists and middle-class reformers was complete. Chartism in Ashton and Stalybridge had acquired its class conscious and independent character, which was to undermine all attempts to effect an alliance with middle-class reformers during the ensuing 20 years.

Chartism survived the arrests of 1839 to demonstrate, by the early 1840s, renewed, even increased vitality. The establishment of the National Charter Association in 1840 marked an important advance in terms of national organisation and efficiency. Furthermore, the rapid growth of the Association in 1841 and 1842 (from 80 associations in February 1841 to more than 400, with 50,000 members, in June 1842), the collection of over three million signatures (more than twice the number of the 1839 petition) for the 1842 National Petition, and the rebuffs given to the Complete Suffrage Union and the Anti-Corn Law League, were all signs of Chartism's robust health.[100] The northwest fully participated in these developments. At Stockport, for example, the 880 National Charter Association membership cards taken out between March 1841 and October 1842 indicated a continuing high level of support for the movement.[101] The 1842 National Petition was signed by over 14,000 of Ashton's 22,678 inhabitants, and by an astounding 10,000 of Stalybridge's 18,141.[102] And the attempts to develop a popular following on the parts of Anti-Corn Law League and the middle-class reformers failed to diminish Chartism's appeal to working people throughout south Lancashire and northeast Cheshire.

It was, however, during the strikes of the summer of 1842 that Chartism in the northwest appeared to have consolidated its hegemony over the working class. As Mick Jenkins has convincingly demonstrated, it was primarily in the cotton towns that opposition to wage reductions and the demand for a 'fair day's wage' were linked to the wider, overriding goal of the enactment of the Charter.[103] Thus whilst not all the cotton towns supported the 'political' nature of the strike,[104] and whilst some Chartists remained equivocal about the relation between the wage question and the Charter,[105] there is no doubt that the official aim of the Lancashire trades was to 'extend the strike nationally and to remain out until the Charter became the law of the land.[106] The strikes thus represented an unqualified success for those local activists, such as McDouall and Leach, who had campaigned for united action by trade unionists and Chartists.

Paradoxically, however, the very advances made in 1842 represented not the consolidation but the highwater mark of Chartism's power and successes, both nationally and throughout the cotton districts. As Epstein observes, 'the year 1842 marked a watershed in the history of popular radicalism . . . The mass politics which had dominated the period 1838–1842 began to lose its hold within sections of the working class'.[107] Thus the rejection of the second petition by parliament left the Chartist movement disillusioned and uncertain as to future tactics and strategy. Similarly, notwithstanding their mass character and far-reaching aims, the strikes of 1842 ended in defeat and, for many, disillusionment with the politics of open confrontation and insurrection. And, partly as a response to these defeats, and partly in response to the onset of mid-1840s economic recovery, some groups of workers (especially the skilled) turned away from ambitious plans for social reconstruction towards the more limited objective of building up and consolidating the strength of their organisations within the confines of the system. In addition there occurred, as Epstein and others have noted, an increasing separation and specialisation of function within what had been a highly united and integrated labour movement.[108] Thus temperance reform, educational improvement, trade unionism and cooperative retailing tended to assume much more solid and independent individual identities, complete with their own organisation and aims. The bond between the various parts of the 'labour movement' became far less intimate, and Chartism increasingly lost its formerly hegemonic position within that 'movement'.[109]

To argue this case is not, however, to agree with some historians that the increased energy expended upon trade unionism, co-operation and education constituted, in the 1840s, a major and conscious ideological break with Chartism (of the 'pure and simple' trade union/co-operator versus 'social theorist' Chartist variety[110]). Especially in the short term, Chartism, trade unionism and co-operation were seen by many activists as complementary forms of activity, with Chartism occupying pride of place. There also existed a considerable overlap in the personnel of these various organisations.[111] In the longer term, however, it does seem to have been the case that two major 'breaks' developed. Firstly, in the mid-Victorian period it became increasingly difficult to sustain 'labour movement' unity. Of particular importance, as noted by Stedman Jones, was the growing divorce between political and industrial forms of action.[112] And secondly, as the trade unions and co-operatives built up their memberships, perfected their organisational structures and made significant advances within the unreformed system,[113] so Chartism lost much of its former relevance and direct appeal. The attainment of universal manhood suffrage no longer constituted the *sine qua non* of real and lasting economic and social improvement. Herein lay some of the key roots of mid-Victorian fragmentation and reformism to be traced in this study.

Although less influential from the early-mid 1840s onwards, Chartism in the late 1840s, even the 1850s, must not be dismissed as insignificant. For whilst the movement failed to recapture its former mass presence in the cotton districts, and whilst by 1848 London, as opposed to Lancashire, had become the central pulse of Chartism, nevertheless northwest Chartism displayed a remarkable resilience, showing signs of life well into the 1850s and informing the character and ideology of the reform struggle of the 1860s.[114] In particular, 1848 constitutes an important, fascinating if elusive, and as yet largely under-researched year in the history of the movement.[115] Notwithstanding the claim that Chartism in Stockport was comparatively inactive in 1848,[116] it would appear to be the case that, in terms of the cotton districts as a whole, there did occur something of a revival. The precise nature, extent and causes of this revival have still to be fully explored by historians,[117] but, a few highly provisional observations can be made, and the more pressing avenues of further research indicated. There exists firstly, a question mark against the extent of Chartism's revival. Was, for example, Stockport typical of the cotton towns in its lack of enthusiasm for the movement in 1848? Or was the picture, both regionally and nationally, more varied? Foster, for example, whilst noting that Chartism's revival in Oldham during 1847 and 1848 'never reached the proportions of 1839 or 1842', nevertheless refers to 'the revolutionary feeling' among factory operatives being 'apparently quite considerable' during March and April of 1848.[118] And an admittedly brief survey of the contents of the Chartist and local press has certainly raised the suggestion in my mind that the build up of Chartist strength in the Manchester district both before and after Kennington Common, and arming and plans for insurrection during the summer months, were quite possibly far more considerable and widespread than is sometimes claimed.[119] Most assuredly, as admirably shown by John Belchem,[120] Chartism's successful alliance with the Irish Repealers both increased the strength of the working-class movement and brought the questions of violence and insurrection very much to the fore.

This naturally leads into a second area of questions. How seriously was insurrection contemplated in 1848? Were, as Belchem argues, the Irish the 'motive force' in the alliance, the leading advocates of violence, or was the responsibility more equally shouldered? How much serious thought was given to the crucially important questions of planning and the co-ordination of activities? Given the obvious and necessary element of secrecy involved in the risings and 'disturbances' of 1848, it is by no means easy to extract ready answers from the available evidence. But the seemingly serious organisational weaknesses revealed, in for example, the isolated Ashton rising of 14 August, and the failure of the plan whereby Chartists and Repealers from the Manchester district would converge on Manchester on 15 (or 16?) August, fire the mills, and initiate a general uprising in the city,[121] surely demand that every scrap of evidence be located and thoroughly interrogated. If nothing else, there certainly resides in the material a fascinating story.

A final area of potentially fruitful investigation concerns Chartist responses to the setbacks and defeats of 1848. More specifically, how typical of the national picture was the reaction of many Lancashire and Cheshire Chartists, by no means all of whom were 'labour aristocrats', in devoting an increasingly major part of their energies to the development of trade unionism, co-operative retailing and educational advancement?[122] This brings us back, of course, to the issue of ideological and organisational 'breaks' raised earlier.

Was there a *conscious* adoption of more reformist and 'collabora-tionist' attitudes, or did the onset of reformism develop far more 'behind the backs' of our former Chartist stalwarts? As we will see in due course, this study tends to support the latter viewpoint.

We will return to an examination of the chronology of post-1848 Chartism shortly. For the moment, it is necessary to delve further into two key aspects of the pre-1848 movement: its social base and its ideological orientation. In terms of the former, a steadily mount-ing body of research has convincingly shown both that Chartism drew great sustenance from an impressive range of occupations and its articulation of the many and varied grievances which beset work-ing people during the second quarter of the nineteenth century.[123] Handloom and powerloom weavers; spinners and many other fac-tory operatives; metal workers (even of an 'aristocratic' character); labourers, schoolteachers; mechanics; 'independent' persons, espe-cially shopkeepers and newsagents; tailors; shoemakers; hatters; and cloggers — these were some of the occupational groups which gave strong support to northwest Chartism. Indeed, so impressive were the extent and depth of support and the increasingly key role played by leaders from manual and borderline occupations,[124] that full endorsement must be given to Gadian's view that, at its peak, northwest Chartism, 'did not so much draw its support from differ-ent occupational groups, but instead represented the political aspi-rations of a whole class'.[125]

Chartism in the cotton districts had a particularly strong follow-ing among those factory workers (mule spinners, calico printers, dressers, dyers and powerloom weavers), lower artisan trades (tai-lors, shoemakers, hatters, and building trades workers) and out-workers (silk and flannel weavers, fustian cutters and, to a lesser extent, cotton handloom weavers) who experienced similar diffi-culties and threats to their status, independence, security, control and wage levels. To take but one example: technological change (especially the introduction of the self-acting mule) posed a 'formi-dable threat' to mule spinners during the 1830s, removing most of the need for skill and strength in spinning. The adult male spinner was not generally replaced by female workers (as had extensively been threatened during the 1830s), but the wages of fine and coarse spinners fell substantially during the late 1830s and early 1840s, unemployment and general insecurity increased, a number of strike defeats were experienced, and the spinners' battle to retain control over production was, by the late 1840s, in tatters. Little wonder that the spinners and the other threatened groups displayed not 'aristo-cratic' aloofness and a high degree of trade sectionalism, but, as convincingly demonstrated by Sykes and others, a marked degree of inter-trade collaboration and close involvement in Chartism.[126] Spe-cific occupational grievances were, of course, allied to those of a more general nature — exclusion from the vote, the hostility of the state to working-class interests, employer 'tyranny', the partiality of the law, the glorification of unrestrained individualism, competi-tion and acquisitiveness and the ideological and cultural onslaught against workers' life-styles, values and practices — which moved large numbers of workers, often differentiated in terms of skill, occupation and income, to join together in struggle in order to rectify their grievances.[127] And out of such grievances and struggles developed a strong sense of class consciousness which involved, 'an identity of their interests as between themselves, and . . . against other men whose interests are different from (and usually opposed to) theirs'.[128] Chartism — with its central message that last-ing improvement for workers was primarily dependent upon the achievement of universal manhood suffrage — represented the flowering of this consciousness.

In the pre-1832 period the class antagonism of workers and their allies had been directed primarily at the aristocracy and the forces of 'Old Corruption': the 'people' or 'productive classes' being placed in opposition to 'corrupt rulers', 'idlers', 'parasites' and 'monopo-lists'. And, as Stedman Jones and Prothero have rightly reminded us, the notion of the 'people' in this pre-Chartist period was not synonomous with manual workers alone: rather, it also embraced those of the middle class excluded from political representation and suffering under the burdens of aristocratic monopoly and privi-lege.[129] However, following the 'betrayal' of 1832 and the marked growth of economic, social and ideological divisions between labour and capital, and whilst there still existed a certain amount of ambi-guity in popular attitudes towards the middle class, nevertheless the 'people' increasingly came to mean the manual working class.[130] And in the manufacturing districts of north, where industrial capi-talism was most advanced and where conflict between labour and capital was most acute, this association of the 'people' with the working class was correspondingly most marked. By the mid-1830s popular anger in the manufacturing districts was directed not only at the forces of 'Old Corruption' but also at the foremost representa-tives of the new system, the factory masters or 'steamlords': indeed, by the end of the 1830s the 'steamlords' had come to be seen as the principal enemy of the 'people' of Lancashire and Cheshire.[131] In such a manner did 'working class' and the 'people' become interchangeable concepts.

Opposition to the factory masters and the severing of political ties with the middle-class reformers at the end of the 1830s were indicative of growing popular antagonism towards the middle class. In the eyes of working-class radicals, the 1832 Reform Bill had given a large section of the middle class a stake in the system. And, as confirmed by the subsequent actions of the Whig administration (the introduction of the New Poor Law, opposition to trade unionism, etc.), the enfranchised middle class had 'ceased to be part of the "people",' having 'joined the system of oppressors and . . . henceforth answerable for the actions of the legislature'.[132] As Stedman Jones observes:

> There was general agreement, that given their contradictory position involving both servility and tyranny, the middle classes as a whole, would only support the claims of the people when pressured by necessity . . . The attempt to create such pressure remained a consistent radical strategy in the post-1832 and Chartist period. The predominant image of the middle classes was of a timid and fearful as well as petty-tyrannical group, who would only ally with the people out of necessity or expediency. Their natural sympathies within the prevailing artificial system lay with property and they themselves were thought to aspire to become idlers.[133]

Working class pressure was brought to bear most strongly upon those sections of the middle class and those borderline occupations not involved in antagonistic productive relations with workers. Thus Chartist leaders, especially O'Connor, distinguished between shopkeepers and manufacturers. Whereas the latter exploited the workers by 'buying cheap and selling dear' (and in numerous other ways), it was in the objective interests of the former to have a well-paid labour force which would, of course, spend more money upon the purchase of necessary provisions. As O'Connor declared, 'You must enlighten the shopkeepers and tradesmen of all denominations, and fight them against the real enemy — the steam Lords'.[134] The support which the working-class movement in Oldham and elsewhere received from many shopkeepers during the

1830s and 1840s lent some credence to O'Connor's view. It is also important to note that O'Connor's view generally prevailed throughout the Chartist movement: the aim was not to engage in unthinking, blanket criticism of the middle class, but to apply realistic, discriminating analysis.[135]

Antagonism towards the 'steam lords', their acolytes, and their political allies and mouthpieces, whether Whig or Tory, was, however, very real. And reference has already been made to a major source of this antagonism, namely the economic and social attitudes and policies of many cotton manufacturers (their commitment to orthodox political economy, their antipathy to collective and independent working-class organisation, their seeming indifference to working-class poverty and suffering, their support for the New Poor Law, their opposition to factory reform, etc.[136]) As a Chartist placard at Ashton declared in 1842, 'If Colonel Thorpe would know who the Chartists are, what they are, and how they became what they are, he must look into our mills and sit on the Board of Guardians'.[137] In the same year William Aitken, a leading figure in Ashton Chartism, took the masters to task for their haughty posturing, their selfish, insensitive and tyrannical actions, and counselled them to 'keep within their own palaces, as the dark nights were coming on . . . the reckoning day was near, and a bloody reckoning it was likely to be'.[138] And Stockport Chartism represented a protest of the dispossessed against, 'the tyranny of those whose God is gold, whose temple is the Bastille and who would crush them for the attainment of wealth'.[139] Given the existence of such heartfelt grievances and antagonisms, and Chartism's programme (with its alternative political economy and support for fundamental social change), it was entirely to be expected that class tensions between workers and employers would not easily weaken. Even during the 'Golden Years', middle-class support for household suffrage and a mellowing of employer attitudes and practices failed to eradicate entirely the 'people's' suspicion of the 'steam lords', however paternalistic and seemingly benevolent the latter had become.

A further source of antagonism, especially important in relation to the issue of an interclass political alliance, was the mistrust in which middle-class reformers were increasingly held by the Chartists. The latter were prepared to accept the hand of friendship from the reforming middle class, if genuinely and sincerely offered.[140] But experience taught the Chartists that this was rarely the case. Thus, as briefly noted earlier, the sense of betrayal in 1832 was compounded by the opposition of the Whig radicals to 'physical force' Chartism in 1838 and 1839, and the arrest, in Stockport and elsewhere, of leading Chartists by those very same Whigs who had been their erstwhile political allies. Indeed, from this time onwards the Stockport Chartists transferred their electoral support from the Whigs to the Tories. This action did not signal a sudden conversion to the principles of Toryism (regarded as the 'traditional foe') by the Stockport Chartists but, given the restricted borough and parliamentary franchises, was adopted as a tactical electoral device to register protest at the actions of the Whig authorities. Thus whilst the Tories were seen as an 'open' enemy, the Whigs were branded as 'a treacherous, deceitful, bad lot'.[141] Similarly, working-class support for the Conservatives in Ashton and Stalybridge in the 1850s and 1860s was, in part, a protest against the overwhelmingly Liberal complexion of local employers.[142]

Mistrust of middle-class reformers also arose in response to four other issues. Firstly, as exemplified by the Leeds Parliamentary Reform Association (1840–41) and some of the middle-class reform groups of the 1850s, the degree of franchise reform supported (usually household suffrage) fell short of the Chartist demand for universal manhood suffrage.[143] Secondly, as vividly illustrated in the history of the Complete Suffrage Union in the early 1840s, even when prepared to accept manhood suffrage, middle-class reformers baulked at an open embrace of the terms Charter and Chartist, with the latter's connotations of violence and extremism.[144] Thirdly, as again illustrated by the Complete Suffrage Union, many Chartists believed that middle-class reformers were reluctant to work alongside workers and their institutions on equal terms: rather, the intention was to place workers under middle-class tutelage and organisational control.[145] Finally, the overtures of some middle-class groups, most notably the Anti-Corn Law League, were dismissed as a selfish attempt on the part of the middle class to use working-class support as a point of pressure upon the aristocracy, and to divert workers away from their true goal, the attainment of the Charter.[146] Given the range and depth of issues which separated the Chartists on the one hand and the middle-class reformers and manufacturers on the other, it is not surprising that mainstream Chartism steadfastly refused to accept the political overtures of the middle class.

Chartism's antagonism towards the factory masters and their allies brings us to an examination of the wider and more complex questions concerning the ideological character and aims of working-class radicalism during these years. To return to questions posed in the previous chapter: what was the ideological content of Chartism? What did a developed sense of class consciousness mean? What was its content?

In response to such questions, it is first of all useful to remember that Chartism belonged to an age when mass labour and post-Owenite socialist movements had not taken root within the European working class. And, as a pre-Marxist movement, Chartism does not easily lend itself to those categories — such as revolutionary and revisionist — which were later developed by Marxists to describe late nineteenth- and twentieth-century movements.[147] A proper sense of Chartism's historical context and of the terminology appropriate to that context are, therefore, of extreme importance in any attempt to define the movement's ideology. It is simply not good enough to dismiss, as is still occasionally the practice in some left-wing political circles, Chartism as 'lacking in theory' (presumably of the 'correct' kind); to do so is to skate over, or completely miss, the actual ideological content of Chartism in favour of some preconceived and idealised notion of how workers should have behaved and thought. Readers may be interested to know that, in their writings on Chartism and in their dealings with workers, Marx and Engels were generally attentive to actual needs and aims.[148]

It is also useful at this juncture to remind ourselves of our earlier endorsement of Stedman Jones's view that, if revolutionary, Chartism was so in a democratic and (at least in some parts of Britain) anti-capitalist, rather than in a consciously socialist manner. Despite its condemnation of the unreformed system, its mounting attacks upon the factory masters and sections of the middle class, and its undoubted, if partial, debt to Owenism, the pre-1850 Chartist movement was not formally committed to socialism or any other single ideological 'ism'. There did not develop a socialist theory of exploitation within production which captured the hearts and minds of large numbers of workers, and Chartism did not aim at the revolutionary overthrow of the state machinery, the expropriation of the mill owners, and the creation of a full-blown socialist society.[149]

In truth , as Asa Briggs informed us some years ago, Chartism was, at heart, an umbrella movement which represented the flowering of early nineteenth-century working-class radicalism, and which embraced, to both its advantage and cost, a variety of aims.[150]

Political enfranchisement, trade union recognition, a 'fair day's wage for a fair day's work', factory reform and repeal of the New Poor Law, an improvement in living conditions and a more equitable distribution of wealth, property and income, an end to 'class legislation' and employer 'tyranny', recognition of the worker's moral worth and his or her right to partake of the benefits of a civilised existence — there were some of the cardinal aims of Chartism.

Such a variety of aims were, however, held together by a vision of an alternative social order which, whilst 'rarely articulated with great theoretical clarity', nevertheless commanded widespread support from fully-fledged proletarians as well as artisans.[151] A 'more or less egalitarian society' in which 'parasites' and 'drones' would have no place, in which the industrious would reap their rightful reward, in which the glaring inequalities between labour and capital would be eradicated, or at least greatly diminished, by the creation and proliferation of units of co-operative production, and in which the values and practices of co-operation, mutuality, and individual and collective independence would occupy pride of place — this was the nature of the Chartist vision.[152] Far from aiming at the creation of a Jacobin republic of 'small equal, independent commodity producers', Chartism, had come by the 1840s to embrace the ideal of a 'commonwealth of associated producers'.[153] Thus, although not offering a formal socialist platform, Chartism did make economic and social demands which presented a very real threat to existing social relationships. And in the cotton districts the primary targets of Chartism's critique were, as Foster rightly emphasises, the factory masters and their allies. Northwest Chartism was thus far more capable of addressing itself to the problems of the factory operative and factory production than the revisionist case, complete with its emphases upon the primacy of the political and the artisan character of Chartism, would have us believe.[154]

Following the setbacks and defeats of 1848, Chartism's mass appeal visibly diminished. This was partly due to the changing social composition of the working class and the social base of popular radicalism. By the mid-1840s many of the occupational groups which had provided Chartism with its driving force had lost their battles against mechanisation and control of production (the spinners and various outworkers), and the growth of 'dishonourable' sections of the trade — and, given such defeats, became far more vulnerable, dependent and accommodative than in the earlier period. As noted in the first chapter, the national labour movement in the post-1850 period was dominated not primarily by fiercely dissatisfied groups such as handloom weavers, mule-spinners, tailors and shoemakers, but by those craft and skilled workers (bookbinders, printers, engineers and others) who had tended to remain aloof from Chartism and Owenism and who were cautious and moderate in their attitudes and behaviour. Within the specific context of the cotton districts, mid-century saw the virtual disappearance of handloom weaving as a major occupation, the emergence of the conservative spinner, and the overall routinisation of the factory system and its patterns of work and authority. In short, we are moving into a different era. No longer did an emerging, raw proletariat confront a largely untried and seemingly unstable system: by 1850 the factory had come to stay, and many of its workers had experienced no other mode of production and patterns of authority and control. The consolidation of the system did not witness a corresponding disappearance in working-class protest; but what it did witness, as noted earlier, was the growth of more limited and narrowed forms of action on the part of experienced Chartists and others.

The sociological underpinnings of the decline of Chartism referred to in the previous paragraph were, of course, accompanied by other changes which will be explored in depth in this study. For the moment it is sufficient to record the falling away of support from the late 1840s onwards. By 1850, and despite repeated efforts to revive local Chartist associations and pleas from the leadership for greater rank-and-file effort, the movement, both nationally and locally, entered its long period of decline. By 1850 'languor and apathy' were everywhere apparent.[155] Two years later the *Star of Freedom* recorded:

> Something is evidently wrong, for if we compare the position of the democratic party now with what it was fourteen years ago, it will require no great philosopher to discover that our influence has greatly declined; vast numbers of the working classes who were then with us are now directly opposed to us. Whole districts have disappeared from the democratic map, while those who remain active in the field are split up into hostile factions.[156]

At Manchester the Chartist executive was split between those urging the necessity of an alliance with the middle-class reformers and those committed to Ernest Jones's socialist and anti-middle class position.[157] Following the triumph of the socialist group in 1852, hopes for a regeneration of Chartism were rekindled. Jones, noting that Lancashire was still the heartbeat of the movement, wrote enthusiastically:

> . . . the brave old Charter has risen up again from his sick-bed, and flinging aside the new physicians with their quack nostrums, and the old women, who were offering shopocratic draughts and aristocratic sympathizing plaster, he thinks a little exercise will do him good, and so he is taking a walk over the hills of Lancashire and Yorkshire.[158]

To some extent Jones's optimism was not unfounded. Independent working-class politics in the cotton districts survived the lean years of the 1850s and continued well into the 1860s. In 1854, for example, Jones lectured in towns throughout the northwest, and in September of that year some 2,000 Chartists attended a rally addressed by Jones and Finlen on Blackstone Edge.[159] During the following year the South Lancashire Delegate meeting drew up plans for the revival of Chartism: further lecture tours were organised; and a Chartist meeting in Stevenson Square, Manchester, attracted 1,000 people.[160] Sporadic flurries of activity, aimed at revitalising the movement, continued up to the end of the decade. In 1856 between ten and fifteen thousand people assembled near Todmorden to greet John Frost on his return home;[161] in 1858 meetings took place at Ashton and Manchester to make preparations for the Chartist conference in London;[162] and at Stalybridge some 800 people crowded into the Chartist Institute to hear Jones and W.P. Roberts denounce the enemies of the movement.[163] In 1859 Abel Heywood, a veteran reformer, stood as an independent candidate at Manchester, and received a high percentage of the working-class vote;[164] and hundreds gathered to hear Jones's eloquent and moving testimony to the memory of O'Connor.[165]

During the 1860s the Manhood Suffrage Associations and the Reform League kept alive the tradition of independence. The Manchester Manhood Suffrage Association was formed in 1858 at a meeting attended by some 4,000 people; and at Salford a meeting called by more than 1,000 inhabitants, the majority being operatives, carried a resolution in favour of manhood suffrage.[166] In 1864 and 1865 Jones and his close political associates, Hooson, Greening and Clayton, refused to join forces with the middle-class National Reform Union. Rather than accepting the latter's support for household suffrage, Jones continued to work through the Manchester Manhood Suffrage Association, and later ran the Northern Department of the Reform League in an effort to generate support for the cause of manhood suffrage.[167]

This continued agitation could not, however, conceal the marked decline in working-class support for independent political action. Despite hopes of revival during the early fifties, the Manchester Chartist executive was forced to note in November 1852, 'the apathy everywhere so lamentably present'.[168] At Stockport the Chartists ran a candidate, John West, at the 1852 parliamentary election, and during the turbulent years of 1853 and 1854 both local strike action and support for Jones's plan for a Labour Parliament were considerable.[169] But, in truth, Stockport Chartism had, by the late 1850s, become a very pale shadow of its formerly robust self. As Reid notes:

> After 1852 Chartism, as a purely political movement, continued in Stockport largely as a result of the labours of a few faithful adherents, and often owed more to sentinent and loyalty than to prospects of its imminent success. Thus much of the history of the movement in the 1850s is simply a record of its mere existence, with periods of more or less regular meetings being succeeded by the temporary abeyance of the movement, and then by attempts from local stalwarts or outside pressures to resurrect it once more.[170]

By March 1856 membership of the National Charter Association in Stockport had fallen to five; and by the end of the decade moves were afoot to ally local Chartism with the middle-class reformers.[171] Elsewhere in south Lancashire and northeast Cheshire a similar pattern prevailed. By 1857 Ashton Chartism had, 'pined away silently to the shadow of its former self', and a marked falling away of support was in evidence at Stalybridge, Hyde and Glossop.[172] And in the 1860s the Manchester Suffrage Association and the Northern Department of the Reform League attracted their greatest support from among the skilled and craft rather than from cotton operatives.[173]

Given the decline in popular support for independent political action, the Chartist leaders were increasingly forced to consider the question of entering into an alliance with the middle-class Liberal reformers. O'Connor had adopted this course in the early 1850s, and Jones, despite his criticisms of O'Connor and his continued mistrust of sections of the middle class, was later to follow a similar path. At the 1858 Chartist conference Jones held out manhood, as opposed to household, suffrage as the basis for such an alliance. Up to 1866 he refused to compromise on this issue, and, as was the case among many Chartist groups in the cotton districts,[174] continued to hold strong suspicions concerning the motives of the middle-class reformers. However, Jones's attack upon the Russell bill of 1866 constituted the last of his 'neo-Chartist outbursts'. In August of that year Jones accepted an invitation to speak at a Reform Union meeting, and the League and Union held joint demonstrations. In 1868 the Northern Department of the League disintegrated, to merge into Gladstonian Liberalism. Jones, accepted as a parliamentary candidate by the United Liberal Party in Manchester, eulogised Gladstone and Bright as 'the two great standard-bearers in this country- the one upholding the flag of religious liberty, the other the banner of political and social freedom'.[175] Thus by 1868 Chartism was dead: Liberalism had become the political creed of the vast majority of labour activists; and, as we shall see later, Conservatism had made major advances within the Lancashire working class.

This chapter has identified some of the key economic, social and political characteristics of the cotton districts between the 1830s and the early 1870s. In conclusion, it may be useful to summarise my findings, to integrate these characteristics, and to make explicit the relationships implied in the text between structure, historical process and the form and content of working-class politics.

Firstly, in relation to economic characteristics, the readers's attention has been drawn to the dominant position of cotton within the economies of Lancashire and Cheshire during both the second and third quarters of the century. Increased industrial diversification (especially into engineering) from mid-century onwards could not mask cotton's overall dominance, and its virtual monopoly position in the employment structures of towns such as Ashton and Stalybridge throughout the third quarter. Reference has also been made to cotton's marked sexual division of labour; its predominantly female workforce; its geographical specialisation during the latter part of our period; and the central importance of the relatively small cotton factory and the solidly wealthy employer within the industry as a whole.

In terms, secondly, of social structure, attention has been concentrated upon the cotton workforce; artisans and skilled workers; and the bourgeoise. It has been suggested that, whilst not constituting an undifferentiated mass of waged labour (as can be seen in its sexual division of labour, and its status, income and occupational hierarchies), the cotton labour force was, by the 1840s, relatively homogeneous in at least two significant ways. Firstly, unlike the labour forces of Kentish London, Edinburgh and elsewhere, cotton's workers were not divided into an élite of craft and skilled men sharply differentiated, both in structure and consciousness, from a mass of unskilled labourers. Rather, and allowing for the presence of 'aristocractic' mule-spinners (whose threatened status and privileged position had led, in any case, to the adoption of extremely 'un-aristocratic' attitudes and actions), cotton's labour force was overwhelmingly semi-skilled and family-based in character. And, secondly, the impressive support given by all manner of cotton operatives to Chartism was indicative of the extent to which divisions and differences within cotton were overshadowed during the 1830s and 1840s by feelings of labour solidarity. However, as we will observe in the course of this book, the consolidation of the factory system and a semi-skilled factory proletariat in cotton in the post-1850 period was accompanied not primarily by labour unity but by the fragmentation of the cotton proletariat along cultural, ethnic and political lines.

Besides cotton, artisan and skilled occupations constituted the main areas of waged employment for manual workers in Lancashire and Cheshire. These occupational groups were, however, far from being so uniformly privileged, aloof and 'aristocratic' in their behaviour towards other workers as often supposed. Indeed, faced by threats to their status, independence, control and skill and wage levels during the 1830s and 1840s many of the lesser skilled and artisan trades in the cotton districts joined hands with factory workers and others in the Chartist movement. Finally, workers were faced in the 1830s and 1840s by a bourgeoisie which was far from unified in terms of both structure and consciousness. However, the 'big' or 'proper' bourgeoisie was more often than not highly unified in the cotton towns (marriage, religion, source of wealth and politics all constituted important bonds), adopted an antagonistic stance toward the claims of workers, and increasingly during the 1850s and 1860s, consolidated its power and hegemony over lesser bourgeois groups.

Thirdly, the political section of the chapter has concentrated mainly upon the rise, ideological characteristics and decline of northwest Chartism. It has been argued that the cotton districts were strongholds of militant, class-conscious Chartism (especially up to and including the strikes of 1842). As illustrated by the case studies of Ashton-under-Lyne, Stalybridge and Stockport, and with reference to Foster's Oldham, anti-capitalist Chartism took deepest root in those Lancashire and Cheshire towns in which the following economic, social, political and ideological conditions prevailed: the employment of the majority of workers in cotton and the relative lack of industrial diversification especially into the 'aristocratic' engineering industry; the existence of 'felt' common grievances which effectively cut across differences and divisons within the working class to produce a strong sense of class solidarity; a Chartist leadership able and willing to relate to, articulate and direct such grievances: the presence of a highly visible, wealthy and class conscious 'big' bourgeoisie directly involved in relations of production with workers, often owning and operating large mills and seen to be opposed to the interests of labour; and the marked concentration of economic and political power in the hands of this bourgeoisie. Finally, brief reference has been made to the decline of Chartism and to some of the socio-economic factors (the changed social composition of the working class, the weakened position of formerly militant groups such as spinners, and the diverting of energies into non-political channels) which underpinned this decline. Reference has been kept deliberately brief on the grounds that the purpose of the remaining chapters on this book is to explore more fully the socio-economic and other factors which lay behind the decline of Chartism and the growth of reformism. We will begin, in Chapter 3, with an investigation of trends in living standards.

Notes

1. For working-class radicalism in the Ashton district see, for example, N. Cotton 'Popular Movements in Ashton-under-Lyne and Stalybridge before 1832', M. Litt., Univ. B'Ham (1977). For south Lancashire as a whole see J. Foster, *Class Struggle* . . ., op. cit., esp. chs. 3 and 4; R.Sykes, 'Early Chartism and Trade Unionism in South-East Lancashire'. in J. Epstein and D. Thompson (eds.) op. cit., pp. 152–193.

2. See the detailed study by C.A.N. Reid, 'The Chartist Movement in Stockport', MA thesis, University of Hull (1976).

3. D.A. Farnie, *The English Cotton Industry and the World Market, 1815–1896* (Oxford, 1979), pp. 135–8.

4. P. Joyce, 'The Factory Politics of Lancashire in the Later Nineteenth-Century', *Hist. Jnl.* XVIII, 3 (1975), p. 529.

5. Loc. cit.

6. M. Anderson, op. cit., p. 22.

7. See the invaluable study by J. Liddington and J. Norris, *One Hand Tied Behind Us* (1978), p. 58.

8. Ibid., p. 59.

9. Ibid., p. 54.

10. M. Anderson, op. cit., p. 23.

11. J. Liddington and J. Norris, op. cit., pp. 84–5.

12. Ibid., p. 93.

13. Ibid., Ch. V.

14. See Ch. 3 below, Table 37.

15. J. Liddington and J. Norris, op. cit., pp. 84–5.

16. Ibid., p. 85.

17. J.L. White, *The Limits of Trade Union Militancy* (1978), pp. 34–5; See also Ch. 1 above, note 45.

18. J. Liddington and J. Norris, op. cit., pp. 95–6.

19. Ibid., pp. 91–2.

20. H.A. Turner, *Trade Union Growth, Structure and Policy* (1962), III, 2.

21. See E.P. Thompson, *The Making of the English Working Class* (1968), preface.

22. D.A. Farnie, op. cit., p. 313.

23. J. Liddington and J. Norris, op. cit., p. 57.

24. See P. Joyce, *Work, Society and Politics*, op. cit., pp. 13–18, 68.

25. For the ease of access offered to small capitalists in the new weaving districts of north-east Lancashire see, D.A. Farnie, op. cit., p. 284.

26. P. Joyce, op. cit., pp. 60–1, 68, 73.

27. Ibid., pp. 12–13; D.A. Farnie, op. cit., p. 318.

28. P. Joyce, op. cit., pp. 144–52.

29. D.A. Farnie, op. cit., pp. 314–18.

30. R. Sykes, *Hist Jnl.*, op. cit., pp. 168–9; D.S. Gadian, *Hist Jnl.*, op. cit., p. 169.

31. Loc. cit.

32. D.A. Farnie, op. cit., p. 209.

33. P. Joyce, op. cit., pp. 158–9.

34. Ibid., p. 158.

35. Ibid., p. 159.

36. D.S. Gadian, 'A Comparative Study of Popular Movements in North-West Industrial Towns, 1830–1850', unpublished PhD thesis, Lancaster University (1976), p. 88.

37. M. Anderson, op. cit., pp. 23–4.

38. E.P. Thompson, *The Making of the English Working Class*, op. cit., Ch. 8; E.J. Hobsbawm, 'The Labour Aristocracy in Nineteenth-Century Britain', op. cit., esp. pp. 285–90: I. Prothero, 'London Chartism and the Trades', *Econ. Hist. Rev.*, 2nd series XXIV, 2 (May 1971).

39. E.P. Thompson, op. cit., pp. 269–79, 289.

40. E.J. Hobsbawm, op. cit.; A.E. Musson, *British Trade Unions*, op. cit., Ch. 6.

41. This is at least the view of I. Prothero (op. cit.) and R. Sykes ('Early Chartism and Trade Unionism in South-East Lancashire' in J. Epstein and D. Thompson (eds.), op. cit. p. 154). Goodway (*London Chartism 1838–1848* (Cambridge, 1982),

pp. 15–18) goes further, claiming that more or less all the trades in London were under threat and that this 'resulted in the temporary political unity of most London artisans'.

42. For engineering see, *Manchester Guardian*, 21 January, 1858; H.W. Lord, 'Metal Manufactures of Lancashire' in *Royal Commission of Enquiry into the Employment of Children, 1862*, 3rd report (1864), XXII, p. 168; J. Foster, op. cit., pp. 224–9.

43. M. Anderson, op. cit., p. 24; D.S. Gadian, thesis, p. 88.

44. J. Liddington and J. Norris, op. cit., p. 101.

45. M. Anderson, op. cit., p. 24.

46. D.S. Gadian, thesis, p. 88; M. Anderson, op. cit., p. 24.

47. J. Epstein, *The Lion of Freedom* (1982), pp. 273–4.

48. J. Foster, op. cit., pp. 162–3.

49. M. Anderson, op. cit., p. 24.

50. J. Foster, op. cit., pp. 163–6; 177–86.

51. See below, pp. 51–4.

52. J. Foster, op. cit., pp. 166–77.

53. Ibid., Ch. 7.

54. D.A. Farnie, op. cit., p. 231; O. Ashmore, 'The Industrial Archaeology of Ashton-under-Lyne in S.A. Harrop and E.A. Rose (eds), *Victorian Ashton* (Ashton, 1974).

55. N. Cotton, op. cit., pp. 20–1.

56. See P. Joyce, op. cit., p. 104.

57. Thus the population of Stalybridge declined by almost 2,000 during the Cotton Famine. Some of those who left the town and the Ashton district emigrated to America.

58. P. Joyce, op. cit., pp. 103–10.

59. As the table in Joyce's book shows, (Table I, p. 104), although the rate of population growth did decline in the Lancashire cotton towns from 1841 onwards, its continued rate of growth was, in many instances, far from negligible.

60. Ibid., p. 103.

61. T.D.W. Reid and N. Reid., op. cit.

62. See Ch. 6 below, esp. pp. 256–65.

63. D.A. Farnie, op. cit., p. 160.

64. Loc. cit. During the decade 1861–71 Oldham increased its population by 20 per cent, Blackburn by 31 per cent, Bolton by 32 per cent, Burnley by 42 per cent and Rochdale by 66 per cent.

65. For the pre-1850 situation, in which a high degree of labour solidarity over-shadowed ethnic divisions in many northern towns see, D. Thompson, 'Ireland and the Irish in English Radicalism before 1850' in J. Epstein and D. Thompson (eds.), op. cit.

66. *Reports of Inspectors of Factories* (Redgrave, 30 April 1863), XVIII, pp. 17, 19, 21.

67. Ibid., p. 19.

68. A. Hall, 'Social Control and the Working-Class Challenge in Ashton-under-Lyne, 1886–1914', MA thesis, University of Lancaster (1975), p. 4.

69. *Reports of Inspectors of Factories* (Redgrave, 30 April 1863), XVIII, p. 19.

70. These percentage would, of course, be considerably higher in terms of the total population aged 13 and over.

71. I have proceeded as follows. From the total of 25,289 males in Stockport in 1851, I have deducted the 7,527 listed as sons, grandsons, scholars, and of 'no stated occupation' in the printed census. This leaves a waged male workforce of 17,762. From a total female population of 28,546 I have deducted the 15,488 listed as wives and widows (of no specified occupation), grand-daughters, daughters, sisters, nieces, scholars under tuition either at home or at school, innkeeper's wife, shoemaker's

wife, shopkeeper's wife, butcher's wife and beershopkeeper's wife. The total waged female workforce is, therefore, 13,058. This may well be an underestimation — some paid work probably not being reflected in the census returns.

72. That is, those women listed in the printed census under the heading 'Household Work and Wives' (that is, wives, widows, innkeeper's wife, etc. — it does *not* include scholars, daughters, etc. who were girls rather than adult women).

73. O. Ashmore, *The Industrial Archaeology of Stockport* (Ashton, 1975), pp. 36–8.

74. See, G. Crossick, *An Artisan Elite*, op. cit., pp. 44; R.Q. Gray, *The Labour Aristocracy in Victorian Edinburgh*, op. cit., pp. 21–7.

75. D.S. Gadian, thesis, op. cit., pp. 89–90.

76. *Stockport Advertiser*, 1 April 1854.

77. For the importance of small doubling firms at Stockport see, D.A. Farnie, op. cit., p. 303.

78. *Reports of Inspectors of Factories* (Redgrave, 31 October 1863), XXII, pp. 17, 28, 33–4.

79. For Kershaw see, *Stockport Advertiser*, 7 February 1851, 29 April 1864.

80. *Stockport Advertiser*, 29 April 1864.

81. O. Ashmore, op. cit., p. 81.

82. For Stockport Conservatism see, for example, *Stockport Advertiser*, 4 January 1849, 24 January, 1850, 9 July 1852; H.J. Hanham, *Elections and Party Management: Politics in the Time of Disraeli and Gladstone* (1978), pp. 314ff; Ch. 7 below.

83. P. Joyce, op. cit., p. 13.

84. P.F. Clarke, *Lancashire and the New Liberalism* (Cambridge, 1971), p. 32.

85. See Ch. 7 below.

86. P. Joyce, op. cit., pp. 187–9; Ch. 6 below; O. Ashmore and T. Bolton, 'Hugh Mason and the Oxford Mills and Community, Ashton-under-Lyne', *Trans, Lancs. and Ches. Antiqu. Soc.*, vol. 78 (1975), pp. 38–50; J. Holland, 'Hugh Mason: Cotton Master, Puritan and Father Figure' in E.A. Rose and S. Harrop (eds), op. cit.

87. P. Joyce, op. cit., p. 144; Ch. 6 below.

88. P. Joyce, op. cit., p. 13; Ch. 6 below.

89. See Ch. 6 below.

90. R. Gray, *The Labour Aristocracy in Victorian Edinburgh*, op. cit., p. 21.

91. See, for example, C.A.N. Reid, 'The Chartist Movement in Stockport', MA thesis, University of Hull (1976); D. Read, 'Chartism in Manchester' in A. Briggs (ed.) *Chartist Studies* (1959); J. Foster, op. cit., esp. Chs 3 and 4; D.S. Gadian, *Hist Jnl.*, op. cit.; D.S. Gadian, 'A Comparative Study of Popular Movements in North-West Industrial Towns, 1830–1850', Unpublished. PhD thesis University of Lancaster (1976); N. Cotton, 'Popular Movements in Ashton-under-Lyne and Stalybridge before 1832', M. Litt., University of Birmingham (1977); R. Sykes, *Hist Jnl.*, op. cit.; R. Sykes, 'Early Chartism and Trade Unionism in South-East Lancashire' in J. Epstein and D. Thompson (eds), *The Chartist Experience*, op. cit.

92. F.J. Kaijage, 'Labouring Barnsley, 1815–1875', Unpublished PhD University of Warwick (1975), Ch. 9; A.J. Peacock, *Bradford Chartism, 1838–40* (1969).

93. D.S. Gadian, thesis, op. cit., p. 69.

94. The obvious point of comparison is Oldham; but Bolton, it seems, was also a centre of militant Chartism, J. Epstein, *The Lion of Freedom: Feargus O'Connor and the Chartist Movement, 1832–1842* (1982), pp. 181–2.

95. C.A.N. Reid, op. cit., Ch. 2; T.D.W. Reid and N. Reid, op. cit., p. 57.

96. C.A.N. Reid, op. cit., Ch. 3.

97. J. Foster, op. cit., Ch. 3; R. Sykes, article, op. cit.

98. D. Thompson, 'Ireland and the Irish in English Radicalism' in Epstein and Thompson (eds), op. cit., p. 124.

99. D.S. Gadian, thesis, pp. 139–44.

100. J. Epstein, *The Lion of Freedom*, op. cit., Ch. 7.

101. Ibid., p. 231.

102. H. Davies 'A Shot in the Dark' in S.A. Harrop and E.A. Rose (eds), *Victorian Ashton* (Ashton, 1974), p. 16.

103. M. Jenkins, op. cit., Chs 6 and 7.

104. For example, the Reids note of Stockport; 'While mass meetings might raise a cheer for the Charter, there was no real commitment to that cause on the part of the vast majority of strikers'. T.D.W. Reid and N. Reid, op. cit. p. 62. The evidence marshalled to support this generalisation is, however, somewhat thin. Even if the Reids are correct in their hypothesis, it seems to be the case that Stockport was untypical of south Lancashire and north-east Cheshire as a whole. See, M. Jenkins, loc. cit.

105. Richard Pilling, one of the central leaders in the 1842 strikes, was equivocal. Thus, 'And I do say that if Mr. O'Connor has made it a chartist question, he has done wonders to make it extend through England, Ireland and Scotland. But it was always a wage question, and ten hours bill with me'. G.S. Jones, 'The Language of Chartism', op. cit. p. 41.

106. J. Epstein, op. cit., p. 295; G.S. Jones, op. cit., pp. 39–40.

107. J. Epstein, op. cit. p. 310.

108. Loc. cit.

109. C.A.N. Reid, op. cit., pp. 211ff; T.D.W. Reid and C. Reid, op. cit.

110. Thus, the Reids argue that in Stockport the 'wages only' movement grew in opposition to Chartism in 1842, and that by the end of the 1840s the former had taken precedence over the latter. Whilst trade unionism did undoubtedly show renewed vigour at Stockport and elsewhere in the cotton districts from the mid-1840s onwards, it is, however, far less certain that such expansion constituted a conscious *ideological* break with Chartism and its wider political goals. It may well have been the case that increased specialisation of *function* and the need for *organisational autonomy* within the constituent elements of the 'labour movement' were of prime importance; and that, at least in the short-term, trade unionists retained their ideological commitment to the Charter. Certainly there was considerable overlap in south Lancashire and north-east Cheshire in the *personnel* of trade unionism and Chartism. The Reids fail to adequately consider the questions of personnel and the need for separate organisational structures in relation to the Stockport labour movement. See, T.D.W. Reid and N. Reid, op. cit.; R. Sykes, Ch, op. cit., esp. pp. 152–3; M. Jenkins, loc. cit. For a similar debate concerning ideology and the labour movement in the very different context of *post-bellum* America see, G. Grob, *Workers and Utopia* (New York, 1969); D. Montgomery, *Beyond Equality* (New York, 1972), pp. 172–96, 441–7.

111. R. Sykes, loc. cit.

112. G.S. Jones, 'The Language of Chartism', op. cit., pp. 44–52.

113. For a more detailed examination of such advances, see Ch. 4 below, pp. 148–54.

114. F.E. Gillespie, *Labour and Politics in England, 1850–67* (Durham, North Carolina 1927); C.A.N. Reid, op. cit., pp. 226ff for late Chartism in Stockport.

115. See, however, the useful pieces by Belchem and Tiller. J. Belchem, 'English Working-Class Radicalism and the Irish, 1815–1850', *North-West Lab. Hist. Bull.*, no. 8 (1982); J. Belchem, '1848: Feargus O'Connor and the Collapse of the Mass Platform' in D. Thompson and J. Epstein (eds), op. cit.; K. Tiller, 'Late Chartism: Halifax 1847–58' in ibid.

116. C.A.N. Reid, op. cit., pp. 230, 333–6.

117. But see J. Saville, 'Chartism in the Year of Revolution (1848)', *Modern Quarterly*, VIII (1952–3), pp. 23–33; D. Goodway, *London Chartism*, op. cit., pp. 61–96.

118. J. Foster, op. cit., p. 205.

119. I have consulted the *Northern Star* for 8 April, 19 August, 9, 16, 23 December 1848; *Manchester Advertiser*, 15, 22 April 1848; *Manchester Guardian*, 31 May, 3 June, 16, 19 August 1848.

120. J. Belchem, 'English Working-Class Radicalism'. op. cit.

121. *Manchester Guardian*, 19 August 1848.

122. See Chs 4 and 5 below.

123. D. Thompson, *The Early Chartists*, op. cit., intro.

124. D.S. Gadian, thesis, p. 266.

125. Ibid., p. 314.

126. For the involvement of the spinners and the lower artisan trades in Chartism see, R. Sykes, 'Early Chartism and Trade Unionism', op. cit., esp. pp. 181-4; J. Foster, *Class Struggle*, op. cit., pp. 100-1, 107, 118; C.A.N. Reid, op. cit., p. 233; T.D.W. Reid and N. Reid, op. cit., pp. 67-8; D.S. Gadian, thesis, op. cit., pp. 330-5. It is important to note (in relation to Joyce's belief in the 'artisanate' character of Chartism) that north-west Chartism appealed to artisans *and* other sections of the working class, including fully-fledged proletarians. For example, by the late 1830s the powerloom weavers in the Ashton district who were firm supporters of Chartism could hardly be described as 'artisans in the factory'. As Cotton observes, the transition from handloom- to powerloom-weaving in the Ashton district had largely been completed by the mid-1820s. See N. Cotton, op. cit., pp. 16-17.

127. E.P. Thompson, *The Making of the English Working Class* (1968), Ch. 16.

128. Ibid., p. 12.

129. I.J. Prothero, 'William Benbow and the Concept of the "General Strike" ', *Past and Present*, no. 63 (1974), pp. 141-6; G.S. Jones, 'The Language of Chartism', op. cit., pp. 13ff.

130. J. Epstein, op. cit., p. 274.

131. G.S. Jones, 'The Language of Chartism', op. cit., p. 29.

132. Ibid., p. 14.

133. Ibid., p. 25.

134. J. Epstein, op. cit., p. 273.

135. R. Sykes, 'Some Aspects of Working-Class Consciousness', op. cit., pp. 178-9.

136. For powerful indictments of the 'steamlords' see the testimonies of O'Connor, Pilling, Leach and others in 'The Trial of Feargus O'Connor', op. cit., esp. pp. v-ix, 248-55, 277—84.

137. W.M. Bowman, op. cit., p. 501.

138. Loc. cit.

139. C. Smith, 'Stockport in the Age of Reform, 1822-1870', MS in Stockport Public Library (1938), p. 232.

140. J. Epstein, op. cit., pp. 275-6.

141. C.A.N. Reid, op. cit., pp. 282-99, 352. Soffner greatly overestimates the extent of working-class support for Conservatism, and underestimates the appeal of independent political action. See, R. Soffner, 'Attitudes and Allegiances in the Unskilled North', *Int. Rev. Soc. Hist.*, III (1965).

142. See Ch. 7 below.

143. J. Epstein, op. cit., pp. 263-71.

144. Ibid., p. 290.

145. Loc. cit.

146. Ibid., pp. 96-7; D.S. Gadian, thesis, p. 199; C.A.N. Reid, op. cit., pp. 174-5. See also the original and stimulating article by Behagg ('An Alliance with the Middle Class: the Birmingham Political Union and Early Chartism' in J.D. Epstein and Thompson (eds., op. cit.) which challenges the traditional picture of Birmingham Chartism as being based upon inter-class harmony.

147. Thus, despite its considerable merits, Foster's book does at times suffer from its heavy reliance upon a Leninist framework of analysis. See, G.S. Jones, 'Class

Struggle and the Industrial Revolution', op. cit., esp. pp. 46–61.

148. Engels did, nevertheless, maintain that Chartism would become socialist. See *The Condition of the Working Class In England* (Marx-Engels, *On Britain* (Moscow, 1953), p. 273).

149. G.S. Jones, 'The Language of Chartism', op. cit., p. 34; also 'Class Struggle', op. cit., pp. 56–9.

150. A. Briggs (ed.), *Chartist Studies*, op. cit., pp. 2–3, 15, 289–91.

151. P. Joyce, op. cit., pp. 313–14; note 124 above; and Ch. 1 above.

152. G.S. Jones, 'Class Struggle', op. cit., pp. 46, 57–8; J. Epstein, op. cit., pp. 249–57.

153. G.S. Jones, 'Class Struggle', op. cit., p. 60.

154. P. Joyce, op. cit., pp. 313–14. The revisionist argument in favour of the primacy of the political character of Chartism properly belongs to Stedman Jones (see, 'The Language of Chartism', especially pp. 15, 28–33, 44). In interpreting Chartism as an essentially political movement, Stedman Jones (followed by Joyce) does, however, tend to underestimate, at least for the cotton districts, the extent to which (i) deepseated *economic* conflicts between employers and workers constituted, despite political 'liberilization', a major obstacle to class reconciliation at mid-century; (ii) the *economic* realities and conflicts of factory production struck at the roots of the notion of the 'productive classes', complete with its view of harmony between workers and manufacturing capitalists; (iii) Chartists such as McDouall ('The White Slaves of Great Britain' in *Chartist and Republican Journal*) and Leach (*Stubborn Facts from the Factories*) explained poverty and exploitation in economic (i.e. non-Marxist but nevertheless production-based) *as well as* political terms. Stedman Jones thus underplays the class character of Chartism.

155. *Northern Star*, 4 January, 1851.

156. *Star of Freedom*, 21 August 1852.

157. For the split within Manchester Chartism see, *Northern Star,* 1 February, 8 March, 19 April, 11 November 1851; *Star of Freedom*, 22 May 1852.

158. *Notes to the People*, vol. II, 1852, pp. 808, 842.

159. *People's Paper*, 6 August, 2, 16 September 1854; *Manchester Courier*, 26 August, 16 September 1854.

160. *People's Paper*, 2 June, 21 July 1855.

161. *Manchester Guardian*, 25 August 1856; *Manchester Courier*, 30 August 1856.

162. *People's Paper*, 2, 9, 16, 23 January 13 February 1858.

163. *Stockport Advertiser*, 8 October 1858; *Ashton Reporter*, 2 October 1858.

164. For Heywood's campaign see, F.E. Gillespie, op. cit., pp. 165, 183.

165. *Cabinet Newspaper*, 21 May 1859.

166. F.E. Gillespie, op. cit., pp. 163–4.

167. M.R. Dunsmore, 'The Working Classes, the Reform League and the Reform Movement in Lancashire and Yorkshire' MA thesis, University of Sheffield (1961), esp. Ch. III.

168. *People's Paper*, 27 November 1852.

169. C.A.N. Reid, op. cit., pp. 363, 365, 371, 382–92.

170. Ibid.

171. Ibid., pp. 398–405.

172. *Ashton Reporter*, 26 December 1857.

173. M.R. Dunsmore, op. cit., pp. 10–11.

174. For example, at Stockport, where working-class antagonism to the Whigs and bourgeois radicals was deep-seated, opposition to the creation of such an alliance was loudly voiced by the Chartists on a number of occasions during the late 1850s and early 1860s (see, C.A.N. Reid, op. cit., p. 410). In the Ashton district popular grievances against the predominantly Liberal cotton masters prevented any smooth mass movement into Liberalism (see Ch. 7 below).

175. For Jones's increased moderation see, M.R. Dunsmore, op. cit., pp. 22–3, 52–3, 68, 82.

3 ECONOMIC GROWTH AND LIVING STANDARDS

Debates and Issues

Recent research has dealt many severe blows to the traditional orthodoxy that Chartism represented a more or less straightforward response to the stimulus of distress, and that the key to the movement's demise lay in the *substantially improved* living standards of the mass of the population during the latter part of the 1840s and the early mid-1850s.[1] Two particularly forceful and effective lines of criticism — evidential and methodological in character — have been developed. In terms of the former, an increasingly weighty and authoritative body of research has demonstrated that advances in real earnings for the vast majority of workers were considerably more limited, in terms of both time and extent, during the third quarter of the century than the conventional wisdom would have us believe. As Church notes, 'only from the mid-sixties does a discontinuous, but nevertheless marked, upward trend become unmistakable'.[2] This upward trend thus occurred at a point in time when Chartism had long since lost its mass support. Wage gains were, moreover, far from evenly distributed, with the lion's share going to the skilled and regularly employed, and with the unskilled and casual workers picking up the crumbs. Some historians — most notably Barnsby[3] and McCabe[4] — have gone further, to suggest that workers in the respective areas of the Black Country and Merseyside derived few, if any, financial benefits from the economic expansion of the 'golden years'. Certainly, as Foster,[5] Anderson[6] and others have convincingly demonstrated, poverty and general economic insecurity continued to affect the lives of the vast majority of working-class families. And environmental conditions — especially in relation to housing and sanitation — and the health of the urban working class remained, by more or less general agreement, shockingly bad.[7] In short, a simple, straightforward picture of 'improvement' is empirically unsound.

In terms of methodology, it has been suggested by a number of historians, but especially Edward and Dorothy Thompson, that to interpret the rise and decline of Chartism and other forms of popular protest solely, or even predominantly as spontaneous, unthinking and visceral responses to short-run economic stimuli ('distress' and 'improvement') is to fall, either consciously or unconsciously, into the trap of a narrow and fallacious economic reductionism.[8] Thus Edward Thompson forcefully and persuasively contends that the economic reductionism of Rostow and his followers is crudely mechanistic in approach and, in application, greatly underestimates, indeed tends to obliterate, the complex mixture of forces and events which shape human thought and behaviour.[9] For example, while undoubtedly fuelled by the basic economic considerations of poverty, hunger and unemployment, Chartism's sources of nourishment went much deeper than immediate distress. It was, above all, the felt unfairness of the *whole system*, the economic, political, cultural and moral grievances of an increasingly organised and articulate working class which gave Chartism its mass strength and appeal.[10] Thus the historian of Barnsley Chartism accurately observes that, 'the function of . . . economic distress was to bring into sharp focus the brutal realities of the class-based economic, social and political arrangement in society as it was then constituted'.[11] Chartism's wide-ranging critique of capitalism could not be erased by economic growth alone. As Tholfsen suggests:

> Beneath the disagreement on tactics and remedies was the conviction that existing political and social arrangements were not entitled to the allegiance of the mass of the people . . . Thus England was caught up in a predicament that could not be resolved merely by prosperity or propaganda. Workingmen were questioning with impressive intellectual and moral force the legitimacy of the system. They were determined not to be fobbed off with stale political economy. Naked laissez-faire, celebrating acquisitiveness and productivity, was patently incapable of creating a sense of community and common purpose, even under prosperous conditions.[12]

We would also be well advised to take careful note of Crossick's observation that:

> Economic progress alone leads to no particular ideological or behavourial consequences. The effects of mid-Victorian expansion can only be interpreted within the wider framework of social relationships and ideological forces; these determined the

consequences of economic development, in specific places, at specific points in time.[13]

Both empirically and methodologically, it is thus no longer convincing to offer the clearcut argument that, 'Chartism was the creed of hard times: as those hard times disappeared so also did much of the appeal of the Charter'.[14] Matters were less straightforward.

To condemn the excessive explanatory weight traditionally attached to the notions of distress and improvement and the assumptions and procedures of economic reductionism is not, however, to underestimate the part played by economic factors in the rise and decline of Chartism and the growth of reformism. Chartism did receive its greatest support during the depression of 1837–42; and it was surely not accidental that once trade and wages picked up in the mid-1840s, so the attitudes of cotton operatives towards the manufacturers mellowed somewhat.[15] In terms of the third quarter, Hobsbawm is probably correct to draw a close connexion between the 'distinct if modest' improvement in all but the environmental conditions of the working class and increased political moderation.[16] Certainly, as will be demonstrated later, many labour leaders consciously attributed their newfound moderation to the material and institutional gains of the post-1850 years.[17] And attention has already been drawn to the key importance of a restabilised and restructured economy in setting limits to labour's field of action.

The crucial points at issue are thus not the importance or otherwise of the 'economic', but the relative weight to be attached to economic factors in terms of an overall explanation of the onset of reformism; and the nature of the relationship, if any, which existed between economic and other factors.[18] The general purpose of Chapters 3 and 4 is to attempt to shed some light upon these two issues by means of: (a) a detailed investigation of the living standards of the cotton operatives between the late forties and mid-seventies (Chapter 3); and (b) an examination of changes in the material experiences of working-class leaders and the fortunes of their institutions, and the effects of such changes upon the consciousness of the leadership (Chapter 4).

Several questions immediately present themselves. Is, for example, Foster correct to claim that economic recovery constitutes only 'a very partial explanation' of the break-up of Chartism during the late 1840s and early 1850s?[19] To what extent did trends in money and real earnings for the cotton operatives conform to the national pattern of generally modest improvement for much of the 1850s followed by more substantial progress from the early 1860s onwards? Or did the experience of the cotton districts resemble more closely that of Merseyside where, according to McCabe, 'it cannot . . . be assumed that there was any rise in real wages . . . for the bulk of the period 1850 to 1875'?[20] Does not the very fact of the Cotton Famine, with its high levels of unemployment and relief, suggest the advisability of a pessimistic conclusion in terms of living standards in the cotton districts? Or is Farnie closer to the truth in his belief that the effects of the Cotton Famine upon the lives of the operatives were far less damaging than traditionally claimed?[21] What were the key developments in the post-1865 decade? Did, for example, earnings in cotton follow the national pattern of marked improvement? Finally, what were the precise connexions between these economic developments and the politics of labour?

The following conclusions are offered. Firstly, it is suggested that the undoubted improvement in cotton operatives' earnings between the late 1840s and mid-1870s was far less continuous and, especially during much of the decade of the 1850s, more limited than claimed by many contemporaries and historians.[22] Further qualifications and corrections to a picture of *unmitigated* improvement result from investigations into levels of poverty and insecurity, housing and sanitary conditions, the people's state of health and the effects of the Cotton Famine upon living standards. And, as Foster rightly argues, in view of the negligible or extremely modest advances in real earnings achieved by many workers during the latter years of the 1840s, and the early- mid 1850s, the notions of economic recovery and improvement constitute, in themselves, inadequate explanations of the decline of Chartism as a mass movement. Conversely, my second line of argument is that the qualifications and corrections outlined above do not totally invalidate the notion of an overall link between economic improvement and reformism during the third quarter of the century *as a whole*. Thus cotton operatives were generally much better off in material terms in 1875 than they had been in 1850, with the post-1864 years being a period of substantial, indeed, in many cases, spectacular rises in money and real incomes. And, given this overall improvement, it is surely not coincidental that reformism took increasingly deep root in the cotton towns. Thirdly, the full strength of this connexion is most forcefully demonstrated not in relation to the mass of operatives but in the changed fortunes and socio-political outlook of much of the labour leadership. Chapter 4 shows that improvements and successes for labour leaders — as reflected in living standards, upward social mobility, the advances made by their institutions, and the enhanced degrees of public recognition afforded both to themselves and their institutions — were far more substantial and enduring than was the case with the mass of operatives. Most significantly, such successes convinced the leadership that further advances were to be achieved within the confines of British capitalism. Reformism and gradualism increasingly appeared to constitute the only 'natural' and 'realistic' ways forward, and Chartist and Owenite plans for immediate and total social reconstruction to be praiseworthy but totally unrealisable dreams. In sum, although the general lack of mass support for class conscious, independent working-class political action in the post-1850 period can be attributed to economic improvement in only a limited way, nevertheless the reformism of the leadership was far more solidly and directly linked to material and institutional advancement.

Living Standards in the Cotton Districts

The Views of Contemporaries

In charting trends in the living standards of cotton operatives, we can usefully begin by examining the views of contemporaries. The most striking fact to emerge in this context is that, with the exception of a few cautionary or dissenting voices,[23] most observers of the working class had little doubt that material conditions improved markedly for the mass of regularly-employed and 'respectable' operatives during the third quarter, and that such improvement exercised a substantial influence upon the growth of labour's enhanced moderation and reformism.

Thus, as early as 1849, A.B. Reach detected, in his investigation of living and working conditions in Manchester, Salford and the surrounding cotton towns, many signs of 'an evident disposition to improvement'.[24] 'Amid all the grime and dinginess' of Manchester there existed, 'no lack of homely comforts, good health, and good spirits'. Reach was especially impressed by the respectability and propriety displayed by the majority of operatives (noting a 'considerable degree of correct feeling' among the women), their 'industrious', 'mild' and 'inoffensive' character, and, apart from the notoriously 'turbulent' and 'fanatical' operatives of Ashton, their peaceable, moral-force inclinations. The views of an 'intelligent operative' upon the newfound opportunities for advancement provided by the introduction of the Ten Hours Bill were eagerly recorded:

> My friend was a Ten Hours Bill man: 'The people had health, and time, and spirits now to clean their houses and teach themselves something useful. The cotton folks were improving. Oh, yes, they were; and the next generation would be better than the present. No one ever thought of schools for children when he was a child. No; he had wrought many and many a time for twelve hours a day when he was not eight years old. The children were lucky now to what they were in them old times. There were good evening classes too for the men and women, only he was afeard that a good many of them, particularly the boys and girls, were too fond of going to the music saloons, where they did not hear no good, and did not do no good . . . Oh, places like them wasn't no good. But there was the Monday night concerts — *there* was music — there was the place for a working man to have a rational night's amusement.[25]

Eleven years later Chadwick provided statistical backing to the growing belief that the poverty and acute suffering of the late thirties and early forties had been superseded by material improvement and growing contentment. On the basis of returns received from employers in Manchester, Salford and (mainly south) Lancashire, Chadwick estimated that the wages of 'nearly all classes of factory operatives' had risen between 10 and 25 per cent between 1839 and 1859.[26]

The onset of the Cotton Famine during the latter part of 1861 belied hopes for sustained economic improvement, and fears of widespread dislocation and distress were confirmed by the high levels of unemployment which prevailed throughout the cotton districts between 1862 and the spring months of 1865. Somewhat ironically, it was, however, the conduct of the operatives during the Cotton Famine — their 'patient suffering' and their apparent disinclination to engage in violent class conflict — which helped to convince the dominant influences in Parliament and the ruling class that it would be foolhardy to continue to exclude the adult male Lancashire operatives from the franchise.[27] Militant Chartist had seemingly given way to 'Rochdale Man' — 'the respectable, self-helping, self-educating working-man with his cooperative society, savings bank and chapel'.[28]

During the post-Famine decade reports of major advances in working-class living standards multiplied, to reach their climax during cotton's boom years of the early and mid-1870s. W.A. Abram, noting in 1868 that, 'far seldomer than of yore do we hear the murmur of popular discontent', attributed the onset of social calm to the 'vastly ameliorated' social condition of the operatives during the preceding 25 years, and the adoption of more enlightened policies by employers. Reductions in the hours of work (from 12–13 to 10 for cotton factory workers); the introduction of the Saturday half-holiday; increases in earnings; a decline in levels of sickness and mortality; the building of better, more spacious cotton mills; and the 'lavish provision' of public parks, pleasure grounds, baths and free libraries by employers and local authorities — all were listed by Abram as indicative of the ameliorative process at work.[29] Abram paid special attention to what he considered to be significant improvements in operative housing — the homes of the best-paid suitably furnished to reflect their superior status, and those of the less-well paid but nevertheless thrifty being 'moderately comfortable':

> The furniture of the living room may consist of a dresser, an eight-day clock, kitchen sofa and a couple of rocking chairs at either side of the fire-place. The walls are usually adorned with two or three framed engravings or coloured lithographs. The better-paid workmen improve upon this a little. Their front apartment on the ground-floor is dubbed a parlour, and its furniture includes a small book-case if the man be studious, or if, as is not infrequent, he has a taste for music, a piano . . . I believe there is no operative population in the world so well and cheaply housed as are the factory workers in a Lancashire manufacturing town of the second or third magnitude.[30]

During the early mid-1870s boom the cotton industry was 'power and glory': timber, iron, coal and clay were 'vulgar inferiority'; and cotton operatives saw themselves as 'the lords of labour: the manual aristocrats'.[31] In these boom conditions unabashed materialism abounded. The *Co-operative News* provided a graphic account of the share-buying mania which gripped all classes in the Oldham area during the opening of the Oldham Limiteds in the early and middle years of the decade:

> The working class are getting rich in this prosperous state of things, and correspondingly independent in their manners. There is a hush upon politics, once so fiercely rife in the town. The three grand things — ecclesiastical, political and social combined — are now divis, premiums and shares . . . The other day a new company was opened at Shaw near Oldham, and the day after the announcement was made nearly one hundred people from Oldham went by train to the scene . . . They rushed out of the train, knocked the ticket collector to one side, and threw their tickets on the ground. They then marched up the street at double quick, but finding this pedestrian competition too slow, they set off in a run through the village, and besieged the secretary in his own house. The crowd was too great to be supplied at once, and application sheets were soon selling at sixpence and one shilling each . . . Of course the shares are now selling at a premium . . . Nearly one hundred companies have been formed in as many months, and the whole town is rapidly becoming one huge joint-stock concern.[32]

These years of intense activity and high expectations could not last indefinitely. And during the last quarter of the century both the fortunes of the cotton industry and the security of its workforce were to be adversely affected by periodic bouts of depression and increased competition from abroad.

It is worth noting at this point that, while all observers agreed that improved living standards did make a significant contribution towards labour's increased moderation, their assessments of the latter varied considerably. Not surprisingly, the vast majority of middle-class observers were delighted and reserved special commendation for the workers' growing 'restraint' and 'respectability'.[33] Other responses were mixed. As we will see in more detail in the next chapter, many working-class leaders, especially those active in the Co-operative Movement, were unceasing in their praises of the newfound openings within English society for material and moral advancement which had been so eagerly grasped by themselves and their members: 'success' and 'progress' became their watchwords. Thus in 1861 the *Co-operator* could joyfully proclaim:

Englishmen have much to be thankful for inasmuch as there is probably no country on the face of the globe where sober, industrious young men can so soon raise themselves to ease and comfort, as in England.[34]

'Thousands of men', according to the *Co-operator*, had achieved, as a result of the Co-operative Movement's phenomenal expansion, 'that independence and contentedness of mind which is the happiest state the natural man can feel, having plenty of clothes and food, and something to spare for the needy'.[35]

Some did not, however, share the *Co-operator's* euphoria. Ernest Jones, while remaining a central figure in the Lancashire labour movement of the 1860s[36] and welcoming the personal and institutional advances achieved, was nevertheless saddened by the labour movement's increasingly narrowed horizons and the decline of mass class-conscious, independent political action. In the early 1850s Jones voiced the fear that unless craft unionism gave way to general unionism and the Co-operative Movement attended to the needs of the whole, rather than a section, of the working class, then a minority of mainly skilled and craft workers would detach themselves from the rest of the class and slip into 'false consciousness'. 'Do we fight against an aristocracy of privilege?', asked Jones:

Well, then, there is an aristocracy of privilege of the vilest die among the highest paid trades, and we ought to fight it too — THE ARISTOCRACY OF LABOUR MUST BE BROKEN DOWN. If you don't, once you have established democracy, these men will organise the reaction.[37]

Significantly, it was Jones himself who was compelled to moderate his socialist and anti-middle class views (much to the disapproval of Engels[38]). Jones's fears foreshadowed Engel's pessimistic judgement of 1858 that,

the English proletariat is actually becoming more and more bourgeois, so that this most bourgeois of all nations is apparently aiming ultimately at the possession of a bourgeois aristocracy and a bourgeois proletariat *as well as* a bourgeoisie.[39]

How matters had changed since 1845 when Engels had predicted that, 'The approach to Socialism cannot fail, especially when the next crisis directs the working-men by force of sheer want to social instead of political remedies'.[40] Finally, in 1870 Thomas Cooper, himself a former Chartist, recorded his 'sorrowful impressions' that, although Lancashire workers had 'bettered their physical condition considerably' since the Chartist period, they had 'gone back, intellectually and morally':

> In our old Chartist time, it is true, Lancashire working men were in rags by thousands; and many of them often lacked food. But their intelligence was demonstrated wherever you went. You would see them in groups discussing the great doctrine of political justice . . . Now, you will see no such groups in Lancashire. But you will hear well-dressed working men talking, as they walk with their hands in their pockets, of 'Co-ops' . . . and their shares in them, or in building societies. And you will see others, like idiots, leading small greyhound dogs, covered with cloth, in a string![41]

Economic Growth

The extent to which contemporary views provided an accurate indication of trends in living standards will be discussed shortly. What we can say with immediate certainty is that contemporary opinion reflected the vast strides made by the economy during the third quarter. For, despite recent qualifications to the traditional notion of the 'Great Victorian Boom',[42] there is no doubting the enormous boost to the economy provided by railway building, the development of capital goods industries and the vast expansion of overseas markets.

The Lancashire economy fully participated in the boom. Coal mining and engineering, two of the county's three leading industries, experienced massive and rapid growth, in terms both of numbers employed and overall levels of output.[43] The third, and most important industry, cotton manufacturing, enjoyed continued expansion, if at a 'less revolutionary pace' than during the first half of the century (see Table 3.1). The 1850s, in particular, constituted a decade of heady growth. Stimulated by the growth of demand in the United States, Australia and India (whose handloom weavers were 'crushed out' by the Lancashire power-loom)[44], by the general rise in the price of finished goods, and improved technology, cotton fully recuperated from its earlier crisis of a falling rate of profit and overproduction to enter, by 1850, upon 'a great wave of credit-

based expansion', almost as intense as 'that of the heroic age of
1780–1840'.[45] Cotton goods produced, while not matching the dizzy
growth rates of the early decades of the century, still attained the
high annual rate of growth of 8–9 per cent between 1845 and 1859.[46]
And cotton goods exported, which grew at 11.8 per cent per annum
between 1830 and 1845, maintained a very respectable 9 per cent rate
between 1845 and 1859. Furthermore, as Table 3.2 demonstrates,
goods exported increased as a percentage of total cotton goods
produced, from 60.5 per cent in 1844 to 74.4 per cent in 1859 (by
1880 they stood at 81.6 per cent).[47]

Table 3.1:   Percentage Changes in the Production of Cotton
Textiles in Each Decade, 1791–1880

1791–1800	+ 86	1841–1850	+ 60
1801–1810	+ 84	1851–1860	+ 57
1811–1820	+ 62	1861–1870	– 4.5[a]
1821–1830	+ 93	1871–1880	+ 52.5
1831–1840	+ 91		

Note: a, This sudden drop was a consequence of the Cotton Famine.
Source: H.A.Turner, *Trade Union Growth. Structure and Policy*, p. 40.

Table 3.2:   Domestic Consumption and Export of Yarn and
Goods, 1829–82

	1829–31 %	1844–46 %	1858–61 %	1880–82 %
Yarn				
Total export:	67.4	71.4	79.7	84.9
Consumed at home	32.6	28.6	20.3	15.1
Goods				
Exported:	53.9	60.5	74.4	81.6
Consumed at home	46.1	39.5	25.6	18.4

Source: T. Ellison, *The Cotton Trade of Great Britain* (1968), p. 59.

The middle years of the century also saw significant increases in
the numbers of operatives employed and mills in operation. The
number of operatives employed in cotton in the manufacturing districts grew from 540,000 in 1844 to 646,000 in 1859 (in the United
Kingdom as a whole there was an increase of 46 per cent in the
numbers of operatives employed in cotton between 1850 and
1878).[48] Between 1850 and 1860 powerloom weaving increased its

employees by 24 per cent and its factories — increasingly concentrated in north Lancashire — by as much as 62 per cent.[49] The number of cotton mills in operation throughout the United Kingdom rose by approximately 38 per cent between 1850 and 1878, while during the same period the number of spinning, weaving and combined weaving and spinning establishments enumerated by the factory inspectorate increased by, respectively, 38.9 per cent, 175.2 per cent and 4.4 per cent. Mills also tended on the whole to be much larger, to employ greater number of operatives and a higher proportion of young female workers than had previously been the case.[50]

The climax to the boom came between 1858 and 1860. During these two years of 'unprecedented prosperity' there took place a sharp rise in earnings and the productive capacity of the industry. In 1860 cotton attained, according to Farnie, 'a new peak of importance in the national economy': raw cotton supplied 17 per cent of the value of total imports and 18.9 per cent of re-exports' cotton manufacture accounted for 38.3 per cent of the value of domestic exports; and the value added by the industry amounted to 7.1 per cent of the Gross National Income.[51]

The Cotton Famine — resulting not, as contemporaries generally believed, from the northern blockade of southern ports, but from over-production and the consequent saturation of markets during the late fifties' boom — was accompanied by severe falls in the value of cotton's product, the quantity of goods exported and home market consumption, and a steep rise in unemployment.[52] However, by the late spring of 1865 signs of the earlier dynamism were once again very much in evidence. The immediate post-Famine period — from 1866–8 — saw a decline in prices, a squeeze on profits (as wages proved resistant to attempted reduction), and a marked increase in the number of liquidations; but the rates of growth of production and exports were impressive, returning in 1867 to pre-Famine levels.[53]

Farnie observes that the crisis of the 1860s dethroned cotton from its pre-eminent position in the national economy, and that the later years of the century were to witness growing competition and uncertainty. Nevertheless, in overall terms the third quarter had been a time of health and growth; and we would be well advised not to place too premature a date upon the industry's fall from grace. Reference has already been made to the boom of the early mid-1870s. In 1880 Britain still held more than four-fifths of the world's trade in cotton goods. And as late as 1913 cotton exports accounted for one quarter of total exports.[54]

Money Earnings

To what extent does statistical evidence support the belief that cotton's dynamism resulted in substantially improved earnings for its workers? At a general level, a resoundingly affirmative reply must be given. The vast majority of occupational grades within cotton did experience, at least in so far as money earnings are concerned, considerable overall improvement between 1850 and 1875. This conclusion is based mainly upon the investigations into wages and earnings undertaken by Chadwick in the 1850s, Wood during the first decade of the present century, and Deane and Mitchell in the 1950s and 1960s.[55] It is to a detailed examination of the findings of these investigators, especially the painstaking and authoritative work of Wood, that we must now turn.

As demonstrated in Table 3.3, Wood recorded increases of 13 and 17 percentage points in the average money earnings of cotton operatives during the respective periods 1850 to 1860 and 1860 to 1874. Taking 1891 (as opposed to Woods' 1900) as their base year, Deane and Mitchell recorded (see Table 3.4) even more impressive increases of 14 points between 1850 and 1860, and 22 points between 1860 and 1874.

Table 3.3: Average Money Earnings in Cotton, 1850–77 (1900 = 100)

1850	=	54
1855	=	59
1860	=	67
1866	=	74
1871	=	80
1874	=	84
1877	=	88

Source: G.H. Wood, 'Real Wages and the Standard of Comfort Since 1850', *Jnl. Roy. Stat. Soc.* LXXII (1909), p. 93.

Table 3.4: Indices of Average Earnings in Cotton in a Normal Week, 1849–74 (1891 = 100)

	COTTON, U.K.	
	Factory Workers	All Workers in Cotton
1849	54	51
1850	54	52
1851	55	53
1852	56	54

1853	59		57
1854	58		56
1855	59		57
1856	62		60
1857	62		61
1858	62		61
1859	64		63
1860	68		68
1861	68		68
1862	67		67
1863		66	
1864		66	
1865		71	
1866		77	
1867		77	
1868		79	
1869		78	
1870		81	
1871		85	
1872		87	
1873		89	
1874		90	

Source: P. Deane and B.R. Mitchell, *Abstract of British Historical Statistics*, pp. 349–50.

Progress was not uniform throughout the cotton districts. Wood demonstrated that the level of average earnings was higher in the Manchester district than in Cheshire and the remainder of Lancashire (see Table 3.5); and that the fine spinning centre of Bolton (with its generally moderate and conservative trade unionism[56]) stood at the top of the wages league table (see Table 3.6).

Table 3.5: Estimated Changes in the Average Earnings of Cotton Operatives in Manchester and District, and Lancashire and Cheshire 1839–80 (1886 = 100)

	Manchester and District	Lancashire and Cheshire
1839–41	65	63
1845	74	72
1849–51	65	63
1855	70	68
1859–61	71	70
1866	81	80
1870	88	87
1874	100	99
1877	105	104
1880	97	96
1886	100	100

Source: G.H. Wood, *The History of Wages in the Cotton Trade during the Past Hundred Years*, p. 43.

Table 3.6:   Estimates of Changes in the Average Earnings of Cotton Operatives Employed in the Chief Centres of the Industry (1886 = 100)

	1845	1849–50	1855	1860	1863–4	1866	1870
Manchester	74	65	70	71	–	81	88
Bolton	68	67	71	81	80	89	–
Oldham	–	64	–	79	–	86	90
Preston	56	54	56	71	71	85	–
Ashton[a]	–	–	–	–	–	–	–
Stockport[a]	–	–	–	–	–	–	–

Note: a. There exists considerable data on earnings in Ashton and Stockport for the years 1833–42, and 1886 onwards. Data for the mid-Victorian period is, however, scarce. Wood maintained that the course of wages at Ashton and Stockport during the latter period was probably similar to that prevailing at Oldham.
Source: G.H. Wood, *The History of Wages*, pp. 67, 115.

In terms of the earnings of the various occupational grades within cotton, Tables 3.7 and 3.8 — based upon Wood's figures — provide a breakdown of monetary and percentage changes between 1839–40 and 1874. Before examining such changes it is necessary to point out that Wood's calculations were based upon average earnings in specific occupations.

Table 3.7:   Estimated Average Weekly Earnings of Various Classes of Cotton Operatives in Lancashire and Cheshire, 1839–40–74[a]

	1839–40	1850	1860	1871	1874
Self-actor spinners	22/6d	21/9d	24/3d	30/-	33/-
Spinners (Manchester and district)[b]	23/4d	21/10d	24/4d	28/6d	33/1d
Self-acting big piecers	10/-	8/9d	10/-	12/-	14/-
Self-acting little piecers	5/-	5/6d	6/6d	7/-	8/6d
Piecers (Manchester and district)[c]	7/-	7/-	8/3d	9/6d	11/3d
Weavers (Manchester and district)	10/6d	11/-	12/6d	14/-	15/-
Weavers' helpers	5/-	5/-	5/-	5/-	5/3d
Blowing and cardroom women	7/-	7/6d	8/-	12/-	12/-
Drawing-frame tenters	7/6d	7/-	8/-	12/9d	14/6d
Throstle and ring spinners	8/-	7/6d	9/-	12/-	13/-
Winders	9/-	8/6d	10/-	13/-	13/9d
Reelers	9/-	9/-	9/6d	13/-	13/-

Warpers	9/-	11/-	11/6d	14/-	15/-
Strippers and grinders	13/-	12/9d	14/9d	21/-	23/-
Dressers and sizers	26/-	25/-	25/-	30/-	37/-

Notes: a. For the data in Tables 3.7 and 3.8 see G.H. Wood, *The History of Wages*, op. cit. pp. 28–9, 42, 131. Wood (p. 131) calculated earnings to the nearest 3d. per worker.
b. Allowing (p. 28) for the numbers employed in the various classes (fine, medium and coarse), and including both hand-mule and self-actor spinners.
c. An approximate estimate (p. 29) for big, middle and little piecers.

calculations were based upon average earnings in specific occupations. And, as the author himself was aware, such calculations concealed (sometimes substantial) variations in earning capacity within the same occupation. Variations were especially marked in weaving and spinning. For example, in 1849 four-loom weavers generally earned between 5/- and 7/- more than two-loom weavers. And throughout the mid-Victorian period the earnings of the former were well above the average for weaving as a whole.[57] Earnings for hand-mule and self-actor spinners ranged from 16/- to 42/- during the late thirties and early forties; while by 1859 hand-mule spinners could take home between 23/- and 45/- for a 'normal week's work'.[58]

Table 3.8: Percentage Changes in the Average Weekly Earnings of Various Classes of Cotton Operatives in Lancashire and Cheshire, 1839–40–74

	1839–50 %	1850–60 %	1860–74 %
Self-actor spinners	− 3.3	+ 11	+ 36
Spinners (Manchester and district)	− 6.5	+ 11	+ 35.9
Self-acting big piecers	− 12.5	+ 14	+ 40
Self-acting little piecers	+ 10	+ 18	+ 30
Piecers (Manchester and district)	even	+ 17	+ 36
Weavers (Manchester and district)	+ 4.7	+ 13	+ 20
Weavers' helpers	even	even	+ 5
Blowing and cardroom women	+ 7	+ 6	+ 50
Drawing-frame tenters	− 6.6	+ 14	+ 81
Throstle and ring spinners	− 6.2	+ 20	+ 44
Winders	− 5.5	+ 17	+ 37
Reelers	even	+ 5	+ 36
Warpers	+ 22	+ 4	+ 30
Strippers and Grinders	− 1.9	+ 15	+ 55.9
Dressers and Sizers	− 3.8	even	+ 48

Tables 3.7 and 3.8 clearly support a view of overall improvement during the third quarter. The earnings of most grades of cotton operatives were lower in 1850 than they had been in 1839–40 (falling for eight out of the fifteen grades listed; remaining even for three; and advancing in only four cases), but from mid-century onwards the general outlook brightened. The decade of the 1850s did, to be sure, see no overall advance in the earnings of weavers' helpers and sizers and dressers, but such experiences were untypical of the workforce as a whole. Thus the other 13 occupational groups listed in Table 3.7 and 3.8 experienced increases in earnings between 1850 and 1860 ranging from a low of 4 per cent for warpers (warpers' earnings had, however, increased by 22 per cent during the generally gloomy 1840s) to a high of 20 per cent for throstle and ring spinners.

An improvement in earnings during the 1850s had, of course, been earlier recorded by Chadwick (Table 3.9).

Table 3.9:   Average Return of Weekly Wages, Cotton Manufacture, 1849–59

	1849	1859	% increase
Hand-mule spinners (Nos. 180's to 220's)[a]	40/-	45/-	12.5
Self-actor minders (Nos. 25's to 40's)	18/6d	22/-	18.9
Self-actor minders (Nos. 4's to 24's)	18/-	20/-	11.1
Weavers — Four Loom	16/-	18/-	12.5
Weavers — Three Loom	13/-	15/-	15.3
Grinders	13/-	15/-	15.3
Doublers	7/6d	9/-	20.0
Drawing frame-tenters	7/-	8/-	14.2
Piecers	9/-	10/-	11.1
Throstle spinners (girls 14 to 18 yrs.)	4/6d	5/-	11.1
Throstle spinners (women 18 yrs. and ups.)	7/6d	9/-	20.0
Strippers	12/-	14/-	16.6
Sizers	23/-	25/-	8.7
Overlookers (in doubling)	25/-	28/-	12.0

Note: a. Not a direct comparison: the 1849 figure is for 800 spindles; that of 1859 for 1,600 spindles.
Source: D. Chadwick, 'On the Rate of Wages in Manchester, Salford and the Manufacturing Districts of Lancashire, 1839–49–59', *Journal of the Royal Statistical Society* (March 1860), pp. 23–4.

It was, however (with the exception of the Cotton Famine), between 1860 and 1874 that the major, in many cases spectacular, gains were achieved. As shown in Table 3.7, spinners, piecers, blowing and cardroom hands, throstle and ring spinners, winders, reelers, warpers, dressers and sizers increased their earnings during this period by between 30 and 50 per cent. Strippers, grinders and draw-ing-frame tenters did even better, obtaining advances of, respec-tively, 55, 55 and 81 per cent. The earnings of the largest group of workers in the mill, the weavers, also rose but at the more 'modest' rate of 20 per cent.

The common but uneven pattern of wage gains in cotton leads us, thirdly, to consider trends in differentials. Of central importance in this context is Hobsbawm's claim that differentials and the socio-cultural between gap 'aristocratic' male spinners and the remainder of the predominantly female cotton workforce widened during the years from the mid-1840s to the 1890s.[59] Hobsbawm attributes these developments to two factors: the increased proportion of unskilled female workers employed in cotton which, he claims, left the male spinners 'more obviously prominent and dominant' (male spinners fell from 15 per cent of the industry's workforce in 1835 to 5 per cent in 1886, whilst the proportion of women and girls employed increased from 48 per cent in 1835 to 60 per cent in 1907); and the increase in differentials during these years between, on the one hand, spinners and, on the other, weavers and piecers.[60] Hobsbawm's case is strengthened by Foster's finding that the post-1850 years in Oldham witnessed 'increasing wage differentials and a sharp rise in the number of low-paid jobs', with the real earnings of the bottom half of the town's labour force falling slightly between 1839 and 1859 'at a time when those higher up the scale enjoyed quite a sharp rise'.[61]

Notwithstanding the massive disparity in earnings between spin-ners and weavers, a picture of a widened gap is open to question. Thus it may be objected on socio-cultural grounds that to place key emphasis upon a division between male spinners (surely dressers and sizers, the veritable aristocrats in cotton, should at least be included with those 'contrived aristocrats', the spinners[62]) and piecers and the large group of female operatives is to underestimate the central importance of the family in the employment structure of cotton. As Joyce has written, the dispersal of the spinner's family across the whole range of occupations within the industry undermines the notion of a clearcut division between spinners and the remainder of the workforce.[63] There also exist doubts as to whether Foster's findings are strictly applicable to cotton. If I am correct in thinking that Foster's conclusions are based upon the earnings of males over 20 years of age, then surely such conclusions, whilst applicable to trends in Oldham's rapidly growing engineering industry, do not provide a comprehensive guide to cotton with its large adolescent and female workforce.[64] Most crucially in terms of the question of differentials, Table 3.10 shows that percentage rises in average earnings for those occupations in cotton which were wholly or mainly filled by females compared, generally speaking, very favourably with the rises gained by the spinners during the third quarter. During the years between 1850 and 1860 female weavers, drawing-frame tenters, throstle and ring spinners and winders did obtain advances in excess of the 11 per cent received by the spinners. And between 1860 and 1874 spinners stood only joint-fifth in the league table of percentage rises for the nine occupational groups listed in Table 3.10. By the same token it is true that weavers, who constituted the largest group of female workers,[65] occupied a lowly eighth position in the same league table during the period 1860–74, receiving an increase of 20, as opposed to the spinners' 36 per cent. This state of affairs stood in contrast to the 1850–60 period when the weavers had outstripped the spinners by 2 per cent.

Table 3.10: Percentage Changes in Average Earnings of Selected Occupations in Cotton, 1850–60, 1860–74

	1850–1860 %	1860–1874 %
Self-actor spinners	+ 11	+ 36
Weavers	+ 13	+ 20
Weavers' helpers	even	+ 5
Blowing and cardroom women	+ 6	+ 50
Drawing-frame tenters	+ 14	+ 81
Throstle and ring spinners	+ 22	+ 44
Winders	+ 17	+ 37
Reelers	+ 5	+ 36
Warpers	+ 4	+ 30

Source: Information extracted from Table 3.8 above.

In terms, therefore, of a direct comparison between the earnings of spinners and weavers, Hobsbawm is, in all probability, correct to note a trend towards widened differentials, although this trend seems to have emerged during the 1860s rather than (as claimed by

Hobsbawm) during the 1840s. A further conclusion to be drawn from Table 3.10 is that the female operatives not employed as weavers did, however, fare much better in terms of percentage rises *vis-à-vis* male spinners than the deteriorating position of the weavers would suggest. In sum, it is evident that the notion of a widening financial and social gap between male spinners and the remainder of the cotton workforce is, at various points, in need of qualification and correction.

Fourthly, a more detailed breakdown of Wood's figures than hitherto undertaken reveals that advances in the average money earnings of the vast majority of grades in cotton were neither so continuous nor so smooth as has so far been implied.[66] Moreover, a picture of *substantial* improvement for the crucial years of the late 1840s and early mid-1850s, when mass Chartism was in decline, is wide of the mark. In terms of the 1840s there was, for example, little overall, continuous improvement. The generally high earnings in cotton during 1839–40 were successfully reduced by the employers in 1841 (a major source of friction in the run up to the industrial unrest of 1842). The mid-1840s witnessed an improvement in trade and an advance in earnings, but the depression of 1847 was accompanied by reductions. By 1849–50 earnings in cotton were generally just above their 1841 levels, but below the levels of 1839–40 and 1845.[67] As noted earlier, between 1839 and 1850 earnings for eight of the fifteen occupational groups in cotton listed in Table 3.8 showed an overall decline (ranging from 1.9 per cent for strippers and grinders to 12.5 per cent for self-acting big piecers), and advanced in only four cases (by 4.7 per cent for weavers, 7 per cent for blowing and cardroom women, 10 per cent for self-acting little piecers and 22 per cent for warpers). Between 1849–50 and the end of 1852 earnings, as shown in Table 3.4, rose steadily but far from spectacularly (from 54 per cent in 1849 and 1850 to 55 per cent in 1852). The bitter industrial battles of 1853–4 did result in the 10 per cent increase. However, by the end of 1854 this increase had largely been lost as a result of a successful employer counter-attack. The following year saw a slight increase — so that by the mid-1850s money earnings in cotton had generally moved five points above the 1850 mark. Earnings remained stationary throughout the industry between 1856 and 1858, but from the latter part of 1858 to the early months of 1861 they showed a considerable rise (from 62 to 68 points on Deane and Mitchell's scale). Our earlier statement that earnings in cotton were significantly higher in 1860 than in 1850 (by

14 points) thus stands, but it is necessary to add the qualification that the intervening years of the decade did not witness continuous improvement. The gloomy years between the end of 1855 and 1857 were, moreover, made worse by spectacular price inflation; and it was only during the last two years of the decade that a marked and sustained improvement took place. Thus simply to compare money earnings at either end of the 1850s is to present an oversimplified and distorted picture of developments throughout the decade as a whole.

Trends in the money earnings of the spinners of Manchester and district clearly reflect the general fluctuations and developments outlined above.[68] During the 1840s spinners' average earnings (allowing for the numbers employed in the various classes of spinning) moved as follows: from 23/4d in 1840 to 21/8d in 1841, and from 23/5d during 1845-6 (an increase of 8 per cent over the 1841 figure) to 21/10d in 1849-50. Thus by the end of the decade, earnings were slightly above the level of 1841, but below the 1840 mark. Spinners throughout much of Lancashire and Cheshire gained the 10 per cent increase during 1853-4, but subsequently suffered the set-back of an 8 per cent reduction — with the result that by 1855 their earnings were just above the 1850 level (22/- during 1854-5 as against 21/10d in 1850). As in the industry as a whole, spinners' earnings remained steady until the 1858-61 period, when they advanced to 24/4d (a 10 per cent increase over the mid-1850s). Major losses were incurred during the Cotton Famine, but from 1865 onwards progress was both swift and spectacular. Between 1866 and 1870 spinners' average earnings stood at 28/6d — an improvement of 17 per cent upon the 1859-61 figure. A further increase of 16 per cent (from 28/6d to 33/1d) took place between 1870 and 1874.

Real Earnings

Our focus has so far rested upon trends in average money earnings. And the main conclusion to emerge is that money earnings in cotton did generally advance during the third quarter, albeit less continuously and, especially during the 1850s, less substantially than many contemporaries believed. But money earnings constitute only part of the total picture of living standards. It is now time to consider the extent to which money improvements were, when set against price and employment patterns, translated into gains in real earnings.

In terms of employment and prices, the overall picture in the cotton districts was (again, with the massive exception of the Cotton

Famine) more stable and healthy than during the frequently crisis-ridden and uncertain years of the second quarter of the century. The vast expansion of overseas markets, the stabilisation of prices for finished cotton goods, and the general dynamism of the national economy during the post-1850 years, resulted in greater security of employment, and, generally speaking, a diminution in the incidence and severity of depression.[69]

The third quarter was not, as sometimes claimed by historians, a period of continuous secular price inflation but, as Church has reminded us, one of high, relatively stable prices intervening between periods of 'spectacular but short-lived' price inflation.[70] Table 3.11 clearly shows that the latter periods were 1853–6, 1866–8 and 1872–4.[71]

Table 3.11:   Trends in Retail Prices, 1850–77 (1850 = 100)

1850	=	100	1864	=	106
1851	=	97	1865	=	107
1852	=	97	1866	=	114
1853	=	106	1867	=	121
1854	=	122	1868	=	119
1855	=	126	1869	=	113
1856	=	126	1870	=	113
1857	=	119	1871	=	113
1858	=	109	1872	=	120
1859	=	107	1873	=	122
1860	=	111	1874	=	117
1861	=	114	1875	=	113
1862	=	111	1876	=	110
1863	=	107	1877	=	113

Source: G.H. Wood, 'Real Wages and the Standard of Comfort since 1850', *Jnl. Roy. Stat. Soc.* 72 (1909), p. 102.

Having taken into account both employment and price trends, Wood and Mitchell and Deane agree that average real wages in the United Kingdom did improve during the mid-Victorian years. Thus, as shown in Table 3.12, Deane and Mitchell conclude that increases of 32 and 25 percentage points took place in the respective periods 1850–73 and 1863–73. Wood (see Table 3.13) reached similar conclusions: 31 points for the period between 1850 and 1873; and 24 for 1863 to 1873.

Table 3.12:   Average Real Wages (allowing for unemployment), UK 1850–74 (1850 = 100)

1850	=	100	1863	=	107
1851	=	102	1864	=	118
1852	=	100	1865	=	120
1853	=	107	1866	=	117
1854	=	97	1867	=	105
1855	=	94	1868	=	105
1856	=	95	1869	=	111
1857	=	94	1870	=	118
1858	=	94	1871	=	125
1859	=	104	1872	=	126
1860	=	105	1873	=	132
1861	=	99	1874	=	136
1862	=	100			

Source: P. Deane and B.R. Mitchell, *Abstract of British Historical Statistics*, p. 343. The authors describe their index of retail prices as 'experimental', and their allowances for unemployment as 'rough and ready'.

Table 3.13 merits several observations. Firstly, there arises the key question as to whether Wood's calculations concerning trends in real wages in the United Kingdom are safely applicable to cotton. Wood constructed his index upon the assumption that a worker earned 20/- per week in 1850. In terms of cotton there were (excluding overlookers) only dressers, sizers and spinners who received individual earnings of 20/- or above per week at mid-

Table 3.13:   Index of Real Wages, UK 1850–74 (1859 = 100)

1850	=	96	1863	=	103
1851	=	·98	1864	=	113
1852	=	96	1865	=	115
1853	=	103	1866	=	112
1854	=	93	1867	=	101
1855	=	90	1868	=	101
1856	=	91	1869	=	107
1857	=	90	1870	=	113
1858	=	90	1871	=	120
1859	=	100	1872	=	121
1860	=	101	1873	=	127
1861	=	95	1874	=	131
1862	=	96			

Source: G.H. Wood, 'Real Wages and the Standard of Comfort since 1850', *Jnl. Roy. Stat. Soc.* 72 (1909) p. 102.

century. What mattered most in cotton were, as Wood was well aware, family, as against individual, earnings. And Wood estimated that the total earnings of the overwhelming majority of cotton operative families were 'close to' or 'slightly above'[72] the United Kingdom average in 1850. The extent to which Wood's figures in Table 3.13 constitute a reliable record of trends in cotton thus depends upon the accuracy of his estimation.

Whilst not having consulted the census enumerators' books to set earnings against patterns of family employment in specific locations, I accept Wood's estimate to be fairly accurate or, if anything, an underestimation of the totals earned by many operative families. For example, the combined weekly income in 1850 for a family of an adult woman in unpaid work at home, an adult male employed as a stripper (12/9d), a teenage girl working in the cardroom (7/6d), and a 14-year-old boy employed as a cardminder (6/6d) would be, in the event of full employment, 26/9d. The members of this family have been placed in relatively lowly-paid occupations. There were many families with adult males employed as spinners and females in weaving whose total weekly income would have been considerably higher. It is also useful to know that a factory inspector, Robert Baker, calculated that average individual earnings in a cotton mill of five hundred operatives increased from 10/3d in 1860 to 13/2d in 1865.[73]

Secondly, Table 3.13 lends itself to the conclusion that, as in the case of money earnings, the most substantial and lasting advances in real earnings were made not during the 1850s but between the end of the Cotton Famine and 1874. Between 1850 and 1860 real earnings rose five percentage points, but fluctuated to a much greater extent than did money earnings. Thus for five years during the 1850s decade real earnings were below the 1850 level, above 1850 for four years, and on a par with 1850 during one year. In marked contrast to money earnings (which in 1855 were five points above the 1850 level), real earnings in 1855 stood well below (by six points) the 1850 level. Especially galling for the operatives was the loss in 1854 of the 10 per cent at a time when prices had begun their steep upward climb. During the following two years prices remained extremely high (see Table 3.11) and money incomes failed to rise. Only between the end of 1858 and the beginning of 1861 did large increases in real earnings take place.

The early sixties saw a fall in real earnings throughout the United Kingdom. Allowing, however, for the setbacks of the Cotton

Famine and the decline in real earnings between 1867 and 1868 (prices rose sharply during 1866–7 and remained at a high level during 1868), the period from 1863 to 1874 was, was, as in the case of money earnings, one of considerable advancement. Between 1863 and 1870 real earnings rose by ten points, and between 1870 and 1874 by an even more impressive 18 percentage points. The 'golden years' had thus taken perhaps belated but increasingly firm root in the cotton districts.

It is perhaps tempting, in view of developments between 1863 and 1874, to simply conclude that the optimistic case is beyond serious criticism, and that pessimistic protests to the contrary are motivated more by ideological bias than proper scientific respect for the evidence at hand. Such a temptation must, however, be resisted for two major reasons. Firstly, closer interrogation of the evidence so far presented suggests that important qualifications, indeed corrections, to a picture of smooth, overall improvement are in order. Increases in real earnings in cotton occurred with neither sufficient speed nor substance to constitute, as Foster rightly points out, anything more than a very limited explanation of the decline of Chartism. Furthermore, there is little doubt that the most substantial increases in earnings took place during the post-1865 period rather than during the 1850s. Secondly, our picture of living standards is, as yet, incomplete and therefore unbalanced. A comprehensive picture must include not only earnings but also poverty and insecurity, housing and health, and people's expectations and judgements concerning changes in their material conditions. And, as will now be demonstrated, an investigation into these areas lends itself to far more pessimistic findings than a solely earnings-based investigation would suggest.

Poverty and Economic Insecurity

There is no doubt that, despite the relatively secure employment and improved earnings of the third quarter, few operative families could expect to be permanently free from the worries of economic insecurity and periodic bouts of poverty. Attention should, in this context, be drawn to the generally discontinuous pattern of wage advancement outlined earlier, the marked fluctuations in real earnings during the 1850s and the disastrous impact of the Cotton Famine upon living standards.

Poverty was, of course, particularly marked during old age, sickness and those periods when women left paid employment to give birth to and care for their babies. As Foster has noted in relation to Oldham, Northampton and South Shields:

> In all three towns poverty was not so much the special experience of a particular group within the labour force as a regular feature of the life of almost *all* working families at certain stages in their development, especially in old age or before young children could start earning.[74]

Even during 'good' years, poverty levels were high. For example, Foster has shown that during the relatively prosperous year of 1849 the incomes of an outright majority of working families in all three towns were either 'already too low for them to buy all the food they needed, or would be if they had to support just one extra adult member'. The above reference is, of course, to primary poverty: levels of secondary poverty would have been much higher.[75] Foster concludes that 85 per cent of Oldham's working-class families were faced with the prospect of periods of semi-starvation, and that, in terms of specific occupations:

> A carter or power-weaver, if his wife could not work, would find himself in poverty if he had any children at all; a cotton spinner or coalminer if he had more than one child; and even the very small group of craft workers would find themselves in poverty if they had more than four children before the eldest started to work.[76]

Anderson and Barnsby have also drawn attention to the persistence of high levels of poverty. The former estimated that in mid-Victorian Preston only about one in seven of all working-class families would be permanently free from poverty.[77] The latter calculated that, although approximately one-quarter of the Black Country's workers had a minimum standard of comfort, 20 per cent existed almost permanently below the minimum level necessary to maintain life, and a majority (53 per cent) lived above subsistence but below the minimum standard of comfort all their lives.[78]

Despite the dominant climate of economic and social improvement, some contemporaries attempted to draw public attention to the continued economic plight of sections of the mid-Victorian working class. In this context Marx's lectures to the International Workingmens' Association and Mayhew's findings for London are well known.[79] Less well known, however, are the investigations made by Edward Brotherton and his middle-class colleagues in the Manchester and Salford Education Aid Society (founded in 1864) into the educational and general economic conditions prevailing among workers in Manchester and Salford during the 1860s. An exhaustive house-to-house survey (which excluded 'Angel Meadow', Manchester's equivalent of the St Giles district of London) conducted by the society in the mid-sixties revealed that approximately 25 per cent of the 2,896 families interviewed had an average income of only 2/- per family member per week, and a further 11.5 per cent averaged 1/4d per family member per week (both cases were exclusive of the payment of rent). Brotherton, himself, maintained that a figure of 3/- per adult head per week (exclusive of rent) was necessary to keep an adult just above the poverty line. The conclusion drawn was that at least 25 per cent of Manchester and Salfords' workers were in primary poverty. 'This state of things is not the result of the Cotton Famine, or any temporary pressure', insisted Brotherton, 'it is the normal condition existing now [1865–6], when the cotton famine is past, and . . . is no doubt also existing, with equal pressure, in all the other large towns of England'.[80]

Surveys conducted by the Manchester Statistical Society also revealed a depressing picture. While approximately 36 per cent of 789 families covered in an Ancoats sample of the mid-sixties received between one and two pounds per week in income from all sources (the comparable figure for Oldham in 1849 was 16 per cent),[81] approximately 56 per cent (48 per cent at Oldham) received less than one pound.[82] This state of affairs had shown no marked improvement by the late 1880s when Scott's study of the standards of living of 2,515 heads of families in Ancoats and Salford[83] revealed that 31 per cent of the Ancoats sample and 45 per cent of the Salford sample were 'very poor'; 14 per cent in Ancoats and 11 per cent in Salford were 'poor'; and 16 and 12 per cent of the respective samples were 'comfortable'. Only the top 15 or so per cent were not troubled by primary poverty.[84]

By the turn of the century little, if anything, had changed. In 1904 the Citizens' Association for the Improvement of Unwholesome Dwellings and Surroundings of the People concluded, on the basis of its investigations into living conditions in parts of Manchester and Salford, that, 'the recent enquiries of Mr Rowntree and of Mr Booth have given results which we believe can safely be applied to Manchester and Salford'. The Association claimed that out of a total combined population of 764,829 (543, 872 in Manchester; 220, 957 in Salford), between 212,000 and 230,000 people in Manchester and Salford were in a state of secondary poverty, and at least a further 75,000 were in primary poverty.[85]

The inescapable and depressing conclusion to emerge from the investigations outlined above is thus that poverty continued to plague the lives of a majority of workers throughout the second half of the nineteenth century. Finally, it is worth nothing that the presence of the poor, more particularly the chronic poor or 'residuum', aroused increasing concern among middle-class contemporaries. 'Limp in body and mind', steeped in pauperism and dependency, the 'residuum' embodied, in the eyes of the middle class, all those 'evil' attitudes and customs — 'drunkenness, improvidence, mendicancy, bad language, filthy habits, gambling, low amusements and ignorance'[86] — which that model of 'respectability', 'Rochdale Man', had consciously rejected. There existed, furthermore, the possibility that, unless checked or reformed, the 'residuum' might mushroom to spread moral degeneration and urban decay. In the process, the 'newly built citadel of moral virtue and economic rationality' might be overrun, and the 'respectable' working class 'tainted' or even 'contaminated' by the dangerously anti-social, perhaps even revolutionary, views of the undermass.[87]

Stedman Jones has brilliantly described the way in which such fears and concerns reached their climax in London during the 1880s. The euphoria surrounding economic growth at mid-century meant that only rarely in the 1850s and early-mid 1860s did the West End cast a nervous glance in the direction of Stepney and Whitechapel; but with the increased uncertainties of the 'Great Depression', growing distress, the increasingly radical stance adopted by London's artisans and, above all, the unemployed riots and demonstrations of 1886 and 1887, concern gave way to outright, blind panic. During the immediate aftermath of the unemployed riot of February 1886 London was visited, claims Steadman-Jones, by 'something akin to the *grande peur*':

> In the morning (Feb 10th) the confidence of the West End had been slightly restored and some shops had begun to re-open. But from mid-day the fog thickened, 'the disorderly' classes again began to assemble in Trafalgar Square and the panic grew. The rumour spread that '10,000 men were on the march from Deptford to London, destroying as they came, the property of

small traders' . . . All over South London, 'the shops closed and people stood at their doors straining their eyes through the fog for the sounds of the 10,000 men who were stated to be marching either to Clapham Common or to the City'. By mid-afternoon, 'the terror was so general in South London that the board schools were literally besieged by anxious parents eager to take their children home under their protection'. But similar situations existed elsewhere. In Whitechapel a mob was said to be marching down from the Commercial Road; at Bethnal Green the mob was said to be in Green Street . . . In the City and the West End, all approaches were guarded. Banks and private firms closed down . . . Troops were confined to barracks in the company of magistrates who were to read the riot act when the mob approached.[88]

Such levels of fear and panic were not approached in the cotton towns. The latter, with their factory-structured rhythms and disciplines of work, and, generally speaking, relatively stable pattern of employment, did not possess large numbers of casual workers among whom chronic poverty was heavily concentrated. London, as the capital of the casual labour market, was fittingly the place where concern was most acute.[89] Fears of the poor were, however, by no means absent from the manufacturing districts. In the 1860s Brotherton was alarmed by what he believed to be the increasing separation between classes in Manchester, the breakdown of social bonds, and an apparent increase in the size of the 'ignorant, half-starved class'. He warned:

the demoralisation which is going on cannot be contemplated by any thinking man without the conviction that ruin to society is inevitable unless some active change can be brought about . . . we have vice, in all its lowest forms, stalking at night and polluting the air, and in all the towns of England there is a continually growing more inert and more degraded mass of population. At length the point will be reached beyond which it will be impossible to move.[90]

Others expressed concern at the large stock of poor housing in Manchester, and the high rates of mortality and sickness which prevailed in the cotton districts throughout the third quarter.[91] It was perhaps not surprising that attention to environmental improvement quickened during the late sixties and the seventies.

As a large, impersonal, and mainly commercial centre, Manchester had much in common with London. But, in the cotton towns proper, middle-class concern with the 'vices' of the poor and, indeed, on occasion with the 'weaknesses' of large numbers of regularly employed operatives, was much in evidence. During the third quarter some towns, such as Ashton and Stalybridge, lost little of their reputations for 'roughness, turbulence and fanaticism' — as places where the middle class often feared to tread.[92] This continued 'roughness' was, predictably, often attributed by the middle class, to the high numbers of 'uncivilised' Irish Catholic immigrants resident in these towns.[93] But native-born workers were at times equally as 'rough' and 'insubordinate' as the immigrants. We can agree with Rose that the picture of 'Rochdale Man' is, in part, caricature. Despite their enhanced reputation for 'moderation' and 'restraint' (a reputation actively cultivated by working-class leaders to improve the public standing of themselves and their members), many cotton operatives did, at times (during numerous industrial disputes, in the Relief Riots of 1863, and sometimes at elections[94]) behave in exceedingly 'unrestrained' and 'riotous' ways. Herein lay the 'other face' of 'respectable' 'Rochdale Man': an aggressive, independent class presence, which was hardly in accord with the images of passivity and deference so beloved of the middle class.

Housing and Sanitation

In terms of housing and sanitary conditions, we can usefully concertrate much of our attention upon developments in Manchester and south Lancashire. Two major trends emerged during the third quarter. There was, firstly, visible, probably increased, evidence of what Reach termed in the late forties, 'an evident disposition to improvement'. Of particular note was the formation, in 1852, of the Manchester and Salford Sanitary Association by 'a number of gentlemen interested in the welfare of the town and anxious to ameliorate the condition of the poor'.[95] The Association sought to promote both 'personal and domestic cleanliness' and public co-operation with boards of health in 'giving effect to regulations for sanitary improvement'. These, and other attempts to draw attention to and improve the physical condition of Manchester, were not without effect. During the fifties and sixties some of the worst housing in the city was demolished, the number of cellar dwellings reduced by half, and the amount of paving and drainage in existence increased and improved.[96] Furthermore, the newer areas of operative housing, such as parts of Chorlton and more or less the whole of Hulme — with their 'comparatively broad and airy streets', better-constructed houses, and more adequate sanitary facilities — represented a distinct improvement upon the older inner-city areas such as Ancoats and Deansgate.[97] Likewise, those operatives who were financially able to move away from the old and often dilapidated central housing districts of the surrounding cotton towns into newer dwelling areas, experienced improvements in terms of both housing and general environmental conditions. Thus Reach found much to admire in the 'new' town of Ashton, where the houses of most of the operatives who lived outside the old town were 'comfortable' and the streets 'more open and better drained than in the great majority of industrial Lancashire towns'[98].

Secondly, despite these undoubted signs of improvement, most commentators in the late forties and throughout the fifties agreed that, in *overall terms*, housing and sanitary conditions were still extremely poor. The older working-class areas of Manchester and Salford continued to be characterised by cramped, overcrowded and poorly-ventilated back-to-back housing, open cesspools and generally totally inadequate sanitary facilities.[99] Reach was compelled to recognise that, 'In the older parts of the borough of Manchester itself, along the great thoroughfare called the Oldham Road, and in the Ancoats district — the latter entirely an operative colony — are situated some of the most squalid-looking streets . . . I have seen'. Outlying parts of Salford were also seen to be, 'very miserable, full of streets unpaved, undrained, strewn with offal and refuse, and pierced with airless culs-de-sac'.[100] In the surrounding towns conditions were often equally bad. Stockport had fewer cellar dwellings than in the late 1830s (this was generally the case throughout the towns of the cotton districts), but retained much of its unenviable reputation as 'one of the duskiest, smokiest holes' in the 'entire district': housing conditions, especially in the courts and alleyways of the town centre and Hillgate, remained shockingly bad.[101] At Bolton, Reach observed that the 'great mass of houses' were built 'in the oldest and filthiest fashion', and at Oldham that, 'the general appearance of the operatives' houses is filthy and smouldering' — 'airless little back streets and close nasty courts' being common in the latter town.[102] At Ashton the 'nucleus of the place' was 'old, filthy and dilapidated in the extreme', with the once-proud handloom weavers inhabiting 'crumbling, crazy, and dirty' houses in the 'filthy and mean' district of Charlestown.[103]

The picture presented by Reach was, however, far from uniformly gloomy. Reference has been made above to improved conditions in parts of Manchester and satisfactory housing provision in many districts of Ashton. Reach also commented favourably upon conditions prevailing in some of the smaller industrial communities, especially those situated in the countryside. Of Egerton, near Bolton, he wrote:

> The village of Egerton, although inhabited solely by a factory population, is as sweet, wholesome, and smokeless as it could be were its denizens the most bucolic hinds of Devon . . . The houses are furnished much in the same fashion as those of the middling Manchester class; but every article of household use looks better, because cleaner and fresher. Here is no grime nor squalor . . . There is no ragged wretchedness to be seen, no ruinous and squalid hovels.[104]

Unfortunately, even if somewhat less idyllic than suggested by Reach, housing and general living conditions in Egerton were still far from representative of those in which the great majority of operatives throughout the cotton districts were forced to live. In the mid-late sixties, the overall situation — certainly in relation to Manchester and Salford — had changed little. As noted earlier, in 1868 Abram drew attention to 'the moderately comfortable' state of the homes of the 'more thrifty' operatives. But against Abram's optimism must be set a number of pessimistic reports and views emanating from sources of varied ideological persuasions. The Education Aid Society claimed that there were many families living in Deansgate who would be, 'infinitely better lodged, fed and clothed in any prison in England than in the houses they occupy'. There followed a description of a Deansgate cellar dwelling:

> In one cellar, with two apartments, lives a family of ten persons — father, mother and eight children. The three oldest are girls, just growing to womanhood. They are millhands, but at present have very little work. There is a wreck of a small table and two or three chairs. I did not see any bed. The place is incredibly squalid and miserable.[105]

Less predictably, the Education Aid Society's indictment of housing and sanitary conditions in many of the working-class areas of

Manchester and Salford was endorsed by that fervent advocate of free-market capitalism, the *Manchester Guardian*. In 1870, 'impelled by our criminal statistics, and the constant recurrence of Manchester's prominent position in the death scale of the Registrar's returns', the *Guardian* despatched a writer into working-class areas of the city to investigate housing and general living conditions. The result was a series of articles, entitled 'In the Slums', which appeared in the newspaper during February and March of that year. The articles presented a depressing and (doubtless to much of the *Guardian*'s middle-class readership) shocking picture of decay, filth, squalor, exploitation and fatalism. The whole city was, 'encircled by a huge cordon of beastliness and filth, enough to strike horror into the hearts of every civilsed inhabitant'.[106] The author was 'almost at a loss' in attempting to convey to his readers the full extent of the poverty and wretchedness prevailing in Angel Meadow. Angel Street, in particular, presented a sorry picture:

> Go where we would, we found much the same thing — greed growing fat on want and rich men feeding upon the poor. Roofs and floors saturated with wet, beds soaked by the rain coming through, no repairs done for years, was the constant tale told both by the houses and their tenants . . . Filth was everywhere, the street was foul and noisome and the back-yards, even under the very water taps, were a reeking mass of odour.[107]

Similar scenes were present in Deansgate (re-named 'Devilsgate' by the reporter), Carter Street, Rochdale Road and other parts of the city.[108] Final, highly distressing testimony to the general unhealthiness of the places visited was that the *Guardian*'s reporter contracted an illness, 'directly traceable to his exploration of the slums'. On 17 March the newspaper warned its readers that the reporter's illness would probably necessitate the postponement of the next instalment of the series. Two weeks later matters took a turn for the worse when it was announced that, 'the writer of the articles . . . continues so ill as to be quite unable to resume literary work'.[109] To the best of my knowledge, the series was not resumed. And a leaf through the pages of the *Guardian* during ensuing months failed to enlighten me as to the reporter's subsequent, and hopefully improved, state of health.

In conclusion, it should be noted that from the late 1860s onwards strenuous efforts were made by the Medical Officer of Health and others to get to grips with the appalling housing and sanitary problems of Manchester. The fruits of such efforts were seen in the closure of Manchester's remaining cellar dwellings, and in the emptying of cesspools, the removal of the underlying black and saturated soil, and the development of a privy and ashpit system.[110] However, despite improvements, the overall housing and sanitary situation remained very poor. As we will see in the following section, the death-rate in Manchester in the 1880s and beyond compared very unfavourably with the rates prevailing in the other major urban centres of the country. And as late as 1904, T.R. Marr's *Housing Conditions in Manchester and Salford* — an attempt to 'avoid highly-coloured pictures of life in the slums, and to put before the citizens of Manchester and Salford the bare facts' — related a familiarly depressing story of working-class districts suffering from damp, cold, badly-constructed and poorly-ventilated houses, and inadequate sanitary facilities. Not surprisingly, infectious diseases severely afflicted these districts.[111] As Marr's urgent plea for major, planned and concerted remedial action demonstrated, the very real improving efforts of the Medical Officer of Health and the likes of Brotherton could not conceal the extremely poor housing and sanitary conditions in which many of the working-class inhabitants of Manchester and Salford and the surrounding towns lived throughout the second half of the nineteenth century.

Health

Given the intimate relationship between housing and sanitary conditions and the health of the people, it is not surprising that developments in the latter followed a similar chronological pattern to those in the former. As the Medical Officer of Health recorded in his 1868 report, Manchester had an 'unenviable reputation' as 'one of the most unhealthy towns in the kingdom'.[112] The city's almost total lack of adequate hospital accommodation;[113] the high incidence of byssinosis and other respiratory diseases and illnesses (it was estimated that in the 1860s some 60 per cent of Manchester's adult population between the ages of 20 and 60 would die from lung disease[114]); and, above all else, the city's high death rate, were responsible for this reputation. As Table 3.14 shows, the death-rate in Manchester remained appallingly high throughout the third quarter — stabilising during the late forties and early mid-fifties; even falling at the end of the fifties and beginning of the sixties; but then increasing to peak, in 1866, at its highest level of the entire third quarter (a level only slightly below that for the years 1838–42).

Table 3.14:   Manchester: Deaths per 1,000, 1838–75

	per thousand
1838–42	33.78
1843–47	34.22
1848–52	32.80
1853–57	32.42
1858–62	30.06
1863–66	33.32
1868	32.55
1875	28.51

Source: *Reports of the Officer of Health for Manchester* (Manchester 1870 and 1876).

As two concerned contemporaries observed in 1867:

Allowing, therefore, for all temporary influences, we do not gain any sign of progress. When the last ten years are taken together, the average annual death-rates for Manchester and Salford are 33 and 26 in the 1,000 — almost exactly the same as in the ten years from 1841 to 1851. It will be seen at once, then, that the death-tax levied upon the the inhabitants of our town is as great as ever.[115]

Standing well above the national average (of 22 per 1,000 between 1850 and 1875), the death-rate in Manchester also compared very unfavourably with the rates prevailing in other large urban centres. Indeed, with the sole exception of the registration district of Liverpool (which was 'something of a byword for its mortality and general ill health'[116]) Manchester outstripped all its major English urban rivals. In 1868, for example, the respective death-rates of Birmingham and Manchester stood at 20 and 32 per thousand.[117] And a comparison between Merseyside (of which the Liverpool registration district was a part) and Manchester between

1851 and 1875 demonstrates (see Table 3.15) that the death-rate of the former was consistently below that of the latter.

Table 3.15:   Deaths per 1,000: Manchester and Merseyside, 1851–75

		per thousand
1851–55	(Merseyside)	28.98
1853–57	(Manchester)	32.42
1856–60	(Merseyside)	26.90
1858–62	(Manchester)	30.06
1861–65	(Merseyside)	30.79
1863–66	(Manchester)	33.32
1866–70	(Merseyside)	30.97
1868	(Manchester)	32.55
1871–5	(Merseyside)	27.22
1875	(Manchester)	28.51

Sources: *Reports of the Medical Officer of Health* (Manchester, 1870 and 1876); A.T. McCabe. 'The Standard of Living on Merseyside, 1850–1875', in S.P. Bell (ed.), *Victorian Lancashire* (Newton Abbot, 1974), p. 128.

As in many of the large towns, infant mortality was extremely high in Manchester. In the late forties, out of every 100 deaths in the city, 'more than forty-eight take place under five years of age, and more than fifty-one under ten years of age'.[118] In some of the neighbouring towns the proportion was higher. At Ashton it was estimated that during the late thirties and early forties, 57 per cent of the total number of deaths were those of children under five.[119] By the mid 1870s the situation was still extremely bad. Thus between 1869 and 1873 the mean proportion of deaths of children aged five and under to the total number of deaths at all ages in Manchester was 47 per cent; and in some of the poorer parts of the city — especially Ancoats and St George's — the proportion exceeded 50 per cent.[120]

As noted earlier, Manchester's high death-rate was closely linked to its appalling housing and sanitary conditions (almost one-sixth of the city's deaths in the late sixties resulted from those infectious diseases which were rife in working-class districts[121]). And, as sanitary facilities improved somewhat after 1870, so the death-rate declined from 32.55 per thousand in 1868 to 28 per thousand in 1875, and to 26.9 in 1890. Nevertheless, the 1890 figure was, with a solitary exception, higher than in any other of the great English towns.[122]

This, and the preceding two sections, have clearly demonstrated that, even during a period of rapid economic growth and advances in earnings, large numbers of cotton operatives and other workers were still afflicted by poverty, ill-health and low life expectancy, and continued to inhabit substandard dwellings in insalubrious areas of Manchester, Salford and the surrounding cotton towns. Above all else, insecurity was a basic, perhaps the key, feature of working-class life. How best to make ends meet? How to cope with the reality or likelihood of unemployment? These were the questions which dominated the daily lives of the vast majority of workers, and which stubbornly refused to disappear even during periods of relative prosperity. During times of depression such worries could all too easily and quickly be transformed into a desperate struggle to 'keep the wolf from the door'. As Pollard has so pertinently remarked, 'an average family lived perilously near the margin'.[123] A dramatic and distressing illustration of the adverse effects of a period of acute depression upon living standards is provided by the Cotton Famine (1861–5). It is to a study of the effects of the latter upon employment, applications for relief, wages, and the general appearance and health of the operative population that we now turn.

The Cotton Famine

Towards the end of 1861 a mood of pessimism began to replace the optimism which had characterised the cotton districts during the two years of 'almost unexampled prosperity' between 1859 and the beginning of 1861.[124] This change in mood was caused primarily by the dull overseas markets for finished cotton goods and the low prices for these goods which prevailed throughout much of 1861. Also of significance was the growth in industrial conflict attendant upon employer attempts to reduce wages,[125] and the increase in the price of raw American cotton which followed the Federal blockade of Confederate ports. Mills began to run short-time or close down in October, and by the end of the year applications for relief were well above the average increase during the winter months. During the spring months of 1862 relief committees were formed in a number of towns to ease the impossible strain placed upon the Boards of Guardians. However, far from declining, the numbers of unemployed and those on relief continued to climb steeply to reach record levels during the winter months of 1862–3.[126]

As Table 3.16 shows, in December 1862, 49 per cent of *all* operatives in the 28 unions of the cotton districts were unemployed, with a further 35 per cent on short-time, and only 16 per cent in full-time work. By March 1863 unemployment had fallen from its December peak, but still stood at the extremely high level of 43 per cent. And, apart from a decline during July 1864 (to the relatively low level of 22 per cent!), unemployment remained at or above the 30 per cent mark during all the months recorded for 1863 and 1864. This truly depressing picture was marginally brightened by the rise in full-time work from the spring of 1863 onwards, and a levelling off in the numbers of those working short-time during 1863 and 1864. However, the winter of 1864–5 brought a sharp increase in hardship; and it was not really until the summer months of 1865 that 'normal' levels of work were beginning to be resumed.[127]

Unemployment was not, of course, evenly distributed throughout the cotton districts. Hardest hit were those towns either heavily dependent upon American cotton, or whose major (in some cases almost sole) source of employment was the cotton industry, or both. In those centres where this dependency was less marked and industrial diversification more in evidence, distress was correspondingly lighter. Most severely troubled (see Table 3.17) of the 28 unions was Ashton-under-Lyne, where both of the former conditions prevailed. In March 1863, 56 per cent of the Ashton Union's operative workforce was unemployed, and throughout 1863 and 1864 (with the sole recorded exception of July 1864) unemployment in the union did not fall below 43 per cent. Conversely, as Table 3.17 shows, Oldham and Manchester, having more varied employment opportunities than Ashton, were less severely affected. (It should nevertheless be noted that unemployment was far from inconsequential in the Manchester and Oldham unions, resting, in both cases, at or above the 25 per cent mark for much of 1863 and the winter and spring months of 1864–5.)

In terms of unemployment within districts, Ashton again topped the league table. Not surprisingly, as shown in Table 3.18, the neighbouring districts of Stalybridge and Hyde also suffered greatly; and Stockport was very badly hit during the winter of 1862–3. Thereafter, the unemployment situation in Stockport eased somewhat (apart from an increase during the winter of 1864–5), but, nevertheless remained, throughout 1863 and 1864, at a higher level than in Oldham and Manchester and Salford. Oldham had a relatively low level of unemployment, but an extremely high incidence of short-

Table 3.16:   Employment in the Twenty-Eight Unions of the Cotton Districts, December 1862-March 1865

	Dec. '62 %[a]	Mar. '63 %[a]	Jul. '63 %[a]	Nov. '63 %[a]	Mar. '64 %[a]	Jul. '64 %[a]	Nov. '64 %[a]	Mar. '65 %[a]
Unemployed	49	43	31	30	30	22	33	26
Short-time	35	32	21	22	24	15	21	18
Full-time	16	25	41	47	46	63	45	56
Totals	100	100	93	99	100	100	99	100

Note: a. A percentage of *all* operatives (not simply cotton), but not of the entire population.

Source: *Fund for the Relief of Distress in the Manufacturing Districts. Central Executive Committee Reports and Returns, 1862–5*. See, especially, J.W. McClure's, *Summary of Returns from 170 Relief Committees* (May 1865). (M/c. Cent. Ref. Lib. P. 3339).

Table 3.17:   Employment in Selected Unions, March 1863–5

	Mar. '63 %[a]		Jul. '63 %[a]		Nov. '63 %[a]		Mar. '64 %[a]		Jul. '64 %[a]		Nov. '64 %[a]		Mar. '65 %[a]	
	F/T.	Ud.	F/T.	Ud.	F/T.	Ud.	F/T.	Ud.	F/T.	Ud.	F/T.	Ud.	F/T.	Ud.
A-u-Lyne	15	56	25	48	21	44	22	43	38	34	25	46	38	37
Oldham	22	35	47	22	45	25	41	22	44	20	42	32	44	28
Manchester	43	31	48	30	56	26	55	29	71	23	56	28	60	28

Note: a. Percentages of *all* operatives (not simply cotton) in the three unions.

Source: Percentages calculated from data in J.W. McClure's *Summary of Returns from 170 Relief Committees* (May 1865).

Table 3.18:   Employment in Selected Districts, December 1862-May 1865 (percentages[a])

	Dec. '62			Mar. '63			Nov. '63			Mar. '64			Nov. '64			May. '65		
	FT.	ST.	U.	FT.	ST.	U.	FT.	ST.	U.	FT.	ST.	U.	FT.	ST.	U.	FT.	ST.	U.
A-u-Lyne	10	36	54	14	30	56	24	25	51	18	24	58	25	15	60	67	–	33
Hyde	0	47	53	17	36	47	10	46	44	16	50	34	33	22	45	40	19	41
Stalybridge	–	–	–	17	27	56	23	38	39	23	39	38	17	32	51	76	6	18
Stockport	21	32	47	26	31	43	58	12	30	40	26	34	53	12	35	81	1	18
Oldham	19	61	20	23	47	30	54	25	21	44	35	21	48	21	31	79	4	17
Manchester and Salford	40	27	33	–	–	–	–	–	–	–	–	–	–	–	–	–	–	–
Salford	–	–	–	45	26	29	57	20	23	53	16	31	63	13	24	59	13	28

Note: a. To the nearest percentage point. Percentages of *all* operatives in these districts.

Source: Compiled from information in J.W. McClure's, *Summary of Returns from 170 Relief Committees* (May 1865).

time working (for example 61 per cent in December 1862 as against Ashton's 36 per cent, Hyde's 47 per cent, Stockport's 32 per cent and Manchester and Salford's 27 per cent). Indeed, between December 1862 and May 1865 the number of operatives on short-time was consistently higher in Oldham than Ashton. Finally, what is most striking, in terms of all the districts listed in Table 3.18, is the depth and persistence of unemployment. As late as November 1864, 60 per cent of Ashton's operatives were out of work, whilst at the opposite end of the league table Salford had a comparable unemployment rate of 24 per cent. Such large percentages could only partially be attributed to the usual increase in unemployment attendant upon the onset of winter. Rather, they constituted awful testimony to the lasting severity of the Cotton Famine.

Mounting unemployment from early 1862 onwards brought in its wake a dramatic increase in the number of applicants seeking relief from either the Poor Law Guardians or the newly-created relief committees. Table 3.19 provides an overall picture of the relief situation in the cotton districts during the Cotton Famine, and clearly shows that (as was the case with unemployment) numbers relieved reached their peak during the winter of 1862-3. In December 1862 fully 23 per cent of the total population of the cotton districts was in receipt of relief; and average pauperism for the whole of the 28 unions in 1862 was 131 per cent in excess of the level for 1861.[128] The 12 months from June 1863 to June 1864 saw a

Table 3.19: Total Numbers Relieved in the Twenty-eight Unions of the Cotton Districts by the Guardians (out-door) in 1861, and by the Guardians (outdoor) and the Local Relief Committees, 1862-5

	Numbers relieved	% of *total population* of the 28 unions in 1861 (2,059,310)
Nov. 1861	47,537	2.3
Nov. 1862	458,441	22.26
Dec. 1862	485,434	23.57
Jan. 1863	451,343	21.9
Jun. 1863	255,578	12.4
Nov. 1863	170,268	8.26
Jan. 1864	202,785	9.8
Jun. 1864	100,671	4.8
Nov. 1864	149,923	7.2
Jan. 1865	119,544	5.8
May. 1865	75,784	3.6
Nov. 1865	48,267	2.3

Source: See, J.W. McClure's, *Summary of Returns from 170 Relief Committees* (May 1865); J. Watts, *The Facts of the Cotton Famine* (1968), pp. 227-8.

decline in the numbers relieved from 255,578 (12.4 per cent) to 100,671 (4.8 per cent), but November 1864 saw a sharp increase to 149,923 (7.2 per cent). Matters began to improve from the beginning of 1865, and by the summer of that year the pre-Famine levels had almost been restored.

Applications for relief were, as one would expect, extremely high in Ashton and its surrounding area. Watts calculated that in February 1862 pauperism in Ashton, Stockport and Glossop stood, respectively, at 213, 263 and 300 per cent above normal levels.[129] Table 3.20 demonstrates that between November 1862 and November 1864 the Ashton union led the south Lancashire league in terms of numbers relieved as a percentage of the total populations of the various unions, followed, in descending order, by Stockport, Oldham, Manchester and Salford.

Table 3.20:   Numbers Relieved[a] in Selected Unions, November 1861-November 1865

	Nov. '61	Nov. '62	Nov. '63	Nov. '64	Nov.'65
A-u-Lyne union					
(popn. in 1861	1,827	56,363	23,568	20,638	1,417
= 134,761)	(1.3%)	(41.8%)	(17.4%)	(15.3%)	(1.05%)
Stockport union					
(popn. in 1861	1,674	34,612	10,661	8,593	1,189
= 94,361)	(1.7%)	(36.6%)	(11.2%)	(9.1%)	(1.2%)
Oldham union					
(popn. in 1861	1,622	28,851	8,371	9,164	1,892
= 111,267)	(1.45%)	(25%)	(7.5%)	(8.2%)	(1.7%)
Manchester union					
(popn. in 1861	4,678	52,447	13,818	9,035	5,046
= 185,040)	(2.5%)	(28.3%)	(7.4%)	(4.8%)	(2.7%)
Salford union					
(popn. in 1861	2,507	16,663	5,600	3,600	2,265
= 105,334)	(2.3%)	(15.8%)	(5.3%)	(3.4%)	(2.1%)

Note: a. Those relieved by the Guardians during the last week of November in 1861 and 1865, and those relieved by the Guardians and local committees in 1862, 1863, and 1864.

Source: *Fund for the Relief of Distress, Report of the Central Executive Committee* (4 December 1865).

Whether as recipients of relief or wages for full- or short-time work, operatives endured a severe loss of income during the Cotton Famine. Those who were totally dependent upon the guardians and relief committees could expect to receive, in December 1862, an average weekly income of only 2/- per person — to which could be added during winter a supply of fuel and clothing, 'if the family have been long out of work'.[130] Many guardians and relief committee members doubtless shared Lord Derby's beliefs that a weekly income of 2/- constituted sufficient safeguard against inducements to indolence and dependency, and that, when translated into family income, was, 'an amount not far short of that which in prosperous times an honest and industrious labourer in other parts of the country would obtain for the maintenance of his family'.[131] However, as W.O. Henderson has observed, Lord Derby's comparison was 'hardly a just one'. What mattered most was not the comparison with labourers elsewhere, but the difference in income between relief rates and the average earnings of cotton operatives before the onset of the Famine. And, as the latter have been set at about 12/4d per week per operative, we can safely support Henderson's conclusion that a large drop in family income occurred.[132]

For those in work, whether upon a full- or short-time basis, there is little doubt that, despite considerable variations in earnings within occupations and between districts, the substitution of Egyptian or Indian for American cotton generally involved harder work (especially to keep the ends pieced up) and a reduction in earnings. For example, in 1863 Alexander Redgrave, a factory inspector, calculated that those operatives employed on Surat cotton could expect to earn up to between 20–30 per cent less than those employed on American cotton.[133] Redgrave also provided information concerning reductions in earnings in a district in which mainly American cotton had been replaced by inferior Egyptian and Surat (see Table 3.21).

Table 3.21:   Effects of the Substitution of Egyptian and Surat for American Cotton Upon Wages in an Unspecified District of the Cotton Belt

	1861	1863
Rovers	11/6d	8/-
Drawers	9/6d	6/-
Winders	10/6d	7/-
Warpers	13/6d	10/6d
Self-actor minders	19/6d	14/-
Piecers	13/-	7/6d
Creelers	6/-	5/-
Two-loom weavers	10/-	6/6d
Three-loom weavers	13/6d	9/6d

Source: *Reports of Inspectors of Factories* (31 October 1863), p. 46. See also Ibid., p. 50.

It is also worth noting that 'constant experimentalising . . . upon different kinds and proportions of cotton and waste' occasioned great fluctuations in earnings.[134] Stability and regularity of earnings were thus conspicuous by their absence.

The operatives' fall in living standards was reflected in various ways: a dramatic growth in withdrawls from co-operative and friendly societies and savings banks; the enforced selling or pawning of clothes, furniture, and even bedding (according to Arnold, 'the pawnbrokers' stores were glutted with the heirlooms of many an honest family'); increased overcrowding; the turning of hands to every conceivable method of scraping together a few coppers (some sold newspapers, religious tracts or back numbers of penny periodicals, whilst others took to street singing); and considerable reductions in expenditure upon food.[135] Few families could still afford to buy much meat. Bread, oatmeal and potatoes became the staple foods, and tea with sugar, but usually without milk, the common drink. In addition, soup kitchens, 'where a quart of good meat soup is given for a penny', were set up in many towns.[136]

There exist, however, directly opposing viewpoints as to the effects of reduced food intake upon the health of the operatives. On the optimistic side contemporaries such as Edwin Chadwick, Arnold, and several Poor Law Medical Officers, and, more recently, Farnie, have contended that the evidence does not support a picture of deteriorating health. Although admitting that, 'the evidence for a balanced judgement is difficult to secure', Farnie nevertheless concludes that there was no general rise in the death-rate comparable to the fall in the marriage — and birth — rates, and that, in overall terms, the operatives' health 'does not seem to have suffered'.[137] Arnold and Chadwick pitched their claims higher. Arnold maintained that health actually 'improved during the years of the Cotton Famine under the influence of compulsory temperance, of restricted diet, of outdoor exercise, and of greater leisure among the married women to devote to the duties of home'.[138] Chadwick baldly declared:

. . . it was not a case of starvation when a man was deprived of beer, gin, or even tea; it was the case of men having bread, simple food with better air, as against a high or ordinary diet with impure air.[139]

In marked contrast some Poor Law Medical Officers and

Registrars of Births, Marriages and Deaths believed that the operatives were thinner and 'not in the same robust health as is common to them in ordinary times'. And the Registrar of Hyde was far from alone in believing that deaths had increased owing to 'privation arising from want of employment'.[140] As Henderson has noted, the most important and well-balanced evidence on the pessimistic side was unearthed by Dr Buchanan in his two months' enquiry into the health of the operatives in 1862.[141] Buchanan's list of 'certain morbid conditions, such as are not accounted for by climatic peculiarities', was long and depressing: insufficient and innutritious diet; 'a loss of strength and flesh' among many operatives; 'pale and emaciated' mothers who, in an attempt to maintain the strength of the other members of the family, 'clemmed' themselves; in Preston 'a large excess of diarrhoea beyond what is usual in other years'; in Stockport, Preston, Blackburn and Salford cases of scurvy among women; high, but perhaps customary, levels of bronchitis and pneumonia throughout the cotton districts during November; in Stockport, Salford, Blackburn and Manchester an 'unparalleled quantity of itch', itself a consequence of the 'exceptional dirtiness of houses and persons'; and epidemics of typhus fever in Preston and Manchester, measles in Ashton, Blackburn, Bury, Chorley and Manchester, whooping cough in Chorley, Manchester, Oldham and Stockport, and scarlatina in Oldham.[142]

Given the lack of reliable evidence on key aspects of health (such as the effects of unemployment upon the mental wellbeing of the operatives), and the ambiguous nature of much of the available data, it is extremely difficult, and probably unwise, to give unreserved support to either the pessimistic or optimistic case. On balance, it does, however, seem that the pessimistic argument is the stronger. There is, for example, and despite optimistic claims to the contrary,[143] little doubt that death-rates rose appreciably in many parts of the cotton districts during the Famine. The Medical Officer of Health for Manchester pinpointed a sharp increase in the city's death rate between 1863 and 1866 (from 30.06 per thousand between 1858–62 to 33.32 per thousand between 1863–6). Indeed, as was shown in Table 3.14, the death toll in Manchester between 1863 and 1866 was higher than at any other time during the period from 1848 to 1875.[144] It might, of course, be argued that Manchester's increase was untypical of trends in the cotton districts as a whole: but similar increases in numerous towns throughout Lancashire would strongly suggest the opposite to be the case.[145] Whether all such increases were invariably and directly linked to the distress of the Cotton Famine is difficult to say. The very timing of the rise in the death roll (during the winter of 1862–3 when distress was at its height) does, however, lend itself to the conclusion that more than coincidence was at work.

Further support for the superiority of the pessimistic case can be gained from Buchanan's report. Based upon detailed and impartial investigation into conditions of health, Buchanan's authoritative findings are much to be preferred to the biased, grossly insensitive and unsubstantiated opinions of Chadwick. On a more impressionistic, but nevertheless valid level, there are, in so far as we can ascertain the views of the operatives themselves, solid grounds to believe that the vast majority of operatives would have opted for regular employment and a 'full' diet rather than short-time working, unemployment, and the 'simple diet' and abstinence from intoxicating drink so beloved, from afar, by their advisers in the middle class.[146]

In assessing the *overall* effects of the Cotton Famine upon living standards we can safely give unqualified support to a pessimistic interpretation. Indeed, we can go further to argue that, with the exception of somewhat ambiguous evidence concerning standards of health, the vast weight of evidence presented in relation to levels of employment, relief and income strictly supports a catastrophic rather than a merely pessimistic viewpoint. Moreover, as will be shown in Chapter 6, cotton operatives were far less quiescent during the Cotton Famine than traditionally claimed. They were loud in their criticisms of the miserly behaviour of sections of the wealthy, and bitterly critical of the patronising and humiliating ways in which they were treated by some of the guardians and relief committee members.[147] It would thus appear to be the case that no small amount of special pleading is present in Farnie's claim that, 'The extent of the distress . . . seems . . . to have been exaggerated by outside observers in order either to make political capital in the Conservative interest or to facilitate the raising of relief funds'.[148]

Conclusions

Three major conclusions emerge from the evidence presented in this chapter. Firstly, there is no doubt that the notion of widespread and lasting economic improvement as constituting the sole or even predominant explanation of the demise of mass Chartism and the onset of reformism is extremely limited and, in itself, inadequate. We have seen that, as was the case at the national level, real earnings in cotton did not show a significant or continuous increase during the late forties and early fifties. Money earnings were reduced by the employers in 1847 and did not rise substantially until 1853–4. Gains won during the latter years were, however, shortlived. As a consequence of the defeat of the struggles at Preston and elsewhere, earnings were once again reduced, to stand (in real terms) in 1855 well below the 1850 level. Between 1855 and the end of 1857 real earnings in cotton failed to rise. The remaining years of the decade did, however, see major advances which, although interrupted by the Cotton Famine, resumed their spectacular upward trend during the post-1865 decade. Substantial increases in real earnings occurred, however, at a time when Chartism had long since declined as a mass movement.

Secondly, the third quarter *as a whole* did, nevertheless, witness overall and significant gains in the real earnings of the vast majority of cotton operatives. As Thomas Cooper and other contemporaries accurately noted, cotton operatives were both much better off materially and much less interested in rapid wholesale political and social changes in 1870 than they had been during the 1830s and part of the 1840s. If we adopt this longer-term perspective upon changes in living standards and politics, then the links between material improvement and the growth of reformism and gradualism do become stronger.

Thirdly, overall economic improvement did not, however, signal *embourgeoisement*. The improvement achieved was, by middle-class standards, not particularly great. And, as we have emphasised throughout this chapter, uncertainty, insecurity, unemployment and misery were, as tragically illustrated by the Cotton Famine, very much still a part of working-class life. Similarly, ill-health and poor housing in insanitary areas continued to be the lot of large numbers of urban working-class dwellers. As Allen Clarke observed in the 1890s:

> While, on the whole, the factory folks are better fed, better housed and better treated than they were fifty years ago, and that while a few of them get good wages, and live in parloured houses, owning a piano maybe (after years of laborious saving), the majority live in small cottages, shabbily furnished, unblest by

literature or music, pursuing an existence that is mainly from 'hand to mouth', an existence that is pithily described in their own Lancashire phrase as 'all bed an' work'.[149]

Notes

1. For varying degrees of emphasis upon the notions of distress and improvement see, A. Briggs (ed.), *Chartist Studies*, op. cit., pp. 56, 291; A. Briggs, *The Age of Improvement*, op. cit., pp. 394, 402–4; G. Kitson Clark, *The Making of Victorian England* (1962), p. 47; A.R. Schoyen, op. cit., p. 206. See H. Perkin (op. cit., pp. 343–4) for criticism of the belief in mid-Victorian working-class improvement.
   2. R.A. Church, op. cit., p. 71.
   3. G.J. Barnsby, op. cit., pp. 220–39. See also E.H. Hunt, *Regional Wage Variations in Britain, 1850–1914* (Oxford, 1973), pp. 27–35.
   4. A.T. McCabe, op. cit., p. 142.
   5. J. Foster, *Class Struggle*, op. cit., pp. 95–9.
   6. M. Anderson, op. cit., pp. 31–2.
   7. E.J. Hobsbawn, *Industry and Empire*, op. cit., p. 118.
   8. See, especially, E.P. Thompson, 'The Moral Economy of the English Crowd', op. cit., esp. p. 78.
   9. Loc. cit. Also E.P. Thompson, *The Making of the English Working Class*, op. cit., p. 10.
   10. D. Thompson, *The Early Chartists*, op. cit., intro.
   11. F.J. Kaijage, op. cit., p. 506.
   12. T.R. Tholfsen, 'The Intellectual Origins of Mid-Victorian Stability', *Political Science Quarterly* (March 1971), pp. 59–60.
   13. G. Crossick, *An Artisan Elite*, op. cit., p. 18.
   14. D. Read, 'Chartism in Manchester', op. cit., p. 56.
   15. Loc. cit.
   16. E.J. Hobsbawm, *The Age of Capital 1848–1875* (1977), p. 221.
   17. See Ch. 4 below, esp. pp. 148–52.
   18. In relation to this issue, I support Edward Thompson's views (*The Poverty of Theory*, op. cit., pp. 350–1) that (a) the nature of the relationship between the 'economic' and 'non-economic' is to be grasped by means of a dialogue between theory and empirical evidence; and that (b) the reductionist notion of sole determining cause be replaced by an emphasis upon the complex but patterned ways in which the 'economic' and 'non-economic' interact, with the former 'determining' in the sense that it sets limits and exerts pressures (sometimes key pressures and limits) upon the latter.
   19. J. Foster, op. cit., pp. 205–6.
   20. A.T. McCabe, op. cit., p. 142.
   21. D.A. Farnie, *The English Cotton Industry and the World Market, 1815–1896* (Oxford, 1979), p. 156.
   22. Hence Pelling's claim that, 'Only in the 1840s and later did the situation begin to improve markedly; and the class which now emerged into comparative prosperity was not, an élite of labour aristocrats but a more homogeneous class of factory workers', requires some correction. H. Pelling, 'The Concept of the Labour Aristocracy', *Popular Politics and Society in Late Victorian Britain* (1979 edn), p. 47.
   23. Engels, for example, maintained that temporary improvement for 'the great mass' was 'reduced to the old level by the influx of the great body of the unemployed reserve, by the constant superseding of hands by new machinery, by the immigration of the agricultural population'. Engels did recognise sustained improvement for two

'protected' sections of the working class, the factory hands ('The fixing by Act of Parliament of their working-day within relatively rational limits has restored their physical constitution and endowed them with a moral superiority . . .'), and '*grown-up men*' organised in the 'great Trades' Unions' ('They form an aristocracy among the working-class; they have succeeded in enforcing for themselves a relatively comfortable position, and they accept it as final.') See Marx, Engels, *On Britain*, op. cit., pp. 27–8. In his inaugural address to the IWMA, Marx argued that, 'the misery of the working masses' had not diminished, despite the fact that a minority of workers had improved their position. See. R. Harrison, op. cit., p. 22.

24. A.B. Reach, *Manchester and the Textile Districts in 1849* (C. Aspin (ed.), Helmshore Local History Society, 1972), pp. 8, 10.

25. Ibid., p. 34.

26. D. Chadwick, 'On the Rate of Wages in Manchester and Salford and the Manufacturing Districts of Lancashire, 1839–1859', *Jnl. Roy. Stat. Soc.* (March 1860), p. 5.

27. R. Harrison, op. cit., pp. 113–14.

28. M.E. Rose, 'Rochdale Man and the Stalybridge Riot. The Relief and Control of the Unemployed During the Lancashire Cotton Famine' in A.P. Donajgrodzki (ed.), *Social Control in Nineteenth-Century Britain* (1977), p. 185.

29. W.A. Abram, 'Social Conditions and Political Prospects of the Lancashire Workman', *Fortnightly Review* (October 1868), p. 428.

30. Ibid., p. 429.

31. A. Clarke, *The Effects of the Factory System* (1899), p. 161.

32. Quoted in B. Jones, *Co-operative Production* (Oxford, 1894), vol. 1, pp. 292–5.

33. See Ch. 5 below, pp. 182–4.

34. *Co-operator*, no. 12, May 1861, p. 174.

35. Ibid., no. 13, June 1861, p. 1.

36. For Jones's political career during the 1860s see Ch. 4 below, pp. 156, 165, 167.

37. J. Saville, *Ernest Jones, Chartist* (1952), p. 194; *Notes to the People*, vol. 2, p. 585.

38. K. Marx, F. Engels, op. cit., pp. 491–2.

39. Loc. cit.

40. Ibid., p. 271.

41. T. Cooper, *The Life of Thomas Cooper Written by Himself* (1877), p. 393.

42. R.A. Church, op. cit.

43. For developments in these industries see, J. Foster, op. cit., pp. 224–37; E.J. Hobsbawm, *Industry and Empire*; op. cit., Ch. 6.

44. K. Marx, F. Engels, op. cit., p. 18.

45. D.A. Farnie, op. cit., p. 135. Much of the following account of cotton's economic progress is based upon Farnie's book.

46. T. Ellison, *The Cotton Trade of Great Britain* (1968 edn), p. 59.

47. Loc. cit.

48. Ibid., pp. 74–5.

49. D.A. Farnie, op. cit., p. 135.

50. T. Ellison, op. cit., Ch. 6.

51. D.A. Farnie, op. cit., p. 136.

52. See pp. 115–25 below.

53. D.A. Farnie, op. cit., pp. 164–5.

54. J.L. White, 'Lancashire Cotton Textiles' in C.J. Wrigley (ed.), *A History of British Industrial Relations, 1875–1914* (Brighton, 1982), p. 210.

55. G.H. Wood, *The History of Wages in the Cotton Trade during the Past 100 Years* (Manchester, 1910); B.R. Mitchell and P. Deane, *Abstract of British Historical Statistics* (Cambridge, 1962); D. Chadwick, op. cit. It may be the case that some of Chadwick's calculations are open to question. According to a contemporary,

Chadwick 'makes out the best case he can for his employers'. This contemporary maintained that Chadwick's general calculations were 'incorrect', and that his specific figures concerning wages in silk were too high. Chadwick's survey was undertaken at the request of the Manchester Chamber of Commerce and the Manchester Statistical Society. See the comments of J.C. in *Weekly Wages*, no. 1, vol. 1 (August 1861).

56. See Ch. 6 below, pp. 289–90.

57. 16s to 17s as against 10s 6d in 1839–40; 16s as against 11s in 1849–50; 16s to 20s as against 12s 6d in 1859–60. The working of four looms was not the norm. The average number of looms per worker was $2^1/5$ in 1850, $2^4/5$ in 1870 and $3^1/5$ in 1877. See, G.H. Wood, op. cit., p. 30.

58. Wood probably exaggerated the earnings of self-actor spinners in 1839–40. As against Wood's figure of 22 6d, Lazonick (op. cit., p. 237) gives the more reliable figure of 16s to 18s. See, also, R. Sykes, op. cit. Earnings in spinning depended upon a number of factors: output per spinner (that is, per pound or 'length' of yarn produced); the speed at which the mules were run; whether employed upon hand or self-acting mules; and the amount of wages paid by the spinner to his assistant, the piecer. For enlightening insights into wage determination and the nature and control of the labour process in spinning see W. Lazonick, op. cit., esp. pp. 232–3, 247.

59. E.J. Hobsbawm, *Labouring Men*, op. cit., p. 292.

60. Ibid., pp. 282, 292.

61. J. Foster, op. cit., p. 204.

62. J.L. White, *The Limits of Trade Union Militancy* (1978), pp. 34–5.

63. P. Joyce, *Work, Society and Politics*, op. cit., p. 51.

64. J. Foster, op. cit., p. 323 (note 3).

65. J. Liddington and J. Norris, op. cit., p. 93.

66. G.H. Wood (op. cit., pp. 9–14, 16, 29, 36, 42) for the earnings of specific grades in cotton.

67. Ibid., pp. 43, 115.

68. Ibid., p. 28.

69. Periods of depression were, however, not absent. For worker hardship during the winter months of 1857–8 see, *Manchester Guardian*, 20 January 1858; A.T. McCabe, op. cit., pp. 142–3.

70. R.A. Church, op. cit., p. 16.

71. The years between 1866 and 1868 constituted a period of high prices which must be added to Church's inflationary periods of 1853–5 and 1870–3.

72. G.H. Wood, 'Real Wages and the Standard of Comfort Since 1850', *Jnl. Roy. Stat. Soc.*, 72 (1909), p. 102.

73. *Reports of Inspectors of Factories* (Robert Baker, 31 October 1865), p. 60.

74. J. Foster, op. cit., p. 96.

75. Ibid., p. 95.

76. J. Foster (thesis), op. cit., p. 109.

77. M. Anderson, op. cit., pp. 31–2.

78. G.J. Barnsby, op. cit.

79. R. Harrison, op. cit., p. 22; E.P. Thompson and E. Yeo (eds), *The Unknown Mayhew* (1971), pp. 52–95.

80. For Brotherton and the Manchester and Salford Education Aid Society see, *Scrapbook of Edward Brotherton, Hon. Sec. to the Manchester and Salford Education Aid Society* (M/cr. Cent. Ref. M 98); E. Brotherton, 'The State of Popular Education and Suggestions for its Advancement', *Trans. Nat. Asstn. Prom. Soc. Sc.* (1865).

81. J. Foster (thesis), op. cit., pp. 335–42.

82. H.C. Oats, 'An Inquiry into the Educational and other Conditions of a District in Ancoats', *Procs. M/cr. Stat. Soc.* (session 1865–6).

83. F. Scott, 'The Condition and Occupations of the People of Manchester and

Salford', *Procs. M/cr. Stat. Soc.* (May 1889). It should be noted that Scott's survey covered districts which were inhabited mainly by factory operatives and the poor.

84. Loc. cit.

85. T.R. Marr, *Housing Conditions in Manchester and Salford* (Manchester, 1904), pp. 4, 23.

86. G.S. Jones, *Outcast London: A Study in the Relationship Between Classes in Victorian Society* (1976 edn), p. 11.

87. Ibid., p. 16.

88. Ibid., pp. 292–3.

89. Ibid., p. 1.

90. *Scrapbook of Edward Brotherton*, op. cit. See also Brotherton's remarks in *Manchester Guardian*, 27 February 1864.

91. See pp. 112–115 below.

92. A.B. Reach, op. cit., p. 72.

93. See Ch. 7 below, esp. pp. 312–13.

94. See, for example, Ch. 6 below, esp. pp. 262–5.

95. A. Ransome and W. Royston, *Report Upon the Health of Manchester and Salford During the Last Fifteen Years* (Manchester, 1867), p. 9.

96. Ibid., pp. 8ff.

97. A.B. Reach, op. cit., p. 3.

98. Ibid., p. 71.

99. A. Ransome and W. Royston, op. cit., p. 15; J.H. Smith, 'Ten Acres of Deansgate in 1851', *Trans. Lancs. and Ches. Antiqn. Soc.* (1980), p. 47.

100. A.B. Reach, op. cit., p. 3.

101. K. Marx, F. Engels, op. cit., p. 76.

102. A.B. Reach, op. cit., pp. 65, 79.

103. Ibid., p. 71.

104. Ibid., p. 68.

105. *Scrapbook of Edward Brotherton*, op. cit., p. 26.

106. *Manchester Guardian*, 16 February, 3 March 1870; *Free Lance*, 12 March 1870.

107. Manchester Guardian, 23 February 1870.

108. Ibid., 16 February, 3, 10, 17 March 1870.

109. Ibid., 31 March 1870.

110. *1874 Report of the Officer of Health for Manchester* (Manchester, 1874), p. 19.

111. T.R. Marr, op. cit., pp. 4ff.

112. *1868 Report of the Officer of Health for Manchester* (Manchester, 1868), p. 3.

113. In 1870 Manchester had three hospitals into which sufferers from febrile infectious diseases were admitted. See, *1870 Report of the Officer of Health for Manchester* (Manchester, 1870), p. 9.

114. A. Ransome and W. Royston, op. cit., p. 21.

115. Ibid., p. 13.

116. A.T. McCabe, op. cit., p. 127.

117. *Co-operator*, 30 January 1869, p. 69.

118. A.B. Reach, op. cit., p. 23.

119. Loc. cit.

120. *1874 Report of the Officer of Health for Manchester* (Manchester, 1874), pp. 4, 16. See also, Brotherton's comments in *Manchester Examiner and Times*, 9 April 1864.

121. *1868 Report of the Officer of Health for Manchester* (Manchester, 1868), p. 3.

122. *1890 Special Report of the Officer of Health for Manchester* (Manchester, 1890).

123. S. Pollard, *History of Labour in Sheffield* (Liverpool, 1959), p. 27.

124. J. Watts, *The Facts of the Cotton Famine* (1968 edn), Ch. 8; *Reports of the Inspectors of Factories* (Redgrave, 31 October 1861), p. 11.

125. See Ch. 6 below, esp. pp. 256-7.

126. J. Watts, op. cit., pp. 119-23.

127. By October 1865 there existed, according to a factory inspector, a scarcity of hands. See, *Reports of the Inspectors of Factories* (Redgrave, 31 October 1865), p. 36.

128. J. Watts, op. cit., p. 115.

129. Ibid., p. 114.

130. Much of the following information concerning wages and health is based upon the admirably clear Ch. V in W.O. Henderson, *The Lancashire Cotton Famine* (Manchester, 1969), pp. 94–118.

131. Ibid., p. 100.

132. Ibid., p. 101.

133. *Reports of the Inspectors of Factories* (Redgrave, 31 October 1863), p. 41.

134. Ibid., p. 50.

135. W.O. Henderson, op. cit., pp. 97-9; J. Watts, op. cit., pp. 123-6.

136. W.O. Henderson, op. cit., pp. 101-2.

137. D.A. Farnie, op. cit., p. 157.

138. W.O. Henderson, op. cit., p. 102.

139. Loc. cit.

140. Ibid., p. 104.

141. Loc. cit.

142. Ibid., pp. 104-5.

143. Optimistic claims issue from the contemporary calculations of J.W. McClure, Secretary to the Central Executive Committee for the Relief of Distress in the Manufacturing Districts. See J. Watts, op. cit., p. 232; W.O. Henderson, op. cit., p. 107.

144. The death rate on Merseyside was also extremely high during these years, peaking in 1866 at 38.97 per 1,000. A.T. McCabe, op. cit., p. 128.

145. At Ashton, for example, the borough's death rate increased from 24.3 per 1,000 in 1862 to 29.3 in 1863. In 1866 it stood at 29 per 1,000. *Ashton-under-Lyne Corporation, Manual, 1877-8*, p. 107.

146. See Ch. 6 below, esp. p. 260.

147. M. Rose, op. cit. See also Ch. 6 below, esp. pp. 258-65.

148. D.A. Farnie, op. cit., p. 156.

149. A. Clarke, op. cit., pp. 153-4.

4   LABOUR LEADERS AND THEIR INSTITUTIONS

Introduction

The various objections lodged in the previous chapter to a picture of unqualified economic and social improvement for the mass of operatives during the third quarter lose much of their force when applied to changes in the material situation of the labour leadership. For, as several historians have commented, it was among the mid-Victorian labour leadership that the language of 'success', 'improvement' and the attainment of a 'stake in society' was most pronounced.[1] The aims of this chapter are fourfold: to identify the precise nature and extent of the 'improvement' desired and achieved by selected labour leaders within the cotton districts; to trace the fortunes of the main institutions of the organised working class — trade unions, friendly societies and co-operative societies — both within the cotton districts and (albeit far more briefly) at the national level between 1850 and 1875; to outline the initiatives and responses of the state, employers, and the established political parties to the claims of mid-Victorian labour; and finally, to assess the impact of the above factors upon the ideological and political direction of organised labour (particular attention being paid to the decline of Chartism, the general growth of reformism, and the specific attachment of labour leaders in Lancashire and Cheshire to Liberalism). In these various ways the chapter aims to add something of value to our understanding of the nature of mid-Victorian reformism and its material, sociological and institutional roots.

Before proceeding to the empirical substance of the chapter, it is first of all necessary to insert an explanatory note on sources and methods. The bulk of the evidence relates to the cotton districts. Thus whilst data concerning labour institutions, ideology and ruling-class responses have been drawn from both the cotton districts and the wider national context, that pertaining to the backgrounds, career patterns, values and politics of the labour leadership is exclusively based upon the cotton districts. More specifically in terms of the leadership, I have put together pieces of information concerning the occupational, social, political and religious characteristics of 144 males who were active in a variety of leadership roles within organised working-class institutions in the cotton districts during the third quarter.[2] This leadership sample does, however, suffer from two major weaknesses. There exists, firstly, the problem of patchy evidence. Many local labour leaders left few, if any, written records of their activities to posterity. This was especially true of working-class women.[3] And it is for this reason, in conjunction with the general withdrawal of working-class women from public activity during the post-Chartist years,[4] that female activists are excluded from the leadership sample. For example, even in the predominantly female sector of weaving few, if any, women appear to have held leadership positions in the union branches which they had undoubtedly fought to establish.[5] Women were present at some co-operative society functions, but usually in a supportive than a directive capacity.[6] In short, female labour leaders are extremely hard to discover during the third quarter of the century — a reflection not of any innate lack of organising ability on the part of women, but of the increasingly widespread popularity within organised labour of the notions of female home-centredness and inferiority.[7] Patchy evidence also defeats the attempt to provide a fully comprehensive picture of all the male subjects in our leadership sample. For example, whilst political allegiance is listed for over 90 per cent of our leaders, occupations are recorded for 64 per cent and religious affiliation for only 50 per cent.

A second area of imbalance lies in the sample's heavy bias in favour of co-operative society leaders (well over 100 of our subjects being active co-operators), and its underrepresentation of the leaders of trade unions and friendly societies.[8] However, an attempt has been made to offset the limited nature of the evidence contained in the sample by reference to the mass of evidence concerning working-class institutions, their leaders and ideologies, and the attitudes of the established political parties and employers contained in the local press and other contemporary sources. The outcome is the presentation of a more balanced and comprehensive view of the world of the labour leadership than contained in the sample.[9]

Seven major conclusions emerge from an interrogation of the whole body of evidence: the heavy, rather than exclusive, recruitment of those in the leadership sample from the ranks of the craft and skilled; the marked degrees of 'success', if rarely the attainment of substantial wealth, experienced by the vast majority of our leaders (irrespective of their starting points in life); the leadership's deep attachment to the values of respectability and self-help; the solid presence among co-operative society leaders of middle-class reformers; the uneven but, in overall terms, striking advances registered by the organised institutions of the working class from the mid-late 1840s onwards both in the cotton districts and nationally; the marked shift at mid-century in the policies of the state, established political parties and some employers towards workers, as reflected in greatly increased efforts to accommodate some of the demands of labour; and the powerful stimuli to reformism and liberal-radicalism provided by institutional and personal advancement and concessions from above. We will now turn to a detailed consideration of these seven areas.

The Labour Leadership Sample: Occupations, Successes and Middle-class Involvement

In terms, firstly, of the occupational composition of the leadership sample, it is noteworthy that of the 92 leaders in the sample for whom occupations are known, 44 (47 per cent) were craft or skilled workers. Engineers, shoemakers, joiners, cabinet-makers and weavers were especially prominent: printers, blacksmiths, bookbinders, millwrights and mechanics less so. Heavy skilled and craft representation did not, however, signify total domination. Seventeen (18 per cent) of the 92 leaders had spent some, or all of their working lives in unskilled or semi-skilled occupations (11 as cotton workers, 2 as coalminers and the remaining 4 as either assistants in the retail trades or semi-skilled operatives in engineering). The craft and skilled leaders were, moreover, by no means uniformly privileged. Many shoemakers and the overwhelming majority of handloom weavers had been adversely affected by the mushrooming of the dishonourable parts of their trades and by technological change. And our typical labour leader had started life in very humble circumstances, commenced work in a distinctly non-aristocratic occupation, and had expended a great deal of time, effort and self-denial in reaching the ranks of the craft and skilled. The domination of the craft and skilled groups is, furthermore, in part a reflection of the bias of the leadership sample towards those institutions — co-operative societies and selected trade unions — in which such such groups were frequently prominent in leadership roles. As we will see in the next chapter, an occupational breakdown of both leaders and members from across a wider range of 'respectable' working-class institutions strongly suggests that such institutions cast their recruitment net well beyond the confines of a 'labour aristocracy'.

Secondly, and irrespective of social origin, all the leaders in the sample had eagerly grasped those opportunities for personal and collective improvement which had been in marked evidence from the mid- to late-1840s onwards. We must search in vain for protests against immiseration and downward social mobility: 'success' had become the great rallying cry of the mid-Victorian labour leadership. Improvements in their living standards, the greatly increased recognition and status advancement achieved both for themselves and their institutions, and a belief that opportunities for upward social mobility and political mobility had multiplied since the days of Chartism — these were the manifestations of 'success' that our leaders were keen to publicise. In terms, for example, of upward social mobility, the language of success, whilst not reflective of the material situation of the vast majority of workers, did nevertheless reflect the very real advances made by the leaders in our sample. Thus 23 of the 44 craft and skilled workers experienced varying degrees of upward occupational mobility: 4 became manufacturers; 8 advanced into managerial positions (often in connexion with thriving co-operative stores); and the remaining 11 enjoyed improved status as teachers, lecturers, editors, pawnbrokers, bookkeepers, agents or clerks. Such advancement was not, moreover, confined to the craft and skilled. Eight of our 17 leaders from unskilled or semi-skilled occupations achieved upward mobility: 5 out of the 11 mill operatives moved into the positions of either manager, manufacturer or foreman; the grocer's assistant became a teacher; and the 2 coalminers became managers within the industry.

Redfern and Foster have demonstrated in their researches that upward occupational mobility for labour activists was often accompanied by advancement to positions of municipal prominence. For example, 29 (24 per cent) of Redfern's sample of 122 figures active in the Co-operative Wholesale Society between 1863 and 1913 became town councillors, justices of the peace, poor law guardians, aldermen, mayors, or members of school or hospital boards.[10] And at Oldham as many as 10 out of 40 councillors, businessmen and magistrates sampled by Foster for 1890 seem to have owed their advancement 'not to industrial promotion or setting up on their own, but directly to positions held (and capital acquired) in labour organizations, particularly the co-op.'[11]

The nature and extent of 'success' can perhaps best be illustrated by reference to the biographical details of some of the prominent figures in our leadership sample. The career of William Marcroft, a leading light in the Co-operative Movement at Oldham, dramatically demonstrates the changed fortunes of one such figure.[12] Born the son of Sally Marcroft and Richard Howard, a weaver, in Middleton in 1822, Marcroft was to be found working as a piecer in a Heywood cotton mill at the age of eight. He was later apprenticed to a fustian cutter, but left after three years to become, once again, a piecer. Marcroft's life at this point in time (the late thirties and early forties) was one of 'acute misery' — far from 'aristocratic' in character. His father seldom in work and his mother broken down by childbearing and poverty, Marcroft was forced to work extremely hard to scrape together every available penny to support the family, and to abandon night school in order to nurse his mother. Marcroft wrote of the winter of 1840–41:

> This was a winter in my life long to be remembered — no money, no school at night, no clothes to go to Sunday school, the food scarce and imperfectly cooked: no comfort at home either day or night.[13]

On the death of his mother in November 1841, Marcroft renewed his educational endeavours at the Mechanics' Institute. He also joined the Oddfellows, the Rechabites and the Machine Grinders' Society, and attended Chartist meetings. In 1844, shortly after being married, Marcroft obtained employment at Hibbert and Platts machine-building works in Oldham as a grinder. It was at this point that Marcroft began his long devotion to the principles of thrift, frugality and self-reliance. He became a keen teetotaller, left the friendly societies to join the Oldham Savings Bank, saved half of his weekly earnings, sent his wife and child to the Unitarian chapel and school in Oldham (where they 'received instruction and encouragement to live an industrious, sober, careful and useful life') and avoided waste of any kind.

Marcroft's connexions with Chartism and teetotalism brought him into contact with the Co-operative Movement. And following the failures of Oldham Chartism in 1848, Marcroft was a leading influence in the re-direction of working-class energies into co-operation. In 1850 he helped promote, and subsequently became a prominent voice within, the Oldham Industrial Co-operative Society.

Following the defeat of the Amalgamated Society of Engineers in 1852, Marcroft turned from his involvement in trade unionism towards co-operative production which he increasingly came to see as the panacea for labour's ills and the prime means of overcoming conflict between labour and capital. This view was strengthened by the granting of limited liability in 1856. Marcroft wrote:

> Now that there is protection trade union men should use their funds to employ themselves in the trades of which they have knowledge, and cease from hoarding up funds to interfere with the system of trade carried on by other people, and thereby combining in the same person the employers and the workers.[14]

In keeping with this belief, Marcroft was a leading spirit in the formation of the Sun Mill Company in 1860. Marcroft acted as director, chairman and treasurer of the company at various points during the 1860s. His strong beliefs in the notion of a 'bonus to labour', in the principle of 'one man, one directorship', and in imposing checks upon the power of management brought him into conflict with the board and management of the Sun Mill who increasingly saw the company simply as a profit-making venture. Marcroft resigned from the board of the company in 1871, and played a relatively minor role in the Working-Class Limiteds boom of the seventies. During the last 20 years of his life (he died in 1894) Marcroft concerned himself mainly with his writing, but he did practise for a time as a dentist.

Marcroft's career is of interest to us in three main ways. Firstly, it illustrates the paths travelled by many Chartists after 1848 into co-operation and temperance. Secondly, it highlights the central importance of the Co-operative Movement to many workers during the mid-Victorian period. (Marcroft probably did more than anyone else in Oldham to promote co-operation. In addition to his central involvement in the Industrial Society and the Sun Mill and House and Mill companies, he was instrumental in the formation of the North of England Co-operative Wholesale Society and the Co-operative Insurance Company.[15]) Thirdly, it underlines the attachment of labour leaders to the principles of self-help and respectability, and the enhanced financial and status gains to be derived therefrom. Whether Marcroft was as contemptuous of the 'non-respectable', 'non-aristocratic' working-class elements as implied by one historian is perhaps open to question,[16] but what is not open to doubt is the marked degree of 'success' achieved by Marcroft and his belief that workers were in the process of securing a place in the system. The Marcroft family enjoyed a style of living 'far more comfortable than that of most of their contemporaries'. Their final house had two parlours, eight bedrooms (one of which was used as a chemistry laboratory and museum) and a bathroom, and upon his death Marcroft left an estate valued at the sum of £14,753.[17]

Few other leaders in our sample accumulated comparable wealth and property. However, in contrast to the 1830s and 1840s, the vast majority did achieve relative security and comfort during the third quarter. William Booth, one of Marcroft's colleagues in the Sun Mill Company and first president of the Oldham Industrial Society, experienced marked improvement. Born of poor parents in 1817, Booth started work in a mill warehouse, but eventually set up in business as a pawnbroker. The success of his business enabled Booth to spend his retirement in comfortable circumstances at Southport.[18] Henry Hewkin, while not experiencing the same degree of financial success as Booth, also found an outlet for his radicalism and ambition in the Oldham co-operative movement. A joiner by trade, Hewkin was a pioneer of the Industrial Society and later became the first chairman of the Sun Mill Company.[19] Rochdale, according to the *Co-operative News*, produced a 'vast number' of comfortably situated people who had started life as 'the poorest of the poor'.[20] Many of these had achieved improved respect and recognition through the agency of co-operation. J.T.W. Mitchell, destined to become 'the strongest and most vigorous personality in the whole co-operative movement', was one such figure.[21] Born the illegitimate son of a working woman in Rochdale in 1828, and reared in humble circumstances, Mitchell obtained his first job as a piecer in a Rochdale cotton mill where he worked from 6 a.m. to 7 p.m. for 1/6d per week. At the age of 17 he joined the Young Men's Class at the Providence Independent Chapel. Impressed by Mitchell's desire to acquire knowledge, the leader of the class, a local flannel manufacturer, gave Mitchell employment in his own warehouse in 1848. Mitchell worked in the warehouse for some 20 years, rising ultimately to the position of manager. By the late sixties Mitchell had set up in business as a flannel dealer. Fired by a desire to help others, Mitchell joined the Rochdale Pioneers in 1853 and quickly made his mark upon the movement. By 1856 he had become a committee member of the Pioneers. During the 1860s Mitchell was a member of the CWS committee, and served as chairman of the

CWS in 1874. He was also a respected and influential figure in municipal affairs. Although unsuccessful in his candidature for a seat upon the town council in 1894, he did serve as a magistrate, and was often called upon to act as an arbitrator in industrial disputes.[22]

Many of the early Pioneers included in our sample had prospered by the 1870s. Samuel Ashworth, Owenite, Chartist, flannel weaver, and the youngest member of the original Pioneers, became the first paid counter-man at Rochdale. In 1866 he resigned as manager at the Rochdale society to become the Co-operative Wholesale Society's buyer.[23] John Potts, auditor of the Pioneers during the late 1840s, advanced to the position of head clerk in the borough treasurer's office, and eventually became chief clerk at Rochdale gasworks.[24] Thomas Cheetham, president of the Pioneers in 1862, became a member of the board of the Mitchell Hey Manufacturing Society, and successfully stood as a Liberal candidate in the 1880 municipal elections.[25] And even many of the men who remained faithful to the tenets of Owenism experienced economic improvement. William Cooper, for example, progressed from handloom weaver to stationer, and thence to account bookmaker.[26]

As at Rochdale, the rapid expansion of the Co-operative Movement throughout the cotton districts provided an important avenue for not only socio-political radicalism but also for personal advancement. In every locality the self-made labour activist was prominent. Thus at Mossley John Schofield moved from piecer to warehouseman, to assistant secretary to the Mossley Spinning Company, and finally to manager of the Hyde Equitable Co-operative Society.[27] At neighbouring Ashton-under-Lyne James Lowndes, an orphan, advanced from shoemaker's apprentice to insurance agent, and thence to clerk to the Board of Guardians and the Assessment Committee, holding the latter position for some 30 years. 'Blessed with shrewd business sense', Lowndes was an agent for the Prudential Insurance Company and chairman of the Ashton Co-operative Society during the 1870s. A director of the Star Corn Mill, Lowndes was elected to the Committee of the Co-operative Wholesale Society in 1885. An active Primitive Methodist, Lowndes served as a Sunday School superintendent for over 30 years.[28] Another influential co-operator at Ashton, John Ridgway, served an apprenticeship as a machinist and later attained the position of manager in the Grosvenor Street Mills. Prominent in the local Mechanics Institute, the Oddfellows, and in a building society, Ridway was a key figure in the local Liberal Party.[29] At Bury Thomas Kilson, born of poor

Irish parents, who had been forced to leave Ireland during the Famine, achieved self-respect and recognition. Starting work as an errand boy at the age of seven, Kilson graduated from piecer to foreman. He joined the Co-operative Movement in 1874 and was elected to serve upon the board of the Co-operative Wholesale Society during the 1890s.[30] The Macclesfield Co-operative Society was dominated for many years by the figure of William Barnett. The son of a whitesmith, Barnett served his apprenticeship as a bookbinder and took a keen interest in education. From 1857 onwards he occupied the positions of trustee, secretary and general manager of the Macclesfield Co-operative Society. A director of the Co-operative Insurance Society, Barnett was also a founder and chairman of the Macclesfield Silk Manufacturing Company. An active Congregationalist, Barnett left an estate valued at almost £4,000 on his death in 1909.[31]

Determined and able men also dominated the labour movement in the Manchester area. Thus the historian of Stockport Chartism records that many of the younger Chartists active in the borough during the 1840s went on to achieve upward occupational mobility during the 1850s.[32] Anthony Brelsford, a prominent figure in the Forresters, was for many years president of the Stockport Co-operative Society, and the first working man to serve as a magistrate in the borough.[33] William Bates was another example of a man who, mainly as a result of strenuous effort, rose to make his mark on the labour movement. Born of poor parents at Bury in 1833, Bates moved to Pendleton in 1838 to work as a 'tear boy' in a calico printing works. Bates's father died in 1843, leaving the mother and five children to be maintained upon the earnings of two members of the family. Bates became involved in Chartism and trade unionism and was also a member of the Pendleton Mutual Improvement Society. During the mid-Victorian period he was active in Co-operation and political reform movements. In 1870 Bates became president of the Eccles Co-operative Society, and in 1873 was elected to the board of the Co-operative Wholesale Society. A strong Methodist, Bates left just over £2,000 on his death in 1908.[34] Tim Pollit, another stalwart at the Eccles society, was a respected Oddfellow, holding the office of Grand Mastership of the Eccles district in 1884.[35] George Owen, born at Salford in 1831, began his working life as a bookbinder but soon advanced to the position of foreman, and ultimately manager. Owen was appointed corresponding secretary to the Manchester and Salford Equitable Co-operative Society in 1859. He later served as president of the Co-operative Printing Society. By the early 1890s he had accumulated sufficient capital to retire in comfort to Buxton.[36] Other leading figures in Manchester co-operation — such as Edward Hooson, J.C. Fox and J.C. Edwards — had also tasted the fruits of success. Hooson, Ernest Jones's closest ally during the 1850s and 1860s, had been assisted by his former employer (Hooson was then a journeyman wire-drawer) to set up in business.[37] James Fox, successfully overcoming the disadvantages of a poverty-stricken background, and a firm believer in temperance and self-help, joined the Manchester and Salford Industrial Society in 1858. A few years later Fox was among the founders of the Hulme Pioneers' Society, serving as its secretary for the first few years. A member of the board of the Co-operative Wholesale Society from 1868 to 1871, Fox also acted as editor of the *Co-operative News* for part of the 1870s. Upon his death in 1877 he left effects valued at under £1,500.[38] John Charles Edwards, born in 1833, worked as a mechanic in Manchester during his younger days. A vigorous supporter of temperance, Edwards was a founder member of the Manchester and Salford Equitable Co-operative Society, of which he became the first president. When the Co-operative Wholesale Society was founded in 1863, Edwards became its first secretary and cashier. An influential member — along with Hooson and E.O. Greening — of the Union and Emancipation Society (set up to demonstrate sympathy with the Northern cause in the American Civil War), Edwards was firmly committed to a Liberal political stance. He died in 1881 leaving a personal estate of under £800.[39]

It is, finally, worth recording that the phenomenon of 'success' was by no means confined to the cotton districts. Both Gray and Crossick note that the tone and direction of the Co-operative Movement in Edinburgh and Kentish London were set by men who were keen to 'rise in society'.[40] And across the Pennines, the Yorkshire labour movement was increasingly dominated by men who had tasted the fruits of self help. For example, R.M. Carter, the central figure in the West Riding reform movement, was a highly successful self-made man.[41] Carter graduated from farm labourer to foreman in a Leeds cloth mill, and subsequently built up a flourishing coal merchants business. He took part in Chartism from 1844 onwards, and upon the decline of the latter turned his attentions to education and co-operation. In 1848 he joined the Leeds Redemption Society, and in 1853 became president of the Leeds District Flour Mill Society. Carter was a supporter of the Leeds Mechanics Institute, and devoted much of his spare time to the accumulation of 'useful knowledge'. In 1850 he was elected to Leeds town council as a 'Chartist' councillor. Accepted as the leader of the advanced Liberal group within the council, Carter dominated the Yorkshire department of the Reform League, and entered Parliament in 1868. Edwin Gaunt, Carter's right-hand man in the Reform League, also achieved prominence in Leeds politics. A cloth worker turned manufacturer, Gaunt was elected as a councillor in 1861, an alderman in 1874, and became mayor of the city in 1885.[42] And one of the foremost co-operators in Leeds, William Bell, exchanged, 'by dint of perseverance', poverty for affluence, and anonymity for influence and respect. One of eight children in a farm-labouring family, Bell left labouring to become a blacksmith's apprentice. In 1849 he moved to Leeds where he rose successively from journeyman to foreman to manager of the Lion Screw Works. An experienced co-operator, Bell was also chairman of the Leeds Woollen Cloth Company.[43]

Our leaders attributed their successes to three major factors: the cultivation of 'sound' personal habits; a strong belief in the benefits and strengths to be derived from collective and democratic forms of organisation; and the ability to set one's face resolutely against the many obstacles which lay in the path of both personal and collective advancement. In sum, the third major characteristic of the leadership was a commitment to a value system organised around the qualities of industry, restraint and moderation; self-respect and independence; unremitting determination (often in the face of great odds); mutuality and self-sacrifice in the interest of the wider advancement of one's organisation, even, on occasion, one's class; and fierce opposition to 'loose' personal habits and to those who continued to oppose labour's claims to its due recognition and status. Somewhat lacking in spontaneity and the capacity for relaxed, informal enjoyment of life, our labour leaders had, nevertheless, been reared in a hard school which taught the necessity of struggle and toughness and the immediate, visible folly of capitulation and personal weakness (better to be an independent, self-respecting co-operator than to be cast on to the scrapheap or to become the deferential plaything of one's 'betters'). In short, much of the emphasis upon industry and discipline was both necessary and admirable in the harsh material climate in which such men had been brought up.

Strong attachments to education and temperance exemplified the key importance of discipline and 'manliness'[44] to the labour leader. Many of our leaders were actively involved in the cause of temperance, often having taken the 'pledge' in the aftermath of Chartism's setbacks and defeats in 1848. At Halifax, for example, Ben Wilson resolved in 1849, 'not to taste of any intoxicating drink or smoke tobacco as long as I lived'. Wilson took his decision 'as an example to others', and in the firm belief that, '. . . if working men could have been induced to invest in the co-operative movement what they were spending on intoxicating drinks it would have greatly improved their condition'.[45] Similar scenes and views were in evidence at Oldham (where some Chartists came to see teetotalism as the 'only safe and lasting remedy' for popular grievances), Stockport, Ashton, Failsworth and numerous other centres throughout the manufacturing districts.[46] Teetotalism did not claim the undivided support of our leaders, but the minority not in favour of total abstinence did, nevertheless, advocate moderation in terms of the consumption of alcohol.

It is extremely important to note at this stage (the matter will be dealt with in more detail in the next chapter) that a commitment to abstinence or moderation did not signify, at least in terms of Ben Wilson and the many other northern Chartists who had a record of *both* 'physical force' and 'respectability', either a sudden conversion to bourgeois individualism and 'class collaboration' on the basis of 'respectability', or, at least consciously and in the short term, an ideological rupture with Chartism.[47] Rather, in turning towards temperance (and Co-operation) such Chartists were exploring, in the light of the setbacks and defeats suffered by Chartism in 1848, other means whereby the 'emancipation of the working classes' could be achieved. As we will see later, the *longer-term* effects of this redirection of energies were of profound significance for the ideological character of the labour movement, both in terms of the decline of Chartism as a mass force and the growth of reformism. But in the short term there is a great but misleading temptation to search out ideological breaks. As in the very different context of post-bellum America, our leaders were intent upon building up efficient and durable organisations which would *both* cater to immediate needs and advance the wider and more distant goals of workers.[48] And the cultivation of moderation or temperance signified allegiance to certain qualities — independence, self-respect, self-control and discipline — which were absolutely essential to the creation of successful labour institutions, and which would enable workers to fashion their own destinies irrespective of any concessions handed down to them by their 'betters'.

The pursuit of education and truth was also seen more as a necessary prerequisite to the collective and personal development of workers rather than as a means of escaping from one's class. Almost all our leaders had struggled to acquire education. J.C. Fox of Manchester had developed an 'insatiable thirst' for knowledge at the tender age of 12, when he began to save his spare coppers to buy literature. Philip Coley, president of the Sunderland Co-operative Society, realised his ambition to become a teacher by 'much burning of midnight oil and assiduous application'.[49] J.T.W. Mitchell and R.M. Carter both devoted their spare moments to the acquisition of knowledge and were supporters of mechanics institutes.[50] And William Bates of Pendleton, 'feeling a longing for education', accordingly formed a discussion class.[51] These were but a few examples of an extremely widespread phenomenon.

Moderation, temperance and the struggle for education were part and parcel of the ethos of 'respectability' which was so pronounced in mid-Victorian Britain. A full discussion of the content and meanings of 'respectability' must await the next chapter. But that we can do at this point is to sound warning of our disagreement with those who see the workers' attachment to respectability as proof of incorporation into the system and the passive acceptance of bourgeois values.[52] As noted above, in their emphasis upon collective improvement and their opposition to condescension and patronage from above, our leaders could scarcely be seen as the unthinking, even willing, victims of a bourgeois cultural trap. Two other factors also militate against a simple picture of 'embourgeoisement'. Firstly, as we have clearly seen, struggle against all|manner|of|adversities had been part of the common experience of the leadership. And part of this struggle had resided, especially during the 1830s and 1840s, in economic, social and political struggles against 'respectables' from other classes. Given the intensity of such struggles and the fact that 'respectability' itself was open to very different, indeed conflicting interpretations according (mainly) to one's class situation, an interclass alliance upon the basis of 'respectability' was, at least in many of the cotton towns, doomed to failure. Furthermore, such areas of struggle and conflict, whilst softened somewhat, did not disappear with the onset of mid-Victorian 'stability'. There were still many battles to be fought — for improved living standards, the vote, greater opportunities for education and around many other

campaigns and issues. Even in personal terms, the undoubted successes of our leaders were, generally speaking, solid rather than
spectacular. The experience of Marcroft was not typical of the leadership as a whole. By no means all 'respectable' Chartists partook
of the financial benefits of the mid-Victorian boom, and beyond the
limits of the labour activist there existed a large number of workers
for whom the successes of respectability lay in the achievement of
the more modest aims of relatively secure employment and an easing
of the chronic problem of economic insecurity.

Nevertheless, despite such corrections and qualifications, there is
no doubt that the thinking and behaviour of mid-Victorian labour
leaders was heavily influenced by the successes they had experienced
since the 1840s. The ideological effects consisted essentially of a
serious questioning of the belief that organised labour was still a
complete outsider with little or no chance of advancement within the
confines of the existing system, and the introduction of a much
greater degree of ambiguity into labour's thinking. Such effects will
be considered in more detail later. Our immediate task is to demonstrate how the very successes of our labour leaders facilitated
the involvement in parts of the labour movement, and especially in
the Co-operative Movement, of all manner of 'self-made men' —
both those who had crossed the manual/white collar divide and
those reformers who were solidly middle class in origin and occupational background.

The significant involvement of middle-class males — the fourth
major feature to emerge from our questioning of the evidence — is
clearly demonstrated in the case of our leadership sample. Thus
manufacturers (often small masters), managers and overlookers
comprised 13 (14 per cent) of the total of 92 occupations listed.
Clerks, cashiers and agents made up 10 per cent; and teachers,
lecturers and architects accounted for 8 per cent.

Of insignificance in terms of trade unionism (which was often
seen as ideologically 'wrongheaded'), middle-class reformers did,
nevertheless, sometimes figure prominently in the running of the
more established and larger friendly societies.[53] It was, however, in
relation to the Co-operative Movement that the middle-class presence was most solidly felt. As Schatz has convincingly argued, the
essentially working-class character of Co-operation (a survey conducted by the Co-operative Union in the late eighties revealed that
only 2 per cent of its societies' members had incomes in excess of £150
per year) should not conceal the fact that middle-class reformers

'took a key role'; and that 'shopkeepers, civil servants and others outside the working class (with incomes most often below £150 in the late eighties) could and did join the societies'.[54] Thus at the Newcastle, Nottingham, Huddersfield and Leicester societies middle-class co-operators were active as founders, propagandists and in attracting wider middle-class support. Co-operative societies, unlike trade unions, were portrayed by their middle-class supporters as cultivators of the true capitalist values of self-help, competition and enlightened self-interest which served the wider public good.[55]

A similar pattern emerged throughout the cotton districts. At Manchester, for example, Henry Pitman, vegetarian, member of the United Kingdom Alliance, and celebrated shorthand writer, served as editor of the *Co-operator* from 1861 until its demise ten years later. Born the tenth and youngest child of a weaving overseer (who subsequently became a manufacturer), Pitman was for some time chief reporter on the *Manchester Examiner and Times* and for a brief period was also on the staff of the *Manchester Guardian*.[56] Henry Whiley, a member of the Central Co-operative Board between 1869 and 1875, was superintendent of the public health department at Manchester.[57] J.M. Percival, one of the founders of the Manchester and Salford Equitable Co-operative Society, was a clerk.[58] Dr John Watts, 'perhaps a model of the reformer-co-operator', and E.O. Greening were both 'advanced' Liberals who exerted considerable influence within the Lancashire Co-operative Movement. Watts was one of 12 children of a Coventry ribbon weaver. Practically paralysed from the waist down at an early age, Watts attended the local mechanics institute between the ages of 13 and 20. During the early 1840s he was an Owenite lecturer in Lancashire, but by the end of the decade had become disillusioned with the practicality of Owenism and became a staunch defender of the 'truths' of orthodox political economy. A strong opponent of trade unionism, Watts was involved in a number of reform campaigns (of 'strictly utilitarian and practical purposes') in the Manchester area during the mid-Victorian period, and gave active support to the Co-operative Movement. He was a member of the Manchester and Salford Equitable Co-operative Society, often spoke at the society's annual meetings, and was the principal leading article writer for the *Co-operative News* during 1872. Co-operation appealed to Watts primarily because it appeared to be a means of turning workers into 'capitalists'. This process would not mean that workers would cease to live by wages, but as Schatz notes, 'that their propertyless status would be papered over with savings, shares in limited companies, and the socially-desirable virtues of "providence and consideration" '.[59]

E.O. Greening was in the mainstream of mid-Victorian Co-operation. Born in Warrington in 1836, Greening was the son of a wire manufacturer whose factory was 'visited' by the Plug strikers of 1842. In 1850 Greening moved to Manchester where he became an apprentice wiredrawer. By the mid-1850s Greening was able to establish his own business, and within a few years he had acquired considerable wealth. An executive committee member of the United Kingdom Alliance, Greening helped to found both the Union and Emancipation Society and the Manchester and Salford Manhood Suffrage League, the latter being a section of the Reform League. In 1868 he unsuccessfully contested Halifax as an independent labour candidate, receiving strong support from local labour activists and old Chartists.[60] During the 1860s Greening became keenly interested in Co-operation, especially the notion of industrial co-partnership which he introduced into his own business. He played a leading role in the establishment of many co-partnership schemes, the most important being at the Cobden Memorial Mills in Sabden and the ill-fated South Buckley Coal and Fire Brick Company.[61] Greening also founded and edited the *Industrial Partnership Record* in 1867 to advance the principles of co-partnership. Upon the failure of his own business in 1870 he devoted the remainder of his life's work to the Co-operative Movement, being a prolific writer, a member of the Central Board of the Co-operative Union, and a founder of the International Co-operative Alliance in 1895. Whilst less critical than Watts of trade unionism, Greening did agree that the main benefits of co-partnership and co-operative production generally were that they would resolve conflict between labour and capital (conflict 'artificially' kept alive by the trade unions), increase productivity, induce company loyalty, better acquaint workers with the responsibilities of capital, and promote capitalist values 'without ever-threatening the rights of property'.[62]

Growing ties between middle-class reformers and co-operators were in evidence not only in Manchester but also in many of the surrounding cotton towns. At Ashton and Stalybridge, for example, Mason, Whittaker and many other prominent employers were keen to cultivate links with the local co-operative societies, frequently addressing co-operative functions and praising the 'improving' endeavours of co-operators.[63] Generally speaking, support for co-operation among manufactures and other employers cut across political allegiances, but in many towns support and encouragement was particularly forthcoming from Liberal employers. It is also significant that by the late 1860s the overwhelming majority of our leadership sample were heavily committed to Liberalism.

Institutional Advancement and Concessions from Above

The fifth conclusion to emerge from our investigation is that the individual successes achieved by our leaders were frequently accompanied by greatly enhanced recognition and advancement for the institutions which they ran. Most marked in relation to co-operation and the friendly societies, post-1850 institutional advancement went beyond the confines of Lancashire and Cheshire to embrace the organisations of workers at the national level. And in turning to consider this wider picture, we can usefully chart the growth in trade unionism, co-operation and friendly societies.

In terms, firstly, of national trade unionism, we know that, despite the paucity of reliable membership figures for the pre-1870 period, the third quarter belonged essentially to the unions of the craft and skilled. These unions came into their own after Chartism, building up their membership, carefully cultivating a moderate and responsible public image, dominating the mid-Victorian trade union movement, and meeting with an increasingly favourable response from the 'new model' employers.[64] Cotton and coal were the main areas of unionisation outside the craft and skilled sector, but the former's dominance lay in the future and advances in union recognition were far more patchy than in the latter sector. In cotton, for example, attempts to unionise the workforce continued to encounter fierce employer opposition. Thus although spinning trade unionism made generally solid progress from the mid-1850s to the mid-1870s and weaving trade unionism advanced in north Lancashire, the successful unionisation of the vast majority of operatives in cotton took place after 1875.[65] Nevertheless, in terms of the overall national picture there is no doubt that substantial advances in both recognition and membership were recorded between 1850 and 1875. By the latter date the trade union movement in Britain could record a total membership of about half a million. Furthermore, with the passing of the Trade Union Act of 1871, the abolition of the Criminal Law Amendment Act of 1871 and the passing of the Conspiracy and Protection of Property Act and the Employers and Workmen Act of 1875, the trade union movement had acquired secure legal status.[66]

By the mid-1860s the vast majority of friendly societies were recognised as models of self-help, respectability and sound, moderate habits — earlier associations with secrecy and subversion having largely disappeared in the flush of mid-Victorian expansion.[67] Indeed, from the 1830s onwards the friendly societies experienced heady growth rates. By 1872 the known membership of all friendly societies making a return was estimated to be 1,857,896. But in 1874 the Royal Commission on Friendly Societies calculated, more realistically, that there were in Britain 4,000,000 members of friendly societies and approximately 8,000,000 persons interested in them as beneficiaries.[68] By the 1870s the affiliated orders had acquired particular prominence and strength, possessing in 1872 a combined membership in Britain of 1,282,275, of which about two-thirds was represented by the Manchester Unity of Oddfellows (426,663 members), and the Ancient Order of Forresters (388, 872 members).[69]

From the mid-1840s onwards the Co-operative Movement recorded striking, indeed often spectacular, advances. And given co-operation's central place in organised working-class activity in the northwest after 1850 and the heavy representation of co-operators within our leadership sample, it is to a relatively detailed examination of the fortunes of co-operation that we now turn. As convincingly demonstrated by Pollard and others,[70] the post-Owenite Co-operative Movement experienced rapid growth at mid-century. The success of the Rochdale Pioneers led to widespread imitation, and by 1850 there existed more than 200 co-operative societies run according to the Rochdale principle, the majority being in the north of England. It is difficult to provide precise figures for the pre-1870 years, but one estimate sets the number of consumer co-operatives in England and Wales in 1863 at 100,000.[71] Co-operation did experience difficulties during the heavy unemployment of the Cotton Famine period; but it was a tribute to the movement's strength that the vast majority of societies in the cotton districts did survive the Famine to resume their rapid growth rates in the post-1865 period. And a further sign of the overall vitality of the movement lay in the setting up of the Co-operative Wholesale Society in 1863.[72] In 1867 the *Co-operator* enumerated 560 co-operative societies in England and Wales with a total membership of 173,600, 72 per cent (125,700) being concentrated in Lancashire and Yorkshire.[73] By the end of

1872 industrial and provident co-operative societies in Britain had at least 301,157 members.[74] And of the 458 distributive societies in existence in England and Wales in 1872, a total of 279 (60 per cent) were located in the northern counties of Lancashire (112 societies), Yorkshire (121 societies), Durham (28 societies) and Northumberland (18 societies).[75] Even more spectacular advances were to take place during the final quarter of the century as co-operation established a secure base in other parts of the country.[76]

In terms of the progress made by individual co-operative societies during the third quarter, Halifax, Leeds Industrial, Bury and the Rochdale Pioneers led the way, having membership and sales figures for 1872 of, respectively, 7,400 and £235,730, 6,756 and £180,750, 6,460 and £193,952, and 6,444 and £267,572.[77] All these societies had started at mid-century from extremely humble beginnings and owed much of their success to the hard work and dedication of small knots of Chartists and radicals. The Halifax society was, for example, started by a few Chartists in a cottage. During its early years the society struggled to keep its head above water, but after ten years of existence had entered calmer, more favourable waters, having in 1859 a membership of 414 and receipts totalling £6,260. During the following year spectacular progress was made, membership and receipts having risen to 1,374 and £16,875, respectively. And between 1862 and 1866 advances were even more striking. By the latter date the Halifax society had 6,000 members and receipts of £168,222.[78]

The four leading societies constituted the outstanding examples of the widespread successes achieved by co-operation throughout the cotton and woollen districts. At the Oldham Industrial Society, for example, receipts increased from £1,168 in 1850 to £80,000 in 1865. Between 1851 and 1865 the Oldham society's share capital rose from £252 to £28,000, and the amount paid out in dividends increased from £131 to £9,448. In 1868 alone the society, with a membership of 2,815, paid out more than £10,000 in interest and dividends, devoted £250 towards the further development of the newsroom and library, received £109,614 for goods sold, and had share capital of £41,622. The society had also begun the construction of 'model cottages' for its members.[79] The Manchester and Salford Equitable Co-operative Society had £100 and 170 members at its birth in 1859. Eleven years later the society possessed capital amounting to £30,000 and a membership of 3,820.[80] The Manchester-based Co-operative Wholesale Society also flourished, increasing its capital and profits from, respectively, £2,456 and £306 in 1864 to £37,785 and £3,584 in 1869.

During the same period the value of the goods sold by the CWS rose from £51,858 to £469,171.[81] At neighbouring Eccles the co-operative society commenced business in 1857 having capital totalling the princely sum of £25 and a membership of 35. But by 1864, at a time when the Cotton Famine still stalked Lancashire, the society could afford the £3,000 needed to build a new central store.[82] And at Ashton, Stockport, Stalybridge and Mossley, centres hit especially hard by the Cotton Famine, co-operation was, by 1865, well on the path towards recovery. Indeed in 1866 the Stockport society (which had been inaugurated in 1860 by 12 workers) could boast of its 'rapid progress', there being, 'no other institution or society in the borough based on a firmer foundation, or one which . . . pays the same interest . . .'.[83] Three years later the Ashton society recorded 'great progress' and noted that 'the principles of co-operation seem to be taken up more and more by the working population of the neighbourhood'[84]. And by 1871 the Mossley society had a fine library containing upwards of 1,000 volumes and made judicious use of its ample capital resources.[85]

Great rejoicing and euphoria surrounded the expansion of co-operation. Looking back upon developments at Halifax, the veteran Chartist and co-operator Ben Wilson wrote in the 1880s:

> What a change since 1849. If, at the last meeting when we broke up our co-operative society in that year, some one had said that in less than twenty years there would be a co-operative society in Halifax with 6,000 members, a capital of £60,000, and having a turnover of £3,000 per week, there was not one that would have credited it.[86]

Co-operative advancement at Halifax had paralleled individual success. The former Halifax Chartists who held a reunion in the town in 1885 contrasted their erstwhile poverty (they had all been 'poor working men earning low wages') with their present affluence (many having become 'men of business').[87] Ernest Jones believed that co-operation had fully demonstrated its durability during the Cotton Famine and that, 'If it could stand such a trial as that it is invincible, it is immortal'.[88] The cultural and material benefits accruing to co-operators were claimed to be considerable. According to Isaiah Lee, himself a keen co-operator, the movement had achieved successes, 'never hitherto attained by any people'.[89] Jones observed that co-operation's advance had enabled its members to become, 'independent men, having a stake in the country as well as the richest lord who lives in the land'.[90] Such sentiments were shared by the *Co-operator*, the official journal of the movement during the 1860s. Thanks to co-operation 'thousands of men' had, according to the *Co-operator*, attained that 'independence and contentedness of mind which is the happiest state the natural man can feel, having plenty of clothes and food, and something to spare for the needy'.[91] 'Englishmen have much to be thankful for', opined the *Co-operator*, 'inasmuch as there is probably no country on the face of the globe where sober, industrious young men can so soon raise themselves to ease . . . and comfort, as in England'.[92] J.C. Edwards looked forward to a time of wider co-operative influence:

> Co-operators are no longer poverty-stricken labourers, but creators of wealth and power, which will make itself felt and enable us to exercise our influence not only in the affairs of our own country, but perhaps in the affairs of the entire world.[93]

Increased satisfaction with their past and present achievements and boundless optimism in the prospects for future progress were the products not only of the considerable advances made by sections of organised workers after the mid-1840s, but also of the greatly enhanced readiness on the part of the state and influential social groups to accommodate some of organised labour's claims to recognition, protection and advancement. During the 1830s and the early mid-1840s the state, established poltical parties and the dominant social groups had appeared to workers as openly hostile to the claims of labour, but from the mid late- 1840s onwards a mellowing of attitudes and policies was increasingly in evidence. This mellowing process, aptly termed by Foster one of 'liberalization',[94] was underpinned by a complex ensemble of factors. Among the latter the following were of special significance: the fears engendered by Chartism, the Revolutions of 1848 and the continued ability of mid-Victorian British workers to mount, on occasion, miltant, strong and well co-ordinated campaigns which, as in the case of the political agitation of 1866–67, 'could only be ignored at the cost of reviving and sharpening the class-consciousness of the workmen and helping on the formation of revolutionary forces';[95] an enhanced awareness, most marked among the New Model employers, of 'the exposed position of property and of its need of find outside support';[96] and the growing recognition that it was both safe and advisable to give a stake in the system to a reformist and generally moderate labour movement.

'Liberalization' took many forms. The enactment of legislation favourable to working-class interests, the public recognition of organised labour, the conscious attempts made by the Conservative and Liberal Parties to attract popular support, and the softened attitudes of, and paternalistic image projected by, many erstwhile hostile employers were some of liberalisation's cardinal features and, as such, are deserving of careful investigation.

Given their detailed treatment elsewhere in this study,[97] the policies of employers and the major political parties can be briefly dealt with at this juncture. In terms of the former, whilst many employers remained anatagonistic towards trade union recognition, a minority did come to terms with unions (especially of the craft and skilled), and the cotton unions as a whole did register significant, if highly chequered, advances in employer recognition during the third quarter. A further significant development in Lancashire was, as Joyce has shown, the widespread growth in employer paternalism from the mid-1850s onwards. However, whilst designed to encourage worker loyalty to the employer, paternalism was often fiercely anti-union in character, and many paternalistic employers were prepared to wage protracted battles to keep 'their workers' free from 'outside' union 'interference'.[98] Thus the overall record of employers in terms of liberalisation was far from uniformly impressive. Whilst a softening of approach can be detected among the 'New Model' employers, the vast majority displayed, as Hobsbawm notes, 'a fundamental reluctance to accept the existence of a labour movement at all'.[99] Given such an attitude, it is not surprising that industrial conflict was frequently in evidence after 1850. Herein lay the weakest link in the chain of liberalisation. In terms of the policies of Conservatives and Liberals, the notion of liberalisation is far more solidly based. As Foster himself demonstrates, serious attempts were made by Liberals to win the support of labour by presenting their party as the organ of the people, the true embodiment of progress and enlightenment. And the merging of late Chartism into Liberalism was a fact of major political importance. On the other side of the political divide the Conservative Party succeeded (as is shown in Chapter 7) in creating a mass working-class base on its policies of 'No Popery' and opposition to Manchester School sentiments.

In relation to the policies and attitudes adopted by the state and its organs towards the claims of labour, attention has already been drawn to the enactment of legislation favourable to the trade union movement during the first half of the 1870s. Such acts gave official seal to the improved standing of trade unions since the bleak days of the 'Sheffield Outrages'. Co-operative and friendly societies also benefited from legislative developments. The Industrial and Provident Societies Acts of 1852 and 1862 provided a legal framework conducive to the relatively unhampered growth of co-ops, and friendly societies received effective legal protection from the legislation of 1850, 1855 and 1875.[100]

In terms of the wider legislative context, it is highly significant that the 'blatant class legislation' of the 1830s (as seen, for example, in the Poor Law Amendment Act), and the more or less total refusal to countenance reforms which went against the grain of orthodox political economy, were not to be repeated. There was a mellowing of attitude and practice. Indeed, Stedman Jones has forcibly argued that the 'the very vehemence of opposition' to the state's intransigence and repression 'forced a change of course'. Peel's reduction of taxes on consumption (continued with 'crusading zeal' by Gladstone), the Mines Act of 1842, the Bank Charter Act of 1844 and, above all, the Repeal of the Corn Laws, the Ten Hours Act and the Second Reform Act, signified to many that the state was no longer the selfish and intransigent tool of aristocrats, placemen and capitalists, but that it was becoming increasingly responsive to the wishes of large numbers of male citizens.[101] Certainly, with official state acceptance of trade unionism and of the mass electorate, this was the viewpoint adopted by many labour leaders. Herein lay a great spur to reformism: recognition implied involvement and 'responsibility', the enmeshment of the labour movement in a 'web of conciliation and collaboration', against which, as Hobsbawm reminds us, 'only the firmest and clearest revolutionary theory or moral commitment can safeguard the labour cadre against mere reformism'.[102] As we will now see, the drift into reformism was both widespread and largely unchallenged in the post-1850 period.

Ideological and Political Effects

The main effects, both in the cotton districts and nationally, of labour's advancement and the process of liberalisation were twofold. Firstly, much of the ideology of Chartism failed to encompass the improved position of many workers and the movement accordingly suffered a severe decline in support. Secondly, a tremendous boost was provided to the growth and spread of reformism and piecemeal gradualism.

In terms of Chartism, there is no doubt that the successes achieved by co-operators and others were increasingly at the expense of continued or full involvement in Chartism. This was in part a result of the fact that workers were prepared to devote far more time and energy to rising movement rather than to a movement, such as Chartism, which showed few signs of regaining its former strength in the post-1848 period. As Stedman Jones has pioneeringly argued, it was, however, also a result of the fact that the mid-Victorian workers' experience ran counter to Chartism's expectations. Thus, contrary to the central Chartist tenets that real and lasting economic and social improvement would be possible only *after* the enactment of the Charter (since Chartism taught that the source of oppression was, at root, political rather than economic in character), and that concessions were highly unlikely to be made by an unreformed Parliament and state machinery dominated by the people's enemies, mid-Victorian labour leaders and some workers had achieved various forms of advancement within the unreformed system and had seen the emergence of a more accommodative state. In sum, there had opened up a gulf between, as Stedman Jones expresses it, 'its [Chartism's] premises and the perception of its constituency'.[103] In the short term Chartism's ideals were not consciously abandoned by our mid-Victorian labour leaders, but the movement's ideology of the primacy of the political did appear somewhat dated and of increasing irrelevance to their situation — hence the falling away of support and involvement. Politics were not forgotten. Indeed, during the 1860s many of our leaders were active in the suffrage campaign. But in comparison with the Chartist period much had changed. Political campaigns no longer occupied pride of place in terms of the various forms of working-class protest, but had become one form of activity among many. The unity and essential interdependence between political and other kinds of struggle had thus been ruptured. And, as Royden Harrison has rightly insisted, mid-Victorian working-class politics were brought into being in relation to increasingly narrowed and limited goals, having lost by the 1860s their earlier association with the creation of an alternative social and political order.[104]

In relation to reformism, labour's advances and the process of 'liberalisation' helped to promote the increasingly widespread belief that the system had changed its stripes, that it had become far more receptive to labour's aspirations, and that the commonsensical way forward lay not in bypassing the system or in planning for insurrection but in grasping those immediate and tangible, if often limted, opportunities for advancement which presented themselves. This changed mentality was captured by Thomas Wright. In 1867 Wright contrasted the working-class 'crusher' mentality — which maintained that all the evils of society were 'entirely attributable to the general wrong-doings and special machinations against them of the rich and powerful' — with that of 'the more literate, intelligent and energetic' workers:

> Hugging themselves in this belief they [the 'crushers'] remain stationary, grumbling at their position, but refusing to 'move on', and are a millstone about the neck of the more literate, intelligent and energetic section of the working class, who have learned, and are striving to carry out the principle that workingmen themselves must be the chief workers in achieving their own elevation, and that self-denial and self-improvement are primary means to the desired end.[105]

Self-help did not, however, signify that genuine help, as opposed to condescending patronage, from other groups and classes would be rejected. And in the eyes of many labour leaders offers of genuine help and friendship had undoubtedly increased since 1850. For example, when Parliament passed legislation in 1862 permitting the formation of a Wholesale Co-operative Society, the committee of co-operators which had lobbied for the legislation saw this as, 'another proof that when the working classes are earnestly bent on measures for improving their condition, the higher classes . . . do not oppose them, but give them a cheerful helping hand'.[106] And Ernest Jones believed that all classes had become more 'reasonable', more readily given to compromise after 1850. In 1868 Jones declared:

> Seventeen years ago each class in this country was fighting single-handed, and perhaps in antagonism to others. We then called our opponents hard names, and our opponents called us the same. But that has changed, and we have learned not to abuse but to reason together; and the result of that reasoning is that rich and

poor, employer and employed, moderate Liberal and advanced, now stand united upon the same platform for one common object, the prosperity of each through the good of all.[107]

The full influence of reformist ideas and practice was reflected in the changed direction of working-class institutions. As a number of historians have observed, the 'break' was most marked in relation to the Co-operative Movement. Certain aims of co-operation — the provision of unadulterated food, opposition to the credit system, and the encouragement of education, independence, personal decency, domestic happiness and the benefits of collective association — remained strong during the third quarter. Pollard has, however, conclusively demonstrated that the wider ideals of consumer co-operation faded, often unconsciously, into 'misty vagueness'.[108] Dreams of the New Moral World retreated before the advance of the more mundane, but more successful preoccupation with 'rising in society' and collecting the 'divi'. The price of 'success' was thus a narrowing of aim. A leading figure at the Stockport society could criticise the 'utopian' aspects of Owenism without fear of rebuke: 'The social schemes of Robert Owen may have had their merits, but it [sic] was dark and incomprehensible, and had signally failed'.[109] And an address presented to Gladstone by members of the Oldham Co-operative Society in 1868 read:

In the earlier part of Mr. Owen's days co-operation was looked upon as a dream of enthusiastic, theoretical writers; now, such of our friends as Mr. Mill, who have long echoed the noblest aspirations of the people, and who view co-operation as the most promising of all agencies in operation to elevate the working class, have the pleasure of finding it the feted theme of Social Science Congresses, and looked upon as the mediator between labour and capital.[110]

Leading co-operators in the 1860s frowned upon social levelling. Co-operation aimed to prosper, 'not by pulling down the rich — excepting those who are rich with ill-gotten gains — but by lifting up the poor'.[111] Official handbooks of the movement stressed that co-operation sought not to, 'set class against class, but rather to build up and promote that sympathy and friendship, which is of such vital importance to the national welfare'.[112] Workers were thus to be encouraged to 'rise' without infringing the property rights of others. The leadership was also unsparing in its criticisms of social and industrial conflict, of antagonistic trade unions and employers, and set itself up as the promoter of industrial peace and harmony. The means whereby anachronistic class conflict was to be ended was co-operative production. Debates concerning co-operative production occupied a central place in the movement from the 1860s to the 1880s. The widespread belief among co-operators was that co-operative production, by extending share ownership to the working class and paying a bonus to the workers involved in production, would 'substitute a citizenship of the workshop for a system of hired servitude'.[113] Thus at the 1875 Co-operative Congress Abraham Greenwood, in his 'teens a Chartist and later a Rochdale Pioneer, declared that it was the task of the movement to continue the work begun by the Pioneers to 'emancipate their class from the position of merely hired labourers'.[114] In practice, however, the content of such rhetoric was far less radical than at first might appear to be the case, and was certainly not, by the late 1860s, Owenite in inspiration. Whilst, for example, a few of the Oldham Limiteds — which were regarded as 'the exemplary forms of co-operative production' during the 1870s and 1880s — did pay a 'bonus to labour' and were governed upon a one-man-one-vote basis, they were basically, as Schatz notes, ordinary joint-stock manufacturing companies.[115] By the 1880s few manual workers held shares in the 'Limiteds,' and 'bonus to labour' schemes were, more often than not, a matter of fierce disagreement within the movement, being short-lived and far from common. Thus the historian of co-operative production could find only 24 out of the 222 productive societies registered between 1850 and 1880 which allocated a proportion of their profits to their workers.[116] In 1862 the abolition of the bonus system by stockholders, at the Pioneers Mitchell Hey Company moved William Cooper, a veteran Rochdale Owenite and co-operator, to declare:

> Working men . . . must speak with bated breath in denouncing the oppression and tyranny of capitalists, else someone will point to the rapacity of certain working men in Rochdale, who, on becoming employers of labour, took the bounty off their work-people at the so-called co-operative mill.[117]

In 1869 the famous Sun Mill Company introduced a bonus to labour. Stockholders voted to end the scheme in 1875, believing that 'it was incapable of affecting the purpose for which it was intended'. It had failed to persuade workers to work harder.[118] In addition, working conditions and systems of management in the Limiteds did not generally differ from those in operation in family firms or partnerships. Finally, some unscrupulous employers were not above exploiting co-operative production as an anti-union device.[119]

In practice, therefore, co-operation increasingly took much of its colouring from the society in which it flourished. As E.O. Greening recognised in 1870, profit-making had become a respectable form of endeavour:

> Societies in 1850 realised that their main object was to make men of their members, and regarded the making of profits, the production of wealth, as only a means to this end. Since that time they have to a great extent 'given in to the prevailing heresy of our day', and treated the making of profits and the production of wealth as the end and not the means.[120]

It is highly questionable as to whether the 'break' in trade union ideology and practice was so sharp as in the case of co-operation. As Royden Harrison has written, 'Whether or not one discerns a basic continuity in Trade Union history during the second and third quarters of the nineteenth century largely depends on what one is interested in'.[121] At the level of local workshop practices matters probably changed little, but, in contrast to the second quarter, the trade union movement was increasingly dominated by the generally cautious and 'responsible' craft unions which had held aloof from attempts at general union and, often, from involvement in radical political movements. At the level of ideology, the wage-earner-capitalist relationship was generally accepted as given, and there took place 'a reconciliation with the new order'.[122] The capacity to wage, on occasion, militant industrial struggles could not obscure this reconciliation. As we will see in Chapter 6, developments in trade unionism throughout the cotton districts paralleled, in many ways, those taking place nationally. Industrial conflict continued to exist, often at a high level of intensity, in the cotton districts and employers, especially in south Lancashire, put up fierce opposition to union recognition (especially of the unskilled and semi-skilled). But against such developments, trade union leaders were intent upon generating a moderate public image, were keen to demonstrate the advantages of reason over force, were careful to keep their unions free from 'political' involvement, and did indeed operate upon the assumption that the system had become an established fact of life.[123]

Friendly society leaders were also keen to publicise their 'soundness', moderation and strong sense of personal and social responsibility. Mainly in order to dispel any lingering doubts as to their loyalty to the system, the friendly societies attached growing importance to the cultivation of a patriotic image. The Oddfellows, for example, exhorted their members to join the Volunteer Force. 'Only think how much it would redound to the credit of the unity', declared the *Oddfellows Magazine* in 1861, 'if . . . among the enrolled corps there were about fifteen thousand Oddfellows, or about five per cent of the Order'. Still, the society could be proud of the fact that, 'everywhere there is a goodly sprinkling of Oddfellows in nearly every volunteer regiment'.[124] The Oddfellows contributed generously to the Patriotic Fund in 1854, and in 1863 various lodges of the order celebrated the marriage of the Prince of Wales. In Manchester meetings were often addressed by prominent volunteers, and the national anthem was sung with great gusto.[125] A similar state of affairs existed in the other affiliated societies. The Forresters boasted of their loyalty to the throne, and counselled their members to be patriotic and peaceful citizens.[126] In sum, the friendly societies thus made strenuous efforts to convince the establishment that their members were 'good conservers of the constitution'.[127]

Protestations of loyalty and patriotism were not confined to friendly societies: rather they were part of the public image projected by more or less all sections of the labour movement during the third quarter. Appeals to patriotism were, of course, not new in organised working-class circles. Chartism had fully and successfully utilised a tradition of radical patriotism to swell support for the movement and to expose the 'unpatriotic' and 'selfish' actions of aristocrats, manufacturers and others opposed to an acceptance of the 'natural' political and other rights of 'the people'.[128] This tradition of radical patriotism did not completely disappear in mid-Victorian Britain; and we would be mistaken to suggest that movements such as the Volunteers attracted large working-class involvement primarily upon militaristic and jingoistic grounds. As Cunningham has convincingly shown, manual workers joined the Volunteers mainly on account of the opportunities offered for recreation. Nevertheless, it is also worth noting Cunningham's overall conclusion that, '. . . the vocabulary of [radical] patriotism came less instinctively to the lips of radicals in the third quarter of the century than it had done throughout the first half; and by the late 1870s the shift of patriotism to the political right had become established'.[129]

The direction and content of working-class radical politics were also reflective of workers' diminished dissatisfaction with their lot. As seen earlier, independent working-class politics were less totally eclipsed than sometimes supposed, and the movement into Liberalism was not untroubled. Nevertheless, when all such qualifications have been made, there is no doubting, by the late 1860s, the ascendancy of liberal-radicalism over the British labour movement. And, despite the strength of working-class Toryism, the labour movement in the cotton district pledged its majority support to the Liberal Party. For example, with the exceptions of Wood and Nicholson of the Manchester and Salford Trades Council, all of the 130 subjects in our leadership sample for whom political ties are recorded were committed Liberals.

Liberalism appealed to the leaders in our sample for a variety of reasons. At a general level, Liberalism was equated with the ideals of enlightenment, toleration, progress and reason, whereas Toryism signified ignorance, reaction, intolerance and an appeal to the 'baser instincts' of rowdyism, bellicosity and hedonism.[130] A political party which represented aristocratic privilege and monopoly ('the privileges of Wellington boots and the humble and reverent submission of clogs'[131]) and which, despite its actions in 1867, had a strong tradition of opposition to an extension of the franchise, was hardly to the liking of labour leaders who prided themselves upon their progressive views and their sturdy independence which 'fears no influence and obeys no master but the dictates of its own reason'.[132] The causes of political and social reform were increasingly identified with the more 'advanced' sections of Liberalism, and the liberal ideal was interpreted by our leaders as one which placed a premium upon personal and collective advancement upon the basis of merit and character.

Nonconformist religion and the cause of civic improvement also constituted significant paths into Liberalism. As is well known, politics and religion often marched hand in hand in the cotton districts, the connections between, on the one hand, Nonconformity and Liberalism and, on the other, Anglicanism and Conservatism being especially pronounced.[133] Hence the significance of the fact that the vast majority of leaders in our sample embraced the causes of civil and religious liberty, and many were active Nonconformists (Unitarianism, followed in descending numerical order by New Connexion Methodism, Primitive Methodism and Weslyan Methodism, attracted the greatest support). Just as our leaders were drawn to a social philosophy which promised advancement upon the basis of merit and character, so they were attracted to religious beliefs 'that placed simple faith above doctrinal erudition and held saving grace free in all and free for all'.[134]

At mid-century all shades of political opinion were present in the various campaigns for civic improvement (the building of public libraries, hospitals and town halls, the opening of public parks, attempts at environmental improvement and the like). Nevertheless, of particular prominence was the role played by ex-Chartists, co-operators and other labour leaders in alliance with members of the Liberal Party. In some towns this was not a new development. As Vincent notes, Rochdale and Leeds had traditions of civic improvement of an inter-class character which stretched back to the 1840s.[135] However, in towns such as Stockport, Ashton and Stalybridge, where there had existed conflict between Chartists and middle-class reformers, a marked break did occur. By the 1860s ex-Chartists in these towns had generally moved in the Liberal camp, and were to be found playing an active role in pressing demands for civic improvement and the abolition of property qualifications for town councillors.[136] Once again, friendly and co-operative societies were often involved — frequently donating to funds for the establishment of hospitals, and impressing upon their members their civic duties as responsibly-minded citizens.[137]

Class tensions and considerations were by no means completely erased from the politics of civic improvement. (Were all members of the community to share equally from the provision of hospitals, libraries and parks? Who was to exercise control over matters of general public concern? These were questions which could generate conflicting class interests.) But, despite such a qualification, there is little doubt that the harnessing of working- and middle-class efforts in the cause of civic improvement did much to ease formerly bitter conflicts and to enhance class harmony. All sections of society would henceforth march together 'in the van of progress'. At the ceremony to celebrate the laying of the foundation-stone of the Ashton infirmary, middle- and working-class leaders spoke enthusiastically about the newfound spirit of common purpose and harmony active within the town. J.M. Broadbent, a worker, typified these feelings:

> He rejoiced to see the different classes of society thus brought together, employers and employed working harmoniously together for the general good — this was how it should be.[138]

A renewed outbreak of industrial conflict, a frequent occurrence in mid-Victorian Ashton, could severely test or break hopes for co-operation between employers and workers at the workplace. But, significantly, co-operation at the political level between Ashton's middle-class Liberals and working-class radicals showed a marked increase during the third quarter. Much the same was true of Stockport. The opening of Vernon Park in 1858 elicited an extremely favourable response from all sections of the press and political opinion in the borough. Above all else, it, much like the Great Exhibition in London, had united the community around a matter of common pride. According to the Conservative *Stockport Advertiser*:

> The twentieth of September . . . was a regular English day in Stockport — a day when they saw all classes of society, from the peer of the realm to the humblest peasant, associated together to promote a great and noble object.[139]

A strong sense of civic responsibility was particularly marked among the ex-Chartists and others among our leaders who attained municipal office. And it was frequently the case that considerations of civic pride and improvement successfully cut across party-political allegiances, and demonstrated to our leaders that their political foes shared much of their public-spiritedness. Thus Charles Rowley could thoroughly recommend his experiences as a town councillor in Manchester:

> You come into close touch and often enduring friendship with your finest neighbours and truest citizens. It is an honourable career, not to be despised or avoided by our best men and women.[140]

The movement of Chartists into Liberalism was rarely free from tensions. As noted earlier, mid-Victorian trade unionists and other labour activists continued to criticise the 'tyrannical acts' and 'excessive powers' of capitalists who were often powerful figures in the Liberal Party, and some of the most prominent and 'advanced' Liberals, such as John Bright, could not bring themselves to accept or condone many of the functions of trade unionism.[141] Nevertheless, in comparison with the 1830s and 1840s, criticisms of the forces of capital were increasingly less fierce, aggressive and generalised (whilst individual capitalists still encountered a great deal of hostility, especially during industrial disputes, the capitalist system as a whole met with far less criticism), and those tensions which did persist did not constitute an insuperable barrier to the successful transition from Chartism to Liberalism.

Three major reasons underlay this transition. Firstly, the various advancements and concessions outlined earlier eased overall dissatisfaction with the system. Secondly, as Vincent has shown, there existed places in the cotton districts where Liberalism bore little relation to the traditional Dickensian picture of mean-mindedness and employer domination. At Rochdale, for example, the majority of millowners were Conservatives, and the local Liberal Party was one of expenditure rather than retrenchment (the latter 'built magnificently and worked municipal socialism for twenty years before Chamberlain'[142]). And thirdly, in the cotton districts as a whole, and even in those towns such as Ashton and Stalybridge where considerable working-class opposition to Liberalism persisted throughout the third quarter, the Liberal Party did attempt to improve its appeal to workers by toning down or sometimes abandoning some of the intransigent Whig dogma of the 1830s and 1840s. This mellowing process was uneven and chequered, and has sometimes been exaggerated by historians; but the fact of its existence and its persuasive influence upon the minds of our labour leaders and many others active in the labour movement is beyond doubt. At Ashton, for example, Charles Hindley, Liberal MP for the borough, was critical of the cold, inhuman teachings of orthodox political economy and looked forward, in 1849, to a time when workers 'would cease to be regarded as looms or spindles, or cast metal, and be treated as creatures possessed of souls as well as bodies'.[143] Hindley's support for the Ten Hours Bill, and his generally sympathetic attitude towards radical working-class political demands, won him the respect and friendship of such veteran labour activists as William Aitken and Thomas Pitt.[144] In 1860 an operative wrote to the *Ashton Reporter* that Hindley had been a man, 'who received no end of abuse from enemies and friends to his devotion to the working classes, for whom he would have parted with his last penny'.[145] The tradition established by Hindley was continued by the *Ashton Reporter*. The *Reporter*, which began publication in 1855, supported the causes of factory legisalation, political reform, educational advancement and, at least in principle if not always in practice, trade unionism. Liberalism was presented by the *Reporter* not as a calculating and dogmatic creed, whose gods were solely profit and the market place, but as a broad reforming and progressive movement in which considerations of need and fairness would be combined with economic efficiency. The *Reporter* frequently took exception to the prevailing notions of political economy on the grounds that they ignored the 'human element' in social relationships.[146] Elsewhere, greater attempts were made to accommodate working-class interests. By the 1860s many Liberal employers in south Lancashire had come to accept, and in some cases to openly welcome, the very factory legislation which they had vehemently opposed in the 1840s (the 'final hour' had not arrived and worker 'morale' had improved[147]). And at the 1868 general election Liberal candidates in Lancashire usually supported the notion of protection for trade union funds. Even Jacob Bright, whilst believing trade unions to be mistaken in many of their assumptions, nevertheless paid tribute to their honesty and readiness to put their case to the public.[148] One of Bright's fellow Liberal candidates at Manchester was none other than Ernest Jones, who had been adopted by the party as a means of attracting the working-class vote, and to dispel fears that Liberalism was inimical to trade unionism and factory legislation.[149]

Indeed, in its mellowed form Liberalism won the support of many leading trade unionists. With the exceptions of Wood and Nicholson, all the members of the Manchester and Salford Trades Council were Liberals in 1870.[150] The Trade Union Political Association, formed in Manchester in 1866 by McCleod of the engineers, Shorrocks of the tailors, Price and MacDonald of the housepainters, and Slater of the typographers to muster trade union support for the cause of political reform, threw its weight behind the policies of the Reform League and the Reform Union. In the opinion of McCleod, Conservatism was no friend of trade unionism.[151] And, despite the gains registered by the Conservatives among working-class voters in the late 1860s, many of the leading trade unionists at Stockport, Ashton and Rochdale remained firm Liberals.

This chapter has attempted to identify and examine some of the important material, sociological and institutional roots of reformism. Special emphasis has been attached to the various gains made by labour and concessions from above. In conclusion, I wish to make three further suggestions.

Firstly, as hinted throughout this chapter, the enhanced reformism of the labour leadership was not synonomous with total 'incorporation' into the system. The leadership's continued emphases upon independence, class, or at least corporate, pride, the benefits of collective endeavour and organisation, and their determination to fashion their own destinies irrespective of instructions from above strongly suggest, as Gray notes, that they were far from being 'passive victims of incorporation'.[152] Conflicts of many kinds — cultural, industrial and political — persisted in the cotton districts and elsewhere in Britain, and belied hopes for *complete* social harmony, class reconciliation and smooth inter-class attachment to a system of common values.[153] To quote Gray once again: 'Compromises were uneasy and double-edged, liable to break down and subject to constant re-negotiation'.[154] Even among the co-operative societies' leaders where, as we have observed, the ideology of success and reformism made its deepest imprint, the sparks of revolt and idealism were by no means totally extinguished. In 1861 Pare and Travis could still write:

> The reason why many of us are such ardent supporters of Co-operation is because we believe the present system of society is altogether wrong . . . We see, as it were, a gulf existing between the present system — which we are compelled to denigrate as a system of unmitigated selfishness — and that system of social and political equality which we feel to be in accord with natural justice.[155]

Mr Rowlinson of the Ashton society often reminded members of the revolutionary potential of co-operation:

> He would like to go a step higher than some of the previous speakers had done, because he felt satisfied that unless they took something else into account other than mere abstinence from intoxicating drinks, and getting knowledge, and stores, and large dividends, the freedom of the working class . . . would not be realised. He contended that no man would be free so long as he

was called another man's property, whether as slave in the shape of goods and chattels, or as a paid or hired servant in the name of wages.[156]

Ernest Jones believed himself to be voicing the general sentiments of the Co-operative Movement in his declaration that, by enabling workers to achieve collective advancement, co-operation, 'would render it impossible for any class ever to enslave workingmen again'.[157] And it is by no means uncommon to find co-operative leaders who, whilst exhorting members to imitate capitalists in the cultivation of self-help, denounced the 'tyranny of capital' and strongly advocated the 'distribution of wealth on equitable principles'. In sum, however diluted its actual content as compared with the pre-1850 period, radical language was not uncommon in the mid-Victorian Co-operative Movement.

This leads on naturally to my second point. During the crucial, formative period from the mid-1840s to the late 1850s the growth of reformism among our leaders often took place unconsciously. Wider ideals were not consciously jettisoned, but, in the context of a re-stabilised capitalism in which there existed increased opportunities for piecemeal advancement, they lost much of their force and faded into 'misty vagueness'. As Pollard suggests in relation to Co-operation:

At no time was there a deliberate break with the past, but the ideals of justice, of fair dealing, of banishing poverty and want, were gradually transferred to the day-to-day operation of distribution and, before long, production in Rochdale, while the ultimate ideal of community life receded even farther into the dim future, even among the leaders. Meanwhile, the successful co-operative society was being swamped by members who were attracted by the immediate benefits, without necessarily believing in any social ideal whatever.[158]

From the mid-1850s onwards a largely unconscious process was increasingly transformed into conscious choice. Piecemeal gradualism appeared to be only natural and commonsensical as compared with the 'wild' and 'visionary' schemes of Owenites and Chartists.

Thirdly, however unconscious the transition at mid-century and however inappropriate the notion of incorporation, there is no doubt that the labour leadership and their institutions were no longer complete outsiders but were in the process of developing a 'stake', albeit ambiguous and, at times, tenuous, in the existing system. As E.P. Thompson has observed:

> Each advance within the framework of capitalism simultaneously involved the working class far more deeply in the *status quo*. As they improved their position by organization within the workshop, so they became more reluctant to engage in quixotic outbreaks which might jeopardize gains accumulated at such cost. Each assertion of working-class influence within the bourgeois-democratic state machinery, simultaneously involved them as partners (even if antagonistic partners) in the running of the machine. Even the indices of working-class strength — the financial reserves of trade unions and co-ops. — were secure only within the custodianship of capitalist stability.[159]

Neither hegemonic nor passive in outlook, a reformist labour leadership both reflected and greatly influenced the narrowed perspective of the working class as a whole. And the advances described in this and the previous chapter were instrumental in promoting such change. The next chapter will turn to an examination of the cultural context in which reformism developed, and explore some of the ways in which economic, social and political development interacted with workers' values and attitudes.

Notes

1. F.M. Leventhal, *Respectable Radical: George Howell and Victorian Working Class Politics* (1971); G. Crossick, *An Artisan Elite*, op. cit., pp. 165–73; R.Q. Gray, *The Aristocracy of Labour, op. cit., pp. 30–44;* R. Harrison, *Before the Socialists,* op. cit., esp. pp. 113–19.

2. The following sources have proved invaluable in the collection of biographical data: P. Redfern, *The Story of the C.W.S.* (Manchester, 1913) contains a collective biography of 122 figures active in the CWS during (mainly) the latter part of the nineteenth century, pp. 375–93; J.M. Bellamy and J. Saville (eds), *Dictionary of Labour Biography*, vols. I and II (1972 and 1974) — particularly useful sources for Co-operators. See, esp. vol. I pp. 32–3 (Ashworth), 40 (Bates,) 72–3 (Cheetham), 77–8 (Cooper), 108 (Dyson), 111 (Edwards), 125 (Fox), 136–9 (Greening), 141–2 (Greenwood), 189 (Hooson), 190 (Howarth), 231–2 (Marcroft), 241–2 (Mitchell), 257–8 (Nuttall), 271–3 (Pitman), 302–3 (Smithies), 340–2 (Watts), vol. II, pp. 332 (Schofield). From its inception in 1871 the *Co-operative News* ran biographical sketches of leading figures in the Co-operative and wider Labour Movement. Particularly enlightening are the sketches in the *Co-operative News* for the following dates: 1875 — May 29, p. 295; August 7, pp. 415–16; November, p. 518;

1876 — January 1, p. 7; 1877 — October, p. 568; 1879 — August 9, p. 521; 1881 — March 19, p. 185, October 29, p. 725; 1882 — November 11, p. 764; 1883 — July 7, p. 611; 1885 — October 31, p. 987; 1886 — January 9, p. 41, March 13, October 2, p. 990; 1889 — June 22, p. 652; 1892 — March 5, p. 243; 1893 — March 11, p. 243, November 18, p. 124; 1894 — April 7, p. 374, May 19, July 7, p. 767, September 15; 1895 — January 12, p. 30, January 19, p. 65, March 23, pp. 289-90, August, p. 839, November 9, p. 1182; 1896 — March 7, p. 230, May 2, p. 431; 1897 — March 6, p. 231, March 27, p. 335; 1898 — Febuary 5, p. 151, September 3, p. 991.

3. I have not, however, carried out the kind of detailed search for information on female activists so successfully undertaken by Jill Liddington, Jill Norris and others. For an example of the thorough investigations of Liddington see J. Liddington, 'Looking for Mrs. Cooper', *Bull. N-West Lab. Hist. Soc.*, 7 (1980-1), pp. 17-39.

4. D. Thompson, 'Women and Nineteenth-Century Radical Politics: A Lost Dimension' in J. Mitchell and A. Oakley (eds), *The Rights and Wrongs of Women* (1976), pp. 136-7.

5. J. Liddington and J. Norris, *One Hand Tied Behind Us*, op. cit., pp. 96-9.

6. Ch. 5 below, pp. 215-20: Later in the century the Women's Co-operative Guild did, of course, provide a forum for discussion and action. J. Liddington and J. Norris, op. cit., pp. 40-2, 136-7, 140-2.

7. D. Thompson, op. cit., p. 138.

8. The 20-odd trade unionists being drawn predominantly from the ranks of the craft and skilled. There did, of course, exist considerable overlap between co-operative and friendly society members. This overlap may have been less marked in terms of trade union and co-operative society *leaders* (as opposed to *members*). During the 1860s and for much of the 1870s, when the Co-operative Movement was enamoured of the notion of industrial co-partnership, many co-operative leaders were critical of trade unionists as perpetuators of unnecessary industrial conflict. Only a handful of the CWS activists listed by Redfern were also cited as trade union leaders. And Schatz observes: 'while the membership of trade union branches and co-operative societies often overlapped, in our limited study of the early seventies we have found no local co-operative leaders who were also trade unionists'. R. Schatz, 'Co-operative Production and the Ideology of Co-operation in England, 1870-1895' (unpublished MS, University of Pittsburgh, May 1973).

9. The *Ashton Reporter, Manchester Guardian, Manchester Examiner and Times* and *Ashton Standard* contain valuable information. See the accounts of the life of a veteran activist, William Aitken of Ashton, in *Ashton Reporter*, 2 October 1869; *Manchester City News*, 28 September, 1869; *Oddfellows Magazine*, July 1857, p. 13.

10. P. Redfern, op. cit., pp. 375-93.

11. J. Foster, *Class Struggle*, op. cit., p. 222.

12. For Marcroft see, R.E. Tyson, 'William Marcroft (1822-94) and the Limited Liability Movement in Oldham', *Trans. Lancs. Ches. Antiqu. Soc.*, vol. 80 for 1979 (1980); W. Marcroft, *The Marcroft Family. A Histroy of Strange Events* (Rochdale, 1889); J.C. Taylor, *The Jubilee History of the Oldham Industrial Co-operative Society Limited 1850-1900* (Manchester, 1900), pp. 18, 37, 102, 129, 138, 170; *Co-operative News*, 15 September 1894; *Oldham Co-operative Record*, no. 3, July 1894; J.M. Bellamy and J. Saville, op. cit., I, pp. 231-3.

13. R.E. Tyson, op. cit., p. 62.

14. Ibid., p. 64.

15. Ibid., p. 75.

16. J. Foster, op. cit., pp. 212-24.

17. R.E. Tyson, op. cit., pp. 62, 78.

18. *Co-operative News*, 22 June 1889, p. 652; *Oldham Co-operative Record*, May 1894.

19. P. Redfern, op. cit., p. 382; *Oldham Co-operative Record*, August 1894.
20. *Co-operative News*, 23 March 1895, pp. 289–90.
21. J.M. Bellamy and J. Saville, op. cit., I, pp. 241–2.
22. *Co-operative News*, 23 March 1895; P. Redfern, op. cit., p. 386.
23. J.M. Bellamy and J. Saville, op. cit., I, pp. 32–3.
24. *Co-operative News*, 19 January 1895.
25. J.M. Bellamy and J. Saville, op. cit., I, pp. 72–3.
26. Ibid., pp. 77–8.
27. *Co-operative News*, 2 October 1886, p. 990.
28. Ibid., August 1895, p. 839.
29. *Ashton Reporter*, 10 January 1885; S. Hill, op. cit., pp. 272–3.
30. *Co-operative News*, 5 March 1892, p. 243.
31. P. Redfern, op. cit., p. 376; Bellamy and Saville, op. cit., I, p. 38.
32. C.A.N. Reid, thesis, op. cit., p. 235.
33. *Co-operative News*, 6 March 1897, p. 231.
34. Ibid., 27 March 1897, p. 335; Bellamy and Saville, op. cit., I, pp. 40–1.
35. *Co-operative News*, 7 March 1896, p. 230.
36. Ibid., 2 May 1896, p. 431.
37. Bellamy and Saville, op. cit., I, p. 189.
38. *Co-operative News*, November 1875, p. 578; P. Redfern, op. cit., p. 379; *Alliance Weekly News*, 11 Febuary 1865; Bellamy and Saville, op. cit., I, p. 125.
39. *Co-operative News*, 19 March 1881, p. 185, October 29 1881, p. 725; Bellamy and Saville, op. cit., I, p. 111.
40. G. Crossick, *Artisan Elite*, op. cit., Chs 8 and 9; R.Q. Gray, *The Labour Aristocracy in Victorian Edinburgh*, op. cit., Ch. 6.
41. For Carter see, M.R. Dunsmore, op. cit., p. 157.
42. Ibid., p. 112.
43. *Co-operative News*, 7 August 1875, pp. 415–16.
44. For the importance of the notion of 'manliness' among nineteenth-century workers see, D. Montgomery, 'Workers Control of Machine Production in the Nineteenth Century', *Labor History*, vol. 17, Fall 1976, esp. pp. 491–2.
45. B. Wilson, op. cit., p. 212.
46. R.E. Tyson, op. cit., p. 63.
47. For meanings of respectability see R.Q. Gray, *The Labour Aristocracy in Victorian Edinburgh*, op. cit., Ch. 7. Also Ch. 5 below.
48. See David Montgomery's criticisms of Gerald Grob's belief that there existed sharp ideological differences between trade unionists and social reformers in the *post-bellum* American labour movement. G. Grob. *Workers and Utopia* (New York, 1969); D. Montgomery, *Beyond Equality* (New York, 1972), pp. 172–96, 441–7.
49. *Co-operative News*, 19 May 1894, pp. 551–2.
50. M.R. Dunsmore, op. cit., p. 112.
51. *Co-operative News*, 27 March 1897, p. 335.
52. See, for example, J. Foster, *Class Struggle*, op. cit., pp. 213–24.
53. See Ch. 5 below.
54. R. Schatz, 'Co-operative Production and the Ideology of Co-operation in England, 1870–1895' (unpublished MS, University of Pittsburgh, May 1973).
55. Ibid., pp. 32–40.
56. J.M. Bellamy and J. Saville, op. cit., I, pp. 271–2.
57. *Co-operative News*, 18 November 1893, p. 124.
58. Ibid., 12 January 1895, p. 30.
59. R. Schatz, op. cit., p. 38. For Watts see, Bellamy and Saville, op. cit., I, pp. 340–1; *Manchester City News*, 9, 16, 23 July and 6, 13, 20 and 27 August 1864 for Watts's attacks upon trade unionism.
60. For Greening see, Bellamy and Saville, op. cit., I, pp. 136–9; M.R. Dunsmore,

op. cit., p. 96; T. Crimes, *Edward Owen Greening: A Maker of Modern Co-operation* (Manchester, 1923).

61. R. Schatz, op. cit., p. 18.
62. Ibid., p. 39.
63. See, for example, *Co-operator*, March 1861 and June 1861.
64. R. Harrison, *Before the Socialists*. op. cit., pp. 6, 13–15, 34.
65. H.A. Turner, op. cit., pp. 123–38.
66. A.E. Musson, *British Trade Unions*, op. cit., p. 63.
67. P.H.J.H. Gosden, *Self-Help: Voluntary Associations in Nineteenth-Century Britain* (1973), p. 63.
68. Ibid., p. 74.
69. Ibid., pp. 39–40.
70. S. Pollard, 'Nineteenth Century Co-operation: From Community Building to Shopkeeping' in A. Briggs and J. Saville (eds), *Essays in Labour History*, vol. I (1960), pp. 74–112; R. Schatz, op. cit.; L. Jones, *Co-operation; its Position, its Policy and its Prospects* (1877); A. Bonner, *British Co-operation* (Manchester, 1970), Ch. 4; G.D.H. Cole, *A Century of Co-operation* (Manchester, 1944), V.
71. R. Schatz, op. cit., p. 81 (Table II).
72. D.A. Farnie, op. cit., p. 154.
73. R. Schatz, op. cit., p. 21.
74. P.H.J.H. Gosden, op. cit., p. 188.
75. Ibid., p. 186.
76. Ibid., pp. 195–6.
77. Ibid., p. 188.
78. B. Wilson, op. cit., p. 226; K. Tiller, 'Late Chartism: Halifax 1847–58' in Epstein and Thompson, op. cit., pp. 213–16.
79. C. Walton, *History of the Oldham Equitable Co-operative Society Ltd. From 1850 to 1900* (Manchester, 1900); *Handbook of the Sixteenth Annual Co-operative Congress 1885* (Oldham, 1885), pp. 73–81; *Co-operator*, 1 February 1867, 30 October 1868, 16 January 1869.
80. Ibid., 15, 29 January 1870, 28 January 1871.
81. For the rapid growth of the CWS see, P. Redfern, op. cit., Chs IV–VII.
82. *Co-operator*, 15 August 1866.
83. For co-operation in Stockport see ibid., no. 13, June 1861, 1 August 1866; *Stockport Advertiser*, 27 April 1861; *Stockport County Express Supplement*, 28 April 1960.
84. *Co-operator*, 30 January 1869.
85. Ibid., 11 March 1871.
86. B. Wilson, op. cit., p. 229.
87. Ibid., p. 40.
88. *Co-operator*, no. 47, January 1864.
89. Ibid., 1 February 1867.
90. Ibid., 23 January 1869.
91. Ibid., June 1861.
92. Ibid., May 1861.
93. Ibid., 1 November 1866.
94. J. Foster, *Class Struggle*, op. cit., 7.
95. R. Harrison, op. cit., p. 133.
96. Ibid., p. 39.
97. See Ch. 6 below for employers; Ch. 7 for Conservatism; and pp. 161–5 below for Liberalism.
98. Ch. 6 below, pp. 296–7.
99. E.J. Hobsbawm, *Labouring Men*, op. cit., pp. 337–8.
100. P.H.J.H. Gosden, op. cit., pp. 63–90, 190–5.
101. G.S. Jones, 'The Language of Chartism', op. cit., pp. 49–52.

102. E.J. Hobsbawm, op. cit., p. 336.

103. G.S. Jones, op. cit., p. 15.

104. R. Harrison, op. cit., p. 3.

105. T. Wright, *Some Habits and Customs of the Working Classes* (New York, 1967), pp. 35-6.

106. R. Schatz, op. cit., p. 44.

107. *Manchester Guardian*, 17 November 1868.

108. S. Pollard, op. cit., pp. 97ff.

109. *Co-operator*, September 1860, p. 50, October 1860, p. 3.

110. Ibid., January 1868, p. 17.

111. Ibid., June 1861, p. 1; S. Pollard, op. cit., p. 98.

112. *Working Men Co-operators* (Manchester, 1914), pp. 21-2; *Co-operator*, August 1860, p. 38.

113. See, for example, E.O. Greening's article, 'How Far is it Desirable and Practicable to Extend Partnerships of Industry?' in *Nat. Asstn. Prom. Soc. Sc.* (1870).

114. R. Schatz, op. cit., p. 42.

115. Ibid., pp. 10-12, 49.

116. B. Jones, *Co-operative Production*, vol. I (Oxford, 1894), p. 147.

117. R. Schatz, op. cit., p. 13.

118. Loc. cit.

119. For the details of such employer schemes see, Kirk, thesis, pp. 190-2; R.A. Church, 'Profit Sharing and Labour Relations in England in the Nineteenth Century', *Int. Rev. Soc. Hist.*, XVI, Part I, 1971, p. 16.

120. *Working Men Co-operators*, op. cit., p. 65.

121. R. Harrison, op. cit., p. 13.

122. Ibid., p. 14.

123. See Ch. 6 below.

124. *Oddfellows Magazine*, January 1861, p. 53, October 1863, p. 194. Originally envisaged as a military institution for the middle class, the Volunteer Force became a largely working-class institution between 1860 and 1870. H. Cunningham, *The Volunteer Force: A Social and Political History 1859-1908* (1975), esp. Ch. 2.

125. *Manchester Courier*, 18 November 1854; *Oddfellows Magazine*, April 1863, pp. 69-70, October 1863, p. 194.

126. *Manchester City News*, 2 April 1864.

127. *Oddfellows Magazine*, January 1861, p. 53.

128. H. Cunningham, 'The Language of Patriotism', *Hist. Wshp. Jnl.*, 12 (Autumn 1981), p. 17.

129. Ibid., p. 18; H. Cunningham, *The Volunteer Force*, op. cit., pp. 122-3; H. Cunningham, *Leisure in the Industrial Revolution c1780-c1880* (1980), pp. 124, 126-7, 182.

130. J. Vincent, *The Formation of the British Liberal Party*, op. cit., pp. 138-41; H.J. Hanham, 'Liberal organisations for Working Men', *Soc. Stud. Lab. Hist. Bull.*, no. 7 (1963); *Ashton Reporter*, 13 October 1860, 19 September 1868, 13 February 1869.

131. *Ashton Reporter*, 25 June 1859.

132. Ibid., 17 November 1860.

133. E.A. Rose, *Methodism in Ashton-under-Lyne, 1797-1914*, vol. 2 (1969), pp. 63-4; *Ashton Reporter*, 13 February 1869; J. Vincent, op. cit., pp. 145ff.; P. Whitaker, 'The Growth of Liberal Organisations in Manchester from the 1860s to 1903' (unpublished PhD thesis, Manchester University 1956), p. 189; P.F. Clarke, op. cit., pp. 53-75.

134. A similar pattern prevailed in America. D. Montgomery, *Beyond Equality*, op. cit., p. 202.

135. J. Vincent, op. cit., Ch. 2.

136. Ibid., pp. 138ff.; R. Harrison, op. cit., p. 20; *Stockport Advertiser*, 31 January 1868; *Ashton Reporter*, 31 October 1868, 2 October 1869, 5 February 1870.

137. See, for example, *Stockport Advertiser*, 7 January 1859, 17 January 1868; *Oddfellows Magazine*. July 1858, pp. 423–7.

138. *Ashton Reporter*, 6 August 1859.

139. *Stockport Advertiser*, 22 April 1859.

140. C. Rowley, *Fifty Years of Work Without Wages* (1911), p. 54.

141. *Ashton Reporter*, 17, 24 November, 29 December 1860.

142. J. Vincent, op. cit., p. 145.

143. *Manchester Examiner and Times*, 27 January 1849.

144. *Ashton Reporter*, 2 October 1869.

145. Ibid., 22 September 1860.

146. Ibid., 26 January 1861.

147. See Aitken's letter in ibid., 30 January 1869.

148. *Manchester Guardian*, 10 October 1868.

149. Jones failed to be elected to parliament. J. Vincent, op. cit., p. 113.

150. L. Bather, 'A History of the Manchester and Salford Trader Council', (unpublished PhD thesis, Manchester University, 1956), pp. 52ff.

151. *Manchester City News*, 2 November 1867.

152. *Soc. Stud. Lab. Hist. Bull.*, no. 40 (Spring 1980), p. 7.

153. See, for example, Chs 5 and 6 below.

154. *Soc. Stud. Lab. Hist. Bull.*, no. 40 (Spring 1980), p. 7.

155. *Co-operator*, July 1861.

156. *Ashton Reporter*, 10 August 1861.

157. *Co-operator*, 2 January 1869.

158. S. Pollard, op. cit.; E.J. Hobsbawm, *Labouring Men*, op. cit., p. 342 (note 4).

159. E.P. Thompson, 'The Peculiarities of the English' in *The Poverty of Theory*, op. cit., p. 71.

5 RESPECTABILITY

Approaches and Debates

The deep attachment of an élite of skilled workers and the labour leadership to the ethic of respectability in mid-Victorian Britain has been well documented by historians.[1] As seen in the last chapter, labour leaders in Lancashire frequently attributed both personal and collective advancement to the assiduous cultivation of the 're-spectable' habits of industry, thrift and sobriety. Yet, whilst we possess a reasonably clear and detailed picture of the culture of the upper sections of the working class, our knowledge and under-standing of the possibly wider appeal of respectability to a mass working-class constituency is extremely limited. Joyce has laid brief claim to the mass character of respectability throughout the cotton districts and the existence of a 'broad, shared culture' among workers which, we are informed, negates Foster's belief in 'internecine cultural strife' between 'aristocrat' and 'undermass'.[2] And various other contributors to the labour aristocracy debate have suggested that respectability probably extended beyond the confines of any such aristocracy.[3] Hobsbawm has made the crucial observation that the distinction between labour élites and the larger bodies of respectable, regularly employed workers remains 'fuzzy', and that, 'If the concept of a labour aristocracy as a separate stratum was vulnerable, this fuzziness constituted its Achilles' heel'.[4] Unfortunately, such interesting and potentially fruitful claims, suggestions and observations have, all too often, been tantalisingly brief and somewhat lacking in adequate empirical support.

The purpose of this chapter is to take a tentative step towards filling this gap in our understanding of nineteenth-century working-class culture. Central focus rests upon the nature, appeal and mean-ings of respectability in the cotton districts. The chapter addresses itself to the following questions. Was respectability the sole or main preserve of an 'aristocratic' élite of workers, or did it cast its net wider? If the latter was the case, what then becomes of the notion of a sharp cultural division between labour aristocrats and the mass of working people? Might it not be pertinent to follow Hobsbawm's lead in asking whether the most important division within the mid-Victorian working class was between 'a much larger stratum of respectable workers, which included the labour aristocracy, and the unrespectable workers or 'the poor'?[5] What were the meanings and content of working-class respectability; and what kind(s) of relationship(s) existed between middle- and working-class 'respectables'? Were, for example, sections of the middle class successful in diffusing their highly individualistic version of respectability throughout the working class? Or was the worker's respectability part of an indigenous working-class culture, which was separate from, and largely impervious to, outside attempts to determine its character and direction?[6]

As the reader will be aware, the frequently scanty and incomplete nature of the evidence available to the student of nineteenth-century working-class culture renders many of the answers attempted to the questions posed above highly tentative in character. An immediate, and probably the major, obstacle facing this particular study is that, while it is relatively easy to piece together information concerning the occupations of the leadership of co-operative and friendly societies and other vehicles of specifically working-class respectability, it is far more difficult to present a clear and detailed picture of the membership of these organisations.[7] Many organisations simply did not record occupations; and, of those that did, the information provided is often incomplete. A survey of material relating to the Co-operative Movement failed to unearth, for example, a single co-operative society in the cotton districts which had kept long-term detailed occupational records of all members, passive as well as active ones. Furthermore, we must remember that while the records of these organisations provide a relatively clear guide to the attitudes of the leadership, they often furnish only fragmentary and fleeting insights into the thoughts and actions of the rank-and-file membership. Given these difficulties of method and the prominence of 'the rising men of the working class' at the leadership levels of the co-ops, temperance societies and adult education institutes,[8] it is perhaps not surprising that Foster has characterised such institutions as 'labour-aristocratic'. Careful attention must also be paid both to the particular variety of respectability proposed and the identity of the proposer. For, as Gray, Crossick and Tholfsen have persuasively argued, the nature and meanings of respectability were often not uniform throughout society but varied, indeed conflicted, according to class situation and experience.[9]

The following were important vehicles of respectability: the family; those 'patronage' organisations run or controlled by the middle class but intended for a mainly working-class membership or audience (many mechanics institutes, temperance societies and Sunday schools;[10] and a host of educational and 'improving' ventures — including the provision of mutual improvement societies and 'workingmen's classes' attached to churches and chapels; sewing and household management classes for women; libraries; reading rooms; and, increasingly, workingmen's colleges[11]); those organisations which were predominantly working-class in character but which attracted middle-class support and, sometimes, membership (e.g. co-ops[12]); and, finally, those run and controlled by and for manual workers (the majority of friendly societies, co-ops and trade unions, many mutual improvement societies, and some religious — especially Primitive Methodist — [13] and political organisations). As we will see in due course, the occupational composition of these institutions was of crucial importance in determining the particular variety of respectability offered.

The methodological considerations outlined above suggest the advisability of paying close attention to the imperfect evidence at hand and of caution in attempting an overall interpretation of mid-Victorian respectability. Fortunately, problems of method and documentation are not insurmountable. There exists sufficient evidence to enable us to put together a tolerably detailed picture. And the past and current researches of historians provide us with a wealth of hypotheses and questions with which to interrogate the evidence. Indeed, before turning to the Lancashire and Cheshire experience, it is first of all useful to consider three mainly distinct and conflicting interpretations of respectability which, in terms of methods employed and analytical perspectives offered, are of particular relevance to this study.

These interpretations can be summarised in the following way. The first interpretation identifies respectability as a basically middle-class system of values and habits which was adopted by labour aristocrats during the post-Chartist period. At the heart of this perspective lie the notions of social control and 'cultural capture'.[14] By way of contrast, the second interpretation sees respectability as a system of shared values which emerged more or less spontaneously to produce a common culture transcending class lines. An insistence upon the complex and ambiguous nature of respectability characterises the third interpretation — mid-Victorian working-class respectability constituting, on the one hand, class pride, independence and opposition to middle-class control and, on the other, conscious dissociation from the non-respectable and acceptance of the broad contours of a socio-cultural world dominated by the middle class. I suggest that the work of Foster exemplifies the first interpretation; that of Laqueur and B. Harrison the second; and, despite some important differences of assumption and approach, that of J.F.C. Harrison, Tholfsen, and Gray and Crossick the third.[15]

In both his dissertation and his book, Foster[16] forcibly argues that in the aftermath of Chartism the labour aristocrats in Oldham were quickly and effectively won over to bourgeois values. These aristocrats, we are told, turned in their co-ops, adult education and temperance societies to 'improvement', and in doing so they came firmly within the cultural orbit of the local bourgeoisie and consciously practised social assimilation. This alleged process involved, 'the ritualistic assimilation of bourgeois values, an acceptance of bourgeois class attitudes, and above all the equation of social evil and the working class'.[17] According to Foster, the spinners and other aristocrats acted as the system's 'messenger boys and interpreters in the labour community'. They 'actively disseminated the culture of their employers', and distanced themselves from the friendly society and pub-based culture of the mass of workers. The labour aristocracy thus became incorporated into the system, and the working class in Oldham hopelessly fragmented along the lines of abstinent, 'improving' aristocrats versus beer drinking and 'non-improving' mass. It is worth noting that Foster is by no means alone in drawing attention to the social control aspect of respectability. Hence J.F.C. Harrison believes that:

> By the fifties and sixties the middle classes had been wonderfully effective in suffusing their ideals and precepts throughout the 'lower orders'. They had established among the more prosperous sections of the working classes the goal of respectability . . .[18]

Despite their various disagreements with Foster, Gray and Crossick also note the widespread existence of a conscious middle-class attempt to spread their version of respectability among workers, particularly the skilled.[19] However, what distinguishes Foster's approach to this issue from that of Gray and Crossick is the former's insistence that the process of social control and the consolidation of bourgeois hegemony proceeded so rapidly, in such a simple, straightforward manner, and with minimal conflict. Far from offering resistance, Oldham's labour aristocrats are depicted as willingly assuming the collaborative role handed down to them by their bourgeois masters.

Laqueur and Harrison do not share Foster's central emphases upon socal control and the capitulation of the labour aristocracy. Rather, these two historians stress the basically consensual nature of respectability — the way in which industry, thrift and sobriety constituted a common point of attachment for members of both middle and working classes. It is suggested that the emergence of shared values did much to reduce the level of class conflict in mid-Victorian Britain. An unstated implication of this viewpoint is that social order is derived, in true Parsonian fashion, from the emergence and general adoption of unifying norms and value systems.[20] An essentially idealist — as opposed to materialist — theory of culture and social life is offered. Thus Laqueur, whilst noting that Sunday schools were, 'to some extent an agency of bourgeois moral imperialism' and that 'on paper the ideal Sunday school child was certain to grow up into the ideal capitalist man or woman',[21] nevertheless ultimately and forcibly rejects the view that Sunday schools acted primarily as institutions of social control and ideological manipulation. In Laqueur's opinion, Sunday schools were increasingly internally controlled and run by the working-class scholars and teachers; the bourgeois boards of managers rarely imposed their political views upon the scholars and teachers;[22] and the values and patterns of behaviour generated within the schools — 'honesty, orderliness, punctuality, hard work and refinement of manners and morals' — may all have been 'congruent with the industrial system and thus in the interest of the bourgeoisie, but they were not therefore middle-class values'.[23] Rather, such values appealed directly to the respectable, and often ambitious, within all social groups. Thus Laqueur can declare:

> It is scarcely surprising that working-class leaders should have adopted so readily the ethic traditionally associated with the entrepreneurial middle class; the personality traits of the successful businessman are, after all, not very different from those of the successful political leader, journalist or trade-union militant.[24]

Furthermore, claims Laqueur, social conflict in early nineteenth-century England issued primarily not from the economic and other determinations of class but from the status considerations of life-style and personality type:

> The great divisions in early C19 society were not between the middle and working classes but between the idle and non-idle classes, between the rough and respectable, between the religious and non-religious. All of these divisions ran across class lines. The puritan ethic was therefore not the monopoly of the owners of capital; it was the ideology of those who worked as against those who did not. Sunday schools were effective in the transmission of certain values precisely because these values were those of the working-class men and women who taught in and supported the schools.[25]

Although not given to such grandiose claims, and more alive than Laqueur to the complex relationships between leisure and work, Brian Harrison nevertheless believes that a common commitment to respectable values increasingly brought together at mid-century liberal-minded workers of the Lovett and Lowery stamp and middle-class radicals such as Bright. Both groups shared:

> . . . a distaste for mobs, and a repudiation of the whole complex of behaviour associated with race courses, fairs , wakes, brothels beerhouses and brutal sports. He [the 'respectable' artisan] was more likely than his inferiors to vote Liberal, if only because his work situation frequently fostered individualism, self-education and social ambition. If he drank at all he drank soberly, without neglecting his wife and family; he often took his recreation with them and believed that the family should keep itself to itself. He was probably interested in religious matters — often a chapel goer or a secularist. He was strongly attracted by the ideology of thrift, with its stress on individualism, self-respect, personal, moral and physical effort, and prudence.[26]

Harrison's views are not without precedent. In the late nineteenth century the Liberal press imbued, albeit belatedly, Chartism with an aura of respectability. W.H. Chadwick, who moved from Manchester Chartism to Liberalism, typified this approach. Reminiscing in the 1890s, Chadwick claimed that Chartism and Liberalism, with their common commitments to political reform, progress, educational improvement and individual freedom, had been natural allies. The less palatable memories of conflict between Chartists and bourgeois radicals and of torchlight parades and drilling had simply been erased from Chadwick's mind.[27]

The third interpretation, which draws attention to the complexities, ambiguities and potential for conflict at the heart of respectability, can best be demonstrated by reference to the work of Crossick and Gray. Three major claims issue from their respective studies of skilled workers in Kentish London and Edinburgh. Firstly, they suggest that while sections of the middle class did employ respectability as a means of social control, many respectable skilled workers did not passively act out roles and values prescribed from above. Rather, both in Kentish London and Edinburgh, workers were adept at interpreting and reformulating middle-class values to suit their own material needs, and at mediating such values through their own institutions. Most significantly, the skilled workers' respectability often owed little to bourgeois initiatives and exhortations: rather it arose out of the realities of working-class experience, both at work and in the local community. Crossick is particularly concerned to identify respectability as part of an indigenous working-class culture.[28]

Secondly, both authors maintain that a common, inter-class attachment to certain words — especially industry, thrift and sobriety — did not necessarily or automatically signify the existence of a harmonious system of common values. Gray and Crossick argue that the meanings attached to such words could, and often did, vary and conflict according to class situation.[29] Thus, far from signifying a surrender to bourgeois individualism, habits of industry and thrift often constituted practical safeguards against threats of poverty and economic insecurity. Similarly, the artisan's desire to 'rise in the world' only rarely amounted to a wish to escape from the working class. More often than not the 'improvement' aimed at was within the class and was both individual and collective in character — the elevation of skilled workers as a corporate group, and recognition of their claims to a decent standard of living, moral worth and the full rights of citizenship.[30] The collective organisations of the worker — trade unions, friendly societies and co-ops — played a vital role in this process. They attached key importance to working-class control and autonomy — free from the cloying and often condescending attentions of their 'betters'

— and reflected a deepseated commitment to independence. Social approval from other groups and classes was welcomed, but there was massive resistance to the more direct forms of control and subordination. Finally, education constituted a vital tool in the development of independence and opposition to dependence and deference.[31]

In short, Crossick and Gray believe that workers were far less collaborationist than argued by Foster, and that an emphasis upon shared values ignores or underplays important differences in material and mental experience. It is claimed that skilled workers in Edinburgh and Kentish London developed a strong sense of corporate consciousness and pride, and that respectability played a central role in this development. Thus any simple equation between respectability and capitulation to the bourgeoise is believed to be wide of the mark. Bourgeois hegemony, argue Gray and Crossick,[32] was negotiated rather than given: and conflict was at the heart of this process.

Thirdly, Gray and Crossick maintain that, despite its encouragement of group pride, respectability did constitute a source of fragmentation within the working class and that, in the final analysis, the institutions of the skilled worker were confined within a social world dominated by the middle class. The respectable skilled élites in Edinburgh and London consciously dissociated themselves from the less economically favoured and less 'respectable' sections of the working class. The latter were exhorted by the former to practise self-help, and respectability was increasingly harnessed to a moderate socio-political framework. The wider structures of power and domination were not directly challenged, and the onus for improvement was increasingly placed upon the shoulders of the individual. In this sense, argue Crossick and Gray,[33] respectable labour aristocrats did transmit individualistic values to the rest of the working class and came to accept bourgeois hegemony.

This is not the appropriate place to enter into a lengthy evaluation of the three interpretations outlined above. (This exercise will be undertaken once the Lancashire and Cheshire material has been considered.) It is, however, important to note at this stage the central issues and questions raised by these interpretations which will concern us throughout this chapter. In terms, firstly, of the social appeal of respectability it is significant that, with the exception of Laqueur, all the authors direct their attention to the appeal of respectability to labour aristocrats or the upper sections of the working class. The culture of the mass of workers does not receive detailed consideration. Secondly, differences of opinion arise as to whether respectability issued *primarily* 'from above' or 'from within'. To put it another way, was 'experience' of greater importance than 'control' in the development of working-class culture? Thirdly, related questions arise concerning the degrees of success achieved by the middle-class in their attempts to spread their version of respectability amongst manual workers, and the nature and means of consolidation of hegemony. The fourth area of concern rests with the extent and ways in which respectability promoted social harmony and/or conflict. Finally, all the interpretations raise important questions concerning interrelationships between life-style and values and the material conditions of existence. In this latter context the greatest weakness of the approach of Laqueur and others of an idealist persuasion is that 'culture' and 'leisure' are often studied in a vacuum — that is, wrenched loose from their material context. The outcome is a skewed and often highly misleading picture of working-class life which, especially in its neglect of the world of work, underestimates the extent of class tensions and conflicts.[34] After all, the economic and social grievances of workers and the social programme implicit in Chartism drove a firm wedge between 'respectable' Chartists and 'respectable' middle-class reformers in many parts of the country, especially in the manufacturing districts.[35]

Respectability in the Cotton Districts

Middle-class Initiatives

What light do the experiences of the cotton districts throw upon the foregoing issues and questions? Firstly, in relation to the notion of social control and middle-class initiatives, attitudes and cultural practices towards workers, two central developments were in evidence. In contrast to the pre-1850 period, the mid-Victorian middle class adopted an increasingly positive evaluation of the habits and customs of a sizeable section of the working class. Furthermore, efforts were quickened to instruct workers in the middle-class version of respectability.[36] Whether these developments were prompted, either consciously or unconsciously, by thoughts of social control will be considered shortly. What can be said with some certainty at this point is that the decline of Chartism as a mass force, the stabilisation of the economy and the growth of a generally moderate labour movement made significant contributions to changes in middle-class attitudes and behaviour. To be sure, there was continued and loud opposition to the 'wrongheadedness' of trade unions, and the supposed growth in the size of the 'residuum' in the major cities aroused the fears and anxieties of respectable opinion.[37] Nevertheless, there was a growing recognition, most marked among Liberal politicians and the Liberal press, that the working class was not an undifferentiated mass, and that large numbers of operatives were daily becoming more 'moderate' and 'temperate', more 'reasonable' and 'responsible', both in their domestic lives and in their outlook upon the world.

This mellowed attitude was lucidly and forcibly expressed by the *Ashton Reporter*, an organ of radical Liberalism.[38] In 1859 the *Reporter* addressed itself to an examination of, 'one of the most important sections of English society — the industrious and intelligent artisans of our cities and manufacturing districts':

It is this class which John Bright, and all the reformers with him, desire to see put in possession of the electoral power, and it is hardly surprising that they should be ignored by other politicians, since their existence is almost unknown to them. Mr Disraeli's idea of a working man is the model labourer of some farmers' club, who is rewarded with a green coat and sovereign for having brought up a large family without parish aid; and he is barely conscious of the existence of a class of men who would count such honours insults . . . Of other political leaders . . . they are ignorant of the condition of the people . . . The philanthropists in their researches also miss this section of the community. They dive below them to the depths of misfortune and vice, and when they have fished up some unhappy specimen of a drunkard or fallen upon some poor waif stranded upon the shores of social misery, they cry out, 'Behold the true state of the working classes!' Never do our statesmen or our would be philanthropists seem to take into consideration the multitude of families where religion, cleanliness and virtue find congenial abodes, or the many thousands of religious and active members of society who labour for their daily bread . . . The working men are no longer . . . regarded as wild beasts, to be salted for the satisfaction of the upper classes . . . We could get along without peers or princes, but we cannot do without working men. Theirs is the one interest hitherto unrepresented which is essential to the stability and prosperity of the state.[39]

The *Reporter* believed that the unenfranchised were, 'freeing themselves from socialist and infidel delusions', and sought not, 'the predominance of their own class above every other', but, 'the removal of class interests . . . justice, and a fair recognition of their well-founded claims to equality in the constitution'.[40] The *Reporter*'s message was thus loud and clear: enfranchise the loyal, industrious and self-respecting portion of the working class or risk their dissatisfaction and a resurgence of class conflict on a scale reminiscent of the 1840s.

During the 1860s the *Reporter*'s views found increased support in the press and among politicians. In 1863 *Fraser's Magazine* noted that workers were 'a more rational and better conducted class than they were fifty years ago, and as a rule will not be guilty of desperate and insensate actions'.[41] John Bright, enraptured by the activities of the 'self-helping, self-educating working man with his cooperative society, savings bank and chapel' and the fortitude and restraint displayed by cotton operatives during the Cotton Famine, believed that it would be foolhardy to exclude these operatives from the franchise.[42] Gladstone agreed: working men had become, 'our fellow-subjects, our fellow-Christians, our own flesh and blood . . .'.[43]

A softening of attitudes towards workers was part of a wider mellowing of that austere *laissez-faire* social vision of the pre-1850 period. As Harrison and Joyce have demonstrated, it was among the larger employers of labour that the desire to bridge the gulf between classes was often at its strongest.[44] Trips and treats, the provision of libraries, reading rooms and other paternalistic ventures, and an enhanced willingness to accommodate the interests of the labour movement were examples of the 'new spirit'.[45] Also important were the playing down of methods of physical force and an accelerated development of the methods of intellectual and moral improvement. As Tholfsen has noted:

No longer obsessed with the coercion and indoctrination of refractory working men, the middle classes instead invited them to join in the common enterprise of social and economic advancement and intellectual and moral improvement. Instead of merely deploring the vices of the working classes, middle-class spokesmen began to talk of the avenues to virtue and knowledge that were open to all . . .[46]

In the cotton towns attempts to reach the working class assumed renewed vigour. Members of the middle class busily established lecture and reading rooms for workers, opened public libraries with much self-congratulation and public fanfare and patronised mechanics institutes, lyceums, mutual improvement societies, co-ops and temperance societies. In the Ashton area many of the leading employers — Mason, Platt, Cheetham, Whittaker, Buckley and Reyner — were prominent figures in the Ashton and Dukinfield Mechanics Institute and at the forefront of the new paternalism.[47]

In Manchester and Salford, Sir John Potter, Canon Richson, Elkanah Armitage, Dr John Watts, W.R. Callender, Hugh Birley, Abel Heywood, John Rylands and Edward Brotherton took an active interest in educational and welfare provision for the working class.[48] The leaders of St Paul's Mutual Improvement Society in Manchester recognised the attempts of sections of the wealthy to bridge the gulf between classes:

Peers, philanthropists, men of science, art and literature now take a deep interest in all their doings, and in most of our large towns there are working men's societies. Nothing is kept sacred from them. They are taken up and down the country to view the scenery. They are constantly invited to visit gentlemen of note at their residences, thus being brought into touch with the classes above them.[49]

A number of motives, both spoken and unspoken, underlay the interventionist strategy of the middle class. Many of the latter were keen to single out Christian kindness and altruism as the principles guiding their action. At the opening of the Manchester Free Public Library in 1852, Sir John Potter declared:

Let it be said that they [manufacturers and merchants] seek not their own advantage, and that they are content merely to make money for themselves. They have afforded you the advantages of lyceums, mechanics institutes, athenaeums, public parks and they have contributed ten thousand pounds towards this library.[50]

In reality, a mixture of fear, guilt, moral obligation and a strong desire to derive full advantage from the newfound moderation of the working class was present in the minds of the middle class. In 1859 F.D. Maurice, the Christian Socialist and an initiator of the Workingmen's College movement, reminded the wealthy of the obligations of property and their Christian duties to the less fortunate. Addressing himself to the effects of social and political upheaval in the 1840s, Maurice admitted:

> It did cause us fear I own; but it was not fear for our own property and position; it was the fear that we were not discharging the responsibilities — greater responsibilities than those which rank or property impose — that our education laid upon us. We believed that what we saw was the handwriting upon the wall, clearly sent to us by God himself; testifying that if either rank, or wealth, or knowledge is not held as a trust for men, if any one of those things is regarded as a possession of our own, it must perish. We believed and felt that unless the classes of this country, which had received any degree of knowledge more than their fellows, were willing to share it among their fellows, England would fall first under anarchy, then under a despotism in which all life would die, death would live, in which all classes would be crushed.[51]

Of crucial importance was the wish to strengthen existing social relationships. Education was designed to give workers a stake in society, a 'feeling that they are understood'. The Mayor of Manchester described the public library as an institution:

> . . . calculated to raise in the scale of civil society, and elevate to the higher ranks those who unfortunately are limited in time and means, to obtain some of the advantages and privileges which those in higher walks and classes of society are endowed . . . I believe that by such means we cement the bonds of society.[52]

Tholfsen has convincingly argued that middle-class efforts to provide workers with a 'stake in society' did not involve significant changes in class structure and opportunities for rapid social mobility:

> Their notion of improvement for all did not involve any blurring

of class lines. They assumed a stratified and static society, which encouraged movement within separate social classes.[53]

In accordance with this middle-class blueprint, the worker, operating with a limited notion of 'success' (the attainment of a basic level of education; the maintenance of a clean, tidy home; constant attention to industry, thrift and sobriety; and a modest improvement in living standards) would aim not at social levelling but at advancement within the existing system. This grand triumph would be achieved under middle-class tutelage. For the middle-class belief in progress was, 'balanced by the hope that rationality and morality would produce men capable of understanding the arguments of their betters, and eager to accept leadership from above'.[54] Deferential virtues — kindness of disposition, gentleness, self-denial and diligence — were to be fostered in the minds of the working class. Schools were to play an important role in this conditioning process:

> . . . supervised by its trusty teacher, surrounded by its playground wall, the school was to raise a new race of working people — respectful, cheerful, hard-working, loyal, pacific, and religious.[55]

Once exposed to the 'elevating' and 'refining' influences of middle-class culture, workers would turn their backs upon the crude and debilitating influences of the public house and its associated influences of gambling, brawling and general bawdiness. Such activities would characterise only the 'ne'er do wells'. Charles Smith, Liberal MP for Stockport, could not suppress his jubilation at the sight of several hundred workers engaged in reading. 'If you have never seen it', he wrote, 'go and get your enthusiasm excited'. Reading and writing were, 'higher pleasures than the beer house or gin shop'.[56] The 'quiet and subdued demeanour' and the 'earnest and rapt attention' of those workers attending the Hallé concerts in Manchester delighted middle-class 'observers'.[57] And David Chadwick, Salford borough's treasurer, stressed the need to:

> . . . encourage and promote the holding of frequent tea meetings and social parties . . . and where the workpeople enjoy the Saturday half-holiday it will be found agreeable to arrange short excursions into the countryside, which the teachers of geology,

chemistry and natural history may render additionally attractive.[58]

The final goal of the middle class was a competitive, individualistic
and acquisitive class-based society in which harmony and 'moderation' would prevail. Increased social intercourse between classes
would mitigate grievances and 'assuage grudges'. The respectable,
educated worker would both adopt the self-help individualism of
his superiors and 'more faithfully discharge his duty' towards his
employer.[59] Successful conditioning would eradicate the remnants
of Chartism and the 'wild visionary' schemes of socialism. John
Potter rejoiced in the knowledge that Owenite meetings would no
longer be held in the building converted into the public library in
Manchester. A.J. Turner, president of the Manchester Mechanics
Institute, expressed his hostility to independent working-class radicalism more forcibly:

> He sincerely believed that in the Mechanics Institutes they were
> raising up the true Conservatives of our country. He said true
> Conservatives. They might be teaching them to understand their
> rights and how to get them, but they were also teaching them how
> to use these rights with prudence and moderation, and he
> believed that they were raising up among them a body of men
> who would love their country, and defend its institutions.[60]

Another speaker advised his audience that, 'It is only books that are
between him [the worker] and the most exaggerated conclusions, the
falsest deductions . . . and the wildest socialism that ever passed
between man and man.[61]

We would be well advised at this point to note that commitments
to education, industry, sobriety and thrift were not the sole preserve
of the middle class. As E.P. Thompson has shown, there developed
during the first half of the nineteenth century an indigenous working-class culture based upon mutuality, self-help, independence and
education which owed little or nothing to bourgeois inspiration.[62]
Education and personal and collective self-help were instrumental in
the development of working-class pride and awareness, vital
elements in the creation of a working-class democratic and
egalitarian social vision which was so strongly at odds with the
middle-class ideals of competition and individualism during the
Chartist period.[63] The cultural endeavours of the middle class at

mid-century posed a serious threat to this indigenous working-class culture. As Tholfsen notes:

> The working-class quest for integrity and self-respect was in danger of being debased into Uncle Tomism. The ideal of independence and emancipation was vulnerable to transmutation into a middle-class version of self-help, exalting an acquisitive materialism at the expense of the old vision of a more egalitarian and equitable society.[64]

In short, the class-conscious Chartist with a passion for knowledge and a belief in the need for fundamental social change was in danger of becoming a moderate, privatised and 'improving' individual.

To what extent did the bourgeoisie succeed in its attempt to re-create the working class in its own respectable likeness? In order to answer this question, we must first of all turn to a consideration of the appeal and character of respectability within the working class.

The Social Base of Respectability

In terms of the social base of respectability, I have gathered together information concerning the occupations of people involved in a number of institutional vehicles of respectability. Despite the various imperfections of the data referred to earlier, there exists sufficient evidence to enable one reasonably to assess the occupational composition of adult education institutions, friendly societies, some co-operative and temperance societies and various religious organisations. To anticipate my major conclusion, I suggest that while the skilled and better-off workers were frequently prominent at the leadership levels of these institutions, nevertheless the general membership was both more mixed and had a far longer occupational tail than some advocates of the labour aristocracy thesis, especially Foster, would have us believe. And, at least in terms of the cotton districts, a picture of a sharp cultural division between 'labour aristocrats' and the rest is not strictly accurate. Rather, it would appear that the crucial cultural division lay increasingly between 'respectables' and 'non-respectables', the latter including many, but by no means all, of the poor, those with 'irregular' habits, and the majority of post-Famine Irish Catholic immigrants.[65]

We can usefully begin by examining the occupational make-up of adult education institutions. There is no doubt that mechanics institutes — when they managed to reach the working class at all[66] — and workingmen's colleges often attracted proportionately few workers below the ranks of the skilled. Ironworkers and printers were conspicuous at Pendleton Mechanics Institute; Liverpool's Institute recruited heavily among clerks and warehousemen; whilst engineers, mechanics, clerks and various professional groups were represented at the Manchester Mechanics Institute.[67] In 1841 membership of the latter included 284 merchants, manufacturers and professional people; 400 clerks, warehousemen, shopkeepers and their assistants; 262 mechanics, millwrights and overlookers; and only 12 millhands.[68]

By 1859 the Working Men's Colleges of Ancoats, Manchester and Salford had a total membership of 500, the majority of whom had skilled, craft, or lower middle-class jobs. At the Manchester Working Men's College, for instance, clerks, warehousemen and bookkeepers made up over half of the members who had paid the entrance fee of 2/6- plus 2/- per class per term: approximately one-third of the members were listed as operatives.[69] At Ancoats, where it was claimed that the teachers were 'mainly workingmen themselves',[70] the fees were set in 1857 at 1/- per month for elementary courses in reading, writing and arithmetic and 2/- per month for the intermediate courses ranging from logic and algebra to French and Latin. The 382 students who attended Ancoats Working Men's College between January and May 1857 included only 36 (9.4 per cent) mill or factory operatives: 86 (22.5 per cent) worked in machine and engine works; 51 (13.3 per cent) in shops or offices; 18 (4.7 per cent) were from the building trades; and 158 (41 per cent) were dyers, print workers, stonemasons, weavers, packers and policemen.[71] The Salford Working Men's College showed a similar bias towards the lower middle class and the higher echelons of the working class. Out of a total membership of 175 in 1858, half were either warehousemen, clerks or packers. Millhands and labourers constituted only 6 per cent of the total, but printers, bookbinders, engravers, draughtsmen, pattern makers, millwrights and mechanics were present in large numbers.[72] Throughout 1859, as demonstrated in Table 5.1, the pattern of occupational representation did not shift in favour of millhands and other non-skilled groups. By 1863 lower middle-class, craft and skilled elements constituted over two-thirds of Salford's membership. And in 1869 the college admitted its failure to reach 'the lower depths of the masses'.[73]

Table 5.1:   Salford Working Men's College: Occupations of Members, 1859

	Term ending March 25		Term ending June 24		Term ending Sept. 29		Term ending Dec. 25	
	Nos. 72	% 40.9	Nos. 70	% 42.4	Nos. 58	% 46.0	Nos. 79	% 42.4
Warehousemen clerks and packers	6	3.4	5	3.0	7	5.5	6	3.2
Printers, engravers and bookbinders	5	2.8	4	2.4	6	4.7	5	2.6
Draughtsmen and pattern makers	23	13.0	21	12.7	14	11.1	24	12.9
Millwrights and mechanics	13	7.3	12	7.2	4	3.1	14	7.5
Carpenters and painters	4	2.2	3	1.8	1	0.7	4	2.1
Shoemakers and tailors	9	5.1	8	4.8	4	3.1	9	4.8
Millhands and labourers	10	5.6	12	7.2	11	8.7	12	6.4
Shopkeepers and shopmen	30	17.0	26	15.7	19	15.0	29	15.5
Miscellaneous occupations	4	2.2	4	2.4	2	1.5	4	2.1
Porters Total:	176	100.0	165	100.0	126	100.0	186	100.0

Source: *Second Annual Report. Salford Working Men's College* (Manchester Cent. Ref.).

Conversely, there exists a substantial body of evidence to suggest that, financial and other circumstances permitting, large numbers of regularly employed, 'non-aristocratic' workers readily partook of available educational opportunities. Even some mechanics institutes had a relatively wide cross-section of working-class members. During the period from 1851 to 1871 an average of 21 per cent of the members of Stockport Mechanics Institute were factory operatives; while at Huddersfield Mechanics the percentage of members employed as factory operatives averaged 32 per cent between 1859 and 1882, and peaked at 47 per cent in 1865. The mechanics institutes at Ashton and Dukinfield, Leeds and Bradford likewise claimed greatly increased operative involvement.[74] Certainly, as Hemming has demonstrated, the introduction of examinable elementary courses (in arithmetic, geography, English history, gospel history, grammar and sewing) into the institutes of Lancashire and Cheshire and Yorkshire at the end of the 1850s elicited an eager response from a large number of operatives and initiated a new, popular era.[75] In 1858 the East Lancashire Union claimed that the great majority of its members were cotton operatives; and 'operatives on weekly wages' made up 39 per cent and 50 per cent of the respective memberships of the Yorkshire Union in 1861–2 and the Lancashire and Cheshire Union in 1864–5. By 1871 the Lancashire and Cheshire Union, with a membership of 16,760, embraced 120 institutes which included not only mechanics 'but also a host of other institutes such as the Blackburn (Saint John's) Mutual Improvement Society, Burnley Church Literary Institute, Compstall Literary Institute, Droylsden Educational Institute, Glodwick Mutual Improvement Society, Oldham Analytic Literary Institute, Ryecroft Mutual Improvement Society and the Tottington Literary Institute.[76]

Strong support for the notion of increased working-class participation in institute life is to be found in my occupational breakdown of the mainly teenage and male students[77] sitting the elementary examinations in the institutes of the Lancashire and Cheshire Union between 1867 and 1871. Table 5.2 shows that not only were the 3,349 candidates recruited from a wide range of occupations, but that over one-third (1,224) were in the single and mainly 'non-aristocratic' industry of cotton. It is true that lower middle-class and a variety of skilled and craft occupations supplied a substantial number of candidates (bookkeepers, clerks, warehousemen, hatters, joiners, mechanics, printers, spinners and teachers contributed a combined

Table 5.2:   Occupations of Students Sitting the Elementary Examinations (higher and lower grades) of the Lancashire and Cheshire Institutes, 1867–71

1.	Apprentice	6
2.	Artist	1
3.	Assistant	10
4.	Baker	2
5.	Bandmaker	10
6.	Band putter on	1
7.	Basket maker	1
8.	Beamer	1
9.	Binder	3
10.	Blacksmith	9
11.	Bleacher	6
12.	Boatbuilder	5
13.	Bobbin carrier	2
14.	Boilermaker	13
15.	Boltmaker	1
16.	Bookkeeper	52
17.	Bookseller's assistant	1
18.	Boxmaker	1
19.	Brassfounder	1
20.	Breaker off	1
21.	Brewer	1
22.	Bricklayer	7
23.	Bricksetter	1
24.	Builder	1
25.	Butcher	5
26.	Cabinetmaker	10
27.	Candlewickmaker	1
28.	Cardmaker	3
29.	Cardroom	23
30.	Carter	1
31.	Cashier	1
32.	Chairmaker	1
33.	Clerk	178
34.	Clogger	14
35.	Cloth worker	11
36.	Coach builder	2
37.	Coal deliverer	1
38.	Cotton operative	49
39.	Creeler	9
40.	Crofter	2
41.	Crucible worker	1
42.	Currier	3
43.	Cutlooker	5
44.	Dealer	3
45.	Dentist	2
46.	Designer	4
47.	Doffer	13
48.	Doubler	4

49.	Draper	6
50.	Draughtsman	4
51.	Drawer in	8
52.	Dresser	2
53.	Dressmaker	9
54.	Driller	1
55.	Dyer	20
56.	Engineer	4
57.	Engraver	5
58.	Errand boy	38
59.	Factory operative/boy	20
60.	Farm	8
61.	Filer	1
62.	Finisher	14
63.	Fireman	1
64.	Fitter	34
65.	Flagger	1
66.	Flymaker	1
67.	Foundry worker	1
68.	Gardener	4
69.	Gasfitter	1
70.	Grinder	6
71.	Grocer's assistant	14
72.	Groom	1
73.	Hairdresser	1
74.	Half-timer	8
75.	Hatter	59
76.	Home(at)	76
77.	Ironmonger	4
78.	Ironmoulder	5
79.	Ironturner	1
80.	Iron worker	1
81.	Jeweller	1
82.	Jobber	2
83.	Joiner/carpenter	74
84.	Knitter	5
85.	Knotter	9
86.	Labourer	45
87.	Lapcarrier	2
88.	Librarian	1
89.	Lodge-boy	1
90.	Loomer	3
91.	Lubricator	1
92.	Machine hand	4
93.	Maker-up	7
94.	Marker-off	1
95.	Mason	5
96.	Mechanic	63
97.	Messenger	3
98.	Milliner	9
99.	Millwright	8
100.	Minder	8
101.	Miner	11
102.	Moulder	9
103.	Newsboy	1

104.	Nurse	1
105.	Office boy	93
106.	Operative-(mill)	85
107.	Packer	21
108.	Painter	6
109.	Paperer	1
110.	Paper sorter	1
111.	Patternmaker	16
112.	Pawnbroker/assistant	2
113.	Photographer's assistant	2
114.	Piecer	222
115.	Planer	1
116.	Plasterer	1
117.	Plater	1
118.	Plumber	8
119.	Porter	3
120.	Postman/boy	3
121.	Printer/works	55
122.	Quarryman	6
123.	Reeder	1
124.	Reeler	13
125.	Roller coverer	10
126.	Ropemaker	10
127.	Rover	2
128.	Salesman/woman	2
129.	Scavenger	4
130.	School(at)	401
131.	Screw cutter	1
132.	Seamstress	2
133.	Servant	9
134.	Sewing machinist	4
135.	Shirtcutter	1
136.	Shoemaker	5
137.	Shop assistant	4
138.	Shopman/boy	18
139.	Shuttlemaker	2
140.	Silk worker	3
141.	Sizer	2
142.	Sorter	2
143.	Spindlemaker	5
144.	Spinner	44
145.	Spooler	1
146.	Stamper	2
147.	Stationer	2
148.	Stitcher	1
149.	Stone cutter	1
150.	Stonemason	9
151.	Storekeeper	4
152.	Stripper	4
153.	Surveyor	1
154.	Tailor	18
155.	Teacher (pupil/assistant)	103
156.	Tenter	26
157.	Throstle spinner	4
158.	Timber dealer	1

159. Timekeeper	2
160. Tinplate worker	11
161. Tobacconist	1
162. Trimmer	3
163. Turner	29
164. Twiner	1
165. Twirler	2
166. Twister	22
167. Upholsterer	2
168. Wagon maker	1
169. Wagon minder	1
170. Warehouseman/boy	237
171. Warper	6
172. Watchmaker	8
173. Watch regulator	1
174. Weaver	618
175. Weigher out	1
176. Wheelwright	5
177. Winder	30
178. Wiredrawer	2
179. Woolsorter	1
Total = 3,349	

Source: Compiled from information in *Journal of the Union of Lancashire and Cheshire Institutes*, April 1867, April 1868, June 1870, June 1871.

total of 865 — one-quarter of the 3,349). However, as seen in Table 5.3, the top 20 occupations represented were by no means uniformly 'aristocratic' in character. Indeed, weavers, the vast majority of whom were, of course, 'non-aristocratic' women, headed the league table.[78]

Table 5.3:   League Table of Occupations

	Number of candidates	Percent of 3,349
1. Weaver	618	18.4
2. At school	401	11.9
3. Warehouseman/boy	237	7.0
4. Piecer	222	6.6
5. Clerk	178	5.3
6. Teacher (pupil/assistant)	103	3.0
7. Office Boy	93	2.7
8. Operative (mill)	85	2.5
9. At home	76	2.2
10. Joiner/carpenter	74	2.2
11. Mechanic	63	1.8
12. Hatter	59	1.7
13. Printer	55	1.6
14. Bookkeeper	52	1.5
15. Cotton operative	49	1.4
16. Labourer	45	1.3

17. Spinner	44	1.3
18. Errand Boy	38	1.1
19. Fitter	34	1.0
20. Winder	30	0.8

Educational provision was not, of course, confined to the Lancashire and Cheshire Union. Beyond the formal and mainly middle-class controlled institutes there existed a number of more informal educational bodies which were often genuinely working class rather than middle class or 'labour-aristocratic' in character. For example, workers from a variety of occupations were present at the educational and political gatherings of the Stalybridge Chartist Institute during the 1850s.[79] And at neighbouring Ashton eight cotton operatives, two iron moulders, a gardener, a stonemason, a bookkeeper, a clog tip maker and a bookbinder formed a Bond of Brotherhood and a Truth Seekers' Class in the wake of the Chartist failures of 1848.[80] Similar proceedings were in evidence throughout the country as workers from diverse occupations turned from independent working-class politics to a more central concern with education. As Ben Brierley noted of the Failsworth Chartists, 'On the break up of the Chartist movement the branch association threw aside its politics and the members turned their attention to intellectual pursuits'.[81] Of particular note was the proliferation of workers' mutual improvement societies throughout the cotton districts (and elsewhere) during the late 1840s and the 1850s. Our knowledge of the activities and occupational base of these societies is limited but nevertheless useful. J.F.C. Harrison informs us that mutual improvement usually involved a small group of workers who met together in each other's homes or in a rented room to hold essay readings and discussions. Instruction was provided by the members themselves and was designed primarily to promote proficiency in reading, writing and arithmetic. In some societies geography, history, languages and science were also studied. In addition to educational improvement, the societies offered a valuable platform on which to practise public speaking.[82] Most crucially in terms of our immediate purpose, it seems that many mutual improvement societies catered to a wide mix of occupational groups. For example, a correspondent of the *Manchester Guardian* reported in 1850 that members of the various mutual improvement societies in the Royton area included spinners, twiners, bricksetters, blacksmiths, mechanics, handloom and powerloom weavers, colliers, piecers, twisters, engineers, turners and stonemasons.[83]

In turning to consider the occupational roots of friendly societies, there is no doubt that these bodies had a wide appeal.[84] There were, however, gradations in status and financial stability, and Gosden observes that the more prestigious affiliated orders, such as the Oddfellows and Forresters, were particularly attractive to the better paid workers.[85] Furthermore, craft and skilled workers were often prominent both as leaders and members. Of the 118 examining officers listed in the Oddfellows' directories for 1875 and 1876, 33 were shoemakers, 21 were tailors, 9 were hairdressers and 5 were blacksmiths: booksellers, engravers, hatters, masons, druggists, carpenters, saddlers, grocers and confectioners were also included.[86] The admissions register of an Oddfellows lodge in Stockport reveals the strong presence of craft, skilled and lower-middle class occupations: of a membership sample of 184 between 1859 and 1873 just over 40 members were middle class and the remainder, with the notable exception of 26 weavers, pursued either craft or skilled occupations.[87] It would, however, be wrong to conclude that the affiliated orders were essentially 'aristocratic' in composition. Rather their appeal was to the broad mass of regularly employed and relatively well-paid operatives. Included in this group would be the majority of cotton operatives: but many casual workers and agricultural labourers would not qualify for membership.[88] The Poor Law Commissioners' Report on Stockport in 1842 noted that the Oddfellows and other respectable friendly societies in the district embraced 'many of the better-paid manufacturing operatives'.[89] Thus labourers and cardroom workers were to be found paying their subscriptions to the Oddfellows along with mechanics, overlookers and engineers. And spinners and weavers (see Table 5.4) together accounted for 36 per cent of the Oddfellows in the Stockport district.

Table 5.4:   Selected Occupations of 1,533 Members of the Stockport District of the Independent Order of Oddfellows, Manchester Unity, February 1840

	No.	Per cent		No.	Per cent
Spinners	301	19.6	Mechanics in factories	66	4.3
Weavers	261	17.0	Joiners and carpenters	43	2.8
Overlookers	107	6.9	Smiths	41	2.6

Labourers	103	6.7	Tailors	39	2.5
Printers of cotton	97	6.3	Carders	35	2.2
Dressers	90	5.8	Publicans	31	2.0
Dyers	84	5.4	Engineers	28	1.8
Crofters or					
bleachers	83	5.4	Carters	23	1.5
Cordwainers	80	5.2	Strippers	21	1.3
			Total = 1,533		

Source: *Report of the Assistant Poor Law Commissioners into the State of the Population of Stockport* (1842), pp. 129–30.

It is , unfortunately, far more difficult to provide a detailed occupational profile of the members of co-operative and temperance societies, few of which kept occupational records. Evidence gleaned from the Co-operative press and the histories of individual co-operative societies does, however, permit the presentation of a reasonably clear view of the former. As already noted in this study and in numerous other works,[90] the Co-operative Movement held a special attraction for the upwardly mobile, 'most intelligent, industrious, careful, and economical portions of the working classes'. Chapter 4 drew the reader's attention to the advances made by co-operative leaders during the third quarter,[91] and the prominence among such leaders of the craft and skilled.[92] It should be further noted that of a CWS leadership sample of 80 males between 1866 and 1900, only 15 per cent were millworkers. Forty per cent were skilled or craft workers, and 20 per cent were overlookers or small manufacturers.[93] Prominent among the founders of the Runcorn and Widnes Co-operative Society were a mason, foreman boxmaker, blacksmith, sawyer, sailmaker, foreman carpenter, dealer, clothier, storekeeper, warehouseman, clerk, timekeeper and a cooper.[94] The Ashton Co-operative Society was set up by overlookers, and the branch manager at the Mill Lane store became sanitary inspector for Dukinfield.[95] At Hyde two overlookers and a warehouseman acted as trustees of the local co-operative society at its inception in 1862, and a shoemaker, newsagent and overlooker performed the same function at Royton Industrial Co-op during the late 1850s.[96] A reference to the early history of the Greenfield Co-op at mid-century records that, 'overlookers, foremen, and spinners at the various mills, small farmers and clothiers and others in like circumstances — this class found the bulk of the capital which started our Society, and this class supplied its most capable workers'.[97]

And we should constantly bear in mind the point made by Pollard and others that the 'Rochdale principle' of no credit without ample security effectively closed the co-operative stores to the poor.[98]

Exclusion of the latter did not, however, signify that the co-ops in the cotton districts were the main or sole preserve of either a craft and skilled élite or Foster's 'authority wielders'. There exists plentiful evidence to suggest that, as in the case of many friendly societies, co-ops catered to the needs of a wide range of workers. Of particular importance at the leadership level was the continued importance of traditional craft workers whose commitment to a variety of schemes designed to improve the position of the working calls outlasted an often severe decline in control and independence at work, earning capacity and occupational ranking. Thus many of the numerous handloom weavers, shoemakers and tailors present in the Co-operative Movement had felt the full effects of technological change or the growth of 'dishonourable' sections of their trades and consequent price cutting and the beating down of wages and trade union defences.[99] The early Rochdale Pioneers' Society was dominated by handloom flannel weavers who were compelled to strike in an abortive attempt to protect their favourable work situation.[100] Handloom flannel weavers also provided much of the impetus behind the formation of the Eccles Provident Industrial Co-operative Society in 1857.[101] The development of co-operation at Middleton, Failsworth and Newton Heath at mid-century owed much to the initiatives of the Owenite, Chartist and Freethinking handloom weavers in cotton and silk.[102] And silk weavers, who eagerly read the pages of the *Northern Star* at their mutual improvement society's meetings in Leigh, constituted the backbone of local co-operation.[103] At the Congleton Equitable and Industrial Co-operative Society silk weavers and shoemakers occupied leading positions; and the Great and Little Bolton Co-operative Society was started by handloom weavers in 1859.[104]

The above constituted but a few examples of widespread 'artisan' influence. However, the occupational base of co-operative leadership was more extensive. Attention has already been drawn to the presence of men from non-skilled backgrounds among working-class labour leaders.[105] Not surprisingly, cotton operatives were frequently in evidence.[106] The co-operative society at Ashton was formed by overlookers and warpers, the latter being a distinctly 'non-aristocratic' group; and cotton operatives played a key role in the societies established at Eccles, Stockport and Stalybridge.[107] Millworkers employed in a woollen cloth mill were active in the Greenfield society; and operatives employed at Pearson's mill provided much of the enthusiasm at the Great and Little Bolton Co-op.[108] These examples could be multiplied several times over. It is, however, in turning to consider the membership of co-operative societies in Lancashire and Cheshire that the full appeal of the movement to the broad mass of operatives becomes most evident. Thus throughout our period co-operative leaders repeatedly claimed that cotton operative support had rendered possible the remarkable successes of the movement.[109] It is further significant that societies suffered most during the Cotton Famine when cotton workers were thrown out of work in large numbers. The Stockport Co-operative Society's lament that 'the recent stagnation of trade, by exhausting the pecuniary means of the operative classes, has caused many withdrawls from the society', was echoed at the Manchester, Hulme, Ashton, Stalybridge and numerous other co-ops during the height of the distress in 1862 and 1863.[110] By September 1862 the Stockport society had only 720 members as compared with 1,020 in June of the same year. At the Stalybridge Co-op the decline in membership was more spectacular — from 1,800 in 1862 to 672 in 1863. At Ashton, where membership fell from 672 in 1862 to 402 in 1863, several cotton operatives withdrew their shares from the society in order to accumulate sufficient funds to emigrate to America. And in January 1863 the Manchester and Salford Industrial Co-operative Society met to consider ways of relieving the distress of those members on short-time work or unemployed. Fortunately, the vast majority of co-operative societies survived the Cotton Famine to prosper in the more favourable economic climate of the late 1860s and early 1870s.[111]

Reliable information concerning the occupations of temperance society members is extremely scarce. Foster has claimed both that the temperance movement established an independent base within Oldham's working class during the 1850s and that temperance was the preserve of those very same 'aristocrats' who dominated the adult education institutes and the co-ops.[112] Once again, however, the evidence marshalled to support these claims is far from convincing. Foster does identify some of the leading figures involved in all three movements, but does not investigate the occupational composition of the wider memberships. Indeed, any attempt adequately to establish the occupations of temperance society members and to measure the appeal of temperance within the working class is, given the paucity of surviving information, probably doomed to failure. As Brian Harrison, the historian of the Victorian temperance movement, informs us, the loss of the vast majority of membership registers means that it is impossible to analyse the mass membership of the teetotal movement.[113] A search for occupational data in the records of various temperance organisations in south Lancashire and northeast Cheshire has unearthed scraps of information which cannot, however, support unambiguous generalisations.[114] We do know that the Primitive Methodists in Ashton, Dukinfield and Stalybridge warmly embraced temperance sentiments, but the congregations in these areas were composed not of labour aristocrats but cotton operatives (Ashton and Stalybridge) and colliers (Dukinfield).[115] There certainly existed close links between the co-operative and temperance movements; and we have observed that many working-class leaders were keen temperance men.[116] The United Kingdom Alliance claimed strong support among Lancashire's 'artisans', and its meetings in Manchester's Free Trade Hall did attract considerable working-class support.[117] We must, however, remember that the Alliance generally exaggerated the extent of its popular support, and that some contemporaries believed temperance to exert only slight influence upon the working class as a whole.[118] Finally, Harrison has shown that the leadership of the teetotal movement was predominantly middle class in character (between 1833 and 1872 only 1 of 311 teetotal leaders was a textile factory worker).[119]

The paucity and sometimes conflicting nature of the evidence thus renders extremely hazardous conclusions concerning the social base of temperance. It may well have been the case that, although opposed to drunkenness and excessive drinking, many 'respectable' workers were not averse to the moderate consumption of alcohol.[120] There also existed working-class opposition to the self-righteous advocates of temperance who did nothing to tackle the structural causes of poverty and oppression.[121]

In terms of the promotion of respectability by religious bodies, two central questions arise: what was the social base of the Sunday schools, and who constituted the congregations of the (especially Nonconformist) chapels and churches? In terms of the first question, there is general agreement among historians that attendance at Sunday school was a mass experience. In 1857, for example, David Chadwick estimated that in Manchester, Salford and the immediate vicinity there existed 240 Sunday schools which embraced 90,000 scholars and teachers.[122] John Foster informs us that on Census Sunday in 1851 almost 40 per cent of Oldham's children between the ages of 4 and 14 spent some part of the day at Sunday school.[123] At Saint Paul's in Manchester some 4,000 children were in attendance at the Bennett and German Street Sunday schools during the late 1840s, and a further 350 scholars attended Saint Paul's day school.[124] Stockport Sunday School accommodated over 5,000 children at its peak in the 1840s, and attendance was likewise impressive at Droylsden.[125] During the second half of the nineteenth century, Albion Congregational Chapel at Ashton-under-Lyne boasted, in addition to a Sunday school of 1,000 children, a Working Men's Class, a Mothers' Class, a Young Women's Christian Aid Society, a Band of Hope, a Literary Society, a Christian Usefulness Society, a Tract Society, and a Dorcas Society. Albion Day School, which opened in 1869, became the largest and most celebrated school in Ashton with its emphasis upon scientific and technical education.[126] In all these schools the scholars were exhorted to pursue useful and respectable lives by means of industry and self-help.[127]

In relation to the second question, church attendance among adults in the cotton districts was, as at the national level, low. Foster estimates that church attendance never involved more than 10 per cent of Oldham's workers between the 1820s and 1851,[128] whilst at Ashton on Census Day in 1851 it was found that approximately half of the borough's 31,000 inhabitants had not been present at church.[129] Foster nevertheless contends that general popular indifference to organised religion must be set within the context of an increase in working-class attendance at church and chapel in Oldham, and, crucially, that at mid-century, 'It was precisely those congregations in which the big employers no longer played a socially dominant role — those of the Methodists — which expanded fastest'. Control of the Methodist chapels was increasingly concentrated in the hands of the petty bourgeoisie and 'the congregations themselves now tended to be limited to a small minority of largely supervisory and skilled workers'. Significantly, contends Foster, 'it is also the same group of workers that is associated with all the new institutions that appear in the middle of the century: adult education, temperance and the cooperative movement'.[130] In such a manner does Foster claim that attendance at the Methodist chapel was a badge of 'labour-aristocratic' status.

To what extent does Foster's claim hold true for other towns in south Lancashire and northeast Cheshire? A largely negative response would seem to be in order. Thus the most important conclusion to emerge from E.A. Rose's detailed studies of the social underpinnings of Methodism in Ashton, Dukinfield and Stalybridge is that whilst Methodism undoubtedly enjoyed strong support among the lower middle-class, skilled and supervisory groups of these towns at mid-century, it nevertheless also appealed to significant numbers of 'non-aristocratic' workers. Primitive Methodism, in particular, was often strongly proletarian in appeal. For example, 38 per cent of the fathers of those baptised at the Dukinfield chapel between 1850 and 1860 were listed as colliers.[131] And, as shown in Table 5.5, textile workers constituted almost 60 per cent of the fathers of those baptised at Katherine Street Primitive Methodist Chapel at Ashton between 1850 and 1870. It is true that there was an increase in lower middle-class influence at Katherine Street towards the end of the century (shopkeepers rose from 2 per cent between 1850 and 1870 to 14 per cent between 1890 and 1910); but this development could not disguise the predominantly proletarian character of the chapel during the third quarter.

Table 5.5: Occupations of Fathers of those Baptised at Katherine Street Chapel, Ashton, 1850–1910

	1850–70 No. 305	1870–90 No. 236	1890–1910 No. 245
Total baptisms			
Father's Occupations:	%	%	%
Textile worker (inc. warehousemen)	59	37	20
Metal trades	7	15	14
Coal miners	7	5	3
Building trades and labourers	9	11	15
Shoemakers	4	—	—
Overlookers	4	1	4
Shopkeepers	2	10	14
Agents, clerks, bookkeepers	2	5	7
Others	5	14	19

Source: E.A. Rose, *Methodism in Ashton-Under-Lyne*, p. 80.

The social composition of the leadership of the Weslyan and New Connexion Methodists at Ashton does give some backing to Foster's claim. The leaders of the Wesleyans were, by mid-century, mainly tradesmen or shopkeepers; and Stamford Street's New Connexion Chapel was (as a result of the departure of the wealthy to Albion

Congregational Chapel) dominated by mill salesmen, small employers and professional men.[132] And at neighbouring Hurst, where 10 per cent of the adult population of the village followed the New Connexion faith of the dominant local employer (the Whittaker family), teachers at the Sunday school were overlookers, warehousemen, bookkeepers and others of similar standing.[133] The Wesleyan and New Connexion congregations in the Ashton area were not, however, limited to supervisory and skilled workers. The New Connexion Methodists at Dukinfield had, for example, a middle-class leadership superimposed upon a mainly operative base; while at Ashton cotton operatives undoubtedly partook of the social and religious life at the Stamford Street chapel. (Twenty-seven per cent of the fathers of children baptised at Stamford Street between 1809 and 1830 were weavers, 20 per cent were spinners and a further 12 per cent belonged to other occupations in textiles[134].) At Fairbottom the Wesleyan chapel not only had no rented pews (a unique situation in terms of Ashton Nonconformity) but also served as the social centre of the local community and attracted the active support of many colliers.[135] Finally, upon his secession from the Wesleyan ministry in 1834, J.R. Stephens continued to enjoy the support of his overwhelmingly proletarian congregations in Ashton and Stalybridge.[136]

In moving beyond Methodism to consider the social base of other Nonconformist groups, the Church of England and Roman Catholicism in the Ashton district, it is advisable to heed Rose's statement that, 'the bulk of every congregation was made up of relatively humble folk, although only the Catholics appealed to the very poor.'[137] By 1851 the Congregationalists in Ashton had outstripped both the Wesleyans and New Connexion Methodists in numbers and wealth. Albion Congregational Chapel, opened in 1835, claimed an average Sunday morning's attendance of between 900 and 1,000 adults at mid-century, and enjoyed the support of the leading Liberal manufacturers of the borough. Albion also attracted wide support. 'The church was composed mainly of working people', noted the minister at Albion in the 1860s, 'but there was a considerable element of their employers and a still larger infusion of . . . the middle class'.[138]

The fortunes and popular appeal of the Church of England in Ashton revived from the low ebb of the 1830s to show a marked improvement during the second half of the century.[139] A total of 7,404 Anglicans attended four churches in Ashton on Census Day in

1851 (the attendance at 15 Nonconformist places of worship was 8,408); and many of these were active at Saint Michael's where a strong congregation and flourishing Day and Sunday schools developed. Attendance at Christ Church in the working-class area of Charlestown was generally poor during the 1850s. But this setback could not conceal the increasingly successful appeal of the Anglicans to those workers 'who often thought of Nonconformity as the religion of the bosses'.[140] A marked increase in Irish Catholic immigration into the district and the increasingly violent and widespread 'No Popery' disturbances of the 1850s and 1860s also enhanced the popular appeal of Anglicanism.[141] The Church Institute, specifically aimed at 'artisans', was opened in Ashton in 1857, and local Anglicans played an important role in the establishment of the Conservative Working Men's Association in 1865.

Despite the problem of 'leakage', the Catholic Church in Ashton and Stalybridge maintained a strong hold over the vastly increased Irish immigrant communities at mid-century. Indeed, the sharp increase in anti-Irish Catholic feelings served to strengthen both a sense of community and the authority of the priest in Irish neighbourhoods. Two points of major importance were the widespread attempt on the part of the priesthood to lead the immigrants into the path of respectability; and the concentration of the vast majority of the latter in unskilled and semi-skilled occupations.[142]

This brief survey of the social appeal of religion in the Ashton area lends itself to two major conclusions. Firstly, the social base of Methodism was not restricted to a labour aristocracy. And secondly, despite the general indifference of the working class to organised religion, all denominations enjoyed relatively wide social appeal.

We should finally note that trade unions were strong purveyors of the ethic of respectability. As will be shown in the next chapter, trade union leaders in cotton constantly exhorted their members to be sober-minded, industrious, self-respecting and independent. Weavers and cardroom hands were to be cast not as impetuous and intemperate creatures, but as mature and responsible trade unionists and citizens capable of shaping their own destinies.[143]

The above discussion supports the conclusion that whilst craft, skilled and supervisory elements were prominent in the institutions of respectability, nevertheless it is a gross oversimplification to suggest that such bodies were the exclusive preserve of a labour aristocracy, and that they provided a shield against cultural contact with the mass of operatives. The central weakness of Foster's thesis is that slight evidence is used to support an unacceptably wide generalisation. The presence of a select group of aristocrats in Oldham's co-operative, temperance and adult-education institutions does not in itself prove that such institutions effectively excluded non-aristocratic workers. Any such proof would require a systematic examination of the membership and appeal of these institutions — but there is no evidence in *Class Struggle and the Industrial Revolution* that this exercise has been carried out. We are mainly presented with interesting but largely unsubstantiated assertions. My major conclusion, albeit based upon limited, and often patchy, occupational data, is that both the institutions referred to by Foster and other agencies of respectability embraced and appealed to a wide range of occupations in cotton and other industries. Included from cotton were both aristocratic spinners and non-aristocratic weavers and others who may well have been members of the same family network. And, as Joyce contends, the deployment of the spinner's family across the whole range of mill occupations offers a powerful counterweight to Foster's notion of cultural fragmentation along the lines of aristocrats versus non-aristocrats. To argue as such is not, however, to endorse Joyce's general claim that 'status fragmentation' within the working class of the cotton districts was of minor significance.[144] As we will observe shortly, during the third quarter of the century there developed sharp distinctions between the mass of regularly-employed 'respectables' and the (mainly poor) 'non-respectables'.

The Content of Respectability

In the foregoing examination of the social base of respectability attention has been concentrated upon a wide range of institutions, both working- and middle-class in character. I now propose to narrow the focus somewhat — to investigate the content and meanings of respectability as practised by those institutions which were largely controlled by workers themselves (co-ops, trade unions, friendly societies and some mutual improvement societies). I will then return to an evaluation of the three general interpretations of respectability outlined earlier.

Working class respectability in the cotton districts had at its core the following characteristics: a strong belief in the emancipatory powers of education; a search for collective and personal advancement and improvement; adherence to the values and habits of earnest endeavour, discipline and restraint, self-respect self-reliance and independence; a positive evaluation of home and family life which usually assumed male dominance; opposition to the loose frivolities and excesses of life (especially of a sensual character); a liking for 'manly' and vigorous outdoor pursuits, such as rambling; and an emphasis upon the strict observance of 'correct' manners and formal rules of behaviour. Sometimes unduly priggish and earnest, respectable workers nevertheless merit admiration in their struggle for security, self-respect and independence in an often insecure and hostile world.

In turning to a detailed examination of the above characteristics, we can usefully begin with education. The most important point to note in this respect is that co-operators, trade unionists and others were keen to continue at mid-century the powerful commitments to education and collective and personal self-help established by Owenites, Chartists and trade unionists during the first half of the century.[145] In 1849 and 1850, for example, a correspondent of the *Manchester Guardian* marvelled at the educational endeavours made by workers in the Tonge and Royton districts.[146] In the Tonge area weavers, bricklayers, labourers, silk weavers, foundrymen and others built up libraries, exchanged books and, attired in their Sunday best, gathered at each other's houses at weekends to discuss the great affairs of the day. Around Royton the correspondent was shown a temperance society, various book societies, a mutual improvement society, a youth seminary and a Chartist reading room. All these societies were run by manual workers at low rates of subscription. At the Chartist reading room, 'a cold, comfortless place', 30 members met nightly to partake of mutual instruction in reading, writing and arithmetic, and to discuss current political matters. Occasionally the local butcher was hired to teach for a fee of 1½d per week, but more often than not the members were left to their own limited devices and the aid of an 'Irish scholar':

> Here a young man was reading in a very laborious, but imperfect manner what appeared to be his lesson — a paragraph from a newspaper or periodical. Three other young fellows sat near him, beside a stove, and a rather tidy looking Irish tailor was whiffing his pipe. He was the headmaster I was given to understand.

The impressive range of reading material at the Chartist reading room included Joyce's *Scientific Dialogues*, Volney's *Ruins of*

Empire, O'Connor's *The Labourer*, Paine's *Rights of Man* and Douglas's *Narrative of Slavery*.

The Thorpe Clough Society, counting among its members spinners, fustian handloom weavers, piecers and twisters, charged a weekly contribution of 1d and combined instruction in the popular subject of botany with literature and politics. A book society in Royton was also in a thriving condition. Founded in 1794 by fustian weavers, shopkeepers and a few small manufacturers, the society proudly displayed on its shelves, *Shakespeare's plays*, Cobbett's *Advice to Young Men* and Gibbon's *Decline and Fall of the Roman Empire*. The temperance society in Royton was started by a few young operatives during a turn-out. The members met weekly to read newspapers and to debate issues such as 'Whether Improvements in Machinery Have Been Beneficial to the Working Classes or Otherwise'. Shakespeare's *Works* and Bamford's *Early Days* took pride of place in their reading matter. A short distance from the temperance society the correspondent encountered 20 members of a recently-formed mutual improvement society who met nightly to study reading, writing, arithmetic and grammar. Sundays were devoted to reading and singing. The members, 'cleanly dressed young fellows', were engineers, bricklayers, moulders, weavers, blacksmiths, mechanics, spinners, twiners and stonemasons. The Haggate Mutual Improvement Society included among its members spinners, twiners, bricksetters, smiths, mechanics and powerloom weavers. Draughts and discussions were the favourite activities at Haggate. Finally, at the Youth Seminary factory workers and colliers, wearing 'clean linen and neat fustian or woollen cloth coats, jackets and trousers', learned to read and write. The correspondent's impressions were highly favourable. He reported to his middle-class readers that there existed in the Royton and Tonge districts a vibrant working-class culture which owed nothing to middle-class inspiration or patronage. He enthused:

There was an air of quietude about the dwellings; a few men were talking in groups, and smoking their pipes on the sunny side of their garden fences; children, with their bright faces and cleanly apparel, were toddling hand-in-hand to school; their mothers setting about the mid-day meal at home; the spaces before the doors were newly swept; door stones strewed [sic] with sand; clean blinds were put to the windows.

To myself one thing is evident and that is that if the working population of this part of the country is not looked after, with a view to . . . the acquirement of knowledge . . . it will look after itself; nay, it is doing so. Their great cry, in short, is that of the dying Göthe! [sic], Light! light! more light! more light![147]

The passion for education was not, of course, confined to Royton and Tonge. By the 1860s the landscape of the cotton districts was peppered with institutions, such as co-operative and mutual improvement societies, which encouraged educational enlightenment. In all of these societies the breadth of vision and reading material was impressive. Ben Brierley proudly recalled his experiences at a society in Failsworth:

We read after, and marvelled at the colossal Shakespeare; we traced the deep subtleties of the philosophic Wordsworth; we revelled in the grand imagery of Byron; and sympathised with the robust humanity of Burns. We reasoned with Locke; and drew ethical sustenance from grand old Jeremy Bentham.[148]

One cannot fail to be impressed by the very real sacrifices made by workers and their families in the cause of enlightenment. The whole exercise, undertaken after long hours of work, was one of unremitting determination. At Failsworth no time was to be squandered on novels and works, 'that would not in the least be to their advantage'. Even walks into the countryside were to be utilised in the quest for knowledge. 'On the walks', wrote Brierley, 'we enlivened the way by discursing upon our favourite books, upon problems in arithmetic and new kinds of weaving. The too common frivolities of youth we avoided'.[149] Educational habits acquired at an early age were rarely forgotten. Robert Howard, who emigrated to Fall River, Massachusetts, after working as a textile operative in Lancashire for 17 years, described his experiences thus:

From the time when I was very young, I was fond of reading, and I remember many occasions when I have gone to my supper and taken my daily paper in my hands, and have slept there until about eleven o'clock. Then I have been determined to read it, and have put my lamp beside me when I went to bed, and have gone to sleep again with the paper in my hand, and lain there just as I put myself down, without stirring, until morning, the result of exhaustion.[150]

Workers invested so much time in education for a variety of reasons. On a practical, day-to-day level, the skills of numeracy and literacy were of obvious advantage to men and women in terms of making ends meet and paying bills, reading newspapers and other literature, and also in the satisfactory performance of one's job. Education also served to enhance one's self-confidence, self-respect and ability to control one's destiny. For many, but particularly for those people involved in the labour movement, education constituted a vital tool in the development of class pride and political awareness. In an earlier part of the century the members of the Blackburn Female Reform Society had combined learning the letters of the alphabet with political education — the letter B represented Bible, Bishop and Bigotry; K equalled King, Knave and Kidnapper; W meant Whig, Weakness, Wavering and Wicked.[151] Engels was delighted to discover Chartist and Socialist reading rooms and classes where, 'the children receive a purely proletarian education, free from all the influences of the bourgeoisie', and in which 'proletarian journals and books alone, or almost alone', were to be found.[152] And Chartists throughout the country gathered in each others houses at weekends to listen to a fellow member read the latest news from Feargus in the *Northern Star*.

The slogan 'Knowledge is Power' was also a commonplace among Chartists and earlier radicals. To J.F. Bray, education represented a means of arriving at an understanding of the root causes of inequality and exploitation in capitalist society:

> Before all things, and above all things, there must be amongst them a wide-spread knowledge of the wrong and the remedy — the means and the end. Until they obtain this knowledge . . . they will continue to be, as they have always been, the tools and the dupes of their fellows.

The knowledge gained would reveal the secret of exploitation in capitalist production:

> The wealth which the capitalist appears to give in exchange for the workman's labour was generated neither by the labour nor the riches of the capitalist, but it was originally obtained by the labour of the workman; and it is still daily taken from him by a fraudulent system of unequal exchanges.[153]

Harney, Jones, O'Brien and O'Connor all believed that education was critical to the development of political understanding and the furtherance of the Chartist cause. And this association between political education and the emancipation of the working class retained much of its strength at mid-century, despite the fact that the content of emancipation had become more diluted. Co-operators continually warned against the dangers of ignorance. 'If you are the slaves of ignorance and vice', cautioned the *Co-operator*, 'You will be merely the "rolling stock" of the capitalist. You will be deprived of your political rights'. Successful co-operation would, 'render it impossible for any class ever to enslave workingmen again'.[154] The members of the Ashton Bond of Brotherhood declared: 'It is knowledge that makes men free, and it is knowledge that makes nations free'.[155] Clearly Ernest Jones was simply expressing a widespread viewpoint in his belief that, 'an educated and enlightened people would never consent to remain a race of slaves'.[156] Thus many mid-Victorian British workers would have found themselves in ready agreement with the belief of the Knights of Labour that, 'The sword may strike the shackles free from the limbs of the slave, but it is education and organization that makes of him a free man'.[157]

Furthermore, in lending itself to self-respect and self-reliance, education engendered independence and acted as a safeguard against dependence and deference. Being 'petted, pampered and patronized' by their 'betters' was totally against the principles of respectable workers. The *Oddfellows Magazine* declared that workers:

> won't submit to be either drilled. petted or coaxed or bullied into the realisation of the pet theories of self-styled philanthropists, or professors of 'social science' of every description. They think themselves capable of managing their own affairs, and consequently dislike such intrusive patronage, however kindly meant.[158]

Self-reliance was at the very core of the Co-operative Movement. 'As soon as you co-operate', declared the *Co-operator*, 'you feel the dignity of labour . . . No aristocrat in creation has a better title to the respect and confidence of his fellows than the honest upright, intelligent workman'.[159] In 1863 the annual report of the Great and Little Bolton Co-operative Society read:

Co-operation instills into the people a spirit of self-reliance —
that is reliance on the power they themselves possess. It teaches
the working classes to look to themselves for the amelioration of
their condition, and no longer to be powerless at the feet of the
so-called higher classes — the capitalists.[160]

And in a letter written to the *Manchester Guardian* in 1858, James
Haslam pointed to the high intelligence and learning of many
workers:

I could name a considerable number of Lancashire operatives
who can reason great and abstract questions of art and science
with as much knowledge, and as logically, as some of the ablest
journalists, although perhaps with less felicity, or elegance of
language.[161]

These powerful feelings of moral and intellectual worth, pride and
the strong desire to exert control over their lives meant that respectable workers simply did not passively act out a role prescribed from
above; and should alert us to the pitfalls of the claim that respectability signified capitulation to bourgeois values and patterns
of behaviour. The consolidation of bourgeois hegemony in mid-
Victorian England was surely a less straightforward process than
sometimes suggested.

Education was not simply the key to independence and political
and social emancipation: it also constituted a tool to be utilised in
the search for personal and collective fulfilment and noble purpose
in life. In short, as Tholfsen has noted, education was seen as intrin-
sically worthwhile, as something able to confer refinement and the
virtues of reason and enlightenment upon the worker.[162] In the
opinion of the president of the Stalybridge Chartist Institute,
education led to 'high and noble results'. Workers at the Institute
were entrusted with a glorious mission — to 'gather the scattered
youth together and mould them to a way of thinking which would
quicken the thoughts, sharpen their perceptive faculties, and qualify
them for the performance of duties which, at present, they are utter
strangers to'.[163] One speaker at a nonconformist 'workingmen's
class' at Waterloo sharply contrasted the pleasures of the intellect
with the pains of ignorance:

The ignorant man had but few sources of elevated or refined joy, for he depended almost exclusively on the gratification of the mere animal faculties for his pleasure, and as those invariably flowed through one channel, the mind soon became completely satiated, and it was a question whether the pain did not counterbalance the momentary joys which he obtained . . . The intellectual man enjoyed a thousand sources of real pleasure, many of them being as pure and delightful, and as refined as could possibly be experienced.[164]

Scholars were exhorted to 'bring back some of their fellow men, who had gone into the mire and mud of degradation'.

At Failsworth 'nobility of purpose' led away from the public house. Brierley recollected that:

Boys at our age, when they left off their tops and marbles, had nothing to supply the place of such recreation except the deleterious amusements of the public house. They danced upon the taproom hearthstone, held contests in what had the name of alehouse singing, and if strongly limbed, grew proud of each triumphant essay in a more masculine kind of pastime. We had a nobler ambition. We felt a consciousness that better things were to be done than we could see practised around us. We accordingly formed ourselves into a mutual improvement society.[165]

Incorporated within the philosophy of the 'civilised worker' were a complex series of rules governing personal and social behaviour. The personal qualities of industry, thrift and moderation were widely praised and practised. For the majority industry, thrift and sobriety constituted not a commitment to bourgeois individualism but a partial safeguard against insecurity and poverty. They also encouraged self-reliance: to be cast into the arms of the Poor Law Guardians involved a severe loss of 'face' and self-respect.[166] Thus co-operative, mutual improvement and other societies busily established penny banks to safeguard members against rainy days; and consistently had as the themes of their prize essays, self-improvement and self-respect.[167] Finally, the advancement of labour was believed to be dependent upon the cultivation of self-discipline and industrious habits by the mass of workers.

Respectable workers also observed a strict moral code. Sexual 'freedom' was believed to be inconsistent with personal decency and self-control; and was often associated with the 'gaudy lights' and licentiousness of the beerhouse sub-culture.[168] Brierley noted of Failsworth:

> We did occasionally indulge in a dance, those of us who knew how, and from what I can remember, this dancing was no sleepy or shuffling affair, but a good healthy flinging up of the heels. No suggestive hugging was tolerated, and he who ventured upon this objectionable practise was as likely to get a slap as not.[169]

Sexual intercourse outside marriage and 'excessive enthusiasm' within marriage were frowned upon. And much of the enthusiasm for rambling and other strenuous forms of exercise may have owed as much to sexual frustrations and repression as to the desire to sharpen one's mind in the clear Pennine air.[170]

Drunkenness was regarded in much the same light as lack of sexual 'restraint'. Both were associated with the erosion of self-respect and independence, and the onset of domestic misery and dependence upon 'the devil's pawnshop'.[171] Ben Brierley winced at the sight of the 'swaggering drunk' in the streets of Failsworth. John Ward, a weavers' official in North Lancashire, did occasionally drink to the point of being 'gaily sober', but would not tolerate his brother's habitual drunkenness.[172] Ward's attitude was shared by many respectable operatives. Thus while both the Oddfellows and the Bolton Spinners' Union defended the workers' right to partake of 'the mug that cheers', they believed drunkenness to be incompatible with a healthy self-respect. In 1855 the Minders' Association at Manchester decided to end its custom of holding meetings in public houses on the grounds that its exclusively male members often squandered their earnings on drink rather than supporting their families who 'might be clemming'.[173]

A keen sense of propriety governed domestic and social life. In terms of the latter, social functions, especially at the co-ops, were often attended by the wives and 'sweethearts' of male members: 'rough language' was outlawed and polite conversation and 'correctness of manners' encouraged. Readings, duets and glees, and piano concerts formed the staple diet of soirées.[174] Members engaged in the 'innocent' amusements of chess and draughts; and pastimes such as horticulture were combined with the more 'muscular pursuits' of walking and gymnastics. 'Ratting' and dog and horse racing were actively discouraged as having a 'degrading and immoral tendency', and as not being conducive to serious thought, earnest endeavour and intellectual stimulation.[175]

The penny readings, piano overtures and duets performed at Hulme Co-operative Society elicited middle-class approval in that, '. . . there was an absence of anything approaching the vulgarly comic'. 'Such events as these', remarked the *Freelance*, 'cannot fail to have a healthy moral effect and demand recognition as part of our system of social discipline'.[176] The Openshaw Co-op held festivals 'embracing tea, addresses, a concert, and a ball'. The *Co-operator* ran articles on 'Tea Parties — How to Conduct Them'. Co-operators were advised to pay careful attention to the financial arrangements of tea parties and to create an atmosphere which would favourably influence the children present.[177] Workers at Saint Paul's Sunday School arranged cricket matches, women's meetings and ran a mutual improvement society. The United Free Gardeners at Stockport held glee evenings; and Manchester Chartists attended lectures at the Chartist rooms on topics such as 'The Life and Genius of Milton' and 'Constantine the Great'; and organised soirées and tea evenings.[178] Puritanical attitudes were much in evidence at Failsworth Mutual Improvement Society: 'no billiards or cards', left members time to read, and, 'as smoking was not practised except by elderly people and "swells", we were never in an atmosphere rendered offensive by the fumes of "thick twist" or cabbage leaf'.[179] The *Oddfellows Magazine* ran articles on the theme of 'Music as a Means of Moral and Spiritual Culture' — the reader being informed that in the 'harmonious beauty' of music were embodied, 'the highest good, and the loftiest, and purest motives of the immortal spirit'.[180]

Respectable workers had a strong, positive evaluation of home and family life. Home provided a source of strength and peace in a troubled world:

> The home of the workman — where love dwells, in which there is mutual confidence and mutual help between husband and wife, and loving care for the children — ought to be the nest of peace. The limitations of means of the workingman is more than counterbalanced by the absence of brooding care, of ambitious views, of anxieties of the exposure of accumulated wealth to a thousand channels, which the rich man always feels.[181]

The deification of the home was a recurrent theme in the lectures given by men at the Stalybridge Chartist Institute:

What little time they spent on their own improvement was amply repaid by the pleasure and happiness derived from arranging their domestic duties . . . and in the instruction they gave to their children . . . What peace and happiness it imparts to that woman who is the wife of him who spends his spare hours in the cultivation of the intellect, and in the study of those domestic arrangements, which tend to promote comfort and amity in the family circle.[182]

Despite his heavy trade union commitments, John Ward took a keen interest in the upkeep of his house, whitewashing 'both upstairs and downstairs' annually, and saving his spare coppers to acquire attractive but serviceable furniture.[183] Thomas Wright spoke of the pleasure of returning home after work:

. . . to the furniture glistening from the recent polishing, the burnished steel fire irons doubly resplendent from the bright glow of the cheerful fire, his well cooked dinner laid on a snowy cloth, and his wife and children tidy and cheerful.[184]

Co-ops did much to encourage domestic pride. During the 1860s members of the Oldham society attended lectures on the themes of marital contentment and the virtues of good household management. Marriage, according to William Marcroft, was not to be entered into lightheartedly. The prospective bridegroom was advised to ascertain the standing of the bride's family: 'Is the family . . . extravagant or careful of the means on which they live? Is the family of healthy stock, industrious and courteous in their manners? Are they a reading family? Good books are intelligent companions'.[185] Certainly in the eyes of many male co-operators at Oldham, Marcroft himself was viewed as a 'model husband'. His home was clean and tidy, his wife well versed in the arts of domestic management, and the whole family dedicated to 'sober and industrious living'.[186] Chauvinistic and unduly serious and earnest, Marcroft's views nevertheless illustrated the importance attached by respectable workers to 'proper' domestic arrangements. A happy, contented home was believed to represent a powerful bulwark against the attractions of the taproom and gambling den.[187] And it was in the home that children were to be instructed in the habits of politeness, careful financial management, industry, sobriety and reasoned thought.[188]

Much of the responsibility for the cultivation of 'sound' and 'respectable' habits within the family was placed on women. Thomas Wright maintained that, '. . . thousands of workingmen are driven by lazy, slovenly, mismanaging wives to courses which ultimately result in their becoming drunkards and disreputable members of society'.[189] 'Respectable' working-class men at mid-century accordingly exhorted married women to become home-centred and to give up paid employment. And the 1850s and 1860s saw a proliferation of classes for women in household management and related subjects. The co-ops and the schools created during the Cotton Famine attached great importance to domestic science and general household management. A series of lectures entitled, 'Woman as Housebuilder, Worker and Citizen' were delivered at the People's Educational Institute at Stalybridge in 1871.[190] In 1858 the Mossley New Connexion Methodist Chapel offered lectures on the themes of 'Personal and Domestic Economy Connected with Teetotalism' and 'The Model Wife'. A 'model wife', although in the opinion of the lecturer primarily interested in domestic matters, would, 'be able to write, and would make herself acquainted with the history of her own country, with a knowledge of geography, and acquaint herself with those worthies of England, both men and women, who shed a lustre on their country'.[191] The *Oddfellows' Magazine* warned against idle gossip and neglect of the needs of the husband:

> Always remember that it is possible to have a decent meal and decent abode, with even scanty resources, by the addition of a little prudent forethought, but quite impossible where the wife sits down to read the 'Ladies Journal', or gossips with her neighbours over the palings, while the beds are unmade, and the breakfast things unwashed.[192]

Many male and female workers doubtless believed that there were positive gains to be derived from the wife staying at home and caring for the children. For example, unskilled child care and the overworking of married women outside the home would be brought to an end.[193] Furthermore, the notion of mutuality — a central feature of respectability — extended into male-female relationships. Rather than spending his spare time at the pub with his fellow males, the husband was to be encouraged to be with his family, both at home and at the various social and cultural functions organised by the co-ops and likeminded institutions.[194]

Such positive gains were, however, overshadowed, if not completely negated, by the increasingly widespread popularity among men of the belief in male superiority and female inferiority. The strength of this belief was reflected in various ways. For example, while women were to be found at the cultural and social events of the co-ops, they took little part in the formal affairs and running of such bodies: all too often women provided the refreshments and made the tea while men engaged in the 'serious' business of debate. Beliefs in women as homemakers, catering to the wishes of husbands, and female inferiority often went hand in hand. Thus in tracing the 'withdrawl from public activity by women of the working class' and their increasing home-centredness at mid-century, Dorothy Thompson notes:

> The Victorian sentimentalization of the home and the family, in which all important decisions were taken by its head, the father, and accepted with docility and obedience by the inferior members, became all-pervasive, and affected all classes. The gains of the Chartist period, in awareness and in self-confidence, the moves towards a more equal and cooperative kind of political activity by both men and women, were lost in the years just before the middle of the century.[195]

True to form, that 'model husband', William Marcroft, openly paraded his own prejudices:

> Home is the heaven gained in female life. There she makes a world as she wills it; order, cleanliness, regularity,and comforts are the four points of her compass. The husband is the altar of her worship, and to guide her children to do right is the pleasure of her life.[196]

It is, of course, far more difficult to know how Marcroft's wife and other women experienced and viewed their changing role. Women, especially working-class women, were not expected to, and many simply did not have the time to keep a record of their thoughts and actions. (And given the important places of women and the home in the culture of respectability, I am conscious of the deficiencies of the present chapter which is based almost entirely upon source material written by men and mainly about men.) Women's voices are not, however, totally inaudible. Part of a remarkable article written by Alice Wilson for the *Co-operator* in 1868 read:

> The very fact of a woman depending upon a man for her daily bread gives him a power over her . . . and in all but the very best natures, the man is thereby rendered egotistical, conceited and unjust.

Wilson advocated the mechanisation of household chores and the establishment of co-operative communities in which men and women would enjoy equality.[197] It does, however, appear that Wilson's views were far from typical. Women's acceptance of 'an image of themselves which involved both home-centredness and inferiority' was, as Dorothy Thompson claims, an increasingly general feature of mid-Victorian society.[198] However, in Lancashire and Cheshire, where female employment in cotton continued to be of major importance,[199] Thompson's claim must be qualified. Despite the popularity of the cult of domesticity, female cotton operatives retained much of their reputation for 'boldness', 'independence', and a complete lack of deference towards 'all those who appeared to be above them in rank or station'.[200]

Assessments and Conclusions

Can the respectable worker's commitment to sober and industrious living be interpreted as a capitulation to bourgeois values or as proof of the maturation of a socially-soothing, shared culture? At first sight the evidence marshalled above would suggest a resoundingly negative reply to both aspects of the question. Like Crossick, I have been at pains to emphasise the indigenous nature of working-class respectability, to see, in opposition to Foster, respectability as a way of life which owed little or nothing to bourgeois initiative and prompting, but which arose in the determining context of the material conditions of working-class existence.[201] Furthermore, respectability was as capable of promoting class pride and conflict as status consciousness and stability. The ends to which respectable values and habits were directed surely depended upon the ways in which cultural patterns and traditions interacted with other structures and practices in concrete situations. During the Chartist period there is little doubt that, at least in the cotton districts, respectability had served to build and strengthen class consciousness rather than to promote an alliance between Chartists and the 'respectable' bourgeois radicals. As we have already seen, economic and other conflicts and divisions between large sections of the middle and working classes were, in the 1830s and 1840s, much too sharp to permit the creation of a viable inter-class political or cultural alliance. And, as a result of his failure to appreciate the depth and tenacity of such conflicts and divisions, and to situate working-class culture in its proper material context, Laqueur presents a highly idealised and untenable picture of inter-class cultural harmony. Brian Harrison also underestimates the various points of conflict between Chartists and bourgeois radicals, tends to divorce 'leisure' from 'work' and the wider material conditions of conflict, and glosses over the sharp break in working-class consciousness at mid-century. At least in the cotton districts. the movement of 'respectable' Chartists into Liberalism was neither so smooth nor so inevitable as Harrison suggests was the case with Lowery and other 'improvement-minded' workers.[202]

We have seen, furthermore, that beliefs in collective improvement, independence, class pride and the liberating powers of education did not suddenly expire among working people in the 1840s, but were continued, albeit in more diluted form, by trade unionists and others during the third quarter. In the 1860s the Oddfellows could still condemn those institutions in which:

> the worker's imagination is oppressed by the spectral parson and the spectral capitalists morally patting him on the head, and bidding him, like the virtuous artisan he is, to attend church regularly and avoid the trade union.[203]

Such evidence, which exists in abundance, surely lends itself to the conclusions that conflicts between working- and middle-class 'respectables' were of a continued and substantial importance hardly recognised by Laqueur and Harrison; and that respectable workers were far less passive, individualistic and collaborationist than suggested by Foster.

To offer these conclusions is not, however, to claim that working-class respectability did not undergo important changes at mid-century. As J.F.C. Harrison and others have noted, it was during the mid-Victorian period that the ambiguous character of respectability became most pronounced. Earlier emphases upon indepen-

dence and class pride were, as we have seen, not consciously jettisoned. They were, however, harnessed to more reformist and,
often, more privatised ends.[204] In particular, as demonstrated in
Chapters 3 and 4, the increased recognition and advances achieved
by the labour movement within a seemingly permanent and dynamic
social system provided the determining context in which moderation
and reformism appeared 'natural'.[205] In the new, stabilised economic system wider ideals faded, often unconsciously, into 'misty
vagueness',[206] and no longer a complete outsider, the organised
working class now had an interest, albeit ambiguous, in the efficient
working of the capitalist machine. As Thompson notes, 'the
workers had come to fear, above all, not the machine but the *loss* of
the machine — the loss of employment'.[207] Labour advances
meant, in turn, that the values of respectability increasingly lost
their association with an alternative social vision, and were primarily identified as the prerequisites of success and improvement
within the existing system. Along with this there developed a tendency on the part of co-operators and others to regard the poor and
those with 'irregular' and 'excessive' habits and tastes less as the
unfortunate victims of the system than as failed, even fallen, individuals in need of stern and thorough instruction in the habits of
industry, thrift and sobriety. The change in tone, from the compas-
sion, solidarity and sense of common suffering so marked in Chartism to the increased harshness and censorious verdicts of the
mid-Victorian period, is worthy of special note. As others have
noted,[208] it was in this latter sense that many working-class 'respectables', especially the leaders of the institutions of respectability,
transmitted individualist values to the rest of the working class, and
demonstrated an overall acceptance of a social and cultural world
whose dominant influence was bourgeois in character. There is,
furthermore, strong evidence to suggest that many 'respectables'
were increasingly concerned to dissociate and distance themselves,
both culturally and physically, from the 'non-respectables'.

Before looking at such evidence, we can briefly cite developments
in working-class education as illustrative of the narrowed and more
success-oriented focus referred to above. These developments are
clearly outlined by Richard Johnson:

> In the decades that followed and in the wake of the political
> defeats [of the 1840s], independent working-class education con-
> tinued; in the better-off sectors it may even have increased. But it

took on more individualised forms ('self-education') or lost its connection with politics ('mutual improvement') or became the cultural preserve of the aristocracies. It certainly lost the ambition of being an alternative system, especially with regard to children. At the same time a new kind of educational agitation began to emerge, linked to popular liberalism and the anti-Anglican alliance. Working-class activists began to demand education through the state, even though initially, like the Chartist rump of 1851, they insisted still on some popular control.[209]

At the Stalybridge Chartist Institute the onus for working-class advancement was increasingly placed upon the shoulders of workers themselves. The system was no longer closed to workers' wishes. In 1859 a speaker at the Institute declared:

> They might talk about the grievances which affected them, the burdens they had to bear, how legislation was managed for a class instead of the great body of the people, and how the aristocracy monopolised all places of office, but all their complaints would be little regarded until they endeavoured to improve their own social and moral position. They would then be adopting a course calculated to ensure success, and those in power would be willing of their own accord to grant the concessions sought by the struggling sons of toil.[210]

During the Chartist period workers had demanded the vote as a matter of right: by the 1860s 'respectable' workers were intent upon demonstrating to the establishment their personal fitness to be admitted to the rights of male citizenship. Education was to be one of the major means of demonstrating this fitness. Thus leading figures at the Stalybridge Institute believed that the tasks of educational and personal improvement should provide the primary focus for the Institute.

The members of the Ashton Bond of Brotherhood discovered that educational endeavours could bring not only mental stimulation but also material success.[211] The Bond dissolved during the 1850s when two of the members emigrated to America and several others left Ashton. Annual reunions were, however, held. And these reunions demonstrated both the marked degrees of upward occupational mobility attained by the members and the changed ideology of the group as a whole. One member, a former bookbinder, enjoyed great success in America in his newfound role of gold digger; the stonemason became an assistant surveyor in an English manufacturing town; one of the self-actor minders attained the position of overseer; and one of the warpers became a 'first-class' photographic artist in Stalybridge.[212] Education had led not to social revolt but to 'improvement'. The aim of the group became, 'to assist its members in attaining such positions in society as will conduce to their temporal, moral and social elevation'. The members eagerly generalised from their own experiences:

> It is just such an institution as we desire to see workingmen creating throughout the town and country; for the Bond teaches that industry, supported by habits of frugality and self-denial, with a firm resolution to do what is right, are the grand elements of success in life . . . join your Mutual Bond of Brotherhood society . . . try to create among the people an earnest desire for intellectual improvement.[213]

Given our limited knowledge of patterns of upward and downward social and occupational mobility among mid-Victorian workers, and the very real difficulties involved in assessing the meanings and implications of mobility both for the workers involved and the wider social structure,[214] it is extremely difficult to assess the typicality of the experiences of the members of the Ashton Bond of Brotherhood. There is, however, no doubt that exhortations to self-help, improvement and the 'success' widely believed to be attendant upon such activities, figured prominently in the organs of the Co-operative Movement and many friendly societies. For example, in 1863 the *Oddfellows Magazine* ran a story entitled, 'Self-help: or Work, Wait and Win'.[215] The hero of the tale, Harry Fairlight, was portrayed as a model man and an exemplary worker. 'Industrious, studious and ingeniously inventive', Harry excelled in every field of endeavour. He was neither greedy, dishonest nor envious. No one could look into his face, 'without being struck by the candid open eye, the smiling mouth, the trustful eyes which shone, as it were, through him'. Although prepared to discuss political and social affairs in a reasoned and sober-minded way, Harry refused to countenance the 'extreme' views of one of his workmates. Predictably, Harry's conduct did not pass unnoticed or unrewarded by management. He was promoted to the position of foreman while his more vociferous but less industrious mates remained at the workbench.

The work experiences of the vast majority of workers were undoubtedly different from those of Harry Fairlight. The former generally did not move into supervisory or managerial positions, and respectability was equated less with an 'escape' from the class than with attempts to achieve greater security, independence and comfort in one's role as a manual worker. On the other hand, it must be noted that stories of the Harry Fairlight variety were far from insignificant — acting as a constant spur to the ambitiously inclined and, perhaps most crucially of all, they did square with the advances and successes of an important minority of workers. Thus we have clearly seen in Chapter 4 that the leaders of the labour movement prospered greatly at mid-century and imposed their philosophy of collective advancement and personal success upon the movement. Other workers became Sunday School and, to a much lesser extent, day school teachers. The reports of the factory inspectors of the 1860s contain congratulatory references to workers who had advanced in these ways. For example, six of the teachers at the Methodist New Connexion day school at Lees had started their working lives as piecers; and most of the teachers in the Droylsden Association of Sunday School Teachers were recruited from the ranks of the upper sections of the working class and from the lower middle class.[216] Some enjoyed spectacular successes. In 1842, 26 members of the writing and arithmetic class at Bradford Mechanics Institute followed the occupations of office worker (3); woolcomber (1); factory boy (4); shop boy (1); in warehouses (10); apprentice to mechanics (3); shoemaker (1); printer (1); joiner (1); and bookbinder (1). By 1859 the career patterns of these same students had changed markedly. Only one was described as 'working class'; 16 had acquired 'responsible positions' as bookkeepers, clerks, schoolmasters, commercial travellers, wool buyers and salesmen; and nine had become 'successful men of business', some of them 'highly so'.[217] By the 1860s the working-class males who attended the Royton Temperance Society in the 1840s had risen to prominent positions: one had become a vicar, and others had risen to become cotton spinners, foremen, managers and schoolmasters.[218] Finally, education and self-help occasionally opened doors to municipal office holding. Some of the working-class members of the Stockport Mechanics Institute became 'leading citizens' in the borough, whilst at Oldham Lyceum workers acquired 'that self-respect and longing for distinction which have enabled them, by perseverance in self-

acquisition, to raise themselves to the highest level in the municipality'.[219] In short, self-help, education and 'success' were increasingly believed to be inextricably linked.

In terms of the relations between 'respectables' and others in the
working class, there is little doubt that the mid-Victorian period saw
an increased concern with status and a decline in those feelings of
class solidarity so marked during the Chartist period. And, as advocates of the labour aristocracy thesis have argued, feelings of superiority and exclusiveness were often most marked among the highest
paid workers. Thus Allen Clarke noted that the boom years of the
early 1870s in cotton heightened the superior attitudes of the
spinners:

> The spinners or minders were the working aristocracy of
> Lancashire; they strutted in the shoes of importance, and talked
> with the voice of superiority . . . No spinner with any self-respect
> in his stomach would drink beer in the taproom with a common
> labourer; he must have his ale clad in shining glass; not paltry
> pot, and enjoy it in the company of his own class, or at least with
> engineers, and other artisans of the elevated grade, who had the
> time o'day and night told to them by gold watches with con-
> spicuous chains to match.[220]

Similarly, Robert Roberts maintained that status divisions constituted a formidable obstacle to working-class solidarity in Salford
well into the first quarter of the present century. 'Artisans' had their
own room in the pub, took a keen interest in their personal appearance, home life and their children's education, occupied different
seats from the 'masses' in the theatre, were opposed to general and
industrial trade unionism on the grounds of unwanted association
with the 'rougher elements', and were careful to keep a clean door-
step and rent book — sure signs of superior social standing.[221]

In neighbouring Manchester, the skilled trades which dominated
the trades council in the 1870s did little to stimulate unionism among
the unskilled of the city; and opposed a proposal to lower admission
prices to organ recitals in the town hall in the belief that a reduction
would result in the attendance of 'certain classes of people, whose
company was distasteful'.[222] Some of the skilled workers of
Manchester also demonstrated a strong desire to distance themselves physically from the less fortunate and the gregarious street life
of the central city areas. In the 1860s Co-operative and friendly

societies began to construct 'model cottages' away from the inner-city slum areas; and by the 1870s many of the newer properties in Ardwick, Hulme and Chorlton was inhabited by the better-paid manual workers and lower middle-class elements. Such residents met with the approval of the Medical Officer of Health in that they were, 'temperate in their habits, spend their incomes on their families . . . and attend to their children'.[223] Developments in Manchester were repeated elsewhere. Both Kentish London and Edinburgh saw the growth of specifically artisan housing areas, increased residential segregation and the adoption of an increasingly privatised life-style on the part of the skilled élite.[224] Doubtless many shared the views of two 'model co-operators' in Edinburgh, who, having removed themselves from the slums to 'a very pleasant part' of the city, were extremely reluctant to return to 'those dingy hovels' and to 'associate in any degree . . . with the people one sees there'.[225]

Attitudes of superiority and exclusivity were not, however, confined to a skilled élite in the cotton towns. In the latter respectability, as demonstrated earlier, had a mass base. And by the 1860s the main cultural division was between this mass of 'respectable' operatives and the 'non-respectable'. The latter came from a variety of occupations and income groups. (Heavy drinking and the upholding of Saint Monday were of continued importance among artisans in unmechanised, small workshop trades well into the second half of the nineteenth century; and uncertain patterns of employment among dockers and seamen — some of whom could earn high wages — were often productive of 'irregular' and 'improvident' habits.[226]) But as respectability was increasingly associated by co-operators and others with 'success', so lack of respectability was frequently identified with 'failure' and 'the poor'.[227] The 'respectables' starkly contrasted their dedication to sober and industrious living with the alleged drunkenness, bawdiness and dependence of the 'non-respectables'. A 'respectable' worker, walking through a poor urban area, declared that the language and scenes to which he was subjected, 'made him feel as if he were going out of heaven into the bottomless pit'. Nathan Booth, a leading figure in the Stockport Co-op, was equally damning:

Look through the principal streets of our large towns and there you will see them standing in groups. Listen to the ribaldry of the language. See them pouring out of the gin shops and public houses, and then sir, if we have any respect for our class, any hope for our race, we shall hail with joy any step, however humble, that may be taken to bridge over that gulf that lies between the more intelligent and ignorant portions of our class.[228]

J.H. Salkeld, a member of the Manchester and Salford Co-op, believed that, 'there will ever be a swinish multitude until counter attractions to the public house are set up'. And John Ridgway, president of the Ashton Co-op, maintained that all co-operators were, 'steady and sober, and different to those men who made a practice of visiting pothouses'.[229]

In truth, many of the poor had become a source of acute embarrassment to the 'respectable'. While Chartists had no wish to be associated with the 'prevailing low songs, low comic humour and vulgar mirth' of urban life, their respectability had served not to divide workers but to instil in them a sense of class unity: and the cause of poverty was firmly attributed to the political and economic system. By the 1860s there was a marked tendency for the poor to be viewed by co-operators and others, 'not so much as a group denied justice by a corrupt system, but as a group of individuals in need of personal reformation'. The *Co-operator*, despite its ardent desire for collective working-class advancement, epitomised this changed focus:

> The poverty of the great masses is not the result of want of means, of opportunities, or of laws excluding them from the attainment of wealth. Their poverty is a poverty of ideas in the first place. Ill furnished minds and badly trained faculties can no more produce thrift and comfort than an undrained marshy wilderness. They have sunk where they are not because anybody oppresses them . . . but because they have no powers of self-guidance as motive powers within them, except those which children, savages and lower animals possess.[230]

This extreme viewpoint did not, of course, receive unqualified approval throughout the ranks of the 'respectable' working class. Among the likes of Jones and Hooson and their followers, and within the co-operative and trade union movements, there was, as we have seen, continued opposition to the manifestly unjust and oppressive features of the social system. Nevertheless, however much respectability, class pride, independence and a belief in collective improvement still marched hand in hand, there is little doubt that respectability did become more privatised, more inner-directed in aim and character. Increasingly large numbers of workers came to believe that salvation — in the form of self- and collective-help — was open to all. And those who failed to grasp the nettle received little sympathy. A letter printed in the *Co-operator* baldly illustrated the estrangement of co-operators from the poor:

> I am sorry to say that many of the sons of toil are wilfully ignorant — probably mistaking ignorance to be bliss . . . They glory in their shame; they will not advance. In fact they seem to be insensitive to every effort put forth for the amelioration of the physical, moral and intellectual condition of the working class, Let us not be daunted by such formidable enemies . . .[231]

This was the far from admirable side of respectability. Smug in their individual and collective successes, some 'respectable' workers equated poverty with personal failings and consciously divorced themselves from the 'non-respectable'. Hence, although not confined to a labour aristocracy and by no means a simple mirror-image of bourgeois values and habits, working-class respectability during the third quarter did increasingly operate within a bourgeois-dominated world and did constitute an important point of division within the working class; a point of division which worked against class solidarity and which — to go a limited way towards accepting the claims of Brian Harrison — did facilitate the emergence of an alliance between reforming 'respectables' from the middle and working class.

In conclusion, I wish both to emphasise the tentative nature of some of my conclusions and to counsel against the presentation of a static picture of working-class culture. In relation to the first point, certain aspects of the increased division between 'respectables' and 'non-respectables' at mid-century require much more detailed investigation and documentation before firmer conclusions can be drawn. For example, the extent to which 'respectable' workers distanced themselves physically from the 'non-respectable' is surely open to further and difficult examination. As noted above, many respectable skilled workers expressed a growing desire to move away from the crowded and noisy inner urban working-class neighbourhoods into the more tranquil and privatised suburbs. But the extent to which this process of residential segregation developed on a national scale has not yet been established. The census enumerators' books and other sources may well reveal that working-class housing patterns varied considerably from region to region, and were variously influenced by factors such as occupation, level of skill, earning capacity, the nature and location of employment, and access to transport. In the cotton towns proximity to place of work and kinship and neighbourhood ties, rather than considerations of status, probably constituted the main determinants of place of residence for the great mass of operatives.[232] Furthermore, as already noted, any simple identification of respectability with the skilled and non-respectability with the poor is open to serious criticism. As the investigations of the Manchester Statistical Society, the Manchester Education Aid Society and others demonstrated, it would be entirely wrong to assume that respectability did not inhabit the homes and streets of the central, and often poor urban working-class areas. The pride and self-respect of working-class women in Ancoats was on open display:

> Pavements have been duly cleaned, doorsteps edged with the inevitable line of white, and passges rendered brilliant with 'elbow grease'.[233]

Competition for respectable standing was a marked feature of working-class life in Salford. Robert Roberts's experience was instructive. 'Our family was in the slum', noted Roberts, 'but not, they felt, of it: we had "connections". Father, besides, was a skilled mechanic'.[234] And Charles Rowley believed that many working-class youths had been 'saved' from the rough-and-tumble of Ancoats street-life by a good, loving home-life and by Saint Pauls with its many religious, cultural and recreational attractions.[235]

In terms of the second point — the pitfalls attendant upon the presentation of a static picture of working-class life — E.P. Thompson is surely correct to insist that what such a picture omits, or at best under-represents, is a sense of process, of change over time, and the growth of connexions between 'disparate and seemingly unconnected events'. Thompson writes:

> If we stop history at a given point, then there are no classes but simply a multitude of individuals with a multitude of experiences. But if we watch these men over an adequate period of social

change, we observe patterns in their relationships, th and their institutions.[236]

It must, furthermore, be noted that the working class is not an undifferentiated whole, *completely unified* by identical objective determinations and a single, common consciousness.[237] Of crucial importance are the ways in which those events and structures conducive to either divisions or shared interests within the working class work themselves out over time in specific historical contexts. In short, change and contradiction lie at the heart of process. Thus Allen Clarke realised that the superior and exclusive attitudes of the Bolton spinners in the early 1870s were not eternally fixed but subject to change. Accordingly, once the mid-seventies boom gave way to growing insecurity and industrial conflict in the 1880s, so the spinners began to preach the virtues of collective solidarity on the part of the entire workforce:

> Later, on, when trade declined and woe came upon labour, all sorts of workers, high and low, were eager to join together to do something remedial.[238]

By the turn of the century all manner of divisions within the working class were, in various northern towns, increasingly in the process of being overshadowed by a renewed sense of class unity. Even in Roberts's status-ridden and Conservative Salford, the years after 1918 saw the growth of class awareness and confidence and an upsurge in support for the Labour Party.[239] Most striking testimony to the process of change was the movement of formerly exclusive 'aristocrats' in engineering into the ranks of the Labour Party, the militant Shop Stewards' Movement and the young Communist Party.[240]

Notes

1. See, for example, G. Crossick, 'The Labour Aristocracy and its Values: A study of Mid-Victorian Kentish London', *Victorian Studies*, vol. XIX, no. 3 (March 1976), pp. 301–28; T.R. Tholfsen, 'The Intellectual Origins of Mid-Victorian Stability', *Political Science Quarterly*, vol. LXXXVI, no. 1 (March 1971); R.Q. Gray, 'Styles of Life, the "Labour Aristocracy" and Class Relations in Later Nineteenth-Century Edinburgh', *International Review of Social History*, vol. xviii (1973); E.J. Hobsbawm, 'The Labour Aristocracy in Nineteenth-Century Britain', op. cit.; J.F.C. Harrison, *Learning and Living (1790–1960), A Study in the History of the*

English Adult Education Movement (1963), esp. V; G. Best, *Mid-Victorian Britain 1851–1875* (1971), pp. 256–64; F.M. Leventhal, *Respectable Radical: George Howell and Victorian Working Class Politics* (1971).

2. P. Joyce, *Work, Society and Politics*, op. cit., pp. 288–9.

3. According to Crossick, 'The values of respectability entered the working class via the skilled élite, but if they were most accepted there, they penetrated further'. G. Crossick, op. cit., p. 314. See also H. Pelling, 'The Concept of the Labour Aristocracy', op. cit., p. 47.

4. *Bull. Soc. Stud. Lab. Hist.*, no 40 (Spring 1980), p. 6.

5. Ibid., no. 18 (Spring 1969), p. 53. The close identification of non-respectability and the poor is, however, surely open to qualification. As Dorothy Thompson has suggested, the 'non-respectables' (with 'excessive', 'irregular' and sometimes 'loose' habits) were drawn from a wide variety of occupations; although some categories (for example post-Famine Irish immigrants and gypsies) were less likely than others (for examples Methodists) to belong to the 'respectables'.

These were, however, as Thompson notes, 'ethnic/cultural rather than occupational categories, although there is clearly an overlap. But many of the poorest — eg, the agricultural labourers (see *Lark Rise*) could be the most respectable.'

I agree with these comments and qualifications; but contend in this chapter that there was an increased tendency on the part of many 'respectable' workers during the third quarter to equate 'non-respectable' behaviour with the (predominantly urban) 'poor'. For a similar conclusion for early twentieth-century Vienna see, J.R. Wegs, 'Working Class Respectability: the Viennese Experience', *Journal of Social History*, vol. 15, no. 4 (Summer 1982), pp. 621–31.

6. For an excellent study of the largely impervious, yet conservative culture of late-nineteenth-century workers, see G.S. Jones, 'Working-Class Culture and Working-Class Politics in London, 1870–1900; Notes on the Remaking of a Working Class', *Jnl. Soc. Hist.*, vol. 7, no. 4 (Summer 1974), pp. 460–508.

7. As one might expect, societies controlled or run by the middle class usually maintained better membership records. See pp. 190–6 below.

8. See Ch. 4 above.

9. T.R. Tholfsen, *Working-class Radicalism in Mid-Victorian England* (1976), pp. 102ff; G. Crossick, op. cit.; C. Reid, 'Middle Class Values and Working Class Culture in Nineteenth Century Sheffield — The Pursuit of Respectability' in S. Pollard and C. Holmes (eds), *Essays in the Economic and Social History of South Yorkshire*, (Barnsley, 1976), pp. 275–95; R.Q. Gray, *The Labour Aristocracy in Victorian Edinburgh*, op. cit., Ch. 7.

10. Although Laqueur (T.W. Laqueur, *Religion and Respectability. Sunday Schools and Working-class Culture, 1780–1850* (1976), pp. 189, 196–7, 214–18) claims that Sunday schools were genuinely popular working-class institutions and the source of an independent working-class culture. However, as Joyce notes, (*Work, Society and Politics*, op. cit., pp. 248–9) the schools were often, 'the agency of a party politics organised and directed by the middle-class party hierarchies and the political clergy'; and that school funds, organisation and teaching were not primarily in working-class hands.

11. The workingmen's colleges were designed to provide 'human studies' and to promote the notion of 'fellowship in learning'. They intentionally differed from the mechanics institutes in their exclusively classroom contact and the discussion of controversial subjects. J.F.C. Harrison, *A History of the Working Men's College, 1854–1954* (1954); D. Chadwick, 'On Working Men's Colleges', *Trans. Nat. Asstn. Prom Soc. Sc.* (1859) pp. 323ff.; *Reports of Salford Working Men's College* (M/cr Cent. Ref).

12. R. Schatz (op. cit., pp. 31–40) for the involvement of middle-class reformers in co-ops.

13. See pp. 198—201 below.

14. For a critique of the functionalist character of the notion of social control see, G.S. Jones, 'Class Expression versus Social Control? A critique of recent trends in the social history of "leisure" ', *Hist. Wkshp. Jnl.*, 4 (Autumn 1977), p. 164.

15. For Brian Harrison see his, *Drink and the Victorians* (1971), esp. pp. 388, 395–9; also B. Harrison and P. Hollis, 'Chartism, Liberalism and the Life of Robert Lowery', *Eng. Hist. Rev.*, vol. LXXXII (1967). See also, P. Bailey, 'Will the real Bill Banks Please Stand Up? Towards a Role Analysis of Mid-Victorian Working-class Respectability', *Journal of Social History*, 12 (Spring 1979), pp. 336–53.

16. J. Foster, *Class Struggle and the Industrial Revolution*, op. cit., pp. 212–24; J. Foster, thesis (1977), pp. 272ff.

17. Loc. cit.

18. J.F.C. Harrison, op. cit., p. 43.

19. G. Crossick, 'The Labour Aristocracy and its Values', op. cit.; R.Q. Gray, op. cit. Ch. 7.

20. For the key importance of shared values in the Parsonian system see, P.S. Cohen, *Modern Social Theory* (1968), pp. 28–30, 45–6, 96–105.

21. T.W. Laqueur. op. cit., pp. 170. 186, 189, 194–7, 214–18, 239.

22. Ibid., pp. 183, 196–201, 239

23. Ibid., p. 239.

24. Ibid., p. 218.

25. Ibid., p. 239.

26. B. Harrison, *Drink and the Victorians*, op. cit., p. 25.

27. T.P. Newbould, *Pages From a Life of Strife-Being Some Recollections of W.H. Chadwick, the Last of the Manchester Chartists* (1911).

28. G. Crossick, 'The Labour Aristocracy and its Values', op. cit., p. 303.

29. Ibid., pp. 301–3.

30. Ibid, p. 305.

31. Ibid., pp. 306ff. See also T.R. Tholfsen, 'The Intellectual Origins', op. cit.

32. R.Q. Gray, *The Labour Aristocracy in Victorian Edinburgh*, op. cit., pp. 5–7, 143; G. Crossick, 'The Labour Aristocracy and its Values.', op. cit., pp. 302–1; T.R. Tholfsen, *Working-Class Radicalism in Mid-Victorian England*, op. cit., pp. 12–17; C. Reid, op. cit., and her, 'Class and Culture', *Bull. Soc. Stud. Lab. Hist.*, no. 34 (Spring 1977).

33. R.Q. Gray, op. cit., pp. 138–43; G. Crossick, op. cit.

34. Laqueur does not examine the extent and nature of industrial conflict which was widespread and deep-seated in many cotton towns during the first half of the century. See R. Sykes, op. cit.; M. Jenkins, op. cit.; J. Foster, *Class Struggle*, op. cit., pp. 107–20. For the mid-Victorian period see Ch. 6 below.

35. D. Thompson, *The Early Chartists*, op. cit., p. 15.

36. For middle-class attempts to spread their ideas among the workers of Manchester in the pre-1850 period see, J. Seed, 'Unitarianism, Political Economy and the Antinomies of Liberal Culture in Manchester, 1830–1850', *Social Hist.*, vol. 7, no. 1 (January 1982), pp. 1–25.

37. G.S. Jones, *Outcast London*, op. cit., Part III.

38. The *Ashton Reporter* supported household suffrage, the co-operative movement and other attempts at working-class self-help (including trade unionism), and insisted upon the need to 'humanise' the tenets of orthodox political economy. See, for example, *Ashton Reporter*, 17 November 1860; 26 January 1861.

39. Ibid., 19 March 1859.

40. Loc. cit. Also 13 July 1861; 4 March 1865.

41. *Fraser's Magazine*, September 1863, p. 317.

42. M.E. Rose, 'Rochdale Man and the Stalybridge Riot. The Relief and Control of the Unemployed During the Lancashire Cotton Famine' in A.P. Donajgrodzki (ed.), *Social Control in Nineteenth Century Britain* (1977), pp. 185–6.

43 H. Perkin, op. cit., p. 319; *Manchester Examiner and Times*, 19 June 1860.

44. P. Joyce, op. cit., pp. 148, 151–2; R. Harrison, op. cit., pp. 35–9.

45. P. Joyce, op. cit., Ch. 4.

46. T.R. Tholfsen, *Working-Class Radicalism*, op. cit., p. 124.

47. P. Joyce, op. cit., pp. 187–9, 200ff.; Ch. 6 below; N. Cotton, op. cit., pp. 168–83.

48. For such activities see, J.H. Hinton, *The Case of the Manchester Educationists* (Manchester 1852); *A Plan for the Establishment of a General System of Secular Education in the County of Lancaster* (Manchester, 1847); B. Templar, *A Paper on Ten Years Experience of the Manchester Free School* (Manchester, 1866); D.K. Jones, 'Socialization and Social Science; Manchester Model Secular School 1854–1861' in P. McCann (ed.), *Popular Education and Socialization in the Nineteenth Century* (1977); P. Bailey, *Leisure and Class in Victorian England. Rational Recreation and the Contest for Control 1830–1885* (1978).

49. *Odds and Ends*, no. 36 (1890). (Manuscript collection relating to Saint Paul's Mutual Improvement Society. M/cr. Cent. Ref.)

50. *Manchester Courier*, 4 September 1852.

51. *Working Men's College Magazine*, vol. 1 (1859) p. 1.

52. *Manchester Courier*, 4 September 1852.

53. T.R. Tholfsen, 'The Intellectual Origins.', op. cit., p. 65.

54. Loc. cit.

55. R. Johnson, 'Educational Policy and Social Control in Early Victorian England', *Past and Present*, no. 49 (November 1970), pp. 96–119.

56. J.B. Smith, *Stockport Letters* (J.B. Smith manuscript collection. M/cr. Cent. Ref.), p. 11.

57. *Working Men's College Magazine*, no. 3 (March 1859), p. 58.

58. *Nat. Asstn. Prom. Soc. Sc.* (1859), p. 334.

59. *Salford Working Men's College Magazine* (1863), pp. 6, 9.

60. *Manchester Courier*, 6 January 1849.

61. Ibid., 4 September 1852.

62. E.P. Thompson, *The Making of the English Working Class*, op. cit., I, 16.

63. T.R. Tholfsen, 'The Intellectual Origins.', op. cit., pp. 58–60.

64. Ibid., p. 67.

65. For Irish immigrants see Ch. 7 below; R. Roberts, *The Classic Slum* (Harmondsworth, 1973), pp. 20–3.

66. For the appeal of mechanics institutes see, M. Tylecote, *The Mechanics Institutes of Lancashire and Cheshire before 1850* (Manchester, 1957); J.W. Hudson, *The History of Adult Education* (1969 edn), pp. viii, 110; E. Royle, 'Mechanics Institutes and the Working Classes 1840–1860', *Hist. Jnl.*, xiv, 2 (1971); J.P. Hemming, 'The Mechanics' Institute Movement in the textile districts of Lancashire and Yorkshire in the second half of the Nineteenth Century', PhD (University of Leeds, 1974), pp. 27ff.

67. *Sixth Annual Report of the Pendleton Mechanics Institute* (1856); *Manchester Courier*, 4 January 1851.

68. J.W. Hudson, op. cit., p. 130.

69. *The Working Men's College Magazine*, vol. 1 (1859), pp. 21–2; *Second Report of the Manchester Working Men's College* (1860).

70. *The Working Men's College Magazine* (Supplement, February 1859), p. 15.

71. Loc. cit.

72. *Report of Salford Working Men's College* (1858), p. 331, and (1860), p. 8.

73. Ibid. (1869 Report), p. 6.

74. J.P. Hemming, op. cit., pp. 102–4; E. Royle, op. cit., p. 310; *Report of the Ashton and Dukinfield Mechanics Institute* (1850).

75. J.P. Hemming, op. cit, pp. 67, 106; J.F.C. Harrison, op. cit., pp. 213–4.

76. J.P. Hemming, op. cit., pp. 95–101.

77. Many of the male and female examination candidates in Lancashire and

Cheshire were in their mid-late teens (*Journal of the Union of Lancashire and Cheshire Institutes, 1867-1871*). Hemming does, however, estimate that approximately 50 per cent of the total institute membership in Yorkshire and Lancashire were, on average, well over the age of 21 (J.P. Hemming, op. cit., p. 538).

78. Hemming estimates that an average of 10 per cent of institute members throughout the textile districts of Lancashire and Yorkshire were females (J.P. Hemming, op. cit., p. 543).

79. See, for example, *Ashton Reporter*, 2 September 1863.

80. *The History of the Ashton-under-Lyne Mutual Improvement Society and Bond of Brotherhood* (1858 Ashton Ref. Lib.); *Co-operator*, October 1860.

81. B. Brierley, *Home Memories and Recollections of a Life* (1887), p. 49.

82. J.F.C. Harrison, op. cit., pp. 49-53.

83. *Manchester Guardian*, 15 December 1849, 5 January 1850.

84. J. Foster observes (*Class Struggle and the Industrial Revolution* op. cit., p. 216): 'the friendly society was the one social institution that touched the adult lives of a near majority of the working population'.

85. P.H.J.H. Gosden, *The Friendly Societies in England, 1815-1875* (Manchester, 1961), pp. 48, 74-5.

86. *A List of the Lodges Comprising the Independent Order of Oddfellows, Manchester Unity*. With the kind permission of the staff at Oddfellows' House, Manchester, I consulted material for 1875-6 (pp. 269-96) and 1878-9 (pp. 278-305).

87. *Admissions Register. Trafalgar Lodge no. 401, 1859-1873* (Stockport Lib.)

88. P.H.J.H. Gosden, op. cit., pp. 74-5.

89. *Report of the Assistant Poor Law Commissioners into the State of the Population of Stockport* (1842) pp. 7, 129-30.

90. G. Crossick, *An Artisan Elite*, op. cit., pp. 165-7 for the occupations of members of the Royal Arsenal Co-op.; Ch. 4 above.

91. Ch. 4 above, esp. pp. 136-42.

92. R. Schatz, op. cit., pp. 32-9, 46: Crossick, op. cit., p. 166.

93. Biographical information on the CWS leadership collected from the following sources: P. Redfern, op. cit., pp. 375ff.; *Co-operative News*, 1875-1898 for sketches of leading lights in the movement; J.M. Bellamy and J. Saville (eds), *Dictionary of Labour Biography*, vol. 1 (1972).

94. W. Millington, *Runcorn and Widnes Industrial Co-operative Society Ltd. Jubilee History, 1862-1912* (Manchester, 1912), p. 19.

95. J. Thompson, *History of the Ashton-under Lyne Working Men's Co-operative Society Limited, 1857-1907* (Manchester, 1907), pp. 12, 19, V.

96. T. Jones and J. Rhodes, *Jubilee History of the Hyde Equitable Co-operative Society Ltd., 1862-1912*, (Manchester, 1912), p. 28; T. Burton, *Royton Industrial Co-op. Society Ltd* (Manchester, 1907), p. 25.

97. D. Lawton, *Village Co-operation. A Jubilee Sketch: Greenfield Co-operative Society Limited, 1856-1906* (Manchester, 1906), p. 13.

98. R. Harrison, op. cit., p. 32.

99. For such changes see E.P. Thompson, *The Making of the English Working Class*, op. cit., [8.]

100. W.H. Brown, *The Rochdale Pioneers, 1844-1944* (Manchester, 1944), pp. 9-11.

101. J. Haslam, *Eccles Provident Industrial Co-operative Society Limited. History of Fifty Years Progress* (Manchester, 1908), p. 21.

102. J.H. Ogden, *Failsworth Industrial Society Limited. Jubilee History, 1859-1909* (Manchester, 1909), pp. 15, 20, 27; S. Partington, *Jubilee of the Middleton and Tonge Industrial Society Limited* (Manchester, 1900), pp. 25-34.

103. T. Boydell, *The Jubilee History of the Leigh Friendly Co-operative Society Limited, 1857-1907* (Manchester, 1907), pp. 90-1.

104. A. Cooke and J. Cooke, *The Jubilee History of the Congleton Equitable and*

Industrial Co-operative Society Limited, 1860–1910 (Manchester, 1910), p. 17; F.W. Peaples, *Great and Little Bolton Co-operative Society Limited. Jubilee History, 1859–1909* (Manchester, 1909), p. 29.

105. See Ch. 4 above, p. 134.

106. J. Thompson, op. cit.

107. J. Haslam, op. cit., p. 21; J.H. Hinchcliffe, *History of the Stalybridge Good Intent Industrial Co-operative Society Limited, 1859–1909* (Manchester, 1909); T.W. Gough, *Stockport Great Moor Co-operative Society Ltd. Centenary History, 1831–1931* (Stockport, 1931).

108. D. Lawton, op. cit.; F.W. Peaples, op. cit., p. 29.

109. R. Schatz, op. cit. (pp. 23–4, 69) for the appeal of co-operation to the mass of regularly employed 'respectables'. Also notes 110 and 111 below.

110. See, for example, *Co-operator*. June, August, September 1862, January March, September 1863.

111. Ibid., June 1865, August 1866.

112. J. Foster, *Class Struggle and the Industrial Revolution*, op. cit., p. 221.

113. B. Harrison, *Drink and the Victorians*, op. cit., esp. p. 147.

114. Among the records examined were those of the Lower Mosley St Day and Sunday schools (see *An Old Scholar, Sketch of the Origin and Progress of the Lower Mosley Street Day and Sunday Schools* (Manchester, 1867). In 1847 a Total Abstinence Society was formed at Lower Mosley Street; after twelve months the society had 220 members); Saint Paul's, Manchester (see M103/14/1/lM/cr. Cent. Ref.); Saint Martin's, German St, Manchester (M 23 1/12) and Saint Martin's Band of Hope Minute Book (M12/10/1, M12/10/2/1 M/cr. Cent. Ref.); Cavendish Street Band of Hope and Total Abstinence Society (M162 M/cr. Cent. Ref.); Lancashire and Cheshire Band of Hope Union (M285/1/2- 1866-9, M/cr. Cent. Ref.).

115. E.A. Rose, *Methodism in Ashton-under-Lyne, 1797–1914* (Ashton-under-Lyne 1969), pp. 42, 80; E.A. Rose, *Methodism in Dukinfield* (the author ? 1978), pp. 41–3.

116. Ch. 4 above, pp. 142–3.

117. B. Harrison, op. cit., p. 223.

118. In the early 1840s a (far from disinterested) publican in Stockport claimed that temperance organisations in the borough had exerted 'very slight influence amongst our operatives generally'. *See Rept. Asst. P. Law Commiss. (1842)*, op. cit., p. 100.

119. B. Harrison, op. cit., pp. 152, 155.

120. See pp. 214–15 below.

121. B. Harrison, op. cit., pp. 388, 404.

122. D. Chadwick, 'On free Public Libraries and Museums', *Nat. Asstn. Prom. Soc. Sc.* (1857), p. 575.

123. J. Foster, op. cit., p. 215; T.W. Laqueur, op. cit., p. 89, Ch. 6.

124. A.B. Reach, op. cit., p. 46.

125. T.W. Laqueur, op. cit., pp. 46, 64, 199; E.A. Rose, *Methodism in Droylsden 1776–1963* (Droylsden, 1964), p. 22.

126. E.A. Rose, 'Ashton Churches and Chapels' in E.A. Rose and S. Harrop (eds), *Victorian Ashton*, esp. p. 70; *Albion Congregational Magazine* (1874).

127. T.W. Laqueur, op. cit., p. 155, Chs 6 and 7.

128. J. Foster, op. cit., p. 214.

129. E.A. Rose, 'Ashton Churches and Chapels', op. cit., p. 68; E.A. Rose, *Methodism in Droylsden*, op. cit., p. 18.

130. J. Foster, op. cit., pp. 214, 220.

131. E.A. Rose, *Methodism in Dukinfield*, op. cit., pp. 41–3.

132. E.A. Rose, 'Ashton Churches and Chapels', op. cit., p. 73.

133. E.A. Rose, *Methodism in Ashton-under-Lyne*, op. cit., pp. 26, 54.

134. Ibid., p. 20; and his *Methodism in Dukinfield*, op. cit., p. 18.

135. E.A. Rose, *Methodism in Ashton-under-Lyne*, op. cit., pp. 32–3; E.A. Rose, 'Ashton Churches and Chapels', op. cit., p. 68.

136. E.A. Rose, *Methodism in Ashton-under-Lyne*, op. cit., pp. 36, 49.

137. E.A. Rose, 'Ashton Churches and Chapels', op. cit., p. 70.

138. Ibid., pp. 68–70.

139. Ibid., pp. 73–4.

140. Loc. cit.

141. Ch. 7 below, pp. 317–23.

142. Ibid., pp. 325–81.

143. Ch. 6 below, pp. 281–3

144. P. Joyce, op. cit., pp. 288–9.

145. E.P. Thompson, *The Making*, op. cit., pp. 781–820; B. Simon, *Studies in the History of Education 1780–1870* (1960), esp. Chs IV and V.

146. *Manchester Guardian*, 15 December 1849, 5 January 1850.

147. Ibid., 5 January 1850.

148. *Ben Brierley's Journal* (June 1873), p. 211.

149. B. Brierley, *Home Memories*, op. cit., p. 36.

150. For the American material I am much indebted to Leon Fink. See L. Fink, 'Rebels for Hearth and Home', unpublished paper (City College, New York, 1972).

151. E.P. Thompson, *The Making*, op. cit., p. 788.

152. K. Marx and F. Engels, *On Britain*, op. cit., pp. 274–5.

153. J.F. Bray, *Labour's Wrongs and Labour's Remedy* (Leeds 1839), pp. 49, 209.

154. *Co-operator*, no. 50, April 1864.

155. *The History of the Ashton-under-Lyne Mutual Improvement Society*, op. cit., p. 16.

156. *Manchester Guardian*, 23 November 1853.

157. L. Fink, op. cit.

158. *Oddfellows Magazine*, January 1865, p. 6.

159. *Co-operator*, no. 29, August 1862.

160. Ibid., September 1863.

161. *Manchester Guardian*, 17, 19 December 1858.

162. T.R. Tholfsen, *Working-Class Radicalism*, op. cit., pp. 102ff.

163. *Ashton Reporter*, 2 September 1863.

164. Ibid., 12 April 1862.

165. *Ben Brierley's Jnl.*, June 1837, p. 211.

166. G. Crossick, *An Artisan Elite*, p. 136.

167. See, for example, *Odds and Ends*, no. 13, 1867, pp. 318–19; *Co-operator*, no. 5, October 1860, p. 62.

168. B. Brierley, *Home Memories*, op. cit., p. 6; *Ashton Reporter*, 13 August 1859, 12 November 1864.

169. B. Brierley, op. cit., p. 50.

170. W. Marcroft, *The Inner Circle of Family Life* (1886); C. Rowley, *Fifty Years of Ancoats*, op. cit., p. 6; B. Brierley, op. cit., pp. 35–6; R.Q. Gray, *The Labour Aristocracy in Victorian Edinburgh*, op. cit. pp. 103–4.

171. *Co-operator*, no. 58, December 1864, p. 100; *Ashton Reporter*, 10 August 1861, 2 July 1864.

172. M. Brigg, 'Life in East Lancashire 1856–60: A Newly Discovered Diary of John O'Neil (J. Ward) Weaver of Clitheroe', *Trans. Hist. Soc. Lancs. and Ches.*, vol. 120 (1968), pp. 108–9.

173. *Manchester Guardian*, 15 November 1855.

174. *Free Lance*, 5 February 1870; *Co-operator*, June 1860, p. 2.

175. B. Brierley, *Home Memories*, op. cit., p. 50; *Ashton Reporter*, 23 October 1858, 8 October 1859, 29 September 1860, 31 December 1864, 28 March 1868.

176. *Free Lance*, 5 February 1870.

177. *Co-operator*, 19 December 1868, pp. 806–7.
178. C. Rowley, op. cit., pp. 5–9; *Northern Star*, 19 April 1851; *Stockport Advertiser*, 7 January 1859.
179. B. Brierley, op. cit., p. 50.
180. *Oddfellows Magazine*, July 1863, p. 145.
181. *Co-operator*, July 1865, p. 99.
182. *Ashton Reporter*, 8 October 1859, 29 September 1860.
183. M. Brigg, op. cit., p. 104.
184. T. Wright, *Some Habits and Customs of the Working Classes* (New York, 1867), p. 189.
185. W. Marcroft, *The Inner Circle*, op. cit., pp. 8–9.
186. Ibid., pp. 13ff.
187. *Report of the Pendleton Mechanics Institute* (1854), p. 5; *Ashton Reporter*, 5 March 1870.
188. W. Marcroft, op. cit., pp. 29–30.
189. T. Wright, op. cit., p. 190.
190. *Ashton Reporter*, 23 September 1871.
191. Ibid., 27 March 1858.
192. *Oddfellows Magazine*, July 1863, p. 139.
193. D. Thompson, 'Women and Nineteenth-Century Radical Politics: A Lost Dimension', J. Mitchell and A. Oakley (eds), *The Rights and Wrongs of Women* (Harmondsworth, 1976), p. 137.
194. *Ashton Reporter*, 25 February 1860. Workingmen also frequently maintained that in staying at home women were to be rescued from the horrors of 'wage-slavery' in factory and mine. The economic argument — that waged female labour constituted a source of cheap competition in the marketplace — was of equal, if not much greater importance than the moral argument to many of these men. See, *Manchester Guardian*, 28 December 1853, *Ashton Standard*, 21 April 1860; and 'Trade Societies and Strikes', *Nat. Asstn. Prom. Soc. Sc.* (1860), p. 220 for a selection of these claims.
195. D. Thompson, op. cit., p. 138.
196. W. Marcroft, *The Inner Circle*, op. cit., p. 11.
197. *Co-operator*, 17 October 1868, pp. 660–1.
198. D. Thompson, op. cit., pp. 137–8.
199. J. Liddington and J. Norris, op. cit., p. 58.
200. This was at least the impression conveyed by Mrs Gaskell in *North and South*. Liddington and Norris (op. cit., pp. 49, 61) are surely correct to suggest that, while the majority of Lancashire mill women enjoyed 'limited independence which working women elsewhere could not match', it was, nevertheless, 'an independence and security that varied from town to town . . . and it was an independence that could really only be fully enjoyed by unmarried women whose domestic responsibilities were still comparatively light'.
201. G. Crossick, 'The Labour Aristocracy and its Values', op. cit.
202. See Ch. 2 above, pp. 58–64.
203. *Oddfellows Magazine*, April 1867, p. 110.
204. G.S. Jones, 'Class Struggle and the Industrial Revolution', op. cit., p. 69.
205. E.J. Hobsbawm, 'Trends in the British Labour Movement' in *Labouring Men*, op. cit., pp. 334–7, 341.
206. Ibid., p. 342 (note 4).
207. E.P. Thompson, 'The Peculiarities of the English' in his, *The Poverty of Theory and other essays* (1978), pp. 70–1.
208. For example, R.Q. Gray, *The Labour Aristocracy in Victorian Edinburgh*, op. cit., Ch. 7.
209. R. Johnson, 'Really Useful Knowledge: Radical Education and Working-class Culture, 1790–1848', J. Clarke, C. Critcher and R. Johnson (eds), *Working*

Class Culture (1979), pp. 99–100.

210. *Ashton Reporter*, 8 October 1859.

211. *The History of the Ashton-under-Lyne Mutual Improvement Society*, op. cit.

212. Loc. cit.

213. Ibid., p. 10.

214. The expectations and overall value systems of those experiencing mobility surely have to be examined in conjunction with quantitative assessments as to the extent of upward and downward occupational mobility. For a critique of the 'capitalist–individualist' preferences of many studies of mobility see, J.A. Henretta, 'The Study of Social Mobility: Ideological Assumptions and Conceptual Bias', *Labor History*, vol. 18, no. 2, (Spring 1977), pp. 157–78; S. Thernstrom, 'Working-Class Social Mobility in Industrial America', P. Stearns and D.J. Walkowitz (eds), *Workers in the Industrial Revolution* (New Brunswick, 1974).

215. *Oddfellows Magazine*, October 1863, pp. 235–7; also April 1864, p. 349.

216. *Reports of the Inspectors of Factories*, 30 April 1858, pp. 11, 66–7; *Ashton Reporter*, 9 May 1857.

217. J.F.C. Harrison, op. cit., pp 211–12.

218. *Working Man*, 27 January 1866.

219. B. Grime, *Memory Sketches* (Oldham, 1887), p. 119.

220. A. Clarke, *The Effects of the Factory System* (1899), pp. 161–2.

221. R. Roberts, op. cit., Ch. 1.

222. L. Bather, 'A History of the Manchester and Salford Trades Council', (unpublished PhD. thesis, Manchester University, 1956), p. 17.

223. *Report of the Medical Officer of Health* (Manchester, 1876), p. 38; also *1878 Report*, p. 8.

224. G. Crossick, *An Artisan Elite*, op. cit., pp. 144–9; R.Q. Gray, *The Labour Aristocracy in Victorian Edinburgh*, op. cit., pp 95–9.

225. *Co-operator*, 17 October 1868; R.Q. Gray, op. cit., p. 98.

226. See, D.A. Reid, 'The Decline of Saint Monday', *Past and Present* no. 71 (1976), esp. III. For the effects of casual labour upon trade unionism, politics and working-class leisure see, E.L. Taplin, *Liverpool Dockers and Seamen, 1870–1890* (Hull, 1974); M. Nightingale *et al.*, *Merseyside in Crisis* (Manchester, 1980), part 2.

227. A further dimension of the division between 'respectable' and 'non-respectable' was the contrast between 'modern' and 'non-modern' work patterns and leisure-habits. As Dorothy Thompson has written (in a letter to the author):

> There is also a category of 'modern' and 'non-modern'. Cruel sports, heavy drinking, loose sexual behaviour could also be seen as old fashioned, belonging to a more picaresque age when people lived more for the moment. Planning, saving and belonging to a friendly society could be signs of a more 'modern' outlook, living in an age of greater certainty. This could mean — I think probably did — that some forms of older cultural behaviour persisted in communities like the miners who lived in a more dangerous, unpredictable way. Or among sailors — a well-paid but often non-respectable sector.'

228. *Co-operator*, December 1862, p. 119.

229. Ibid, February 1863, p. 146; *Ashton Reporter*, 11 February 1871.

230. *Co-operator*, 1 June 1865, p. 41, 15 July 1865, pp. 65–6.

231. Ibid., March 1861, p. 142.

232. For consideration of such questions see, J. Foster, thesis, op. cit., pp. 228ff. Various reports produced in the 1860s suggested that, although the poor and very poor were increasingly concentrated in certain areas of Manchester (Angel Meadow, parts of Deansgate etc.), many working-class communities in the city contained a wide mix of occupations, with unskilled and skilled living side by side on the same streets.

See Manchester Statistical Society, 'An Inquiry into the Educational and other Conditions of a District in Deansgate', Session 1864–5; 'An Inquiry into the Educational and Other Conditions of a District in Ancoats', Session 1865–6; 'Report on the Educational and other conditions of a District at Gaythorn and Knott Mill', Session 1867–8; *Free-Lance*, 18 January 1868, p. 227, February 1868, p. 48; E. Brotherton, *Scrapbook*, op. cit., letter IV. For the increased concentration of the poor in the inner city areas of Manchester towards the end of the nineteenth century see, *Report of the Medical Officer of Health* (Manchester, 1890), Appendix 3; J.C. Thresh, 'An Inquiry into the Excessive Mortality in No 1 District, Ancoats', *Manchester Statistical Society*, Session 1889; Revd J.E. Mercer, 'The Conditions of Life in Angel Meadow', *Manchester Statistical Society*, Session 1896–7; T.R. Marr, *Housing Conditions in Manchester and Salford* (Manchester, 1904), pp. 54, 58, 61, 67.

233. *Alliance News*, 14 January 1865, p. 11.

234. R. Roberts, op. cit., p. 14.

235. C. Rowley, *Fifty Years* op. cit., pp. 8, 49–50.

236. E.P. Thompson, *The Making*, op. cit., p. 11.

237. Historians, such as A.E. Musson, who wrongly áttribute a simple, undifferentiated view of class to Marx and Marxist historians, have little trouble in unearthing differences and divisions between 'artisans' and labourers' during the first half of the nineteenth century. Such divisions are then used to 'prove' that class solidarity and consciousness are the inventions of ideologically-motivated Marxists, rather than concrete historical realities. What such an approach lacks is a sense of process and change, of the ways in which (as Thompson and others demonstrate) a sense of class belonging, whilst not embracing every proletarian in the land, did, as a result of concrete political, economic, cultural and ideological developments, embrace increasingly large sections of workers. It is ironic that Musson employs an undifferentiated view of 'artisans'. As Rob Sykes and others have shown, there existed within this supposedly homogeneous group of 'artisans' varying experiences and levels of consciousness, with those trades badly hit by the growth of a 'dishonourable' sector or technological change providing strong support for Chartism and other radical forms of protest. On a more abstract level, Musson's empiricist methodology rests upon the patently false assumption that theory stands or falls solely upon its fit or correspondence to *every single piece* of empirical evidence. On such matters see, for example, the conflicting approaches and claims of Foster and Musson in *Social Hist*, 3 (1976). See also A.E. Musson, *British Trade Unions*, op. cit., pp. 15–21; E.P. Thompson, *The Making*, op. cit., esp. Preface; D. Thompson, *The Early Chartists*, op. cit., intro; R. Sykes, op. cit. For critiques of empiricism see, for example, G.S. Jones, 'The Poverty of Empiricism' in R. Blackburn (ed.), *Ideology in Social Science* (1972); T.W. Adorno, 'Sociology and Empirical Research' in P. Connerton (ed.), *Critical Sociology* (1976). For a discussion of the issue of correspondence between theory and empirical evidence see, E.P. Thompson, 'The Poverty of Theory' in his *Poverty of Theory*, op. cit., esp. pp. 197–242.

238. A. Clarke, op. cit., pp. 161ff.

239. R. Roberts, op. cit., esp. Ch. 10. Roberts probably exaggerates the effects of the First World War in the shift leftwards of the working class in Salford.

240. E.J. Hobsbawm, *Labouring Men*, op. cit., pp. 289, 301, 327; J. Hinton, *The First Shop Stewards Movement* (1973).

6 MASTERS AND OPERATIVES

In their *History of Trade Unionism* the Webbs claimed that the years around 1850 constituted a 'watershed' in the development of trade unionism and industrial relations in Britain during the nineteenth century. According to the Webbs, the third quarter, with its moderate, conciliatory and pragmatic 'New Model' unions and its increasingly tranquil and harmonious industrial relations, stood in marked contrast to the radical, even revolutionary, unionism and chronic industrial conflict of the 1830s and 1840s.[1]

As every student of nineteenth-century labour history knows, historians have long debated the notion of a 'watershed'.[2] The purpose of this chapter is not to rehearse such debates, but to examine the validity of some of the Webbs' claims in relation to developments in industrial relations in the cotton districts. Central, overriding concern rests with an attempted evaluation of the extent to which relations between workers and employers in (mainly) cotton and (to a lesser extent) other industries underwent a major shift during the third quarter. Did industrial conflict diminish in terms of frequency and intensity? Did some agreement as to the 'rules of the game' take place — with employers more prepared to deal with trade unions and the latter more intent upon developing their organisational and bargaining strengths than upon fundamental social reconstruction? To what extent did the unions of the unskilled and semi-skilled in cotton assume the bureaucratic, centralised and moderate, pacifistic features and attitudes attributed by the Webbs to the 'New Models'? Finally, can developments in the field of industrial relations thus furnish any clues as to the increased reformism of workers and their institutions after 1850?

As the often conflicting judgements made by the mid-Victorian press and twentieth-century historians of Lancashire labour demonstrate, questions concerning the overall direction and temper of industrial relations in the cotton districts do not lend themselves to easy, instant answers. The majority of historians have little doubt that major changes and 'improvement' were in evidence at midcentury. Chapman, for example, believed that between 1850 and 1870 employers and workers 'came of age':

The trade-union movement was . . . in comparison with that of previous periods, peaceable and law-abiding. The operatives were ceasing to regard masters' associations as the malevolent combinations of their oppressors, and the masters were ceasing to regard trade unions as organised insubordination.[3]

H.A. Turner arrived at similar conclusions. He maintained that, although industrial relations were never totally placid, they showed a definite improvement in comparison with the 1830s and 1840s. Turner noted that there were no county-wide strikes or lock-outs in Lancashire after 1854, and that strikes were far less frequently accompanied by acts of incidental violence than in earlier years. Moreover, cotton unions, according to Turner, lowered their sights. Sporting the 'New Model' title of 'Amalgamated', they underwent 'a reconciliation with the new order', which expressed itself in 'attempts to adapt it to their needs rather than to overthrow it'.[4]

Finally, Joyce has argued that 'very considerable' changes occurred in relations between labour and capital during the 1850s and 1860s. Alongside the 'new paternalism' of the employer there developed moderate conciliatory and (especially in weaving) bureaucratised and centralised cotton unions. Industrial relations in cotton increasingly assumed institutionalised form, and a new 'calm' replaced the open industrial warfare of the pre-1854 era. It is Joyce's central contention that the emergence of a system of 'good labour relations' was of necessary, and, therefore, fundamental importance in the widespread growth of paternalism and deference.[5]

The mid-Victorian press was, however, for less inclined to record major and enduring 'improvements' in the tenor of industrial relations. This is not to suggest that no gains were recorded. At various times throughout the period the press wholeheartedly congratulated employers and employed upon their 'newfound harmony' and their spirit of tolerance. Indeed, on several occasions the press spoke enthusiastically of the possibilities of lasting social harmony and industrial peace. In 1856, for example, the *Manchester Guardian* boasted of, 'the prosperity, contentment, and re-union of social affection' which had resulted from 'the legislation in recent years'.[6] In January 1857 the *Ashton Reporter* proudly proclaimed that there was 'no discord between the various classes of the community'.[7] And in April of the following year one of the most prominent manufacturers in Ashton received warm applause when he declared at a meeting that: 'There was a feeling of sympathy which now existed between master and workman . . . which but a few years ago was entirely unknown.'[8]

Such sentiments reached a climax in the periods of good trade and favourable employment opportunities in 1859 and 1860. In December 1859, for example, the *Ashton Reporter* could record 'with pleasure' the year's events in the district: a 'happy feeling of reciprocity' characterised relations between employers and workers.[9] Optimistic reports and forecasts were, however, not exclusively confined to periods of economic upswing. Many reporters believed that rather than re-opening old class wounds the Cotton Famine produced 'a new feeling of respect' induced by 'common suffering'. In 1862 Alexander Redgrave, the factory inspector, observed that relations in industry had 'never been better'. 'What is passing now in Lancashire and other manufacturing districts,' he declared, 'is a triumphant instance of the increased intelligence and higher tone of the operatives.'[10] And in the post-Famine years many newspapers welcomed the efforts of employers and unions to create Boards of Conciliation and Arbitration.[11]

We would, however, be wrong to assume that press coverage of trends in industrial relations was uniformly or permanently favourable. All too often chronic fluctuations in trade and the temper of industrial relations[12] compelled the press to retract its erstwhile prognostications of industrial peace and harmony, and substitute circumspection and sober realism for exaggerated optimism. Hence the generally favourable newspaper reports of 1850 gave way in the conflict-ridden years of 1853 and 1854 to gloomy expectations of perpetual industrial warfare.[13] In a similar, although less pronounced manner, the depression and severe unemployment of the winter of 1857 burst the optimistic bubble of 1856. 'The working classes are seriously dissatisfied,' noted the *Ashton Reporter*, 'prosperous times may abate the more prominent symptoms [of discontent] but the first sign of adversity exacerbates them.'[14] In 1860, the *Ashton Standard* warned that short periods of prosperity could not erase class hostilities which had accumulated over the previous 50 years. Beneath 'the smiling outside' of prosperity, and despite the 'flattering terms' in which men and masters had spoken of one another, there remained 'much of the old feeling'. It will require another generation at least,' concluded the *Standard*, ' . . . even under the most improved conditions, before the title of cotton master can come to be regarded as synonomous with that of a good, kind, and humane employer of people.'[15]

The *Standard*'s prediction proved to be accurate. Throughout the decade of the 1860s industrial conflict was much in evidence. In the spring of 1861 powerloom weavers and employers throughout southeast Lancashire and much of northeast Cheshire were locked in bitter conflict. During the supposedly harmonious years of the Cotton Famine, both the *Times* and the *Ashton Standard* noted that worker complaints concerning low scales of relief and employer parsimony were 'rife', and that 'mutterings deep if not loud' were to be heard 'in all directions'.[16] In 1866 the *Manchester City News* protested that 'internecine industrial warfare' was 'the one blot and the reproach of our national intelligence'.[17] And by 1869 the *Ashton Reporter* had abandoned its earlier optimism. 'Their distrust of each other dates many years back,' claimed the *Reporter*,

> and the growing intelligence, of which we ever and anon are reminded by warm hearted and enthusiastic masters and men, seems to leave them, on the whole, very much as it found them. During periods of cotton prosperity exciting speeches are delivered respecting the oneness and identity of their interests, but when a recurrence of bad trade takes place we see really nothing whatever significant of the altered relations or improved intelligence of those classes, who were almost ready to embrace each other when times were good . . . The actual appreciation of each others interests, and the recognition of each others rights appear as far off as ever.[18]

While I might wish to modify the sentiments expressed in the *Reporter*'s concluding sentence, I nevertheless believe that its evaluation of the tenor of industrial relations in the third quarter of the century was far more accurate than that advanced by Chapman. In this chapter I will offer the thesis that despite the moderate and narrowly 'economistic' aims of increasingly bureaucratised cotton trade unionism, despite the efforts of union leaders to promote arbitration, goodwill and stability, despite numerous instances of 'enlightened' conduct among employers and despite the fact that class conflict was more subdued in the 1860s than in the 1830s and 1840s, industrial conflict persisted, often at high levels of intensity, throughout the mid-Victorian period, and constituted the major source of friction between the working class and the manufacturing middle class. Therefore, although advances were registered, any attempt to explain working-class accommodation to the capitalist order primarily or mainly in terms of a substantial 'improvement' in industrial relations is, at least for the cotton districts, unconvincing.

The chapter is organised around the themes of conflict and reconciliation. A detailed examination of the nature, pattern and causes of conflicts between masters and operatives is followed by an investigation into areas of 'improvement' and reconciliation. Both parts of the chapter pay close attention to the attitudes and behaviour of trade unionists and employers and the incidence of industrial disputes. The chapter is underpinned by the belief that generalisation concerning trends in industrial relations during the third quarter must be supported by a far more substantial and detailed evidence than has often been the case in the past.[19]

Conflict

Industrial relations in Lancashire and Cheshire were rarely placid or harmonious. Conflicts persisted throughout the period 1850–70, albeit at varying levels of intensity. Unrest, in the form of strikes and lock-outs, surfaced most acutely in the years 1853–4, 1861, 1867, and 1869. Apart from 1853, these were years of bad trade and attempted wage reductions. However, conflict was not confined to these years.

Hence the enactment of the Ten Hours Bill in 1847 and the demise of Chartism as a mass movement after 1848 did not initiate a period of unmitigated industrial peace and worker contentment. In the good year of 1849, when demand for labour quickened, the *Manchester Examiner and Times* could still warn its readers that 'the most dangerous feature' of the country was 'the isolation and antagonism, the distrust or alienation' that existed between different social classes.[20] To be sure, the cotton industry was not troubled between 1849 and 1853 by major widespread conflicts, but bitter local disputes did surface. For example, Elkanah Armitage's factory at Salford was hit by a seven months' strike in 1850 and 1851 which was attended by considerable violence and ill-will. Armitage's property was attacked, 'knobsticks' beaten and ill-feeling prevailed on both sides. Many of the trades in Manchester held large demonstrations to protest against Armitage's non-union policy, and his haughty indifference to the plight of his workers.[21] The local employers complained, in turn, of worker violence and 'union dictation'. Blackburn and northeast Lancashire also witnessed fierce local struggles. However, in comparison with the late thirties and early forties, relations in the cotton industry as a whole were relatively peaceful during the late forties and early fifties.

The industrial storm centre of these years, both nationally and in Lancashire, was the engineering industry, where employer attempts to mechanise production, increase the number of semi-skilled machine operatives, and introduce piecework and systematic overtime met with fierce resistance from the skilled engineering workers.[22] The latter believed that a systematic employer attempt was being made to undermine their security, control, high-earning capacity and status, and to replace highly-skilled men by semi-skilled minders. The upshot was a period of acute industrial conflict during 1851 and 1852.[23] In Lancashire the struggle against the 'abuses' centred around Hibbert and Platts, the largest and most advanced engineering establishment in Europe. In May 1851 a partial worker victory was gained when Hibbert and Platt agreed to abolish systematic overtime and piecework. However, the issue concerning the employment of 'illegal' men was not resolved, and provided the spark for the national confrontation of January 1852 when the employers enforced a lock-out. The issues of systematic overtime, piecework and 'illegal' man continued to divide masters and workers, but the central points of conflict were the questions of union recognition, and the 'legitimate' exercise of power and authority at work. Thus both Hibbert and Platt and the vast majority of engineering employers throughout the country were pledged to resist 'any interference in the management of their business', and were, therefore, opposed to the threat posed by trade unionism, however moderate, to the employer's 'right to manage'. Aided by a widespread anti-union campaign in the press — the *Guardian*, for example, condemned the 'monstrous demands' of the union, which would put the 'idle and industrious . . . on the same footing' and lead to 'communism'[24] — the employers carried the day. By the end of April 1852 most of the skilled men had signed the 'document' renouncing trade union membership. Systematic overtime, piecework and the employment of semi-skilled machine operators were henceforth to be introduced at the discretion of the employer.

Class discord was not confined to the engineering industry. Conflicting worker and employer interpretations of the Ten Hours Bill of 1847 generated much bitterness and conflict. Employer attempts to nullify the effects of the Bill by operating a system of juvenile relays (which enabled them to work the legally unprotected adult males beyond the ten hours) triggered off protests in several cotton towns during 1849 and the early 1850s, and brought forth widespread calls and petitions for a 'True Ten Hours Bill' and the abolition of relays.[25] In February 1850 the operatives' cause suffered a severe blow when the judges of the Court of Exchequer upheld a ruling by the Manchester magistrates that the relay system was within the law. Agitation, especially under the auspices of the militant Fielden Association, continued, and in August 1853 Palmerston's bill prohibited relays and, in effect, introduced a standard ten and a half hour day for all grades of cotton factory workers. Only as a result of Disraeli's legislation of 1874 did the cotton operatives win a genuine ten hour day.

Although Palmerston's bill went some way towards mitigating worker frustrations, the whole question of legislative interference in cotton continued to excite passions on both sides well into the 1850s. In 1855, for example, the National Association of Factory Occupiers — claiming to have the support of the employers of some 250,000 workers — set its sights against the 'unjust, not to say insulting Acts'. The Association fought compensation cases in the courts and waged a fierce polemical battle against 'the unscrupulous statements and objectionable misrepresentations of the humanity mongers'. Dickens, with his 'philoperative cant, conceit, insolence, and wilful one-mindedness', was a favourite target for employer invective. As late as 1858 Horner, the factory inspector, claimed with no little authority that the 'leading' men in Lancashire were 'averse to all legislative interference with their concerns'.[26]

The Ten Hours agitation of the early 1850s was a prelude to the most conflict-ridden years of our period, 1853 and the first half of 1854. Demands for wage increases which started in coal and iron spread to the building industry and the docks, and even included policemen in Manchester. The nature and extent of the conflict can best be illustrated by a study of events in cotton.[27]

During the depression of 1847 cotton employers throughout Lancashire and Cheshire enforced a 10 per cent reduction in wages, but promised, at least according to the operatives, that the cuts would be restored once trade revived. Taking advantage of the improved state of trade in 1853, the operatives requested the employers to honour their pledge. The campaign was initiated at

Stockport in March. From the outset the operatives' committees at Stockport adopted an extremely conciliatory tone, speaking in 'very respectful terms' of the masters and asking for nothing 'unreasonable', merely the promised 10 per cent.[28] Care was taken to impress upon the public mind the 'loyal' and 'orderly' character of the workers. A weavers' committee placard, recounting the events of 1848, read: 'Did we break out into revolution, destroy property, or endanger the peace? No! No! . . . Property was never more safe and respected.'[29]

Such protestations of loyalty and moderation failed to impress the employers of the borough. It was obvious from the outset that the employers would not readily meet the workers' demands. Some employers had no recollection of any promise. Two further difficulties, which were to prove a constant thorn to all attempts at settlement, revealed themselves. Firstly, the employers were reluctant to recognise the workers' committees, preferring to bargain with their 'own' workpeople. By June, the weavers' committee had received only one communication from the Masters Association, which was an outright refusal of recognition.[30] The second problem revolved around the question of averages. The employers believed that an increase of wages could be justified only on the grounds that average wages in Stockport had failed to keep abreast of those in 35 towns and districts in Lancashire and Cheshire. The employers accordingly set to work to investigate wage rates in the 35 towns. The operatives, while by no means hostile to the idea of averages, argued that a 10 to 12 mile radius around Manchester would provide a more realistic basis of comparison. Nevertheless, an operative committee was set up to conduct a survey of both the 35 towns and the towns in the vicinity of Manchester. The committee's findings reinforced the operatives' case that wages in Stockport were found to be 8½ per cent below those in the 35 towns, and 12½ per cent below those in Ashton, Hyde and Oldham.[31]

These statistics were produced at the end of April. By the end of May, however, the employers had neither produced a rival set of figures, nor acknowledged the figures produced by the operatives. Moreover, many workers had been treated 'with contempt' and their committee with 'derision'. And a worker offer to submit the dispute to arbitration was flatly turned down by the employers, who simply warned the operatives against the evils of trade unionism, and against a repetition of the strike of 1842.[32]

By June, therefore, tempers were frayed. The 'moderation' and 'sweet reason' which had characterised the activities of the weavers' committee, gave way to frustration, bitterness and condemnations of the intransigence of capital. Threats to strike were widely circulated. George Cooper, one of the leading figures in the Stockport movement, cautioned the employers to beware, and 'not to tread so heavily upon their workpeople'.[33] By the middle of June 14,000 workers had turned out. At the beginning of July some 15 of the 52 mills in Stockport had conceded the advance demanded. Even at this stage, however, the employers remained unwilling to have any dealings with a committee representing the workers. When they finally relented, an 'animated interview' took place. The employers offered an advance of 10 per cent upon 1848 prices to the spinning and cardroom and blowing hands, but only 5 per cent to the weavers. Despite the readiness of the spinners' executive to accept the offer, a mass meeting of workers rejected the employers' averages, and the strike continued. However, at the beginning of August the operatives finally returned to work, all sections having received the advance demanded.[34]

The victory at Stockport gave added impetus to the 10 per cent movement in other towns. In June many of the weavers at Blackburn struck work for a 10 per cent advance in wages. By August their demands had been met.[35] At Manchester the police, and the dressers, dyers and finishers, struck in support of wage increases in July. The dyers' strike, which lasted 17 weeks, inflamed passions on both sides. Employer attempts to replace the 1,600 workers on strike with 'knobsticks' resulted in an attack on one factory, and frequent and bloody scuffles between striking workers and the strike breakers. And throughout August the trades in Manchester rallied to the support of their fellow workers by holding 'monster' sympathy demonstrations. The employers, nevertheless, carried the day: the dyers' union was effectively destroyed, and known union sympathisers blacklisted throughout the Manchester area.[36]

The employers' determination and intransigence in the dyers' strike was part of a general employer counter-offensive, which started in the summer months and gathered pace throughout the winter. In July, for example, the Manchester Spinners and Manufacturers Association, supported by some 360 firms, was inaugurated. Its overriding aim was to protect the 'freedom and independence' of the employers against 'the very extraordinary claims' being made upon them by 'bodies and associations engaged in the cotton trade', which wished to 'dictate and interfere' in the functions reserved for management.[37]

Throughout the autumn and winter months the number of strikes and lock-outs escalated. In September the weavers at Manchester struck work in support of their claim for 10 per cent and union recognition. At the end of the month the Preston manufacturers formed an association to 'annul the actions of the workpeople', and in October enforced the lock-out which was to last 28 weeks.[38] In November the *Peoples Paper* estimated the numbers locked out or on strike in Lancashire to be between 60 and 70 thousand.[39] Lock-outs were in force at Wigan, Burnley, Preston, and in the Bacup region; workers were on strike at Manchester, Bury and Darwen; and negotiations were in progress in many towns in southeast Lancashire. In the same month the *Guardian* warned its readers that the times were 'pregnant with danger': hostilities between workers and employers had become 'more alarming and serious, because more extensive', than 'anything ever recorded in the history of strikes.'[40]

Hostilities were most marked at Preston. From October 1853 workers and employers throughout Lancashire and Cheshire increasingly concentrated their attentions and resources upon Preston.[41] In December a general association of employers was formed to render financial and moral assistance to the Preston masters; a scurrilous anti-union campaign was mounted in the press; and the countryside scoured for potential sources of 'free' labour. For their part, the operatives elected delegates to guide the struggle at Preston, organised demonstrations of solidarity throughout the manufacturing districts, and initiated a regular system of contributions. The upshot was the most bitter and protracted struggle of our period involving 26,000 workers and lasting 28 weeks.

As at Stockport, the operatives of Preston believed their demands for 10 per cent and union recognition to be consistent with principles of equity and justice. However, steadfast employer refusals to countenance such demands created an atmosphere torn by class hatred. The Preston masters were commonly seen as 'greedy tyrants', 'hypocrites', 'inhuman monsters', the 'most oppressive' and 'gormandizing' in the county. In the opinion of Mortimer Grimshaw, one of the central figures in the struggle, human considerations had no place in the collective employer conscience: 'The Manchester Guardian was their Bible, the Examiner and Times was their Testament . . . Gold was their God, silver their Jesus Christ, and copper their Holy Ghost.'[42] Traditionally the last to concede advances, the first to enforce reductions, and aided by the Poor Law Guardians, who in the event of a strike 'emptied their workhouses of all that could crawl from the gates', the Preston employers did in a very real sense give credence to the popular image of the tyrannical and cold-hearted capitalist.

As frustrations mounted throughout the winter months, threats of violence grew. Swinglehurst, for example, suggested that the disturbances in Spain 'should teach the masters a lesson'. 'Might not they too', he continued, 'have to take up arms and defend themselves?' He hoped not, 'but patience had limits. Let them have a cessation of labour in this country for two days only, and England would be free.'[43] By April the Preston operatives had become desperate, 'knobsticks' having been brought in and the leading delegates arrested. The lock-outs at Burnely, Padiham, Colne and Bacup, and the strike at Stockport against employers' attempts to deduct the 10 per cent won by the operatives in 1853, severely reduced the contributions going to Preston. In May the Preston operatives were literally starved back to work on the employers' terms, and reductions in cotton operatives' wages were enforced throughout Lancashire and Cheshire.[44]

The significance of the struggles of 1853 and 1854 was that they belied hopes for industrial harmony and marked a revival of general class conflict. Throughout 1853 and 1854 the overwhelming majority of cotton (and other) employers were extremely reluctant either to concede wage advances or to recognise trade unions. The latter were generally viewed by employers as coercive bodies which sought to challenge the capitalists' control and authority in the workplace. And, faced by employer hostility, workers and trade unionists became increasingly antagonistic towards and more wide-ranging in their criticisms of employers *as a class*.[45] Heightened worker militancy and awareness reflected themselves in a hardening of language and attitudes towards capital, and in the growth of (albeit temporary and limited) support for the notion of co-operative production and Ernest Jones's idea of a Labour Parliament. During the course of the 10 per cent campaigns workers' became progressively less conciliatory in their attitudes and language. In refusing to abide by the conventions of 'reason' and 'commonsense', capitalists were thought to be acting in a 'greedy', 'unscrupulous' and 'tyrannical' manner. In such circumstances, not only individual capitalists, but the capitalist class as a whole, and the society they represented, were more widely criticised. *An Address to the Cardroom Hands of England*, issued by the Stockport operatives, typified this approach:

> We live in an age of selfishness and co-opposition, and dwell in a land of exaction and oppression . . . That some members of society should become poor through their idleness, extravagance or imprudence is not surprising; but for whole communities to become poor by industry is monstrous. To labour in want, and to labour in fear of still greater want even in the midst of abundance is that which renders the condition of the British labourer worse than that of the West Indian slave.

Emancipation would come through organisation and struggle. The Address continued: 'Then arouse yourselves, fellow operatives, from your apathy and inactivity — be no longer the willing slaves of the tyrannical manufacturers, nor the tools of the merciless speculators'.[46] The goal to be attained was no longer a 'fair day's wage for a fair day's work', but 'the abolition of wage slavery'. 'If working people persevered in their union', declared one Stockport operative, 'employers would become an obsolete race, and the working people would employ themselves.'[47]

By no means all workers would have shared the Stockport operative's faith, nor would some have subscribed to his views. However, many of the operatives involved in the conflicts of 1853 and 1854 yearned for a society in which competition and industrial strife would be things of a corrupt past. While many of their dreams remained unfulfilled, or gave way to resignation, it is significant that the idea of co-operative production, as a means of abolishing 'wage slavery', was widely circulated at this time and received support from workers at both Preston and Stockport.[48]

Similarly, the ideas of Ernest Jones were not without influence. Towards the end of 1853 Jones and a few Chartists, such as Edward Hooson of Manchester, conceived of a scheme whereby workers throughout the country would elect delegates to a labour parliament.[49] The aims of the parliament were twofold. Firstly, by levying a rate of one penny per week on wages, the parliament would render financial assistance to workers on strike or locked out. Secondly, and more significantly, by purchasing land and machinery, the parliament would create a co-operative society based on common ownership. Despite the collapse of the Labour Parliament in

1854 — lack of support and inadequate funding were major problems[50] — Jones and his comrades did register some successes during the wave of strikes and lock-outs. Jones addressed enthusiastic audiences at Wigan and Stockport, and local branches were set up at Stockport, Rochdale and Stalybridge. Support was forthcoming from some of the weavers' delegates; and representatives of the cardroom hands from Bolton and Stalybridge, the weavers from Preston, and Bury, the Leek silk twisters, operatives from Stockport, the cordwainers from north Lancashire and the dyers from Manchester attended the meeting of March 1854. By the summer, however, hopes of 'emancipating the mass of our countrymen from the curse of wage slavery' has faded. The eventual failure of the 10 per cent struggles deflated hopes for radical social change and brought in their wake bitterness and resignation to capitalist rule.[51]

The intensity and scale of the unrest of 1853 and 1854 were not to be repeated. Nevertheless, industrial relations were by no means harmonious during the remainder of the decade. At the end of 1855, for example, the self-actor minders and piecers in Manchester struck work against a 10 per cent reduction. The strike followed what had become a familiar pattern. The workers' addresses in favour of short time rather than a reduction in wages were couched in conciliatory language, a fact which did not escape the attention of either the fiercely anti-unionist *Manchester Guardian* or the employers themselves.[52] Nevertheless, the employers refused to reconsider their decision, claiming that the rates paid to piecers and self-actor minder were higher than those paid in other areas, and complaining of 'the past dictatorial conduct' of this class of self-actor minders and piecers, who would only work the mule 'in a manner they deem to be proper'.[53] Worker frustrations grew. 'If we quiety succumbed to this reduction', declared one operative, 'other reductions would follow . . . until we reached the utmost limit of bare existence.' The masters were accused of seeking a reduction not on account of 'bad trade', but from their own 'cupidity'. Another delegate anticipated a struggle on the scale of that of 1829: 'He had gone there determined not to speak violently of the masters, but with the system they were pursuing . . . now was not the time to be mealy-mouthed with them [the employers] because there was no chance of filling up the gulf which they had made, seeing that they manifested such a determination in their purpose.'[54] The masters had 'a concentrated organisation by which they were determined to crush and degrade their workpeople': the piecers and self-actor minders lacked strong trade union defences. In these circumstances the strike was doomed to failure. By the middle of January the men were beginning to drift back to work. By February the strike had ended in ignominious defeat; attempts to resurrect trade union organisation had been crushed, and the number of mules assigned to each worker increased.[55] Further isolated and unsuccessful strikes against reductions took place at Preston and Blackburn during 1856.[56] Throughout 1857 and for the greater part of 1858 relative quiet prevailed. In August 1858 weavers at three factories in the Ashton district struck work against reductions, but no general turn-out ensued.[57]

Following the revival of trade in 1859, workers throughout Lancashire and Cheshire submitted demands for increased wages. The intensity and momentum of the movement and employer reactions to newfound worker confidence were reflected in the writings of one employer, James Garnett of Low Moor, Clitheroe.[58] In the early months of 1859 Garnett noted that 'great uneasiness' prevailed among the operatives. 'Every class is clamouring for an advance of wages', he declared, 'and now that times are good they are unmanageable'. Against his better judgement, Garnett conceded an advance of 5 per cent to the spinners in April. In May, when the spinners requested a further 5 per cent increase, he 'indignantly refused'. A week later Garnett received a letter from the Central Committee of Self-Actor Minders threatening a strike unless the advance was extended to include the piecers. Following a strike in the late summer, he conceded a further advance to the spinners. In October the hands in the blowing room gave notice of a strike because their requests for an increase had not been met. During the same month Garnett met deputations from the weavers, warpers, twisters and cardroom hands, all asking for increases. However, in spite of industrial unrest and the advances made, Garnett wrote that the year of 1859 had been one 'of almost unprecedented prosperity'. In January 1860 weavers' complaints concerning inferior materials snowballed into a strike in support of payment of the Blackburn Standard List. Garnett was extremely reluctant to have any dealings with Pinder, the union representative, or to recognise any form of trade unionism — 'the real question was whether an employer was to be master of his own concern, or whether he was to be ruled by an irresponsible committee, sitting he knew not where, and composed of he knew not whom.' Nevertheless, he was forced to deal with 'this dictatorial spirit'. By February he was complaining that the 'insubordination' of the workers was 'beyond all bounds'. In March, winders and warpers received a 5 per cent advance to bring them into line with the Blackburn list.[59] And in July the spinners and cardroom hands, taking advantage of the tight labour market, secured an advance, despite Garnett's repeated complaints concerning the 'tyrannical' powers of trade unionism.

The twin issues of union recognition and enforcement of the Blackburn Standard List, which dogged relations at Low Moor, were of crucial importance in the Padiham strike of 1859. In 1858 the East Lancashire Amalgamated Power Loom Weavers Friendly Association initiated a campaign to recruit members for the union, to secure a general enforcement of the Standard List paid at Blackburn, and to establish the union secretary's right to inspect machinery in the mills. Although successful in its first aim — membership grew rapidly in 1859 — the union's other two proposals encountered fierce employer resistance. The Padiham dispute, which lasted 29 weeks, provided the real test of strength.[60] In 1859 the employers of Padiham offered their workers an advance of 10 per cent, but the workers rejected the offer on the grounds that it was 2½ per cent below the Blackburn list. A strike became inevitable when the Employers Association 'positively refused' to allow Pinder, the union secretary, to inspect the looms in their factories. Eventually, after a 29-week strike and its attendant conflict and ill-will, the union triumphed. The employers agreed to pay the standard rate and in effect to negotiate with union representatives.

Trade unionism also made spectacular gains in south Lancashire and Cheshire in 1859 and 1860. Following a strike at Ashton Bros., Hyde, in June 1859 vigorous attempts were made to form a union which would embrace powerloom weavers and cardroom hands. The response was magnificent. Public meetings held to outline the benefits of trade unionism were 'literally crammed'. At one meeting alone 700 members were enrolled; by the end of June the union could claim a membership of some 2,000.[61] In August the North Cheshire Amalgamated Factory Operatives' Union was formed. Claiming that employers had combined to 'keep them poor and powerless', the union called on 'the oppressed sons of toil' to assert their 'manliness': by the middle of August the union had a membership of 3,000 workers.[62] In 1860 Reverend Verity and J.R. Stephens held boisterous meetings in the Ashton area, exhorting the workers to support the operatives of Padiham and to join the Amalgamated.

Verity asked enthusiastic and crowded meetings to combine 'in order to vindicate humanity from its mighty tyrants, and redeem themselves from their grasp'. Stephens's criticisms of industrial capitalism were as cutting as they had been in the 1830s: 'All that independence as citizens, as yeomen, as independent freemen', he cried, 'had disappeared; they now lived on wages . . . and if work be suspended they were thrown into the streets, helpless and powerless, and as a consequence, compelled in thousands . . . to accomplish by union what they could not accomplish in their individual capacity.'[63] Such polemics had the desired effect — membership of the Amalgamated rapidly increased.

Industrial conflict in southeast Lancashire and Cheshire was not, however, particularly marked during 1860. To be sure, the Oldham spinners threatened to strike in support of their wage claim, and one or two mills in the Ashton area experienced turn-outs. On the whole, however, employers readily conceded the advances demanded by the operatives.[64] And in his report for April 1860, Alexander Redgrave, the factory inspector, noted with obvious satisfaction: 'Probably at no time have the operatives been in the enjoyment of so many advantages as at the present; labour is in demand; wages are good; the hours of work are moderate.'[65]

By March 1861 Redgrave's optimism was redundant. At the first sign of trade stagnation in the early months of 1861 employers throughout the cotton districts cut wages by 7½ per cent. In February Blackburn was in 'a very excited state'. No longer willing to tolerate 'union dictation', and totally unsympathetic to worker suggestions for short-time, the Blackburn cotton employers enforced a lock-out. By the middle of February 16,000 workers stood idle. By mid-March lack of funds had compelled the vast majority of Blackburn's cotton operatives to return to work empty-handed.[66] However, apart from Stockport, where 'nothing but a feeling of harmony and contentment' prevailed, conflict in 1861 was most pronounced in southeast Lancashire and northeast Cheshire. At Bolton 12,000 operatives turned out. In March the employers declined an offer of arbitration put to them by the executive committee of the South Lancashire Weavers Union — whereupon the normally mild-mannered committee registered its strong disapproval of 'such haughty and serf-like treatment', which 'only tends to irritate and embitter the antagonistic feelings of the operatives against them'.[67] In refusing to accept reductions in wages, workers were effectively locked out in March. By April 30,000 workers in southeast Lancashire and northeast Cheshire were out of work, Ashton and Stalybridge being the worst hit with unemployment figures of 4,500 and 4,200 respectively.[68]

The general proceedings reminded one contemporary of the 'great agitation in the palmy days of Chartism'. Open air meetings, often numbering between 5,000 and 12,000 operatives, and processions accompanied by banners and the music of the Bolton Fife and Drum Band, were held in the Ashton area throughout March and April.[69] More significant was the fact that some operatives made conscious efforts to imitate the pattern of 1842. One of the more moderate leaders at Ashton claimed that the overriding aim of the operatives was 'to induce all to come out in South Lancashire'.[70] Despite official union disapproval, a massive body of weavers visited Ashton, Stalybridge, Dukinfield, Hyde and Glossop in turn, in March, calling upon the weavers still at work to join them. Glossop 'presented a scene such as seldom before witnessed', the town reverberating to the sound of 12,000 weavers singing 'Britons Never Shall Be Slaves'. And only speedy union intervention prevented the planned marches to Oldham and Stockport from taking place.[71] The speeches made at the 'monster gatherings' also bore a striking resemblance to those made in 1842 and 1853. Probably the most charismatic figure in Ashton and Stalybridge was Jonathan Bintcliffe, whose fiery denunciations of 'capitalist oppression' drew a warm response from his audience. 'It had come to this', declared Bintcliffe, 'that the classes who had produced the wealth of the country, must not be allowed to eat of the wealth they had produced.' The working class had been 'gathering honey', not for themselves, 'but for certain old drones, filled their pockets, and enabled them to make whips to lash their backs with; because for every pound they increased their masters in wealth, they gave them pounds worth of power to thrash them with.' Bintcliffe's sentiments were in no sense those of an isolated and frustrated extremist. The so-called 'moderate' leaders agreed that 'the present position was for life and death', and spoke freely and frequently of the pressing need to abolish 'wage-slavery'.[72] And when the operatives were finally driven back to work by starvation in May and the weavers' union destroyed by the employers, proposals for the creation of producer co-operatives were widely aired at crowded meetings. The opening of the co-operative Stalybridge Spinning and Mill Company in June was heralded as the first step towards the 'total abolition of wage-slavery'.[73]

The northern blockade of the southern ports of the United States of America, which cut off supplies of Lancashire's life blood, cotton, brought with it unprecedented unemployment from the end of 1861 to 1864. Ashton, the town hardest hit by the Cotton Famine, had at the beginning of 1861 a regularly employed cotton workforce of 11,000. By January 1863 there were 1,263 cotton operatives on full time, 3,111 on short time, and 6,482 unemployed in Ashton. The situation had not greatly improved by December 1863, there being 2,128 on full time, 2,772 on short time, and 5,956 unemployed. In 1862 approximately, 1,700 workers left Ashton for the United States.[94] Unemployment, which thus reached the 60 per cent mark, failed, however, to produce a social revolution. Indeed, it was the conduct of the operatives during the Cotton Famine — their 'patient forebearance' and their disinclination to riot — which won the praise of politicans of all shades, and which convinced many of working-class fitness for the vote.[75] These years were often seen by contemporaries as the highwater mark of class harmony and social cohesion. The *Times* correspondent outlined his viewpoint in 1863:

> It is generally supposed that the unemployed operatives are enduring the crisis calmly and contentedly, fully persuaded not only that it was unavoidable, but that every effort is being made to meet it. It is presumed that the stringency of the Poor Law is being relaxed to meet the exceptional features of the case; that the Relief Committees are, on the whole, fulfilling their trust to the satisfaction of the recipients; that with a few exceptions, the wealthier masters are paying considerable weekly allowances to their hands, and are allowing them to live in their cottages rent free.[76]

This 'official' viewpoint which, with the publication in 1866 of Dr John Watts' book *The Facts of the Cotton Famine*, became standard orthodoxy, is in many respects superficial. Grievances did not simply melt away. J.H. Bridges, the *Times* correspondent in the north, realised that beneath a carefully cultivated exterior of placidity, there lay 'deep and widespread irriation'.

The sources of worker discontent were threefold. Firstly, operatives bitterly resented the failure of the authorities to revise the system of poor relief introduced by the Poor Law Amendment Act of 1834.[77] Outdoor relief for the able-bodied had never been completely abolished in the cotton districts, but operatives were particularly incensed by the low scales of relief, the physical separation of the sexes, and the 'humiliating' and 'degrading' tasks of the 'labour test'. These grievances were aired at large and boisterous meetings throughout 1862. At a demonstration in Manchester in July Mr Schofield captured the general mood of the audience in declaring that the operatives, 'for no cause of their own', were being treated 'worse than felons in gaol'. 'Women would rather go into the streets', he continued, 'than be put under the same tyranny again.'[78] At Preston, Banks, the spinners' leader, protested that stone breaking and oakum picking were tasks intended for the 'idle and profligate' rather than for 'honest, independent, self-respecting workingmen', who never shunned hard work. The delegate meeting of operative spinners in July resolved that 'to exact any kind of degraded labour from applicants for relief' was to 'aggravate rather than mitigate their misfortune.'[79] In short, there was a consensus of opinion among cotton operatives that stone breaking and oakum picking were degrading tasks incompatible with self-respect.

The guardians' insensivity to unemployed workers was compounded by a frequent failure to treat applicants with civility and respect. Bridges found that at Manchester and Preston approximately one minute was devoted to the consideration of an applicant's case. Applicants had no means of redress: the guardians' word was final. Many guardians were also notorious for their stringency. Doubtless widespread was the opinion expressed by one officer that the employer practice of supplementing poor relief with albeit meagre wages was 'incompatible with the spirit of the Poor Law'.[80]

Operatives were sometimes supported in their criticisms of the system of poor relief by members of the middle class. In April 1862, for example, a joint deputation of workers and employers met with the guardians at Ashton to present the workers' case. In the following month some employers at Stalybridge signed a petition which called for a relaxation of some of the more obvious and patently irrelevant aspects of the Poor Law. Similarly, a delegation of spinners, which presented a list of their complaints to the government in August, thanked Palmerston for the 'kind and courteous manner' in which he had received them. Thanks were also extended to those employers sympathetic to the spinners' cause.[81]

At a wider level, a picture of unrelieved hostility between workers and employers is wide of the mark. Some employers heeded the *Manchester Guardian*'s advice that the presence of adversity, 'should cause distinctions of social position to be merged in the common desire to bring succour to the suffering class'. Very real efforts were made by such employers to alleviate the operatives' plight — free clothes and food were distributed; rent arrears were conveniently overlooked; mills were run at a loss; and generous contributions made to local relief funds.[82] Nevertheless, the second source of operative bitterness revolved around the miserly attitude adopted by some of the wealthy members of the community. Worker complaints were loudest and most persistent in those towns most severely hit by the Famine. In April 1862 the *Ashton Reporter* received a particularly ominous letter, which read:

> Unless some united action be taken by those who have wealth and influence at hand to alleviate the sufferings of the operatives, who have hitherto borne their privations with the utmost fortitude and resignation, I believe that at no distant day the smouldering embers of dissatisfaction, which are beginning to ooze through the fissures of the troubled minds of the operatives, will explode with a violence too terrible to be conceived.[83]

The widespread indifference displayed by many of the wealthy to the sufferings of the operative population in the Ashton and Stalybridge area was the subject of a series of operative meetings held throughout 1862. In May Jonathan Bintcliffe warned the masters that, 'starving people were no longer themselves', and that 'it was dangerous to allow them to remain destitute in a country where there was enough for each and enough for all'.[84] When the mayor of Ashton convened a public meeting to protest against the harshness of the system of poor relief, few of the wealthy attended. Some accused the workers of 'ingratitude, indolence, and pauperism', and only a dozen of the 36 mill owners in the borough of Ashton contributed to the local relief fund. Indeed, by May of 1862 the relief fund was exhausted: it did not recommence operations until September. This position contrasted unfavourably with that of neighbouring Mossley, where relations between workers and employers were excellent, the latter having contributed generously to the fund.[85] Ashton operatives were not alone in their bitterness. In August 1862 the operatives at Oldham, threatening to 'repeat '42', were held in check only by their moderate leaders, whose antipathy to worker violence matched that of the authorities.[86]

Thirdly, both the central executive committee in Manchester and local relief committees were increasingly accused of partiality, arbitrary exercise of power, and of a marked tendency to imitate the parsimonious, and 'inhumane' activities of the Poor Law Guardians. Scales of relief were painstakingly designed so as not to be conducive to 'idleness and dissipation', and many of the committee members' actions were characterised by a gross insensitivity to the operatives' self-respect, pride, independence and intellectual capacities. At Preston every article of clothing distributed by the relief committee was stamped with the word 'lent'; and the committee's handbook reminded the recipient that clothing could be reclaimed 'should the recipient be found unworthy of it'.[87] Bridges saw hundreds of spinners and minders herded together with beggars and vagabonds. When a committee member entered the room the male operatives were roughly ordered to doff their caps. The various grievances of the operatives were summarised in a resolution adopted by 2,000 Stalybridge workers in March 1863. The resolution read:

> . . . the mode of administration is becoming every day more analagous to the practice of the Poor Law Guardians. Language of a harsh, brutal, and disgusting kind is habitually used . . . not merely by the agents of the committee, but by some of the gentlemen who comprise it; and not merely to men, but to their wives and daughters. The conduct of the committee has been marked by innumerable instances of capricious favouritism and arbitrary injustice, and in none of these cases have your memorialists any security for a fair and impartial hearing . . .[88]

Operatives also resented the fact that non-attendance at the schools set up by the committees resulted in non-payment of relief. Whilst welcoming the opportunity to receive educational instruction, and conscious of 'the benevolent motives' of the promoters of the schools, workers were angered and insulted by the dictatorial and mistrustful way in which the schools were run. They were, in fact, treated like rebellious children, whose primary aim was non-attendance rather than educational enlightenment. Leaves of absence, even for the purposes of visiting sick relations, attending funerals, or seeking work, were granted at the absolute discretion of the schoolmaster. Bridges witnessed the pitiful sight of 500 men in a reading school in Ashton kept under lock and key throughout the whole day.[89] Finally, many employers consistently opposed attempts to use public funds for the purpose of emigration. Rather they 'wished to reduce wages permanently by keeping on the spot a stock of superfluous labour.' And those who were fortunate enough to find work, often found that their wages were below the standard rate.[90]

The accumulation of these various grievances produced an atmosphere of suspicion and discontent, which came to a head in the early months of 1863. Throughout the latter part of January and the whole of February angry crowds in Stalybridge condemned the local committee's 'cruelty, plunder, and partiality', but more particularly its decision to deduct four pence per week from each operative's income. In February women in the education and sewing classes at Oldham struck school against 'the unequal distribution of relief'. Similar turn-outs followed at the Stalybridge schools. At Ashton and Dukinfield workers reacted to relief cuts by quitting the schools, and marching through the streets.[91]

Rioting broke out in March. The relief committee at Stalybridge, deciding that the operatives were incapable of spending their money in a judicious manner (much of it allegedly was 'squandered' on drink), introduced a payment-by-ticket system. Under the new system the committee retained a day's wage in hand, and paid workers in the form of tickets, which were to be cashed at authorised provision stores.[92] In the eyes of the operatives, the innovation represented the culmination of a whole series of measures designed to insult their intelligence, and limit their freedom of action and choice. They accordingly drew up a petition against the new measure, and sent a deputation to Manchester to present their case to the central executive committee. The committee promised to raise the matter at their next meeting. While the members of the deputation were apparently satisfied with this response, the workers at Stalybridge were impatient for immediate redress of their wrongs.

On Thursday 19 March, the day before the ticket system was due to take affect, an 'indignation' meeting was held on the Plantation Ground at Stalybridge. The operatives unanimously agreed not to accept the new system. Friday saw 'outrages of a most disgraceful character'.[93] Towards midday the principal streets of the borough presented signs of 'considerable commotion'. Although no outbreaks of violence took place, large groups of operatives were to be seen in earnest discussion. In the early afternoon Bates and Kirk, two leading committee members, notified the operatives of their willingness to reconsider the whole question of tickets. However, the operatives demanded unequivocal and immediate action. Tempers became heated and the cab in which Bates and Kirk were travelling was attacked; they escaped without suffering serious injury. This skirmish formed the prelude to 'extensive disturbances'. At four o'clock when the schools closed a large crowd of men and women formed a procession and walked through the streets 'shouting and hooting'. Although 'urged by the women to attack the police', the crowd first marched to the Central Schools at Castle Street Mills, and joined the scholars there in breaking windows and damaging part of the machinery. The arrival of a body of policemen prevented further destruction at the mills. The crowd then turned its attention to the police station, where many of the windows were smashed. The windows in the homes of several of the relief committee members suffered the same fate. Returning to the centre of the town the operatives gained entry to the rooms of the relief committee and hurled stockings, waistcoats and jackets to their grateful companions outside. In spite of repeated police attempts to disperse the crowd, the relief stores were ransacked and almost fired. The disturbances were finally brought to a halt by the arrival of the hussars.

Rioting erupted again on Saturday. When the relief committee refused to comply with the operatives' request for the abolition of the ticket system, a large crowd, demanding 'money and bread', ransacked several of the provision stores. Sunday passed off relatively peacefully, notwithstanding threats to 'fire the mills' and 'plunder the shops'. By Monday Stalybridge was once again in an 'excited state'. Approximately 12,000 operatives gathered in the streets. According to the *Guardian*, their 'amusements' appeared to be 'to jostle the more respectable inhabitants, thrash the Stalybridge police, and beat the shop doors and window shutters to the no small terror of the inmates.'

On Monday the riots spread beyond Stalybridge. Three hundred operatives marched from Stalybridge to Ashton, where provision dealers threw bread and cheese into the streets. Driven out of Ashton, sections of the crowd proceeded to Dukinfield where they 'pretty well cleared' the shops. Similar scenes were enacted at Hyde.[94] At Stockport 'some excitement' prevailed. The authorities, fearing a 'visit' from the Stalybridge crowd, swore in 1,000 special constables. The 'visit' did not materialise, but large numbers of the Stockport operatives, angered by the relief committee's decision to increase the hours of labour, 'collected in knots' around the various relief stores in the town. Some windows were broken, but no extensive damage was committed. On the following day 500 of the pauper labourers paraded through the streets of Stockport, calling on the scholars to join them. Once again, however, there was little violence.[95]

Indeed by Tuesday evening the riots in Stalybridge were at an end. The operatives, deciding to accept the ticket system for one week's duration, returned to the schools. The newspapers attributed much of the blame for the riots to the Irish. This view contained a grain of truth in so far as 28 out of the 29 sent for trial from Stalybridge were Irish. The riots were, however, symptomatic of the resentments felt by thousands of operatives, both English and Irish. And it is significant that when the police at Stalybridge attempted to transfer the prisoners from the police station to the railway station, they were confronted by a crowd of some 15,000 English and Irish operatives, demanding the release of their comrades.[96]

The return to work of the operatives at Stalybridge did not signal an end to the unrest in other towns. Although rioting did not spread to Manchester, the atmosphere in the city was far from placid. At a mass meeting held in Stevenson Square in March, Mr Rawlinson, while describing the Lancashire operatives as 'the most enlightened, patriotic, and moral' in the country, nevertheless warned the authorities that it was 'dangerous to play with people possessing a strong arm, and a powerful will'. Another speaker served notice to the Poor Law Guardians that if they refused to increase the scales of relief 'the riot in Stalybridge was but the sounding of the tocsin, that would reverberate throughout the whole of the country.'[97] In April disturbances broke out at Preston. On Monday 20th, the 1,000 operatives set to work to clear land for a new cattle market struck work against the decision of the guardians to lengthen the working day.[98] The operatives paraded effigies of the guardians up and down the market ground, and then, amid 'groans and effected sorrow', buried them. On the following evening both the operatives employed at the cattle market, and those on the Moss, proceeded to the police station, where a deputation met with the mayor. When the workers heard that their demands had not been met they attempted to break into the police station. Some windows were smashed and the military called in.

On the following day, which was pay day, workers at the cattle market threatened to kill the labour master in the event of not receiving the full wage. They marched to the Moss, brought the labourers out, and as a combined body of 2,500 walked into Preston. 'Three hideous groans' were uttered in front of the home of one of the guardians, and the windows and doors of a school run by the guardians smashed. Dispersed by three companies of infantry carrying fixed bayonets, a group of the operatives late reassembled and attacked an office in the stoneyard. The windows were broken and hammers thrown into the nearby canal. This, however, proved to be the final gesture of defiance. That evening approximately one half of the labourers employed at the cattle market accepted reduced wages. And when Banks of the spinners union made a plea for peace, the men returned to work. No further rioting ensued in the course of 1864 or 1865. And while the public works programme initiated in 1864 came too late to eradicate the bitter memories of 1863, nevertheless it went some way towards preventing the outbreak of further worker unrest.[99]

At the end of the Cotton Famine industrial relations reverted to a familiar pattern. Demands for wage increases were made in good years, and wage reductions enforced during bad years. Throughout 1865 and 1866 cotton operatives sought to recoup the losses suffered in 1861. Although a 'mutual distrust' existed between workers and employers at Stalybridge in 1866, employers throughout Lancashire and Cheshire generally conceded the 7½ per cent increase with a minimum of resistance.[100] Other trades were, however, afflicted by either strikes or lock-outs. 1866 was the year of the great iron-founders dispute, mainly concentrated in the northeast of the country. There were strikes or lock-outs in Manchester among operative joiners, tailors, bakers, gasworkers, engine drivers, firemen and plasterers' labourers. At Stockport the masons struck in support of a pay claim, and brickmakers' strikes, accompanied by their usual violence, occurred with 'alarming regularity'.[101]

By January 1867, relations in the cotton industry were assuming a 'serious aspect'. Employers justified a reduction of 5 per cent on grounds of worsening trade prospects. At Preston 4,000 operatives struck work; and at Darwen and Blackburn the air was thick with rumours of strike action. In the middle of January delegates representing the cotton spinners of Lancashire, Derbyshire and Cheshire attempted to prevent an escalation of industrial unrest by asking the employers to accept arbitration. Their proposal was met with a mixture of 'indifference and contempt'.[102] Strikes rapidly spread to southeast Lancashire and northeast Cheshire. Workers at various factories in the Ashton area turned out in March. In October the majority of self-actor minders at Bolton, failing to arrive at a satisfactory agreement with their employers, followed the example of the Ashton operatives. Stockport, which in the eyes of one contemporary was destined to be 'the stormy petrel of reductions', experienced the most acrimonious struggle. In March the weavers' committee sought an interview with the masters, but were flatly refused on the grounds that trade unions were not recognised. The ensuing strike involved 20,000 operatives. However, hampered from the outset by lack of organisation and adequate financial support, the operatives reluctantly returned to work at the beginning of April at the reduced prices.[103]

In contrast to the stormy year of 1867, 1868 was unusually quiet, no cotton strikes of note being recorded. However, a massive miners strike, affecting every mining community in south Lancashire, disrupted the general calm. In the Wigan area alone, 10,000 men struck work against a reduction of 15 per cent. Rioting was widespread. At Wigan the troops were brought in when colliers attacked 'knobsticks' and destroyed machinery.[104]

With the stagnation of trade in 1869, the cotton manufacturers proposed a reduction of ten per cent. Operatives were generally unwilling to accept the reduction and a major struggle took place at Preston. There the spinners' and minders' representatives were particularly incensed by the unilateral decision of the employers to enforce a reduction, believing that the latter had promised to enter into discussions with the union before making reductions.[105] Once again, worker proposals for arbitration fell on deaf ears. By the first week of April some 3,000 operatives were on strike. The employers then asked the operatives to accept a 5 rather than a 10 per cent reduction. Although a general meeting refused to accept the offer, the operatives subsequently relented and voted to return to work in the second week of April. A confused situation then developed. Some firms refused to admit the operatives, and others insisted on enforcing the original reduction. of 10 per cent. Finally, after a seven-week strike, the defeated operatives returned to work.

The building industry in Manchester was also beset by chronic industrial unrest in 1869. Demanding a nine-hour day, and resisting employer attempts to introduce an hourly payments system, which in the eyes of the workers would be 'a stepping stone to the overthrow of all the rules that regulated relations', Manchester plasterers, joiners, bricklayers and stonemasons struck work in support of their demands. They encountered fierce opposition not only from the press and their employers, but also from the Free Labour Society, a powerful open-shop organisation in Manchester, which spread its net far and wide in an effort to attract 'free' labour into the building industry. Actively supported by bookbinders, printers, glassworkers, bakers and mule-spinners, the building operatives were nevertheless defeated. By November few trade unionists could find work and those who were hired were forced to sign the 'document' and work under the hourly payments system.[106]

The industrial climate was far more placid in 1870 and 1871. In southeast Lancashire the majority of employers restored the 5 per cent which had been deducted in 1869, and consented to close their mills at twelve o'clock on Saturdays. The major exception to this pattern was Oldham where employers reacted to demands for early closing by locking out 20,000 cotton operatives.[107]

Conflict: Summary and Conclusions

This necessarily lengthy review of industrial conflict during the 'golden years' strongly suggests that a view of substantial improvement in industrial relations is erroneous. Conflict was never far below the surface, and bitter and protracted strikes and lock-outs were a regular feature of the period. Moreover, we have seen that during periods of acute and widespread conflict workers' demands sometimes transcended narrow bread-and-butter issues.

The major source of disagreement between masters and men was the question of trade union recognition. In this context Clements' contention that 'whatever the ostensible point at issue, the masters usually aimed to destroy unions' is particularly pertinent.[108] Many employers persisted in their opposition to trade unionism, irrespective of the latter's claim to moderation. The issues at stake were power and control; the very existence of trade unionism representing a threat to the employer's 'right' to exercise total control in his factory. 'Hands have no rights except for services rendered', declared one employers' mouth piece, '. . . any decision as to the mode of management must arise with the master and be controlled by him. And suggestions made, or any outlays for profits are his property, and the workman has really no claim to any share of the profits arising therefrom.'[109] Failure to abide by the rule that 'the master may do what he likes in his own factory' would lead, in the eyes of many employers, to 'subversion of the rights of property' and to communism.[110]

Hence during every dispute in our period the employers bitterly defended their right to absolute control. They claimed during the engineers' lock-out that the demands of the Amalgamated Society of Engineers, 'precluded the exercise of all legitimate authority . . . in their own workshops'. At Stockport in 1853 the masters refused to countenance operative proposals for the creation of a permanent Board of Conciliation (which would be empowered to intervene in all cotton disputes) on the grounds that 'masters must manage their mills for themselves'. The same pattern was repeated at Preston. Union committee members were branded as troublemakers, 'reckless men, who have never shown sympathy for the operatives, save by loud professions and mercenary declamations. Flattering the passions and desires of their followers . . . they grew rich and bloated on the hard-earned wages of the operatives.'[111] During the minders' strike at Manchester in 1855 one millowner, on hearing that the memorial sprang from the trade committee, '. . . tore it to pieces and threw it into the fire'.[112] The dispute at Padiham in 1859 revolved around the question of power — the need to 'check the schemes and intentions of the amalgamated societies of operatives'. The Burnley Master Spinners and Manufacturers Association warned employers throughout the county of the progress made by trade unionism:

> The extent to which these combinations have arrived is perhaps not generally known; but it is impossible for anyone to be acquainted with the perfection in which they exist, and the immense power with which their demands can be supported, without feeling great alarm at the prospect of the conditions under which the trade must be carried on if these societies are permitted to continue in active operation. We are perfectly satisfied that any effort, however powerfully supported it may be, to regulate the rate of wages, or to establish any uniform rate or standard, will prove fruitless, if not absolutely injurious to the masters themselves. We believe that this question must be left to each master and operative for arrangement . . .[113]

The masters of Lancashire and Cheshire responded to the warnings of their counterparts in Burnley by forming the Lancashire Master Spinners' and Manufacturers' Defence Society to resist 'a spirit of dictation, which must prove baneful to all their interests'. The life of Pinder, the union secretary was 'in jeapordy' when he attempted to gain access to the mills.

Although the East Lancashire Amalgamated Powerloom Weavers Friendly Association survived the Padiham dispute and the employer offensive of 1859–60, weaving trade unionism was systematically destroyed at Ashton and Stalybridge after the lockout of 1861: as late as 1870 the weavers at Stalybridge had failed to repair the damage. At Stockport in 1867 the employers refused to meet union representatives. At Manchester 'nearly all the principal firms in the town', as well as 'not a few' in the Ashton area, signed a petition put out by the Free Labour Society in 1869 condemning 'the baneful effects of trade unions'.[114] At Preston the employers 'bullied, domineered, and blustered over all around them'. 'Should a man appeal to the master or any of his officials', declared Banks, 'he is told, in a vulgar, overbearing manner, that if he does not like it he can go about his business, or come into the warehouse, and be paid off.'[115]

Mainly as a result of employer opposition, advances in union recognition in cotton were patchy during the third quarter. Some two-thirds of the local cotton unions traced by Turner were formed after 1875; and no modern cotton trade union can trace a continuous history before 1850.[116] As noted earlier, the major attempts at unionisation occurred in weaving and spinning. The adoption of the Blackburn Standard List in 1853 and the formation of the East Lancashire Amalgamated Powerloom Weavers Friendly Association in 1858 (the First Amalgamation) were, of course, significant landmarks in the history of weaving trade unionism. But advances in weaving were by no means uniformly smooth. By 1863 the Amalgamated had established branches in six of the most important weaving centres in north Lancashire, but developments in the southern part of the county were far from promising. Although a weavers' organisation had been in existence at Oldham since the 1850s, and despite the efforts of the South Lancashire Weavers' Union to organise workers in 1860–61, weaving trade unionism in south Lancashire encountered fierce employer resistance and remained weak and shortlived throughout the 1850s and 1860s.[117] A further wave of union organisation among weavers began in 1870 (especially in southeast Lancashire), but it was not until 1884 that the second Amalgamation marked the triumph of mass unionism in weaving throughout the county.[118] During the 1850s and 1860s there existed several spinners societies, but they tended to be local, independent and suffer from hostility between the old hand-mule spinners and the new minders. It was not until 1870 that the present Spinners Amalgamation was formed; and only in 1880 did the hand-mule spinners of Bolton merge the remnant of their body with the union of the self-actors.[119] Apart from the organisation of weavers and spinners, most of the unions of other grades of operatives were created only after the mid-1870s. Among cardroom hands, for example, only a few local organisations (mainly groups of male strippers and grinders) survived for any length of time before the Amalgamation of 1886.[120] And it was not until 1890 that the Twisters Amalgamation was formed.

Employer opposition to trade unionism also reflected a wider commitment to the 'laws' of political economy. While favourably disposed to the benefit functions of trade unionism, orthodox political economy both abhorred the 'restrictions' which, it was claimed, trade unionism imposed on individual 'liberty', and doggedly insisted that wage levels were determined not by trade union pressure but by the 'natural' forces of supply and demand. Hence the Free Labour Society, formed in Manchester in 1869 by some of the 'leading manufacturers, merchants, and magistrates', had as its primary object the preservation of workers' 'rights' to 'dispense their labour on whatever terms and under whatever circumstances they may individually and independently see fit.' It was alleged that by attempting to set wage levels for groups of workers, trade unions not only undermined individual 'freedom of choice', but also abolished distinctions between the 'thrifty' and the 'improvident', and sought to reduce all to the 'same common level'. Similarly, the *Manchester Guardian* and, in a more sophisticated way, Jevons, never tired of preaching the futility of trade union attempts to raise wages, and were defenders of the bourgeois notion of equality in the marketplace.[121]

The trade union approach to orthodox political economy was, on the whole, pragmatic: trade unionists accepted those aspects which could prove useful to them, and which could be turned to their own advantage.[122] For much of the time, however, trade unions, despite their overtures of friendship towards capitalists, adopted an openly hostile stance towards political economy. This was to some extent forced upon them in a period when newspapers churned out anti-union propaganda, and when trade union recognition had by no means been permanently secured. William MacDonald, president of the Operative House Painters in Manchester, was not alone in believing an 'objective' social science discipline provided an effective cloak for the class interests of the employers. According to MacDonald, doctors of political economy were, 'mere partisans of the strongest side, on a level with paid agitators, or special pleaders.' 'False opinions in the garb of science', were propogated to, 'maintain class interests, and not the welfare of society.'[123] A Manchester factory operative also criticised the 'class' nature of political economy in a letter published in the *Guardian* in 1851:

> The working classes are frequently amused by the condescension of writers who . . . undertake to make plain to 'the humblest capacities' the simplest elements of political economy. We have observed with a levity which might possibly be construed as ingratitude how some men will stoop from the high stools of philosophy to lecture us poor men on the simplest elements of social and commercial polity . . . These pompous teachers always assume us to be ignorant of our own interests, perverse in our intentions, and consequently ever in the wrong.[124]

MacDonald noted, with no little irony, that unions were criticised for attempting to force wages above their 'natural level' during periods of economic upswing, but that 'it is remarkable that there is never any complaint on the descending scale, when wages are below their natural level'. 'This must certainly happen sometimes', he continued, 'yet it is kept a profound secret.'[125]

Custom and tradition served to convince trade unionists that improvements in the workers' economic position owed less to the forces of supply and demand than to trade union struggle. Indeed, the uninterrupted flows of supply and demand, far from alleviating the workers position, forced wages down to 'starvation rates'. According to MacDonald, the bakers and agricultural labourers, 'who had never disturbed the growth of capital, nor driven it into other channels,' were nevertheless treated as 'slaves and drudges', working long hours for a mere pittance. Conversely, those operatives who put their trust in trade unionism enjoyed higher rates of wages, shorter hours, and 'a better state of things altogether'.[126] In short, it was believed that trade unionism exerted a considerable influence on wage levels, irrespective of the vicissitudes of supply and demand.[127] Implicit in this line of argument were the assumptions that economic gains for the working class did not *automatically* flow from the workings of supply and demand, and that there existed a conflict of interests between employers and workers.

So long as employers pursued a policy of buying labour as cheaply as possible, so, it was argued, would workers continue to have recourse to trade unions and, at times, the strike weapon in their fight for a high wage economy. Similarly, worker demands for 'a fair day's wage for a fair day's work', and the 'right to work' were at odds with an economic philosophy which maintained that levels of employment and wages were determined by market forces. And worker support for emigration did not signify a sudden or long-term commitment to the principles of bourgeois economics, but represented an immediate and practical response to periods of acute unemployment.[128]

Reconciliation

Whilst fully alive to the extent and nature of industrial conflict during the third quarter, we must, however, be careful not to present an unbalanced picture. Why, for example, did some contemporaries believe that relations in industry had mellowed somewhat since the 1840s? Why did demands for the abolition of 'wage-slavery' and social reconstruction fail to make a deeper and more lasting impression on the working class? Why did industrial unrest fail to generate widespread support for independent working-class politics? And why did leading trade unionists rub shoulders with employers in both the Liberal and Tory parties? In order to go some way towards answering such questions, this second section considers areas of 'reconciliation' and examines in greater depth the attitudes and practices of trade unionists and employers.

I have already noted that trade union leaders, although ready to do battle with their adversaries, nevertheless cast themselves in the mould of 'respectable', 'fair-minded', 'public-spirited' and 'reasonable' men. Indeed, perhaps the most remarkable feature of this period was the persistence with which trade union leaders sought to impress upon the public mind the 'moderate' nature of their goals.[129] They aimed neither at the destruction of capitalism, nor the perpetuation of industrial conflict, but at the creation of a well organised, and 'sophisticated' industrial relations system, in which strong trade unions and strong employers, by dealing 'openly' and 'fairly' with one another, would go some way towards substituting industrial harmony for discord. Hence we must search in vain for a leading trade unionist who, in principle at least, supported strikes.

'We hope the time is fast approaching', declared the executive committee of the North Lancashire Weavers Union in 1856, 'when such things will be unknown amongst us.'[130] In the opinion of the secretary of the Bolton Spinners' Union, strikes were 'inimical and subversive to the rights of labour' — they both engendered unnecesary class hatred, and all too frequently exhausted union funds, thus rendering the workers 'helpless at our masters' feet'. The Manchester and Salford Trades Council had as its primary task 'the elimination of strikes and lock-outs'. The Ashton spinners saw strikes as 'the scourges of civilisation'. And in 1860 the executive committees of the South Lancashire Weavers Union hoped to 'bid farewell to strikes and their concomitant evils'.[131]

Union representatives firmly believed that employer recognition of trade unionism would serve both to diminish the number of strikes and lock-outs and facilitate the emergence of industrial harmony. Unions eagerly held out the hand of friendship to the employers. The former wanted to bring about 'a good feeling with all'. In 1853 the committee of the Manchester and Salford Shoemakers Union refuted the suggestion that they wished to 'commence a general crusade' against the masters. Their aims were, on the contrary, 'to engineer a reciprocal feeling between the two classes'.[132] The Operatives Painters, Plumbers and Glaziers Association of Stalybridge had as its principal object not, 'creation of a despotism, but a desire to work amicably' with their employers.[133] The spinners' and minders' leaders at Mossley maintained that the interests of workers and employers were 'synonomous and inseparable': 'when the masters' interests prospered, the people prospered.'[134] The weavers executive in the Ashton area sought not to 'create dissatisfaction between employer and employed'. And a representative of the Ashton Cardroom Hands Union spoke of the necessity to 'cultivate the best feelings' between the union and the employers.[135]

In seeking to develop friendly relations with capitalists, union leaders believed themselves to be acting not from 'sectional' or 'selfish' motives but in the interests of the public good. Hence William MacDonald claimed that trade unionism was 'consistent with the welfare of the workman, the capitalist, and the public at large'. The greatest accolade paid to Thomas Pitt, a veteran trade unionist, was that 'he had always an eye to the welfare of capital as well as labour'. Pitt declared, '. . . each side has its rights and privileges, and he was satisfied that if they were all duly attended to,

that prosperity and happiness would be shared by all.'[136] Many
unions set themselves up, therefore, as guardians of 'impartiality'.
They became, in part, buffers between the employers and rank and
file workers. Ensuring that 'no imposition to be practised by
employer and employed', spinning trade unionism in particular was
often as much concerned to discipline and restrain the more militant
spirits among the rank and file as to combat the policies of
employers.[137] Appearing before the Royal Commission on Trade
Unions, William MacDonald boasted that the Operative House
Painters Alliance had 'stopped and prevented a good number of
strikes'. The branch of the Amalgamated Society of Engineers at
Ashton saw itself as 'the medium of preventing . . . bickerings and
petty strifes'.[138]

All unions were quick to rebut charges that they were intent on
bringing down property, or encroaching on 'managerial prerogatives'. In 1853 Mawdsley of the spinners disclaimed, 'all right, intention, and desire to interfere with their employers, either with regard
to the management of their concerns, or as to whom they should or
should not employ.'[139] The Ashton Operative Joiners sought 'not to
destroy property, but to protect their rights and privileges, and if
possible to draw masters and men closer together'. The Strippers
and Grinders Union at Stalybridge voiced a general union sentiment
in declaring that it sought 'no unfair advantages, but merely recognition, and a fair day's wage . . .'[140] At a dinner at Ashton in 1860,
William Aitken, former Chartist and longstanding defender of
working-class interests, recollected that some unions had once
wished to destroy property, but the spinners had 'far nobler' purposes, 'a fair day's wage for a fair day's work' and the establishment
of a better feeling between the employers and the employed.[141] And
William MacDonald believed that far from contesting supremacy
with their employers, unions had in general been too humble and
passive.

As a token of their good faith, union leaders encouraged their
members to conduct their dealings with employers in 'a proper
manner'. 'Bitter and acrimonious words', 'insulting language', and
'acts of insubordination' were frowned upon; politeness, reason
and calmness were actively encouraged. The newspaper caricature
of the ignorant and bloated union representative was to be exposed
as a cheap propaganda trick. Union members were at all times
advised to oppose acts of violence. In 1860 the Amalgamated
Society of Engineers condemned weaver harassment of 'knobsticks'

at Colne. During the riots at Preston in 1863 the Spinners and Minders Association, being 'actuated by a desire to preserve the reputation of their association', looked with 'feelings of deep regret' on the riotous behaviour of the operatives, and counselled its members to assist the authorities to 'maintain the peace of the borough'. And in 1867 the Manchester and Salford Trades Council held demonstrations to protest against the acts of violence committed at Sheffield.[142]

The 'improved tone' of the operatives and their representatives did not escape the notice of the press. The *Guardian* noted that workers showed a greater willingness to listen 'with patience and attention' to the arguments put forward by employers. And in 1860 the *Ashton Standard* declared, 'The base slanderers of the working classes are little aware of the character and influence of the men whom they make it their business to defame': trade unionists were bringing 'a vast amount of mental ability and moral worth' into the executive councils of the various trades.[143]

Whilst sincerely offered, the moderate and conciliatory declarations of mid-Victorian trade unionists should not be uncritically accepted. Particular concern rests with the extent to which such declarations affected concrete trade union practice, especially in terms of dealings with employers. On the one hand declarations of public-spiritedness and responsibility could, and did, serve the important ideological purpose of improving the trade union movement's standing in the face of critical, indeed often hostile, public opinion.[144] On the other (as the earlier sections of this chapter have been at pains to demonstrate), even the most moderate sounding trade unionist would strike long and hard, when occasion demanded, against the 'unjust' and 'tyrannical' acts of capitalists. On balance it does, however, appear to be the case that increasingly strenuous efforts were made by the vast majority of union *leaders* to translate moderate intentions into practice. Two factors are, in this respect, of crucial significance. Firstly, as Turner has claimed, the cotton unions did seek to effect a reconciliation with the existing social order after mid-century.[145] Thus whilst the language of discontent and class conflict flared up in 1853 and 1861, and whilst trade unionists could denounce the actions of individual capitalists, union criticisms of the capitalist class *as a class* and of capitalism as a social system were far less prevalent than during the Chartist years. Secondly, many union leaders did adopt the belief that by offering the olive branch to employers the latter would come to se the folly of their anti-union ways and come to terms with the claims of labour. In other words, capitalists were afforded elbow room for a 'change of heart' towards the claims of trade unionism and for class reconciliation — options for manoeuvre and reform were rarely ruled out of court by trade union leaders. In this sense the union leaders did bear a striking resemblance to the picture drawn by the Webbs. The union leaders, rather than the employers, were, generally speaking, the pragmatic moderates, the patient and longsuffering tutors in the slow and often painful process of building a 'modern' system of institutionalised collective bargaining.[146]

These general points concerning trade union moderation and pragmatism can best be illustrated with reference to the development, structures and policies of cotton weaving and cotton spinning trade unionism. During the nineteenth century important differences emerged between weaving and spinning trade unionism. In general terms unions in weaving were 'open' (i.e. mass-based), whilst those in spinning were 'closed' (i.e. exclusive).[147] The key to the character of both types of trade unionism lay in the nature of the workplace situation and social relations in cotton production. For example, the bargaining strength, high wages and status of the spinners issued not from the nature of the job performed (spinning was not a craft occupation with a formal system of apprenticeship) but from control of the labour supply into spinning (the spinners regulated piecer promotion according to the principle of seniority); a certain amount of job control (over the number of mules to be supervised per man and the ratio of piecers to mules); and from employer goodwill (the spinners being utilised as recruiters, supervisors and intensifiers of the labour of the piecers). In these various ways the supply of spinners was regulated, the employer search for efficiency and profitability satisfied (the spinner-piecer and minder-piecer systems constituting effective and trusted methods of labour management and speed-up) and the spinners demands for high wages generally secured.[148]

To argue in this way is not, however, to suggest that employers were always willing to abide by this system. Reference has already been made in the first and second chapters of this book to the fierce 'control' struggles which raged between labour and capital in spinning during the 1830s and early 1840s — which greatly weakened the control, status, job security and bargaining strength of the spinners.[149] And at various points throughout the last quarter of the nineteenth century — when foreign competition intensified, profit margins were threatened, and the search for cost-cutting intensified — cotton employers attempted to parcel out the spinners' work to the piecers at lower rates of pay.[150] What is, however, of extreme significance is the fact that from the mid-1840s to the mid-1870s cotton employers did not generally mount concerted or sustained campaigns to dispense with the labour of adult male spinners and the internal subcontracting system based upon the hierarchical relationship between spinner and piecer. Overall employer abidance by the *status quo* stemmed from four major influences. Firstly, for much of the 1840s the substantially weakened position of the spinners and their strike defeats greatly offset earlier objections to the employment of adult males as spinners due to their high wages and strong trade unions.[151] Secondly, and perhaps most crucially for the employers, the spinner-piecer system provided, as pioneeringly and convincingly argued by Lazonick, a convenient, effective and proven method of labour recruitment and management. And, given the exigencies of capitalist competition and the time, expense and possible labour unrest involved in the development of a new system, many employers were prepared to abide by custom and practice.[152] Thirdly, employer interest in continuity was greatly reinforced by the fact that massive profits were to be derived from the expansion of overseas markets for cotton goods at mid-century. Why, in short, risk interruptions to production and possibly reduce profits at a time when fortunes were to be made and consolidated? Finally, by the 1860s the spinners had recovered much of the ground lost during the 1830s and 1840s. As Lazonick notes, during the 1850s and 1860s there developed 'a highly organised "craft" occupation of minders' which had successfully raised its wages to a relatively high level, built up reasonably strong trade union defences and which would put up stubborn resistance to threats to its privileged position.[153] As a result of these four influences, employer attacks upon the position of the spinner became increasingly rare during the course of the third quarter of the century.

By the 1860s spinning trade unionism — both of the hand-mule spinners and self-actor minders — reflected the increase in bargaining strength, confidence and 'craft' consciousness which had taken place since the dark days of the early 1840s. Mid-Victorian spinning trade unionism was exclusive — charging relatively high dues, generally indifferent to the plight and unionisation of other grades of cotton operatives, and conducting its industrial disputes and negotiations with employers on a separate basis.[154] Most

spinning unions also preached caution and moderation, and emphasised the benefit features of trade unionism (themselves offering
members a wide range of financial benefits, including compensation
for accidents at work, and unemployment pay). There existed, however, a division within spinning between the 'skilled' hand-mule
spinners and the 'unskilled' self-actor minders. The hand-mule
spinners were often contemptuous of the minders and usually
excluded them from their trade unions.[155]

Weaving trade unionism was 'open'. Rather than attempting to
control entry to the occupation (the unskilled nature of weaving and
plentiful supplies of labour worked against the adoption of such a
policy), weaving trade unionism sought to improve the weavers'
financial position by enforcing a standard rate of pay for the job.
The crucial importance of the Blackburn List of 1853 was that it
established the precedent of a standard list which could could be
used as the point of reference in future negotiations. Weaving trade
unions also charged low dues and stimulated unionisation among
other cotton operatives.[156]

These contrasting patterns of development had important implications for union policy and structure. In the weavers' case, the
attainment of the standard rate presupposed institutionalised collective bargaining and union recognition. Hence, many of the pro-
longed weavers' disputes of our period revolved either directly (as at
Padiham in 1859) or indirectly (as in southeast Lancashire in 1861)
around the questions of union recognition and enforcement of the
standard list. Furthermore, as a direct consequence of its low dues
policy, weaving trade unionism was forced, during long disputes, to
solicit the financial aid of weavers in other areas, the labour movement in general, and often the public. The Preston dispute of 1853–4
was financed in such ways. These methods of raising money necessitated not only close co-operation between weavers' organisations
throughout Lancashire and Cheshire, but often a judicious use of
the strike weapon. Once a number of strikes took place simultaneously there was a danger that funds would be exhausted. This is
precisely what happened in 1854, when, rather than remaining work
and continuing their contributions to the weavers at Preston, the
Stockport weavers struck work. In doing so they deprived the
Preston workers of financial support: both groups were subsequently forced to capitulate to the masters' terms through lack of
funds.

Both those considerations — the need for union recognition and adequate financial backing — weighed heavily on the minds of weavers' leaders in the post-1854 period, when they were wary of repeating the mistakes of 1853 and 1854. Indeed much of the moderation of the weavers' leadership in the post-1854 period must be explained in these terms. In 1861, for example, weavers' leaders in southeast Lancashire were reluctant to endorse the call for a general strike on the grounds that sufficient funds did not exist to support such a strike, and that defeat would effectively cripple the union.[157] Similarly, the East Lancashire Power Loom Weavers Friendly Association often adopted a conciliatory tone towards employers and carefully cultivated a moderate and respectable image in the hope that employers would recognise the Association and abide by the standard list.[158]

Bureaucratisation and centralisation constituted the two most important structural developments in weaving trade unionism in the 1850s and 1860s. The emergence of a permanent and salaried union officialdom was the direct outcome of the establishment of the Blackburn Standard List.[159] The Blackburn List fixed a price for a 'typical' (i.e. standard) unit of output. The list also involved a meticulous adjustment of piece rates to meet changes in technical circumstances which, since lists were to be enforced in a variety of districts, proved 'of almost infinite combination'. The union negotiator had, therefore, not only to be a master of the complexities of the Blackburn List, but also a skilled adjustor of piece rates, a shrewd calculator of prices, and an astute mathematician. In short, negotiations required an amount of expertise which many rank-and-file workers were not qualified to offer. In 1858 the East Lancashire Amalgamated Power Loom Weavers' Friendly Association therefore appointed an adroit negotiator, Mr Pinder, as full-time secretary of the union. Subsequent secretaries were to be appointed on the basis of their performances in a competitive examination. Pinder was responsible for negotiations with employers, which entailed inspection of looms in the factories concerned and the setting of rates.[160]

Furthermore, the 'Amalgamated' drew up an elaborate grievance procedure and attempted to concentrate powers of decision-making in the hands of the district and executive committees. The power to authorise strikes, for example, was removed from the rank and file to the district committee which, in the event of failing to resolve the dispute, would place the matter in the hands of the executive committee.[161] In this way a highly complex and sophisticated bureaucratic organisation (so admired by the Webbs) was brought into existence.

Spinning trade unionism differed markedly in terms of strike tactics, methods of funding and structural developments from weaving trade unionism. The increasing strength of the spinners during the mid-Victorian years, their control of the labour supply, their utility to the employers as managers of labour, and their strategically placed position within the industry (yarn could not be woven until spun — hence the spinners could bring production to a sudden halt) meant that employers were generally far more reluctant to mount a concerted anti-union campaign against the spinners than against the more vulnerable weavers. Consequently, industrial conflict in the post-1854 period was far more frequent and intense in weaving than in spinning. Furthermore, spinners more regularly won their demands without resorting to militant strike action.[162] Those strikes which did occur were often financed solely from the coffers of the spinners' societies, and were rarely accompanied by the mass appeals for solidarity and financial aid, or by the violence, which sometimes accompanied weavers' strikes. The employers' practice of importing 'knobsticks' during weaving disputes was also less commonly resorted to during spinning disputes.

Bureaucratisation and centralisation also developed more slowly in spinning trade unionism.[163] Spinners' societies were generally local and independent in character. Between the short-lived amalgamation of 1842, which embraced mule-spinners, minders and twiners, and the amalgamations of the 1870s there were two attempts made to create a general association. In 1853 the Equitable Friendly Association of Hand-Mule Spinners, Self-Actor Minders, Twiners, and Rovers of Lancashire, Cheshire, Yorkshire and Derbyshire was formed, only to decline in importance and influence in the following year. In 1860 the 1853 federation was revived, but it remained without its own officials and had no regular funds. The perennial problem facing attempted federation was the reluctance of strong local societies to make regular contributions to an organisation over which they did not exercise total dominance, and which could be used to the advantage of the poorer societies.

However, during the 1860s some spinners' societies imitated the policies of the East Lancashire Amalgamated Power Loom Weavers Friendly Association. In 1868 the Oldham Society appointed a full-time secretary. After the Preston dispute of 1869 federation took on a more solid appearance. In 1870 the Amalgamated Association of

Operative Cotton Spinners, Self-Acting Minders, Twiners, and Rovers of Lancashire and the Adjoining Counties was established. This organisation imposed a levy on affiliated societies, appointed a full-time secretary, and attempted to centralise decision making in the hands of the executive committee.[164]

Despite their different patterns of development, both spinning and weaving trade unionism were remarkable during the mid-Victorian years for their 'moderate' and 'reasonable' attitudes. Recognition and wage increases were to be won, if possible, by stealth rather than by force and open class conflict. Hence in the midst of the Stockport dispute of 1853 the weavers' leaders were extremely reluctant to sanction a general offensive against the employers. They preferred to counsel patience and to reiterate their demand for the establishment of a permanent Board of Conciliation. In the opinion of one of the workers' leaders, the Chairman of the Stockport Masters' Association had, 'always acted with the greatest courtesy and kindness . . . he was sure there was no operative in Stockport who did not respect his name'.[165] This opinion was of course voiced at a time when the masters had flatly and persistently refused to recognise the weavers' committee.

In 1856 and 1857 attempts were made to recoup the losses suffered by weaving trade unionism in 1854. However, far from adopting a militant policy towards employers, the revived weavers' organisations proceeded with caution. In August 1856 the executive committee of the North Lancashire Power Loom Weavers Association pledged itself to, 'encourage to the best of our ability a friendly feeling, a mutual understanding between employer and employed'. The *Manchester Guardian* was 'exceedingly glad' to find that the weavers' address furnished further proof of 'a growing dislike of disturbances, and the practice of turning out for an advance of wages'. During the disputes of 1856 the union did everything in its power to prevent the outbreak of strikes.[166]

The East Lancashire Amalgamated Powerloom Weavers Friendly Association made repeated efforts to gain the confidence of the employers, even at the risk of alienating some rank-and-file weavers. In 1860, for example, 30 of the 50 worker grievances submitted to the union executive were considered 'improper' and rejected. Eight grievances were resolved without recourse to strike action. Pinder, although initially in danger of his life, was eventually accepted by some employers on the grounds that he was more impartial in outlook, and less prone to violent anti-employer outbursts than rank-and-file workers.[167]

In the 1860s the Amalgamated's officials prided themselves on their moderation and 'common sense'. In February 1861 the Blackburn employers asked the operatives to terminate their strike and return to work with the guarantee that they would meet to discuss the whole question of wage rates. The masters' proposal was supported by the Amalgamated's officials. E. Holt, for example, spoke of 'the advantages which the weavers had secured' by the masters' promise 'not to reduce their wages again without first consulting them upon the subject'. The masters' proposal was neither as explicit nor as binding as Holt imagined. Indeed, the weavers opposed the union committee's proposed return to work.[168] Similarly, when the Clitheroe employers agreed to arbitration in March 1861 on the condition that (pending a decision) workers resume work at the old prices, rank-and-file reactions were decidedly more circumspect than those of their union representatives. According to George Cowell the offer constituted, 'the first instance on record in which the masters had made such a concession . . .' When Cowell visited Clitheroe he was surrounded by operatives who 'evinced hostile feelings towards him'. The operatives believed that Cowell had been duped by the employers who had no intention of giving an advance or of abiding by arbitration.[169]

The South Lancashire Weavers Union prided itself on its ability to restrain the more 'extreme' impulses of its members. In 1861 the executive committee endeavoured to arrive at 'an amicable arrangement' with the employers, but its proposal for arbitration was rejected by both employers, and the rank-and-file operatives.[170] In spite of the union's disapproval, the weavers in the Ashton and Stalybridge area then struck work. The union executive, conscious of the need to improve its public image, and fearful lest a general strike develop, did everything in its power to contain and control the strike. Mr Crossley, the Blackburn delegate, was not alone in, 'deprecating the course taken by the operatives . . . trembling for the result, and fearing that it would equal the plug-drawing scenes of 1842'. At the end of March the executive hurriedly despatched representatives to Hyde and Newton to persuade the operatives there not to march to Stockport. The committee also posted placards in Ashton and Stalybridge warning the operatives not to proceed to Oldham to bring the weavers out and affirming that, contrary to popular impression, the Oldham Association would withdraw from the union rather than support a general turn-out.[171]

The South Lancashire Weavers Union's claim that it did not wish to impinge on the employers right to 'hire and fire' was clearly demonstrated during a strike at Ashton Bros., Hyde, in 1860.[172] The dispute arose when Briscoe, the secretary of the cardroom hands' union, was dismissed on the grounds that he had lied to his employer. Briscoe had apparently absented himself from work on account of illness, but his employer claimed that he had left work to render assistance to workers on strike at a nearby mill. The operatives, convinced that Briscoe had been sacked because of his union activities, struck work. However, the weavers union, in the person of the secretary Patrick Maloney, accepted the employer's version of events. 'If a master must be compelled to allow his workpeople to ride roughshod over him in that way', declared Maloney, 'the sooner he got without him [Briscoe] the better. If he was a master, he would take good care they did not ride roughshod over him'. While the union committee 'always endeavoured to do justice to both sides', Briscoe's threats to bring the operatives out in support of his case were (in Maloney's opinion) 'beyond all reason', 'impudent', and 'conducive to a vast amount of misery'. Briscoe was not reinstated, and the operatives, although exasperated by Maloney's actions, returned to work.

The spinners, more so than the weavers, were anxious to avoid 'hostilities' in their dealings with employers. The moderation of the mid-Victorian spinners issued in part from vulnerability (following defeats on the 'control' issues of the 1830s and 1840s) and dependence upon employer goodwill for the preservation of their privileged status in cotton. However, vulnerability and dependence constitute only partial explanations. For we must not forget that as the minder-piecer system became an established and accepted fact of life during the mid-Victorian period, so employer dependence upon the spinners as recruiters and supervisors of labour accordingly increased. In short, there emerged a system of *mutual* dependency between spinners and employers, a structured relationship in which the spinners were far from being the naked, vulnerable proletarians depicted by Joyce and others. Furthermore, as noted earlier, the financial and trade union gains made by the spinners during the expansionary economic climate of the mid-Victorian period, their control over the labour supply and their strategic position within the production process meant that their overall strength and bargaining clout had greatly increased since the mid-1840s. In effect they once again constituted a key group of workers in production which would not easily be dislodged from their strong position. In sum, by the 1860s the moderation of the spinners and their unions derived more from their powerful position than, as claimed by Joyce, from their more or less total subordination to the forces of capital.[173]

The spinners' moderation and caution manifested themselves in many ways. Consistent advocates of arbitration, they often offered little resistance to reductions in wages made during years of bad trade. Not wishing to deplete their funds, the spinners at Ashton opposed strike action in 1853, and in 1861 they accepted a reduction of 10 per cent on the grounds that it was necessitated 'by the state of the trade'.[174] The committee of the Bolton spinners maintained that at times of bad trade the 'workers should suffer as well as the masters'. In fact the Bolton spinners union endorsed strike action only once in our period, in 1861. And even in that instance the Bolton spinners' deputation to the general delegate meeting opposed strike action.[175] When rank-and-file minders turned out against a wage reduction at Bolton in 1869 they were 'strongly advised' to return to work by the Minders' Association, which maintained that 'the exigencies of trade' had necessitated the reduction. The strike at Oldham in 1871 (in support of early closing on Saturdays) was denounced by the spinners' executive committee on the grounds that it would place an intolerable burden on financial resources and 'ruin the organisation'. Many of the spinners ignored the executive's warning, but it is significant that thereafter the committee attempted to concentrate all decision-making powers into its own hands. 'It is a matter of utter impossibility', declared the committee, 'for a great body of members to know which is the best step to take in a great crisis; but the committee, being composed of *practical* men, would be certain to act in the best way.'[176] Even in good years, many spinners' societies were careful not to take 'unfair advantage' of their employers. In 1856 spinners' leaders at Preston assured the employers that 'our interest is closely allied with yours', and claimed that it would be both 'suicidal and dishonest' to ask for an advance 'not warranted by the state of the trade'.[177] In keeping with this perspective, spinning trade unionism aimed neither at the 'overthrow of capital' nor at encroachment upon managerial prerogatives.

Moderate trade unions could not in themselves bring about a more harmonious system of industrial relations. The attainment of this goal depended upon the responses of employers. And whilst we have seen that the majority of employers remained extremely hostile to the friendly overtures made by the unions, some accepted the olive branch, mainly for pragmatic reasons, and pursued more 'enlightened' policies than their predecessors in the 1830s and 1840s. This 'new employer spirit' manifested itself most clearly in the areas of factory legislation; wages; trade union recognition; the creation of Boards of Conciliation and Arbitration; and in the spread of employer paternalism. We will examine each of these areas in turn.

In the early 1850s a great number of employers opposed legislative interference in their concerns. Nevertheless, some employers, even at this early date, did not conform to the popular image of the tyrannical, intransigient master. In 1850 a minority of employers in the Manchester area permitted operatives to circulate Ten Hours petitions in their factories. At Stockport 'only a sordid few' were implacably opposed to all legislative interference.[178] And, as the decade of the 1850s progressed, employer attitudes mellowed. In June 1854 operatives from Manchester, Ashton and Stalybridge met to pay their respects to those employers in the district who had closed their mills at six o'clock.[179] Three years later at Oldham operatives drew up an address in which they tendered 'their most grateful acknowledgements' to those employers who had adhered to the spirit of the Ten Hours Bill, and to those who had struggled 'to improve the mental and social condition of the people'.[180] By the end of the decade most commentators on industrial relations agreed that employer attitudes towards factory legislation had undergone a remarkable transformation: masters who had once opposed it, 'now saw it as their best friend'.[181] Productivity, far from declining, had increased; and Senior's special pleading had been discredited — profits were booming.

Few contemporaries failed to be impressed by 'the progress in the habits, and mental acquirements' of the operatives which resulted from the shortening of hours of work. In 1870 Banks contrasted the prevailing situation with the 'unbearable conditions' which had once been the operatives' lot:

Factory operatives used to follow their ordinary employment . . . which now-a-days would appear to be almost unbearable. But here they were, at about half past seven o'clock on a Saturday evening, enjoying themselves to their hearts content; but prior to the curtailment of the hours of labour, the operatives would barely have left work . . . Now, however, they had time to devote for purposes of recreation, enjoyment, and learning.[182]

Bull had spoken in a similar vein 12 years earlier. 'Prior to the Ten Hours', he had declared, 'the child was driven by the overlooker, the overlooker . . . by the master, and the master . . . by the devil.' That state of affairs had fortunately been 'annihilated', and 'since the passing of the Ten Hours Bill there had been such harmony, and comfort, and good understanding between masters and men, as never before existed'.[183] In the opinion of William Aitken, the shorter working day had 'once again united the silken cord of amity' between masters and men. Moreover, once reconciled to the benefits of a shorter working day, many employers offered only token resistance to further reductions. In 1866 the bookbinders thanked their employers for reducing the hours of labour. In 1871 the iron and brass workers at Stalybridge celebrated the introduction of a nine-hour day; and in the same year cotton operatives in the Ashton district expressed their gratitude to those employers who, following Hugh Mason's lead, had consented to close their mills at twelve noon on Saturdays.[184]

An increasingly large number of employers were prepared to grant wage advances during upswings in the trade cycle. As early as 1844 the Masters Association at Stockport had volunteered a 5 per cent advance, whereupon they received the 'congratulations and heartfelt gratitude' of the powerloom weavers.[185] In 1860, Verity, while bitterly critical of the 'Manchester School' employers, declared that some employers in the Ashton and Stalybridge area 'treated their operatives well, and were liberal in their scale of wages'. In 1859 shoemakers in the Manchester area toasted those employers who had conceded an advance of wages. In 1861 the Amalgamated Committee of Factory Operatives publicly thanked the employers for 'so speedily' complying with a request for weekly payments, and for 'the kind, reasonable, and courteous manner' in which the workers' deputation had been received.[186] During years of booming trade and profits it made good financial sense to concede wage increases rather than risk the interruptions to production and profits attendant upon strikes. Thus in 1859, 1860, 1865 and 1870 workers in southeast Lancashire won their demands without recourse to protracted strikes.

Pragmatic considerations also sometimes helped to check, if only in a minority of cases to completely negate, the ideological opposition of employers to trade unionism. As the *Ashton Reporter* observed in 1855, employers were generally less likely than during the 1830s to treat workers and their union representatives with 'supercilious contempt' and to 'pitch their memorials into the fire'.[187] Employers increasingly tolerated trade unions under one or more of the following conditions: on those occasions when unions proved resistant to attempts at destruction; when union recognition outweighed the costs of repeated industrial conflict; when unions performed a stabilising and integrating role at the workplace, often providing a buffer between employers and workers and, on occasion, disciplining the latter group; and when union recognition was part and parcel of employer attempts to control and stabilise the market mechanism (usually adopted under conditions of extreme competition).

Especially in terms of craft and skilled unions, outright refusals of recognition did, on many occasions, give way to gradual and grudging acceptance and perhaps eventual support. William MacDonald claimed in 1867 that, '. . . trade societies have promoted objects at first resisted by employers, which afterwards all parties have allowed to be beneficial'.[188] MacDonald's own union, the Operative House Painters Alliance, had an excellent working arrangement with the employers of Manchester. There was mutual agreement on work rules and disputes procedure, and both sides abided by a decision taken in 1866 to submit future disputes to arbitration. In actual fact the trade was relatively free from major disputes, and when they did arise solutions were speedily found. When the employers at Blackburn refused to recognise the union a delegation of Manchester unionists eventually persuaded them to recognise both the union and the principle of arbitration.[189] MacDonald's impressions of the employers were extremely favourable. 'I like to meet employers' he said, 'and have generally been well received by them. The best employers, the men who derive the largest profits from the business, are great supporters of the society in Manchester, and I believe anywhere else. They . . . employ the best men, and they pay the best wages.'[190]

By the 1860s building trades unions had, on the whole, been successful in their efforts to achieve recognition, and to draw up working agreements with the employers. In spite of the activities of the Free Labour Society, and the strikes and lock-outs which afflicted the Manchester building industry in 1866 and 1869, many employers had come to accept the inevitability of trade unionism. By 1866 the Operative Carpenters and Joiners Society could boast a membership of some 10,000 in the Manchester area.[191] For their part, the masters, while anxious to preserve their 'supremacy', 'desired to pay the men well, and to treat them respectfully'. During the 1866 dispute negotiations between the two sides were 'conducted with that new courtesy for which the recent parliaments of capital and labour have been so pleasantly characterised.'[192] Conciliation, which had been adopted in the early 1860s, was again resorted to in 1869.[193] By 1868 the Operative Joiners Society at Ashton had, 'to a great extent succeeded in allaying the bad feeling which once existed . . . and had brought about a better feeling, so that strikes were almost a thing unknown to them'. During the course of the year the society had expended a mere 9/10d on strike benefits.[194] By 1865 employers were attending the annual dinners given by the Operative Painters, Plumbers, and Glaziers Association, which embraced workers in Ashton, Stalybridge, and Hyde. Flattering compliments were paid to the workers and their union. 'By promoting intelligence, and virtue', enthused one employer, 'trade unions enhanced the value of their members, and such enhancement promoted the interests of the employers.' Another swore, 'to protect the interests of the employed', and in return, 'he knew the employed would do what they could to promote the interests of their employers.' By 1870 arbitration had been accepted by both sides in principle and practice. 'Thirty years ago no such thing would be listened to', declared one worker, 'but now it was seen that the men could hold their own.'[195] Our conclusion must, therefore, be that industrial conflict in the building industry around Manchester was on the whole institutionalised — that is contained within a framework accepted by both employers and unions.

The most powerful force in improving the industrial climate in the Manchester area was the Manchester and Salford Trades Council. Formed in 1866, and dominated by the 'aristocratic' crafts, such as bookbinders, printers, glassblowers and fine-spinners, the Council's primary aim was to eradicate the 'disastrous social evils' of strikes and lock-outs.[196] In 1868 the members of the Council and the Manchester Chamber of Commerce met to discuss the possibility of establishing a Court of Conciliation and Arbitration. And, despite the disruptive activities of the Free Labour Society, a court, consisting of an equal number of employers and workers, came into existence in the same year. By 1876 the court had never been called upon to adjudicate in a case, but its power as an effective strike deterrent was recognised on all sides.[197] The Trades Council itself exerted considerable influence in bringing about amicable settlements in many trades, and generally generating 'a better feeling between employers and employed'. Its greatest triumph, was, however, to remove from the public mind many of the prejudices which had existed against trade societies.[198]

Developments in cotton were not nearly so dramatic as those effected by the Trades Council in Manchester. Even in cotton, however, our earlier pessimistic conclusions must be modified. The powerful and eminently respectable spinners' organisations were able to cultivate good relations with employers in a number of towns. At Bolton the United Cotton Spinners Association was recognised by several employers in the late 1840s, and strikes rarely occurred throughout the 1850s and 1860s. The Bolton Master Spinners paid the standard rate, and the operative spinners put their trust in the union's ability to achieve wage advances in periods of good trade.[199] Although the president of the spinners' union was snubbed by the employers in the streets of Ashton as late as 1870, most of the employers abided by the standard rate, and dealt 'fairly' with the union. In 1860 the Chairman of the Self-Actor Minders Association at Ashton was 'exceedingly glad to find that the good feelings which had long existed between masters and men', was not likely to be broken. In 1853 and 1861, rather than striking with the weavers, the spinners accepted reductions in the hope that trade would soon revive. And throughout the 1860s the spinners at Ashton and Stalybridge attempted to improve their public image by inviting local officials and employers to meetings to discuss various aspects of trade unionism.[200] By 1870 many erstwhile opponents of trade unionism had come to respect and admire the spinners' point of view. The ultimate triumph came in 1871 when a Board of Conciliation, consisting of six spinners and six masters, was created.[201] At Oldham relations were less harmonious. It was only after 'several keenly fought battles' that the employers finally agreed in 1869 and 1870 to recognise the union and pay the standard rate.[202]

The other grades of cotton operatives encountered much stiffer employer opposition. As noted earlier, it was not until the 1880s that the mass of weavers throughout the cotton districts were effectively organised, and that arbitration in weaving was adopted on a large scale.[203] Nevertheless, a picture of unrelieved conflict in weaving during the third quarter requires qualification. Indeed, in those districts of Lancashire where a fiercely competitive market situation prevailed, trade union recognition by employers was part-and-parcel of employer attempts to regulate and standardise prices and wages within cotton. Such was the situation in the Blackburn district, where employers in weaving sought to control competition by means of the adoption of a standard list of prices and wages (the famous 1853 List) to prevail throughout the district, and by means of trade union recognition. The role of the weavers' officials in this system of industrial relations was, firstly, to come to some agreement with the employers concerning wage and price determination, and, secondly, to 'police' the agreement — to ensure that weavers throughout the Blackburn district abided by the agreed list of wages and did not step out of line so as to threaten a system based upon uniformity and parity.[204]

Blackburn was, however, far from typical of the cotton districts as a whole. In many other areas — where market pressures were often far less acute — the majority of cotton employers tended to persist in their fierce anti-unionism. Thus attention has been drawn to the major setbacks suffered by weaving trade unionism in south Lancashire and northeast Cheshire at the hands of employers who, generally speaking, operated in a much less competitive situation than their Blackburn counterparts; protracted (if ultimately unsuccessful) employer resistance to attempts to raise the wages of weavers at Padiham to the Blackburn level (1859); and to the repeated disputes at Preston concerning union recognition.[205] Even at Blackburn weaving trade unionism during the 1850s and 1860s did not provide an effective counterweight to the massive power of local capital. Despite the widespread union belief that the List was the product of joint negotiation and agreement, the employers retained, in practice, their 'right' to act unilaterally in terms of changes in wages and prices. In the eyes of the employers, weaving trade unionism played the important, but essentially subordinate, role of exercising control over the wage (and other) demands of the rank-and-file weavers, taking special care to outmanoeuvre and isolate the more militant spirits among the latter. And when the union failed to control the workers in the interests of capital — as was frequently the case during the 1860s — the Blackburn employers simply bypassed the union officials in their dealings with the workers of the district. In turn, the weavers' officials (as noted earlier), aware of their relatively weak bargaining power, rarely challenged the fundamental claims and expectations of capital. In such ways weaving trade unionism in the Blackburn district was, in reality, placed in a subordinate position within a structure of seemingly formalised and 'modern' industrial relations in which employers and union officials apparently met upon equal terms.[206]

The unions of strippers and grinders also met with strong employer opposition during the third quarter. However, towards the end of the period there were signs of a significant, if uneven, mellowing in employer attitudes. The Strippers and Grinders Union at Stalybridge had, for example, often been on the receiving end of anti-union campaigns; but by 1871 leading officials and employers of the borough were regular attenders at the union's parties. The novelty of such meetings was fully grasped by J.F. Cheetham, himself a leading employer, who on more than one occasion had chafed against the 'invisible and irresponsible' machinations of union committees. Cheetham said:

> The presence of employers that night was very suggestive of the altered spirit of the times, and it was something significant that the masters should be on such an occasion the guests of trade unionists. Their dealings together had not been so pleasant in the past . . . He believed that the old antagonism between employer and employed was dying out, and giving place to a knowledge of the identity of interests between them. Even now, however, there was much to be done to secure more harmonious feeling . . . but they had both seen the unpleasantness of strikes, and the retaliation known as lock-outs, and they must turn their attention to the promised courts of conciliation and arbitration.[207]

At Oldham the strippers and grinders had found, 'they could now meet the masters, and exchange views with them' — arbitration having, at least temporarily, been adopted.[208]

The Amalgamated Beamers, Twisters and Drawers Society, with its headquarters at Blackburn, also enjoyed 'fairly good' relations with employers in the immediate post-Cotton Famine era; and the cardroom and blowing room hands, while not extensively organised, made strenuous attempts to imitate the 'respectable' spinners by insisting on 'correct' behaviour both in work and at home. According to one unionist, the epithet 'dirty card-room hand', so widely used by other operatives, would soon be obsolete.[209]

Employer recognition of trade unionism and the creation of boards of conciliation and arbitration constituted important stabilising mechanisms in industry. As Patrick Joyce has demonstrated, the 'mighty reassertion' of employer paternalism was designed to have a similar effect.[210] From the mid-1850s onwards we find that an increasing number of employers cast aside their parsimonious attitudes of the 1830s and 1840s.[211] The annual works dinner, trips to the countryside and seaside, and the provision of libraries and reading rooms, canteens and baths at the work-place — all financed by the employer — became an increasingly notable characteristic of employer policies in this period. Most marked among the large employers of labour (who were best able to afford it[212]), paternalism can be interpreted as an attempt to develop worker loyalty to the employer at a time when class conflict and mass commitment to the Charter had already lost much of their earlier force.[213]

In the Ashton area the press draw attention to a 'change of heart' on the part of local employers during the mid and late 1850s. For example, in 1855 Mr Broadbent, a manufacturer at Ashton, invited his employees to dine with him and announced his decision to set up a reading room in the factory. In 1857 the clerks, overlookers and engineers at the Old Mill Dukinfield were invited to their employer's residence at Alderley Edge. And in June of the same year J.H. Marsland, a mill owner at Stalybridge, treated his workers to a trip to Blackpool.[214] These were instances of what was to become a widespread phenomenon. In 1857 the *Ashton Reporter*, whilst admitting that, 'much . . . yet remains to be done before employers and employed faithfully perform their reciprocal obligations and duties', was nevertheless impressed by the fact that it had witnessed, 'a great change going on in the right direction, which had a tendency to bring about that feeling of respect, esteem, and gratitude between manufacturer and operative.'[215] In the following year the factory inspector noted that the wealthiest employers gave active support and encouragement to schools for the factory operatives, and that this action constituted, 'the best guarantee of an inseparable interest between all parties'.[216]

Some of the trips were organised on a large scale. Robert Platt, cotton manufacturer and a leading figure in Stalybridge Liberalism, ran annual worker outings to his estate at Handforth in Cheshire. In August 1858, 900 workers, carrying banners bearing inscriptions such as 'Long Life to our Employers', and 'Brittania Rules the Waves', congregated in front of Platt's mills, which were decorated with flags.[217] The procession, headed by the Stalybridge Old Band, walked through the town to the railway station, where they boarded the special trains hired by Platt. On their arrival at 'Deanwater', Platts stately mansion, they were greeted by salvos of artillery fire. The day was spent in sports competitions and eating and drinking.

The food bill in itself was astronomical. In 1858 300 pounds of beef, 160 pounds of ham, 250 pounds of assorted meats, 600 pounds of potatoes, 300 pounds of plum pudding, 100 pounds of rice, and 144 gallons of ale were consumed at one sitting. In Platt's opinion, the attainment of social harmony took precedence over financial considerations: 'He didn't like to treat workers as inanimate machinery', and 'it mattered little to him whether he acquired a few thousands more or a few thousand less than ordinary, so that those under him did their duty, and were contented and happy.'[218]

Platt's example was followed by other employers. In April 1860 the *Ashton Standard* gleefully reported that 'scarcely a week passes, but we chronicle a treat to the workpeople in some part of the district'.[219] At Stockport dinners and trips were 'happily becoming more frequent'. Five hundred workers at Park Mills sat down to tea and entertainments in the Oddfellows Hall in January. On entering the hall the employers, who had paid for the tea, were met with, 'the most boisterous enthusiasm'.[220] Mossley acquired a reputation for employer generosity. Upwards of 800 workers were treated to a trip to Liverpool, while others journeyed to Blackpool and Belle Vue. The operatives at Mayhall's factory enjoyed three parties in the course of 1860. Nathaniel Buckley and Sons, proprietors of Carr Hill Mills, encouraged gatherings of workers and masters because they 'brought|them|together|into a close unity with one another'.[221] At Dukinfield the spinners in James Ogden's mill were feasted at the employer's expense. In February 1860, 600 operatives at Chadwick's Mill in Dukinfield sat down to a tea of currant and plain bread, and ham and beef sandwiches 'in abundance'. At all these functions employers expressed a desire to treat the workers well, and spoke of the pressing need for harmony in industry.[222]

The rash of trips and 'treats' was temporarily halted by the Cotton Famine. Nevertheless, even in these years, the factory inspector could write enthusiastically:

> Scarcely a week elapses but that in the course of my official wanderings I come across some quite unobtrusive kindness, on the part of the masters to their hands, scarcely known beyond the gates of the factory where it originated, which shows that they have now come nobly forward, with one or two exceptions, to endeavour to allay the distress.[223]

In the post-Famine years the trend was resumed. In 1868 Platt gave some of the older workers in his employ weekly pensions for life. In the following year he provided much of the capital needed to build public baths in Stalybridge. Another Liberal employer followed Platt's public-spirited example by contributing £900.[224] Meetings and tea-parties were characterised by 'cordial and mutual feelings of respect'.[225]

Hugh Mason, mayor, leading Liberal, and owner of extensive mills in the borough of Ashton, epitomised the change in employer attitudes and policies. In the 1840s Mason was the archetypal 'purse-proud' Liberal master whom Chartists criticised so vehemently. Spouting self-help and restraint, Mason would have no truck with either trade unions or factory legislation. In 1847 he was at one with Senior, and in the early 1850s he reputedly positioned himself at the door of one of his mills so as to note the names of workers who left work at six o'clock.[226] During the course of the 1850s and 1860s his attitudes underwent a remarkable transformation. In 1859 he admitted that the Ten Hours campaign, 'had been nobly fought, and fairly won', and that 'he would never be a man to lift up his pen or utter one word to diminish the triumphant victory of that great struggle.' By the 1860s his harsh political economy of the 1840s had been softened by humanitarian concerns:

> He was not indifferent to the teachings of political economy, but he should be very sorry if the rigid and abstract rules of political economy alone prevailed in his workshops. It would be impossible for him to buy the labour of his workpeople, and for the workpeople to sell him that labour, the same as an ordinary commodity over the counter of a shopkeeper. He felt a deep interest in the welfare of his workpeople . . . The bond which united them was not the cold bond of buyer and seller.[227]

Despite his occasional condescension and nauseating paternalism — he saw himself as a 'father' creating an estate of 'happily housed workers' — he increasingly emphasised less the rights than the duties of capital, holding his position of an employer to be 'far more sacred than that of a mere capitalist'. 'Brothers and Sisters' at the Oxford Colony, they were, in Mason's opinion, 'marching together for one common end — the mutual welfare of the workpeople and the employer.'[228]

Mason spent large sums of money to achieve that 'common end'. In July 1859 the workers at the mills of T. Mason and Sons were 'treated' to a trip to Alderley Edge, where they enjoyed milk, 'pop', and cider.[229] At the beginning of 1860 Hugh Mason convened a meeting of his operatives to discuss his plans to open a library, reading, lecture and smoking rooms at the mills. In March 1861 a gathering of some 600 workers celebrated the official opening of the rooms, which had been paid for at Mason's expense. During the Cotton Famine he was a prominent figure on both the Central Executive Committee in Manchester and the local relief committee at Ashton. In December 1861 he was the first figure of any standing to appeal for more liberal contributions, declaring that the operatives must not be forced into the 'Bastille'.[230] In 1862 he castigated the local millowners for their miserly attitudes. And it is significant that the *Times* correspondent excluded Mason from his general indictment of the employers. Indeed, unlike many other spinners in the area, he did not reduce wages at the first rumblings of the Cotton Famine and attempted to keep the mills running full time throughout the years 1861 to 1864. Concerts were held in the reading rooms at Oxford Mills to raise money for the local relief fund, rent arrears were conveniently forgotten, and free food and clothing were distributed to the workers. During 1863 and 1864 Mason consistently fought to secure increased scales of relief; and he played a leading role in the campaign for public works.[231] By December 1864 the *Ashton Reporter* described him as, 'the most energetic, public spirited, and capable man the town has ever raised.' Further benevolent acts followed the Cotton Famine. In 1865 he volunteered an advance of 10 per cent; in the following year he told the Manchester Chamber of Commerce that trade unions were necessary responses to employer associations; in 1868 new reading rooms and baths were opened at the mills; and in 1870 he both supported the Saturday half holiday, and chaired a meeting of the local miners' association, at which he argued for better inspection of the mines and the eight-hour day for miners.[232]

Mason's actions, which did much to win workers to the Liberal cause, were rivalled by those of the Whittaker family at Hurst, an out-township of Ashton. The Whittakers, steeped in paternalism, employed the majority of the 4,000 workers of Hurst. They ran the New Connexion chapel, and were strong advocates of co-operation, teetotalism, education and, as was to be expected in such a cultural setting, were leading Liberals. Like Mason, John Whittaker had a keen appreciation of his responsibilities as an employer: 'He was of the opinion that those who possessed property . . . had certain duties to perform towards the great mass of their fellow creatures; and he had no doubt that what was being done in recognition of this principle would greatly contrast with what was done twenty or thirty years ago.'[233] In August 1857 Whittaker hired two trains to transport 2,000 Sunday school scholars and workers to Liverpool. In 1860 banners and ribbons 'of every shape and size' were draped from the windows of the houses in the village to celebrate John Whittaker's 21st birthday. Over 1,000 workers sat down to a dinner paid for by the firm. In 1861 three trains carried the workers to the home of Oldham Whittaker at Anglesey, where they enjoyed a large meal. Oldham Whittaker maintained that, unless the employers took an interest in the welfare of the workers, the latter would never respect the rights of property.[234]

During the Cotton Famine Whittaker's generosity equalled Mason's.[235] By August 1862 Whittaker had given £500 to the Manchester Central Committee. Clogs, free food and clothes were distributed to the needy; £50 per month were donated to the local relief committee; and the mills were run at a loss. In the post-Famine Years regular trips to Anglesey took place, and in 1870 Whittaker offered his workers an advance of wages.

Many employers explained their paternalism in terms of Christian duty and humanitarianism. Whilst not wishing to assess the depth of religious sentiment among the likes of Mason and the Whittakers, it is evident, as Joyce notes, that 'their paternalist innovations were not the pure milk of benevolence'.[236] Practical economic, social and political considerations were of the utmost importance. The newfound stability of cotton during the third quarter and the massive wealth of the large employers made paternalism possible. And many employers doubtless saw paternalism and welfarism as means whereby a repetition of the class conflict of the Chartist period could be avoided. The desired end was employer hegemony over a contented and disciplined workforce which, by its 'restraint', would greatly increase profits.[237] Furthermore, many paternalistic measures were deliberately designed to counteract the 'disruptive' influence of trade unions. In 1854 the manager of a railway company at Manchester, while making some provision for the educational and cultural needs of his employees, systematically purged the workforce of 'troublemakers'.[238] Platt's seemingly magnanimous gestures were accompanied by vicious attacks on trade unionism and a defence of the *status quo*. In responding to a worker vote of thanks in 1857, Platt declared that his actions would in effect 'beat all trade unions out of court'.[239] The workers who played the leading role in drawing up and presenting the addresses to Platt had obviously been given political clearance by the employer. Part of the address of 1857 read, 'That there should be distinctions of class in society seems to be quite necessary, and it appears to be an arrangement made by the All Wise Governor of the universe . . .'[240] Dan Lynne, the key speaker on such occasions, preached deference, and non-unionism: 'They wanted no third party to interfere between them and their employer; they acknowledged no paid secretary or committee in a back room, drinking brandy and water, and smoking cigars at the expense of the public.'[241] The manager at Chadwick's Mill at Dukinfield took advantage of a gathering of workers to declare that, 'while it was his desire at all times to redress every grievance, however small, he wanted to do this without bringing in any foreign aid whatsoever'.[242] Buckley, proprietor of Carr Hill Mills, was renowned for both his generosity and his dislike of trade unionism and strikers. And when some of the workers at one of Whittaker's mills, claiming that Whittaker was 'robbing them', struck work in 1866 Reginald Whittaker's sweet and caring disposition turned sour. Accusing the operatives of 'ingratitude', he threatened to move his business elsewhere.[243] Similarly, Mason would not tolerate trade unionism in his mills.[244]

Despite such qualifications, there is no doubting 'the warmth and genuineness of operative responses to paternalistic overtures'.[245] Mason's every action at the Oxford Mills evoked warm employee responses. In June 1861 the operatives held a tea party to present Mason with a testimonial. In the chairman's opinion, Mr Mason had proved that he did not consider those employed, '. . . as mere beasts of burden, but as intelligent beings . . .' In 1865 the workers of Ashton gave Mason a clock in recognition of his services to them during the Cotton Famine. One speaker at the gathering of some 600 claimed that, 'it had been Mr Mason's constant endeavour to elevate the working classes, morally, socially, and intellectually, and thus to make them worthy of the name of freemen'.[246] During the following three years further tributes to Mason's role as an employer, and his public spiritedness were made. One address ran:

We cannot refrain from giving free expression to our esteem for your character as an employer of labour. Whilst you are fully alive to the *rights* of property and capital, you have ever been foremost in acknowledging the *duties* that belong to them. Year after year you have stood in the front rank with those who have acknowledged the rights and claims of the working classes.[247]

And in May 1871 between 600 and 700 Oldham operatives marched to Mason's residence at Ashton to thank him for his advocacy of the Saturday half-holiday.[248]

The Whittaker family was likewise showered with presents and eulogistic worker testimonials. In 1860 John Whittaker's operatives presented him with a silver inkstand in recognition of 'those acts and principles which have endeared you to every person, from the highest to the humblest'.[249]

The provision of education for the operatives and the general social harmony prevailing at Hurst were the subject of a poem written by Elijah Moss in 1862:

OUR FACTORY SCHOOL

Tune: 'Artichokes and Cauliflowers'

You factory folks of Lancashire, a song we'll sing to you,
Of a school now formed at Higher Hurst, and every word is
   true,
Our masters are determined to care well for their hands,
If only they will come to school, and there obey commands.

Chorus: Then old and young attend the school, your teachers there
obey,
   There's military exercise, and military pay.

Our mules and looms have now ceased work, the Yankees are the
   cause,
But we will let them fight it out, and stand by English laws;
No recognising shall take place, until the war is o'er,
Our wants are now attended to, we cannot ask for more.

Potatoes, ham, and bacon are now to us being sold,
With comforts such as these we have no fear of winter cold:
Everyone seems hearty glad, and sings with joyous glee
For men and masters now do meet in love and unity.'[250]

In 1867 the executive committee of the Strippers and Grinders

Union exempted the Whittaker Mills from strike action on the grounds that the family paid higher wages, and treated their workers better than other employers in the area.[251] And when a member of the Whittaker family received an assassination threat in 1870, the workers at the mills reiterated their allegiance to the firm, and offered a reward for information leading to the identification and apprehension of the would-be assassin.[252]

Finally, whatever the reasons underlying paternalism and welfarism, the end product was often enhanced operative allegiance to the master. This crucial fact was demonstrated by the growing number of occasions on which workers made presentations to their employers, and paid glowing tributes to the 'new-found employer spirit'. In 1857 the operatives at the Old Mill Dukinfield invited their employer to dine with them, and presented him with a gold pen and an address which ran:

> As an employer of labour you have been kind . . . and have completely divested yourself of those petty acts that give so much uneasiness to working people, and lead to the worst feelings between employers and employed. We earnestly hope that the influential class of men, who have so many hearts beating in their employ . . . will follow your noble example, and endeavour to improve the moral and social conditions of the people.[253]

Workers at Marsland's Mill in Stalybridge looked upon their connections with their employer 'with the warmest feelings of respect and gratitude'. In 1859 operatives at Mossley thanked the employers of the district for 'lending a helping hand to the suffering and distressed'. Workers at Hampson's Mill at Droylsden were 'fully impressed with a sense of your kindness towards us'. In 1860 John Kenworthy, a millowner at Ashton, was given a silver inkstand by his workers 'as a confirmation of the growing attachment and esteem' which characterised relations between them, and in recognition of his 'continued kindness and interest in their welfare'.[254] In 1864 a group of workers at Ashton 'highly eulogised' the manufacturers of the borough — thanking them for their 'past conduct' and observing that 'many had done their duty better than a great many of the manufacturers in Lancashire and Cheshire'.[255] In 1857 Robert Platt's workers, noting that a worker address to an employer was 'quite a novel thing' in the history of the locality, presented Platt with a testimonial in recognition of his 'many acts of kindness and generosity'.[256]

These were isolated examples of what was a widespread phenomenon. Although a few addresses had been presented to employers in the mid-1840s they greatly multiplied throughout the mid-Victorian years. All of them followed a similar pattern: employer kindness was praised and the 'sudden growth' of a 'family spirit' in industry welcomed.[257] Some of the addresses may have been 'doctored' by managers and overlookers before being presented for public consumption, and some employers doubtless followed Platt's practice of selecting the older, more deferential workers to read them. Nevertheless, it appears that most addresses were genuine expressions of worker gratitude.

Conclusion

In surveying the industrial relations scene during the third quarter, we have encountered a variety of interconnected and at times seemingly contradictory forces: on the one hand continued employer opposition to trade unionism, nagging industrial conflict, and disagreements concerning the merits of orthodox political economy; on the other the growth of moderate and pragmatic trade unionism, the creation of boards of conciliation and arbitration, and the emergence of a 'new employer spirit'.

The existence and complex interactions of this wide range of forces do not lend themselves to easy, instant conclusions. We can, however, state categorically that the continued (sometimes major) presence of industrial conflict rules out unqualified acceptance of the Webbs' notion of a 'watershed'. Furthermore, the thesis shared by Chapman, Turner and Joyce of long term overall 'improvements' and changes is by no means watertight. We can agree with these historians that by 1870 trade unions in cotton were generally more moderate and secure than they had been in the pre-1850 period, that employer concessions to their workers and organised labour were generally more widespread, and that industrial relations in the cotton districts had become less violent in character. However, this is not to suggest, as does Chapman, that employers and workers had 'come of age'; nor is it to give support to Joyce's belief in the growth of a deferential proletariat and the attainment of a new level of 'institutionalised calm' in cotton. As we have seen in this chapter, advances in union recognition in cotton were patchy during the third quarter, and many employers were reluctant to deal with trade unions (especially those of the semi-skilled and unskilled). Bureaucratisation and centralisation in union affairs were insufficiently developed before 1875 to permit us to speak of 'institutionalised calm'. (Even during the last quarter of the century, when collective bargaining in cotton became far more extensively institutionalised, it is debatable as to whether such a state of affairs came into existence. H.A. Turner, for example, informs us that, 'the uncertain years from 1872 lead into a major slump . . . and initiate a generation's extensive conflict'.[258]) And, as demonstrated in the numerous local disputes and the wider clashes of 1853-4, 1861 and 1867, industrial conflict persisted, sometimes at a high level of intensity, throughout the 'golden years' and constituted the major obstacle to the attainment of social harmony. Despite their moderate leaders and trappings, trade unions both in cotton and elsewhere never received the kind of widespread middle-class approval and support bestowed upon the Co-operative Movement. Trade unions continued to be both potential and actual organs of class struggle — run by and for workers and resistant to direct middle-class control and ideological penetration.

Trends in industrial relations signalled, therefore, not the emergence of worker deference and class harmony, but continued worker independence and struggle. Simultaneously, however, industrial struggles were not generally linked to political agitation and were not directed against the wider social system. Rather, industrial conflict was increasingly conducted within a more widespread acceptance of the seeming permanence of 'wage slavery'.

Notes

1. S. and B. Webb, *The History of Trade Unionism*, op. cit., esp. III, IV, V.
2. See, for example, R. Harrison, *Before the Socialists*, op. cit., I; A.E. Musson, *British Trade Unions*, op. cit., Ch. 6.
3. S.J. Chapman, *The Lancashire Cotton Industry* (Manchester, 1904), p. 237.
4. H.A. Turner, *Trade Union Growth, Structure and Policy* (1962), pp. 119-25.
5. P. Joyce, *Work, Society and Politics*, op. cit., pp. 64-82.
6. *Manchester Guardian*, 28 August 1856.
7. *Ashton Reporter*, 3 January 1857.
8. Ibid., 10 April 1858.
9. Ibid., 24 December 1859.
10. *Reports of the Factory Inspectors* (Redgrave), 30 April 1862, p. 101; and ibid. (Baker) 31 October 1862, pp. 143-4.
11. See, for example, *Ashton Reporter*, 2 December 1871.
12. While relations often worsened during the periods of bad trade and increased unemployment, periods of good trade did not necessarily mitigate grievances. Hence

the most bitter disputes of the period were fought in the 'good' year of 1853.

13. *Manchester Guardian*, 5 November 1853.

14. *Ashton Reporter* 2 October 1858.

15. *Ashton Standard*, 23 June 1860.

16. Ibid., 1 November 1862; *The Times*, 14 March 1863.

17. *Manchester City News*, 18 August 1866.

18. *Ashton Reporter*, 20 March 1869.

19. For example, both Chapman's and Turner's conclusions and generalisations are based upon somewhat thin evidence. Most noticeable, perhaps, is their lack of detailed investigation into the incidence and nature of local disputes.

20. *Manchester Examiner and Times*, 6 January 1849.

21. For an account of the dispute see *Manchester Guardian*, 20 September 1850, 15 January, 26 April 1851.

22. For the development of the engineering industry see, J.B. Jeffreys, op. cit., pp. 12-15; K. Burgess, *The Origins of British Industrial Relations* (1975), Ch. .1.

23. For accounts of this conflict see J.B. Jeffreys, pp. 28ff; *Trade Societies and Strikes, Report of the Committee on Trade Societies Appointed by the National Association (1860)*; K. Burgess, 'The 1852 Lock-out in the British Engineering Industry', *Soc. Stud. Lab. Hist. Bull.*, no. 24 (Spring 1972), pp. 7-11.

24. *Manchester Guardian*, 24 December 1851.

25. See, for example, J.T. Ward, *The Factory Movement, 1830-1855* (1962), pp. 378-402; *Manchester Guardian*, 27 January, 18 April, 17 May, 14 July 1849.

26. *Reports of Factory Inspectors* (Horner) (2391), vol. XXIV (30 April 1858), p. 9.

27. For conflicts in cotton in 1853 and 1854 see H.I. Dutton and J.E. King, *Ten Per Cent and No Surrender: the Preston Strike 1853-1854* (Cambrige 1981), esp. Chs 2-5, 10.

28. *Stockport Advertiser*, 8 April 1853.

29. Ibid., 18 March 1853.

30. Ibid., 3 June 1853.

31. Ibid., 29 April 1853.

32. Ibid., 3 June 1853.

33. Ibid., 29 April 1853.

34. For details of the strike see ibid., 24 June, 1, 15, 29 July, 5, 12 August 1853.

35. *Manchester Guardian*, 25, 29 June, 6, 17, 20 August 1853.

36. Ibid., 2 July, 6, 31 August, 17 September, 15 October, 6 November 1853.

37. Ibid., 9, 13 July 1853.

38. H.I. Dutton and J.E. King, op. cit., esp. Ch. 5.

39. *Peoples Paper*, 5 November 1853.

40. *Manchester Guardian*, 5 November 1853.

41. See H. Ashworth, *The Preston Strike* (Manchester, 1854); *Manchester Guardian*, 26 October, 23 November 1853. 18, 22 January, 11, 25 February, 4, 15 March, 5, 18 April, 8, 10 May 1854; Dutton and King, op. cit., esp. Chs 5 and 10; R. P. Bradshaw, 'The Preston Lock-out: A Case Study of a Mid-Nineteenth Century Lancashire Cotton Strike, and its Role in the Development of Trade Union Organisation amongst Textile Workers' (unpublished MA, University Lancaster, 1972).

42. H. Ashworth, op. cit., p. 38

43. *Manchester Courier*, 29 April 1854.

44. *Stockport Advertiser*, 14, 21, 28 April, 12 May 1854; Dutton and King, op. cit., pp. 181-94.

45. For ways in which involvement in mass struggles can sometimes raise consciousness above a purely 'economistic' level see J.F. Nettl *Rosa Luxemburg* (1966), Ch XII; J. Brecher *Strike* (San Francisco, 1972).

It is instructive to note that Dutton and King (pp. 54-5) believe that workers' aspirations and rights were considerably lower in 1853-4 than during the general strike of 1842. ('In little more than a decade a remarkable transformation had taken place'). A marked contrast is drawn between the allegedly moderate, generally peaceful and 'narrowly economic' character of the former, and the violence 'and commotion', 'distinct revolutionary overtones' and mass commitment to the Charter characteristic of the latter. I agree with Dutton and King that violence, industrial unrest and support for independent working-class politics were more extensive in 1842 than 1853–4. I would also highlight the increasing separation between industrial and political forms of action.

In some ways contrasts can, however, be overdrawn. The 'revolutionary' character of the 1842 strike and the degree of mass political commitment to the Charter on the part of the strikers are surely open to question. Certainly (as Dutton and King note) the Trades Delegates' meeting in Manchester supported the resolution in favour of the Charter, but there existed differences of opinion within the Chartist movement itself in 1842. Pilling, for example, saw the strike primarily as a 'wages question' and was reluctant, for tactical rather than ideological reasons, to introduce a potentially divisive political issue into an industrial dispute. And O'Connor feared that the strikers were playing into the hands of the Anti-Corn-Law League. (See *The Trial of Feargus O'Connor* op. cit., pp. v-ix, 254–5. Also T.D.W. Reid and N. Reid, op. cit., p. 70; M. Jenkins, op. cit., p. 236.)

It may also be the case that the ideological differences between the actions of 1842 and 1853–4 were less great than often supposed. As Dutton and King themselves note (p. 55), anti- employer sentiment (as reflected in language) was extremely strong in 1853–4. Furthermore a leader such as Cowell, whilst committed to the Charter, was reluctant 'to introduce political questions into the ten per cent campaign, for this would guarantee failure'. In other words, Cowell's opposition to political commitment was on 'political' rather than 'ideological' grounds. Dutton and King remark (p. 55): 'A revolutionary general strike had been doomed to failure in 1842; now it would have been suicidal. Better to strive for attainable goals, even if they fell far short of what they felt might legitimately be demanded.'

The central question concerning 1842 and 1853–4 is whether, as argued by the Reids and others, the growing concentration upon trade unionism and industrial agitation marked a conscious ideological break with independent working-class political action, or whether political, industrial and other forms of working-class agitation were increasingly kept separate for mainly tactical and organisational reasons. See Chs 2 and 4 above pp. 57–8, 154–5.

46. *Peoples Paper*, 3 September 1853.

47. *Manchester Guardian*, 17 September 1853.

48. For proposals for co-operative production at Preston see ibid., 10 May 1854. For an extended discussion of co-operative production see Kirk, thesis, II. Dutton and King, op. cit., pp. 57–8.

49. See *Peoples Paper*, 5 November, 3, 10 December, 1853; *Manchester Guardian*, 12 October 1853.

50. *Peoples Paper*, 2 September 1854. For the hostile attitudes of some of the Preston delegates towards 'political involvement' see ibid., 18 March 1854. The opposition of the weavers' delegates to involvement with the 'mass movement' was, however, mainly pragmatic rather then ideological in character. As Dutton and King note (p. 61), '. . . those who fought against association with the Labour Parliament did so, in the main, for pragmatic rather than ideological reasons; less because they disagreed with its principles, than because they doubted its practicality'.

51. *Peoples Paper*, 3, 17 December 1853; 7, 21 January, 11 March, 20 May 1854; *Manchester Guardian*, 3, 10 December 1853.

52. *Manchester Guardian*, 8, 21 November 1855.

53. Loc. cit.

54. Ibid., 29 November, 16, 20, 27 December 1855.

55. Ibid., 1, 7 February 1856.

56. Ibid., 6, 19 June, 1, 11, July, 4 August, 1 September 1856.

57. Ibid., 2, 10, 27 August 1858; *Ashton Reporter*, 2 October 1858.

58. O. Ashmore, 'The Diary of James Garnett of Low Moor, Clitheroe 1858–1865', *Transactions of the Historical Society of Lancashire and Cheshire*, vol. 12 (1969).

59. The Blackburn Standard List, known as the 'Cotton Operatives' Charter', was drawn up at Blackburn in 1853. The list laid down standard rates for weavers, spinners, and other factory operatives, and included a disputes-conciliation procedure. The list was significant in that it reflected the fact that Blackburn masters had recognised the workers' collective organisations, and that it served as the basis of wage calculation for weavers' organisations throughout Lancashire. For a fuller discussion see H.A. Turner, op. cit., pp. 128, 131.

60. W.A. Jevons, *Trade Societies and Strikes* (1860).

61. *Hyde and Glossop News*, 11 June 1859.

62. Ibid., 20 August 1859.

63. *Ashton Reporter*, 8, 15 September 1860.

64. Ibid., 24 March 1860; *Manchester Guardian*, 27 September 1859; *Ashton Standard*, 21 April, 12, 19 May 1860.

65. *Reports of Factory Inspectors* (Redgrave), 30 April 1860 (2689), vol. XXXI, p. 29.

66. *Manchester Guardian*, 15, 20, 28 February, 16 March 1861.

67. *Ashton Reporter*, 30 March 1861.

68. Ibid., 6 April 1861.

69. *Penny Observer*, 30 March 1861; *Manchester Guardian*, 26, 27 March, 9, 26, 29 April 1861.

70. *Manchester Examiner and Times*, 29 April 1861.

71. *Manchester Guardian*, 26, 27, 29 March 1861.

72. *Ashton Reporter*, 30 March, 4, 11, 25 May 1861.

73. Ibid., 1 June 1861.

74. *Reports of Inspectors of Factories* (Redgrave), 30 April 1862, p. 10; April 1863 (3206), vol. XVIII, pp. 17–19; 31 October 1863 (3309) vol. XXII; 30 April 1864 (3390), vol. XXII; M. Bowman, op. cit., p. 23; Ch 3 above.

75. R. Harrison, op. cit., pp. 113–4, 118; D.A. Farnie, op. cit., p. 157.

76. *The Times*, 14 March 1863.

77. M.E. Rose, *The Relief of Poverty 1834–1914* (1972), esp. p. 18.

78. *Manchester Guardian*, 30 July 1862.

79. Ibid., 29 July, 2, 6 August 1862.

80. *The Times*, 20 March 1863.

81. *Ashton Reporter*, 12 April, 3 May 1862; *Manchester Guardian*, 12 August 1862.

82. See below, pp. 293–5

83. *Ashton Reporter*, 12 April 1862.

84. Ibid., 24 May 1862.

85. Ibid., 31 May, 23 August, 13 September 1862.

86. Ibid., 16 August 1862.

87. *The Times*, 14 March 1863.

88. Loc. cit.

89. Loc. cit.

90. Loc. cit.

91. Ashton Reporter, 14, 21 February, 7 March 1863.

92. Ibid., 21 March 1863; J. Watts, *The Facts of the Cotton Famine* (1866), pp. 263ff; M.E. Rose, 'Rochdale Man', op. cit.

93. *Manchester Guardian*, 23, 24, 25 March 1863.

94. Loc. cit.

95. *The Times*, 25 March 1863.

96. *Manchester Guardian*, 23 March 1863.

97. Ibid., 24 March 1863.

98. Ibid., 22, 23, 24 April 1863.

99. *Ashton Reporter*, 8, 18 June 1864.

100. Ibid., 5 May 1866; *Manchester Guardian*, 3 March, 14, 23 April, 4 July 1866.

101. For strikes among brickmakers see *Royal Commission on Trade Unions*, Reports, vol. 3, 'Manchester Outrages Inquiry', pp. viii, xxvi; *Stockport and Cheshire County News*, 9 June, 14 July 1866.

102. *Ashton Reporter*, 5 January 1867.

103. *Cheshire County News*, 8, 22, 29 March, 5 April 1867.

104. *Manchester Guardian*, 1, 2, 4, 7, 20, 21, 25 April 1868.

105. Ibid., 10, 20, 22, 29, 31 March, 2, 5, 7, 8, 9, 12, 26, April 1869.

106. For accounts of strikes in the building industry see ibid., 12 April, 5 May, 9 June, 9, 11 August, 27 October, 3 November 1869.

107. Finally, however, the employers agreed to submit the question to arbitration. *Ashton Reporter*, 6, 13 May 1871; *Webbs' Trade Union Collection*, Sec. A., vol. 36, pp. 7, 8.

108. R.V. Clements, 'British Trade Unions and Popular Political Economy 1850–1875', *Economic History Review*, 2nd series, vol. xix, no. 16 (1961).

109. *Manchester Guardian*, 14 December 1853.

110. H. Ashworth, op. cit., pp. 15–16; Dutton and King, op. cit., Ch. 4.

111. H. Ashworth, p. 214; *Manchester Guardian*, 17 May 1854.

112. *Manchester Guardian*, 15 November 1855.

113. *Ashton Reporter*, 9 July 1859.

114. Ibid., 16 January 1869.

115. *Manchester Guardian*, 6 July 1869.

116. H.A. Turner, op. cit., pp. 114, 124.

117. E. Hopwood, op. cit., pp. 37ff; H.A. Turner op. cit., pp. 134.

118. H.A. Turner, op. cit., pp. 112–13, 124.

119. Ibid., pp. 115–16; W. Lazonick, op. cit., p. 246.

120. H.A. Turner, op. cit., pp. 144–7.

121. For the Free Labour Society, see *First Annual Report* (Manchester, 1870). For the tenets of orthodox political economy see R.V. Clements, op. cit.; *Manchester Guardian*, 1 April 1868 for Jevons.

122. R.V. Clements, op. cit., p. 98.

123. W. MacDonald, *The True Story of Trades' Unions: Being a Reply to Dr John Watts, Professor Jevons and Others* (Manchester, 1867), p. 13.

124. *Manchester Guardian*, 17, 19 December 1855.

125. W. MacDonald, op. cit., p. 11.

126. This was a stock argument of trade unionists. Loc. cit.; *Ashton Reporter*, 3 December 1870; *Manchester Guardian*, 1 April 1868; *Manchester City News*, 28 December 1867.

127. Many workers doubtless supported the view put forward by one trade unionist that wages were determined by the power of organised labour. See *Ashton Reporter*, 29 March 1859; also the debates on wages and emigration in *Co-operator*, June 1863, p. 7, August 1863 p. 38, January 1864. For the importance of custom and practice in the determination of nineteenth-century wage levels see, E.J. Hobsbawm, 'Custom, Wages and Work-Load' in *Labouring Men*, op. cit., pp. 344–63.

128. R.V. Clements, op. cit.

129. *Manchester Guardian*, 6 June 1856 for the spinners; *Ashton Reporter*, 18 February 1871 for the strippers and grinders.

130. *Manchester Guardian*, 4 August 1856; *Ashton Reporter*, 30 August 1856.

131. For the Trades Council see L. Bather, *A History of Manchester and Salford Trades Council* (unpublished PhD thesis, Manchester University, 1956), p. 22; Ashton Spinners — *Ashton Reporter*, 10 September 1859; Bolton

Spinners — *Manchester Guardian*, 27 April 1861; Weavers — *Manchester Courier*, 9 August 1856 and *Ashton Reporter*, 24 March 1860.

132. *Manchester Guardian*, 15 June 1853.

133. *Ashton Reporter*, 14 July 1866.

134. Ibid., 12 March 1870.

135. *Ashton Standard*, 24 March 1866.

136. *Ashton Reporter*, 14 February 1857.

137. *Webb Trade Union Collection*, see Sec. A, vol. 36, p.261 for Hyde spinners.

138. *Royal Commission on Trade Unions*, op. cit., vol. 1, Reports, p. 81; also *Ashton Reporter*, 11 August 1866.

139. *Manchester Guardian*, 9 November 1853.

140. *Ashton Reporter*, 12 September 1868, 18 February 1871.

141. Ibid., 29 December 1860.

142. For reports of 'courteous behavious' see *Manchester Guardian*, 4 August 1856; *Ashton Reporter*, 29 December 1860. For demonstrations against violent conduct see *Manchester City News*, 27 July 1867.

143. *Ashton Standard*, 22 September 1860.

144. Especially during the late 1860s in the wake of the 'Sheffield Outrages' and the setting up of the Royal Commission of Enquiry into trade unionism. See A.E. Musson, *British Trade Unions*, op. cit., pp. 61–3.

145. H.A. Turner, op. cit., p. 119.

146. During all the major disputes — Stockport 1853–4 and 1867, Preston 1853–4, 1856, 1869, and south-east Lancashire in 1861 — trade unionists advocated arbitration. In February 1867 100 representatives of factory operatives throughout Lancashire and Cheshire supported a resolution calling for the creation of Boards of Arbitration. See *Manchester City News*, 16 February 1867.

147. For an excellent discussion of the two types of trade unionism in the cotton industry see, H.A. Turner, op. cit., esp. pp. 126–38, and III, 2. Much of the following discussion of trade union structure and development is based upon Turner. See also, *Webbs' Trade Union Collection*, sect. A, vols. 35, 36, 37.

148. W. Lazonick, op. cit.; J. Hinton, *Labour and Socialism*, op. cit., p. 5.

149. See, for example, W. Lazonick, op. cit., pp. 236–40.

150. Ibid., p. 248.

151. Ibid., pp. 239–40.

152. Ibid., pp. 243, 245.

153. Ibid., pp. 245–6.

154. H.A. Turner, op. cit., pp. 127, 139, 140.

155. Ibid., pp. 114ff.

156. Ibid., pp. 128–9; E. Hopwood, *A History of the Lancashire Cotton Industry and the Amalgamated Weavers' Association* (Manchester, 1969), pp. 33ff.

157. See below, pp. 282–3.

158. See below, pp. 281–2.

159. H.A. Turner, op, cit., pp. 129ff.

160. Employers were often reluctant to allow Pinder into their factories.

161. *Webbs' Trade Union Collection*, sect. A, vol. 37, p. 51.

162. This is not to suggest that spinners were never involved in bitter strikes. The Preston dispute of 1869 was particularly acrimonious.

163. H.A. Turner, op. cit., pp. 135–6

164. Ibid., p. 136.

165. *Stockport Advertiser*, 29 April 1853.

166. A delegate meeting of weavers adopted a resolution which read: 'It was not their desire to create dissatisfaction between employer and employed, but to use legal means, and so systematize proceedings as to prevent . . . the disturbances that had occurred.' *Ashton Reporter*, 30 August 1856; *Manchester Courier*, 9 August 1856.

167. O. Ashmore's comments in *Hist. Soc. Lancs. and Ches.*, op. cit., p. 87;

Ashton Reporter, 15 September 1860.

168. *Manchester Guardian*, 2, 16 March 1861.

169. Ibid., 25, 27 March 1861.

170. Ibid., 29 March 1861.

171. Ibid., 26, 27, 29 March 1861.

172. For the role of the weavers' leaders in this dispute see, *Ashton Standard*, 23 June 1860.

173. W. Lanzonick, op. cit., p. 246. Joyce's structuralist argument is essentially static, largely ignoring changes in the bargaining strength of the spinners between the 1840s and 1860s.

174. *Ashton Reporter*, 23 November, 1861.

175. For the Bolton Spinners see *Manchester Guardian*, 26 March 1861; *Webbs' Trade Union Collection*, sect. A, vol. 36.

176. *Webbs' Trade Union Collection*, sect. A, vol. 36, 'Short History of the Oldham Spinners', pp. 8, 29.

177. *Manchester Guardian*, 6 June 1856.

178. *Stockport Advertiser*, 16, 21 March 1850.

179. *Manchester Guardian*, 26 June 1854.

180. Ibid., 14 January 1857.

181. *Ashton Reporter*, 8 October 1859.

182. Ibid., 12 March 1870.

183. Ibid., 8 October 1859.

184. For the bookbinders see *Manchester City News*, 13 January, 1866. For the early closing movement see *Ashton Reporter*, 6 May 1871.

185. *Stockport Advertiser*, 17 June 1853.

186. *Ashton Reporter*, 8 September 1860, 9 February 1861.

187. Ibid., 24 November 1855.

188. W. MacDonald, op. cit., p. 5.

189. *Royal Commission on Trade Unions*, op. cit., Repts., vol. 1, pp. 84, 86.

190. Ibid., p. 85.

191. *Manchester City News*, 22 September 1866.

192. Loc. cit.

193. *Manchester Guardian*, 13 April 1869.

194. *Ashton Reporter*, 12 September 1868.

195. Ibid., 24 September 1870, 2 August, 1865.

196. L. Bather, op. cit., p. 22; *Manchester Guardian*, 14 October 1868.

197. L. Bather, op. cit., pp. 23–4.

198. *Manchester Guardian*, 26 January 1870.

199. *Webbs' Short History of the Bolton Spinners*, op. cit.

200. For Ashton Spinners see *Ashton Reporter*, 23, 31 March 1860, 8 December 1866, 23 March 1867.

201. Ibid., 2 December 1871.

202. *Webbs' Trade Union Collection*, vol. 36, 'Short History of the Oldham Spinners', pp. 13, 68.

203. *Webbs' Trade Union Collection*, vol. 37, p. 53.

204. I am grateful to Andrew Bullen for drawing my attention to the importance of market conditions in the overall determination of the pattern of industrial relations in cotton in Lancashire and Cheshire during the second half of the nineteeth Century.

205. At Preston the employers finally agreed, at the end of the 1860s, to confer with the secretary of the union. *Manchester Guardian*, 8 April 1869.

206. Upon this point, I am, once again, grateful to Andrew Bullen for his expert knowledge of Blackburn and north Lancashire.

207. *Ashton Reporter*, 18 February 1871.

208. Loc. cit.

209. *Ashton Standard*, 24 March 1866. For the beamers' and twisters' amalgamation see Webbs' *Trade Union Collection*, vol. 36, pp. 143ff.

210. For an excellent, if controversial account of employer paternalism see P. Joyce, *Work, Society and Politics*, op. cit., esp. Ch. 4. Also Kirk *Bull. Soc. St. Lab. Hist.*, no. 42; H.I. Dutton and J.E. King, 'The Limits of Paternalism: The Cotton Tyrants of North Lancashire', *Social History*, vol. 7, no. 1 (January 1982), pp. 59–74.

211. The question of timing is important. It appears to be the case that employer paternalism, while sometimes practised during the second quarter (for example, during the mid-1840s trade upswing), became a widespread phenomenon in Lancashire only from the mid-1850s onwards.

212. The prosperity and economic stability of the mid-Victorian years provided an essential foundation for the creation of paternalism. Dutton and King, op. cit., pp. 61–2, 72 (note 83); Joyce, op. cit., pp. 147–52.

213. It seems, therefore, that paternalism was a response to a defensive, and in some ways defeated (as opposed to an insurgent), working class. Dutton and King note that, on balance, the decline of independent working-class radicalism was 'more likely to have been a cause than an effect of the growth of paternalism in Lancashire'. Dutton and King, op. cit., p. 74.

214. *Ashton Reporter*, 27 June 1857.

215. Ibid., and 22 August 1857.

216. *Reports of Factory Inspectors* (Baker) 31 October 1858, p. 65.

217. *Ashton Reporter*, 4 September 1858.

218. Ibid., 3 September 1859.

219. *Ashton Standard*, 14 April 1860.

220. *Stockport Advertiser*, 6, 13 January 1860.

221. *Ashton Reporter*, 5, 12 November 3 December 1859.

222. *Ashton Standard*, 26 February 1860.

223. *Reports of Factory Inspectors*, 31 October 1862 (3076), vol. XVIII p. 21.

224. *Ashton Reporter*, 4 January 1868, 9 January 1869.

225. See, for example, *Manchester City News*, 6 January 1866.

226. For Mason see *Ashton Reporter*, 30 April 1859, 14 January 1871. For a sketch of Mason's life see ibid., 1 March 1864. P. Joyce, op. cit., Ch. 4; J. Holland, 'Hugh Mason, Cotton Master, Puritan and Father Figure' in S.A. Harrop and E.A. Rose (eds)., *Victorian Ashton*, op. cit.

227. *Ashton Reporter*, 18 April 1868.

228. It is also significant that Mason believed that it was possible for an employer 'to pay the highest wages that were paid in the district, and still have the highest return for those wages'. Loc. cit.

229. Ibid., 9 July 1859, 28 January, 11 February 1860.

230. Ibid., 30 March, 29 June, 14 December 1861.

231. For Mason's activities during the Cotton Famine see M. Bowman, op. cit., pp. 450ff; *Ashton Reporter*, 8 February, 31 May, 13, 20 September 1862, 2 July, 17 December 1864.

232. For Mason's work during the post-Famine period see *Asthon Reporter*, 28 April 1866, 2 February, 30 March, 18 May 1867, 25 June, 10, 24 December 1870, 6 May 1871.

233. *Ashton Reporter*, 6 March 1858. For allegations of Whittakers' acts of 'tyranny' towards his workpeople in the 1840s see *Ashton Chronicle*, 19 August, 1848, no. 12.

234. *Ashton Reporter*, 22 August 1857; 14 April 1860; 24 August 1861.

235. Ibid., 16 August, 27 September 1862; 30 May 1863.

236. P. Joyce, op. cit., pp. 148–9.

237. At a dinner given by an employer one worker was heard to say: 'Our master thinks to put us off with a plate of beef and a glass of beer, but he will find himself

mistaken. What we want is more wages, and we will have it too before we have done.'
See *Ashton Standard*, 23 June 1860.

238. *Manchester Courier*, 7 January 1854.

239. See *An Address Delivered at the Presentation Tea Party Given by his Work-people to Robert Platt Esq., J.P.* (Stalybridge, 1857), p. 10, Ashton Public Library.

240. Ibid., p. 5.

241. *Ashton Reporter*, 3 September 1859.

242. Ibid., 25 February 1860.

243. For Buckley see ibid., 27 October 1860. For Whittaker see ibid., 28 July 1866.

244. J. Holland, op. cit., p. 7.

245. P. Joyce, op. cit., p. 149.

246. *Ashton Reporter*, 29 July 1861, 15 April 1865.

247. Ibid., 28 April 1866.

248. Ibid., 6 May 1871.

249. Ibid., 14 April 1860.

250. *Reports of Factory Inspectors*, 31 October 1862 (3076), vol. XVIII, pp. 43-4.

251. For the strippers and grinders see *Ashton Reporter*, 6 July 1867.

252. Ibid., 2 April 1870.

253. Ibid., 7 February 1857.

254. Ibid., 27 June 1857, 24 December 1859, 11, 25 February 1860.

255. Ibid., 18 June 1864.

256. See *An Address Delivered to Robert Platt*, op. cit.

257. See, for example, *Ashton Reporter*, 5 November, 1859, 12 November 1860, 7 April 1866.

258. H.A. Turner, op. cit., pp. 123-4.

This study has so far concentrated its attentions upon a relatively narrow range of (mainly) economic and social explanations of the decline of Chartism and the growth of reformism at mid-century. The purpose of this final chapter is to widen our horizons somewhat by incorporating the important, but often neglected, themes of ethnic allegiance and ethnic conflict into our explanatory framework. The thesis expounded is that a massive, unprecedented increase in the level of Irish Roman Catholic immigration into the cotton districts during the post-Famine years of the late 1840s brought in its wake a sharp rise in conflicts and tensions between sections of the immigrant and host communities. Such conflicts revealed themselves most forcibly and dramatically in the extremely riotous years of 1852 and 1868, but persisted, albeit at varying levels of intensity, throughout the period from 1850 to 1870. Set within the wider context of economic and social re-stabilisation, ethnic antagonisms within the working class greatly reduced the capacity for class solidarity and the potential appeal of independent labour politics. And a working class fragmented along ethnic (and wider cultural) lines greatly facilitated the (re)-assertion of bourgeois controls upon the working class, and helped to attach workers more firmly to the framework of bourgeois politics. Just as the majority of labour activists were drawn, for a number of reasons, to the 'progressive' Liberal camp,[1] so ethnic frictions pushed sections of the English workforce into the receptive arms of anti-Catholic Conservatives and Orangemen; strengthened the authority of the priesthood in Irish Catholic communities; and were instrumental in persuading large numbers of immigrants to support their Liberal defenders.

Before examining these trends in more detail, it is first of all necessary to define the terms 'ethnicity' and 'class'. 'Ethnicity'[2] is used here to refer to collectivities of people who share a common origin, ancestry, and *cultural* heritage, and who express their common interests in ideas, value systems and institutions. Ethnicity is used, therefore, both as a structural category (the behaviour of people in specified social situations, within structural constraints and determinations) and as a cultural phenomenon (consciousness). Ethnicity further implies: the existence of 'boundaries', which ensure internal group cohesion and create an external category of non-members; and can carry with it connotations of varying degrees of conflict both within and between ethnic groups. It should also be emphasised that ethnicity is viewed as a dynamic phenomenon. Ethnic feeling is not automatically *given* in a static or unhistorical manner: rather ethnic allegiance can diminish or increase over time depending upon specific historical determinations and the ways in which objective determinations are experienced by people.

As with ethnicity, 'class'[3] is interpreted not as a static thing but as a historical relationship, as something which happens over time. Class is also rooted both within objective determinations (mainly the *productive* relations into which people enter involuntarily) and in consciousness (in the ways in which people, 'live their productive relations, and as they *experience* their determinate situations, within "the *ensemble* of social relations", with their inherited culture and expectations, and as they handle these experiences in cultural ways'[4]). Class, as E.P. Thompson has insisted, owes as much to agency as conditioning. And while class experience is largely determined, class consciousness is far less so. Again, consciousness is not given in a simple, mechanistic way by objective determinations, but is rather the result of lived experience within certain specific structural constraints.

How, then, does class stand in relationship to ethnicity? The preceding sketch suggests that while any analysis of class which ignores or underplays cultural traditions and the ensemble of social relations is inherently unsatisfactory, nevertheless particular importance should be attached to social relations of production. By way of contrast, ethnicity, while cognisant of material factors, takes as its point of departure cultural traditions, origin and ancestry. This is not to imply, however, that classes and ethnic groups must always stand in mutual opposition and separation: the relationship is often more complex, fluid and dynamic than this. For example, while one could not deny the importance of ethnicity in moulding social structure and attitudes in the United States, one would take issue with any suggestion that workers in America have always been motivated by ethnic as opposed to class interests. Ethnic groups, as with classes, are not usually undifferentiated and monolithic wholes: a sense of cultural distinctiveness can be combined with a very real sense of class.[5]

Responses to Irish Immigration, 1830–1870

We can now turn to the situation in Lancashire and Cheshire at the middle of the nineteenth century. I propose, firstly, to outline reactions to Irish immigration between 1830 and 1870; secondly, to examine the material roots of assimilation and conflict; and, thirdly, to trace the socio-political effects of escalating tensions in the post-1850 period.

Contemporary attitudes towards Irish immigration have been well documented. My purpose here is not to rehearse these attitudes in detail, but to focus upon the major points of emphasis.[6] As is well known, contemporary reactions were, for the most part, unfavourable. Irish immigration was widely believed to constitute an example of 'a less civilised population spreading themselves, as a kind of substratum, beneath a more civilised community'. Schooled in a poverty-stricken agrarian society, the Irish were reputedly separated from the 'host' society by economic situation, politics, religion and culture. Concentrated on the bottom and lower rungs of the occupational ladder and huddled into their cramped quarters in the major urban areas, the Irish constituted, according to Faucher, 'the most abject part of the population', prepared to tolerate a lower standard of life than all but the very poor of the English workforce. The Catholic Church's antipathy towards Chartism and trade unionism, the popularity among sections of the immigrants of the anti-Chartist O'Connell, and the use of the Irish as strike-breakers, served to reinforce beliefs that Irish involvement in the labour movement was of little significance, and that the Irish were a direct threat to the English workers' standards of living. The Irish reputation for 'rough, intemperate and improvident' behaviour, their supposed lack of 'industrious and regular habits' and their attachment to an 'alien' religion completed the picture of an ethnic minority at odds with the host population. Even Marx, the major advocate of international proletarian solidarity, believed that the secret of the impotence of the working class in the post Chartist years lay in the growth of acute tensions between English workers and Roman Catholic Irish immigrants. In 1870 he wrote:

Every industrial and commercial centre in England now possesses a working-class *divided* into two *hostile* camps, English proletarians and Irish proletarians. The ordinary English worker hates the Irish worker as a competitor who lowers his standard of life. In relation to the Irish worker he feels himself a member of the *ruling* nation, and so turns himself into a tool of the aristocrats and capitalists of his country *against Ireland*, thus strengthening their domination over himself. He cherishes religious, social and national prejudices against the Irish worker . . . The Irishman pays him back with interest in his own money. He sees in the English worker at once the accomplice and stupid tool of the *English domination in Ireland*.

This antagonism is artificially kept alive and intensified by the press, the pulpit, the comic papers, in short, by all the means at the disposal of the ruling classes. This antagonism is the *secret of the impotence of the English working-class*, despite their organisation. It is the secret by which the capitalist class maintains its power. And that class if fully aware of it.[7]

An emphasis upon strains and divisions has also figured prominently in some of the more recent research. Werly, for example, has seen the emergence of Irish quarters in Manchester in the 1830s and 1840s as symptomatic of a lack of immigrant integration into the life of the city.[8] And Treble maintains that Irish involvement in Chartism was not strong.[9]

And yet, while problems of assimilation undoubtedly existed, we must be careful not to present an unbalanced picture for the two decades before 1850. Relations between English and Irish workers were more complex and fluid than many contemporaries realised. The researches of Thompson and Foster,[10] and to a much lesser extent Treble, suggest that although the mass of immigrants constituted an 'uneasy element' within the emerging working class, nevertheless patterns of integration and the capacity for united class action were by no means absent.

A growing sense of class solidarity was most evident in relation to the labour movement. As E.P. Thompson has noted, a number of the Irish were the descendants of the United Irishmen rather than adherents to the popular Catholicism of O'Connell. Many Irish weavers were at Peterloo and English reformers had supported Catholic emancipation.[11] And Irish participation in Chartism has, as the impressive researches of O'Higgins, Dorothy Thompson and Kaijage demonstrate, often been greatly underestimated.[12]

Several Irishmen held leadership positions in northwest Chartism and the movement at Oldham did attract significant immigrant support. At a national level Chartist leaders, with their belief in international proletarian solidarity, made strenuous efforts to attract Irish immigrants to the cause. Such efforts met with a mixed response and limited successes. We are dealing here with a chequered history, a story of fits and starts, of rebuttals and renewed attempts at unity. In south Lancashire, for example, the cordial relationship developed between the Chartists and members of the Repeal Association in the 1830s was, for a time at least, badly damaged by the events of 1841 when Chartists and Irish supporters of O'Connell clashed on the streets of Manchester, Stockport, Hyde and Stalybridge.[13] After 1841 repeated efforts were made to wrest control of the Repeal Associations away from O'Connellite influence, but without any notable success. However, even in the immediate post-1841 years Chartist influence over sections of the immigrant community was by no means negligible: Irish operatives took part in the General Strike of 1842 and O'Connor enjoyed some popularity amongst immigrant workers. Furthermore, institutional links between Chartists and Repealers were resurrected in 1848 when the increased emphasis placed upon socio-economic demands by Mitchell and his followers and their disillusionment with the results of 'moral force' agitation facilitated the creation of an alliance with the Chartists, which lasted throughout the spring and summer months.

Exaggerations and oversimplifications were also present in contemporary claims that English workers automatically reacted with hostility to Irish competition in the labour market. For those workers influenced by Chartism, this was not necessarily the case. Indeed the *Northern Star* claimed in 1841 that many workers had 'taken the very competition by the hand, and treated them [the Irish] not as aliens but as brethren.'[14] According to Richard Sheridan, a handloom weaver, responsibility for the ills of his craft lay less with the poor, unsuspecting Irish than with the employers' cheap labour policies:

> . . . the capitalists have sent over false reports that they wanted hands, in order to induce the Irish to come over that they might lower wages. I am at a loss to know whether the Irish gentleman or the English capitalist has done more for the destruction of the working classes, both of England and Ireland.[15]

The solution for Chartists lay in the creation of an alliance of English and Irish workers against the divisive acts of capitalists and landlords.

Neither were the Irish totally devoid of trade union experience.[16] To be sure, trade union traditions among the mass of immigrants from rural Ireland were weak, but some of the craft and skilled workers from urban areas had been schooled in trade unionism. As members of the shoemaking and tailoring unions in Manchester, the Irish played a part in virtually every trial of strength with employers in the 1830s and 1840s. Irishmen were amongst those who attempted to form a national weavers' organisation in 1841, and in Manchester Irish building trades labourers were solidly organised. Noted by many employers for their 'rebellious and insubordinate' character, the Irish, in cotton at least, were as likely to be strikers as strike-breakers.[17]

It is also easy to overestimate the extent to which Irish ghettos were formed, and the level and incidence of ethnic conflict during the Chartist period. Irish quarters did come into existence in some towns, but these rarely constituted large formal ghettos from which non-Irish families were totally excluded. And in other towns, for example Oldham, it appears that Irish and English operatives were quite happy to live as neighbours.[18] Indeed, after living in England for some time the Irish became, according to some contemporaries, more acceptable workmates, social companions and marriage partners for the English.[19] And, despite frequent battles between English and Irish railway navvies and the O'Connellite disturbances in 1841, instances of overt anti-Irish direct actions were rare in south Lancashire in the 1840s. Irish 'rows' often amounted to internal faction fights among the Irish, and were not usually directed against host communities.[20]

We must take care, therefore, not to exaggerate the extent of tensions and separations for the Chartist period. Whilst perhaps not fully accepting E.P. Thompson's conclusion that 'it is not the friction but the relative ease with which the Irish were absorbed into working-class communities which is remarkable'[21], we can suggest that a limited process of assimilation was at work in the cotton districts and that strong and widespread class feeling greatly reduced the potential for the development of serious ethnic divisions and conflicts.

With the increase in immigration in the late 1840s this scenario changed dramatically. While the capacity for toleration and even joint action did not totally disappear, the increasingly fragile nature of class unity and the mounting undercurrent of anti-Irish sentiment were demonstrated by a widespread upsurge in anti-immigrant feeling. In the late 1840s petitions flowed into London from the North complaining of the social dislocation and distress associated with the massive increase in immigration. In 1847 hundreds at Liverpool died from disease and fever. And the cholera epidemic, which swept northern towns in 1849, often originated in Irish quarters.[22] Competition in the labour market increased and newspaper reports of skirmishes between English and Irish operatives multiplied. At Stockport hundreds of Irishmen regularly congregated in the streets, 'speaking in the most hostile terms of the English and daring any John Bull man to come out and fight'. And at Ashton and elsewhere the Irish were accused of 'taking the bread out of the mouths of Lancashire workingmen'.[23]

As tensions mounted, Chartist pleas for toleration and understanding of the plight of the poverty-stricken Irish increasingly fell on deaf ears. As we have seen, after 1848 Lancashire Chartism, while by no means defunct, became a pale shadow of its former self: a force capable of challenging religious and cultural prejudices within the working class no longer enjoyed a mass base. With the increase in immigration and the demise of Chartism the various small but vociferous and largely middle-class Protestant organisations redoubled their efforts to generate anti-Catholic sentiments among workers:[24] scurrilous anti-Papist tracts were distributed; a sustained drive for working-class recruits was undertaken; and a series of well-attended and sensationalist lectures exposing the Pope's desire for 'universal domination', his antipathy to 'English liberties', and the manifold 'horrors and superstitions' of Roman Catholicism were delivered at Manchester, Stockport and Ashton. The Irish were portrayed as Papal puppets, intent upon lowering wages and 'transforming England into a great workhouse'.[25]

Extreme Protestants did not succeed, at this stage, in creating a strong working-class following, but their prophecies of imminent Papal domination in England were strengthened by the Pope's restoration of the catholic hierarchy in England and Wales in September 1850. This action triggered off a loud and aggressive Protestant backlash, which, while mainly middle-class in character, served to legitimise and render respectable anti-Irish Catholic feelings among workers and to highlight Irish attachment to an 'alien' religion. Serious anti-Popery disturbances broke out in London, Cheltenham and Birkenhead, and in south Lancashire irate Church of England Protestants held crowded and agitated meetings.[26] Hugh Stowell, a leading figure in Manchester and Salford Protestantism, warned that the Catholic Church intended, 'to get England under her power . . . to persecute and prosecute every Protestant . . . to set up the inquisition in our land . . . and to make Queen Victoria a Papist.'[27] No major outbreaks of rioting resulted from the Protestant backlash in the area, but the signs were ominous. A Lancashire clergyman, who claimed some intimacy with the feelings of operatives, predicted in 1850 that, '. . . our manufacturing and coal-supplying districts will soon rise to expel Popery, by which they mean the Irish Papists, considered by them as the cause of their misery.'[28] In December 1850 there was a street brawl in Manchester's 'Little Ireland' between English and Irish operatives; at Stockport Irish Catholics attempted to disrupt Protestant meetings and Church of England services;[29] and at Ashton and Stalybridge local Orangemen combined virulent attacks on Roman Catholicism with support for the economic and social grievances of English workers.[30]

Mounting unrest reached a climax in 1852 when anti-Irish disturbances occurred in a number of towns. The most serious riot took place at Stockport in July when the authorities' decision to permit the Catholics to hold their annual scholars' procession on the last Saturday in June sparked off several days of violence.[31] Irate Conservatives and Orangemen maintained that the holding of the procession contravened a royal proclamation of June (which forbade the exercise of the rites and ceremonies of the Catholic religion in other than their usual place of worship), and swore to have their revenge. On the Sunday the borough was relatively peaceful, but on Monday evening a crowd of some 100 English factory lads carried an effigy of Canon Frith, the Catholic priest, through the streets of an Irish neighborhood, tore it apart, and then did battle with the outraged Irish inhabitants. The events of Monday formed a prelude to the more serious rioting of Tuesday evening, when, following further street battles in Hillgate and the stoning of a Church of England school, a crowd of several hundred English workers, shouting 'Pull the Papist bastards out', attacked and ransacked Irish houses in Rock Row. The crowd, which increased to some 2,000 people, then proceeded to carry out extensive damage at the Catholic chapel at Edgeley, and was only prevented from ransacking the Catholic chapel of Saint Michael's by the arrival of troops and special constables. On Wednesday Stockport was still in an agitated state. Some English operatives, to the cry of 'Five pounds for an Irishman's head', carried out further attacks against Irish houses, but encountered stubborn Irish and police resistance.

The remaining months of the year witnessed numerous street battles, and on their return to Stockport in August the Englishmen found not guilty at Chester Assizes were received by 'one of the most enthusiastic gatherings that ever occurred in Stockport'.

The riots in Stockport, in which one man was killed and some 100 seriously injured, represented a settling of old scores, a battle for mastery of the borough. A favourite stamping-ground for 'pulpit-drum ecclesiastics' during the 'Papal Aggression Crisis', the town, according to the superintendent of police, had experienced 'for some years' increasing religious tensions. Pot-house brawls between English and Irish inhabitants were 'as common as daylight', and since the late 1840s cotton manufacturers had allegedly practised discriminatory employment policies in favour of Irish operatives. By June 1852 the conduct of some Irish mill workers had allegedly become so overbearing that many English operatives were refusing to work alongside them.[32] The Irish were disliked because they were 'bloody Papists, bloody rednecks'. Irish homes in Rock Row were daubed by the invading English workers with the slogan of 'England for Ever', and English rioters marched to the tune of 'Rule Brittania', a pattern to be repeated in the course of every major disturbance during the following 20 years. Perhaps the most important clue to the outbreaks of rioting was provided by an English factory operative. 'There never will be any good done with them,' he declared, 'it is the Irish who keep wages down.'[33]

The inflamed atmosphere at Stockport was highly infectious. In July the Irish districts in Manchester were in an 'excited state'. Hulme experienced fights between English and Irish labourers and factory operatives, and at New Cross (an area of some Chartist influence) Protestant candidates who stood at the parliamentary elections received some enthusiastic working-class support.[34] Wigan, a centre of deepseated and persistent ethnic conflict, witnessed a running battle between some 500 English and Irish people on election day.[35]

The remaining years of the decade were often tense and sometimes riotous. At Stockport weekend battles and skirmishes continued to plague the lives of 'respectable citizens', and the Protestant Association registered a sharp increase in its popularity among the cotton workforce. At Stalybridge and Ashton, where contemporaries noted a marked decline of Chartism and a widespread growth of anti-Irish feeling, repeated clashes took place. In September 1854, for example, a full-scale riot erupted at Ashton[36] when between 200 and 300 men and youths retaliated against Irish attacks on the homes of English operatives by invading the Irish quarter of Flag Alley. In the ensuing years the Ashton Protestant Association built up a considerable following among the town's cotton workforce. At the 1857 parliamentary election Booth Mason, a prominent local Orangeman, stood at Ashton on a platform of 'No Popery' and support for manhood suffrage. Mason received the show of hands at the hustings but was defeated at the poll.[37] At Oldham ethnic polarisation was one aspect of the decline of working-class solidarity in the 1850s. Here, as at Preston, Blackburn and Wigan, Protestant street preaching and Orange parades often resulted in violence.[38]

Despite the upsurge in conflict in the 1850s some towns, and most significantly Stockport, did experience a lowering of ethnic tensions towards the end of the decade and in the early 1860s. During the Relief Riots at Stalybridge in 1863 English and Irish operatives acted in concert. When the police attempted to transport the Irishmen arrested during the disturbance from the police station to the railway station a crowd of 'not less than fifteen thousand' English and Irish operatives made an abortive attempt to rescue the prisoners.[39] Stockport remained untroubled by major conflicts in the 1860s, and in 1864 relations between host and immigrant communities at Ashton and Stalybridge were said to be relatively tranquil. When Booth Mason stood as parliamentary candidate for Ashton in 1865 his anti-Irish Catholic tirades failed to spark off a riot.[40]

Conflict ebbed in part because of the increased alacrity with which the authorities in the urban areas swore in special constables and enlisted military aid at the first hint of trouble. Furthermore, local Nonconformist Liberals saw the Irish as potential allies against Church of England Conservatives, and accordingly set out to cultivate the friendship of leading figures within the Irish communities. Liberals spoke at major Catholic social functions and praised immigrant attempts at assimilation. Local Liberal organisations thus constituted an important countervailing force against the anti-Catholic fulminations of Orangemen and Tories.[41]

The Catholic Church (particularly the priesthood), while prepared to defend and propagate the faith on all occasions, also made strenuous efforts to render the Irish more culturally acceptable to the 'respectable' sections of the host society by promoting habits of industry, thrift and sobriety within the flock. Temperance drives (often short-lived) were undertaken, branches of the Catholic

Young Men's Society established (to spread habits of 'regularity, discipline, and manly Christian piety'), and the adoption of 'innocent amusements' and 'respectable behaviour' encouraged within the rapidly expanding Catholic schools and mutual improvement societies. In this way the Catholic Church tried to transform the 'pre-industrial' attitudes and behaviour of the Irish: 'respectability' became the keynote.[42]

Countervailing influences met, however, with limited successes. Ethnic frictions varied in intensity but rarely subsided completely. Ashton, Stalybridge and Oldham experienced some tensions in the generally more placid years between 1860 and 1865. In June 1861 a Catholic chapel at Ashton was stoned, and during wakes week some 200 colliers and Irishmen were involved in disturbances at Hurst Brook. At Oldham the early summer months of 1861 saw frequent skirmishes and a full-scale attack against a Catholic chapel.[43] At Stockport, despite the 'improving' endeavours of the priesthood, the mass of Irish retained their reputation for 'unruly behaviour', and (in all probability) the borough was spared serious rioting in 1868 only because Murphy did not visit the town. And at Stalybridge a youth who assaulted the Catholic priest in May 1862 was almost lynched by an irate Irish crowd. The priest was again assaulted during the Whitsuntide procession, and order was temporarily restored only when the mayor pleaded for greater toleration.[44]

In 1862 the Liberal *Oldham Chronicle* bemoaned the continued estrangement of the Irish from all things English:

> They live in the midst of our civilisation without partaking of its spirit . . . If they only blended harmoniously with the population amongst whom they are located, no-one would have any right to complain of their presence in England. But they will not blend at all.

The Irish, according to the *Chronicle*, still retained their, 'unruly, wild habits', were opposed 'in their feelings and their interests' to the English and constituted 'the drudges of the land and a dangerous element in society'. The editorial concluded: '. . . if the Irish will not learn to live peacefully in their adopted land, there may possibly arise in this country . . . the cry of "England for the English." '[45] By the end of 1868 the *Chronicle's* fears had been realised: thousands of Lancashire operatives had rallied behind the Conservatives' election battle-cry of 'No Popery' and serious rioting had taken place in several towns.

Three factors provided the background to the dramatic developments of 1868: the growth of Fenianism; severe economic distress in the winter of 1867; and the success with which extreme Protestants exploited anti-Catholic feelings. The upsurge in Fenian activity in the 1866 and 1867 (the planned seizure of arms from Chester Castle and the Clerkenwell and Manchester 'outrages'[46]) served, despite the opposition of the Catholic Church towards Fenianism[47] to strengthen the view of the Irish as subversive aliens. By the end of 1867 the manufacturing districts were rife with the rumours of imminent insurrection. According to Ben Brierley, 'an armed body of Fenians were seen in every cloud of mist . . . outposts of the "brotherhood" were discovered in every clump of trees . . . whenever the Irish accent was heard a dark suspicion was engendered.'[48] At Stockport there were fears of a repetition of the events of 1852, and at Manchester Fenian threats to fire workhouses and other buildings created considerable alarm: operatives were armed and special constables sworn in for duty.[49]

The belief of the priesthood that Fenian activities could serve only to deepen the rift between hosts and immigrants was, for the most part, justified. Fenianism did enjoy significant support and sympathy among the Irish in Lancashire. Despite the favourable responses of the International Workingmens' Association and leftwing elements in the Reform League, the mass of the host population reacted with anger towards revolutionary nationalist aspirations. In London and Birmingham demonstrations of sympathy towards the plight of convicted Fenians paled before the aggressive outbursts of English crowds. At Manchester the trial of the 'martyrs' took place within an atmosphere of mounting anti-Irish hostility.[50]

Anti-Fenian sentiments and high unemployment in the latter part of 1867 combined to produce the prospect of an 'ugly winter'. According to the *Spectator*, only 'occasion' was needed to transform the 'inextinguishable feud' between immigrant and native workers into 'a fatal war of races and creeds'.[51] In southeast Lancashire and northeast Cheshire 'occasion' arrived in the form of a group of Protestant demagogues headed by William Murphy of the Protestant Electoral Union.[52] In December 1867 Murphy and his colleagues, aided by Booth Mason and other local Orangemen, commenced a series of scurrilous anti-Catholic lectures at Ashton and Stalybridge which continued throughout 1868. The lectures consisted of sensationalist exposés and violent denunciations of

Roman Catholicism (the association of Popery with mumbo-jumbo, political despotism and Fenianism, and the alleged gargantuan sexual appetites of the priests were favourite themes) and attacks upon the immigrant Irish Catholics as puppets of the Pope, sympathisers with Fenianism, and as a profitable source of cheap labour for Liberal employers. Murphy, surrounded by his personal bodyguards, the 'Stalybridge lads', swaggered into lecture halls holding aloft a revolver and proceeded to work through his repertoire of horror stories. Many of those present carried an assortment of weapons to the meetings, and invariably greeted Murphy's entrance with loud renderings of 'Rule Britannia'. Toleration had no place in such an atmosphere. For the greater part of 1868 Ashton and Stalybridge endured chronic disturbances.

The full history of these turbulent episodes cannot be recounted here.[53] What I can do is to highlight some of the incidents. Between January and April large English and Irish crowds, increasingly decked out in Orange and Green, repeatedly clashed on the streets. Frequent sorties were made against heavily-defended Catholic chapels and Irish neighbourhoods, and Liberal pro-disestablishment meetings were reduced to chaos by Murphyite intruders. In April a full-scale riot occurred at Stalybridge when a crowd of several hundred men and youths, shouting 'We'll pull the bloody cross and the bloody Virgin down,' stoned a Catholic chapel. In May riots 'unprecedented for brutality and destruction of property', occurred in Ashton. Several uproarious Irish Church meetings were followed on 9 May by a 'Great Protestant Demonstration' in Ashton Town Hall. Approximately 1,000 sat down to tea, and were afterwards addressed by Booth Mason and the Reverends Heffill and Touchstone on the theme of 'Papal aggression'. The audience, many of whom had travelled from Stalybridge and Dukinfield, was a sea of orange. No immediate disturbances resulted from the meeting, but on the Sunday afternoon young factory lads and lasses, 'displaying party colours', began to taunt Irish Catholics in the streets of the borough. A group of Irishmen responded by assaulting English inhabitants. A crowd of some 1,000 outraged operatives had their revenge by attacking 'Little Ireland': homes were ransacked and furniture thrown into the streets. The crowd, which had increased to over 2,000 people, then wreaked havoc at Saint Ann's Catholic chapel: windows were smashed, the confessional curtains torn down, the altar damaged and images of the Virgin Mary and the crucifix smashed to pieces. The Riot Act was read and the crowd dispersed, only to regroup later to launch an assault against Saint Mary's. On that occasion the police broke up the crowd before entry to the chapel had been gained. Ashton remained in a 'most excited state' throughout Monday. Despite the attempt of the authorities to quell the disturbances — 500 special constables were sworn in and the aid of two companies of the 70th Regiment enlisted — rioting flared up again. Only by Wednesday had order been restored. A total of 34 people were arrested during the disturbances and hundreds injured.

Rioting of this magnitude did not spread to Stalybridge in May, but the borough had acquired a notorious reputation for ethnic strife. The *Ashton Reporter* noted that over the previous six months Stalybridge had been, 'in a chronic state of excitement . . . There have either been street rows on a large scale or riots on a small scale, to be chronicled every week . . .'[54] The remaining months of the year, while less turbulent, witnessed a multitude of battles at Ashton and Stalybridge.[55]

As in 1852, anti-Catholic disturbances were widespread in 1868. Rochdale, Oldham, Preston and Blackburn all experienced major outbreaks of rioting, and in September a Murphyite meeting in Manchester resulted in a brawl involving 300 people.[56] As late as 1871 the *Ashton Reporter* could observe that the 'disreputable spirit of Murphy' was 'by no means extinct'.[57]

The preceding narrative points to the magnitude, and the pervasive and tenacious nature of ethnic conflict. We simply cannot accept the viewpoint of one writer that 'the amount of overt anti-Catholic opinion in Lancashire was never terribly great during the whole of 1846– 1871'.[58] Despite variations in the scale and intensity of conflict, relations between English and Roman Catholic Irish workers from 1850 onwards were tense and discordant rather than relaxed and harmonious. Rioting embraced hundreds and at time thousands of operatives. Far from being of incidental importance, ethnic animosities thus constituted a staple feature of working-class life and the popular politics of the period.

One further point needs to be emphasised. Contrary to the view expressed at the time by many Liberals, the riots cannot be dismissed as the work of the 'rags and tatters', or as a manifestation of youthful rebellion.[59] For, whilst conflicts were often triggered off by the provocative actions of teenage factory lads and lasses, there is no doubt that working-class adults, many of them 'respectable' factory operatives, were heavily involved in all the major disturbances of the period. Hence at Stockport in 1852 adult factory workers formed a significant proportion of the crowds who fought with the Irish in Petersgate and who attacked the Catholic chapels. And the riots of 1868 in Ashton, Stalybridge and the surrounding areas involved hundreds of male and female adults.[60] Similarly, whilst many of the Irish rioters were classified as 'common labourers' — a fact which should occasion little surprise in view of the high percentage of unskilled workers within the Irish community — the English combatants were not on the whole recruited from the 'lower depths'. Of those persons arrested during the Stockport riot, 15 were factory operatives, 4 were tailors, 26 (mainly Irish) were labourers, one was a mechanic and another was a greengrocer.[61] The Murphyite meeting in Hulme in 1868 was attended by factory operatives and 'respectably-dressed' young men, many of whom were probably clerks and warehousemen. And at Ashton, Stalybridge, Dukinfield, Hyde and Oldham, factory lads stood side by side with 'the better class of artisans'. Among those arrested in 1868 we find weavers, strippers, moulders, colliers, piecers, carters, brickmakers, overlookers, dyers and a clogger. Finally, the 'Stalybridge lads' counted among their numbers a stonemason, a tin-plate worker, a labourer, a painter and two self-actor minders.[62] The rioters were thus drawn from a wide variety of occupations.

The Material Effects of Irish Immigration

An explanation of reactions towards the Irish, and more particularly of escalating conflict after 1850, requires further examination of the material effects of Irish immigration. I have accordingly investigated a number of key areas: patterns of immigration; Irish influences in the labour market (did, for example, the English and Irish compete for the same jobs? Did the Irish receive lower wages?); patterns of residence (to what extent did ghettos develop?); and cultural, religious and political relations between immigrants and hosts.

Irish immigration into Britain, whilst by no means negligible in the pre-Chartist period, observed its most dramatic increase in the late 1840s. Outside London, the manufacturing centres of Lancashire and Cheshire were areas of heavy concentration. Of the 400,000 Irish-born inhabitants of Great Britain in 1841, 105,916 resided in Lancashire and 11,577 in Cheshire. By 1851 these figures had almost doubled to 191,506 in Lancashire and 22,812 in Cheshire. By 1851 Irish-born amounted to 10 per cent of the population of Lancashire and 5 per cent in Cheshire. Between 1841 and 1851 Irish-born, as a proportion of the population of the borough of Stockport, increased from approximately 7 to 10 per cent; in the borough of Liverpool from 17 to 22 per cent; and in the district of Manchester from 12 to 17 per cent. By 1851 Irish-born constituted almost 7 per cent of the district of Ashton-under-Lyne and 8.3 per cent of the district of Salford. Apart from decreases in the boroughs of Manchester and Liverpool, these percentages remained roughly constant or increased between 1851 and 1861. By 1871, 6.66 per cent of the population of Lancashire were Irish-born; the total percentage of Irish, including those born outside Ireland, was of course considerably higher.[63]

We are dealing at mid-century, therefore, with a vast increase in the numbers of (overwhelmingly) Irish Roman Catholics from rural backgrounds entering the Lancashire mill towns. Yet increased numbers, in themselves, do not constitute a satisfactory explanation of worsening relations. Manchester, for example, with a higher percentage of Irish-born than Ashton or Stalybridge, was less troubled by serious rioting. We must turn, therefore, to the economic, social and cultural characteristics of the Irish to understand host reactions.

As contemporaries realised, the immigrants were generally of low socio-economic standing. Evidence presented in the 1836 Report and other sources demonstrates that the Irish found little employment at the skilled level; rather the vast majority worked at low-status jobs.[64] Of importance at a general level were three areas of employment: labouring (in the building trades, the docks and on the railways); a variety of crafts and depressed occupations such as handloom weaving, tailoring, shoemaking, hawking and dressmaking; and factory work — in cotton the Irish were concentrated in the low-paid jobs in the carding, blowing, tenting and the weaving sections of the industry.

The general pattern of employment is well known; what is often less clear is the local employment situation. I have accordingly consulted the census enumerators' book for occupational data relating to Stockport, Ashton and Stalybridge for the years 1841, 1851 and 1861. The major finding to emerge from this source is a greatly accelerated trend towards employment of the Irish (particularly girls and unmarried women) in cotton, and a relative decline in the numbers employed in the casual artisan trades. And although many male family heads still worked as labourers at mid-century, a growing number of younger men and male teenagers joined Irish females in cotton factories. In short, by the early 1850s the majority of the employed Irish in south Lancashire and northeast Cheshire were cotton operatives. At Stockport in 1851, for example (see Table 7.1) 57 per cent of 2,281 Irish living in the centre of the town were to be found in cotton. Employment in cotton factories was not a totally new phenomenon: we find a number of Irish-born tenters, throstle spinners and weavers listed for Stockport in 1841. What must be stressed, however, is the mass influx into cotton at the end of the 1840s. At Stockport women and girls were heavily concentrated in throstle spinning, in weaving and tenting. Boys and girls worked as bobbiners and doffers, and young men were either piecers or involved in a variety of occupations in the card and blowing rooms. Few attained positions of high remuneration (there were, in the 1851 sample, only two self-actor minders, three male spinners and two overlookers). Shoemaking and tailoring accounted for 5 per cent of the total employed and labourers made up 17 per cent. Representation at the skilled manual and non-manual levels was negligible.

Table 7.1:   Occupations of a Section of the Irish in Stockport, 1851

Bakers	3	Managers	1
Blacksmiths	5	Messengers	2
Blowing room	14	Milliners	4
Bobbiners	54	Nurses	6
Bookbinders	2	Overlookers — cotton	2
Bricklayers	1	Painters	3
Brushmakers	1	Pedlars	12
Cabinet makers	1	Picture-frame makers	1
Capmakers	16	Piecers	25
Card room	27	Printers	5
Charwomen	4	Reedmakers	2
Clerks	1	Reelers	6
Confectioners	1	Rope makers	11
Coopers	3	Saddlers	1
Cotton mixers	8	Sawyers	1
Dealers	6	Schoolmasters	1
Doffers	63	Self-actor minders	2
Domestics	53	Shoemakers	54
Dressmakers	18	Spinners (male)	3
Errand boys	3	Staymakers	25
Factory hands — cotton	568	Stonemasons	5
Fruiterers	2	Strippers and grinders	17
Gardeners	1	Tailors	77

Glaziers	6	Tenters	87
Greengrocers	1	Throstle spinners	329
Hatters	1	Tradesmen	1
Hawkers	69	Warehousemen	3
Housekeepers	50	Warpers	1
Joiners	7	Washerwomen	32
Knitters	2	Weavers — powerloom	98
Labourers	400	Weavers — handloom	2
Lap carriers	11	Whitesmiths	1
Lodging house keepers	7	Winders	52
		Total = 2,281	

Notes: The table relates to the occupation of the Irish in the central area of Stockport, mainly in St Mary's Ward and Middle Ward, both areas of heavy Irish settlement. It is not a survey of the *total* Irish employment situation.

The table covers Irish-born. The sons and daughters of Irish-born are included.

A strikingly similar pattern emerged at Ashton and Stalybridge (see Tables 7.2 and 7.3). Of 1,392 Irish occupations sampled in Stalybridge in 1851, 960 (69 per cent) were in cotton, with dense clustering in the card room, in tenting and in piecing. Whilst there were 25 male spinners, immigrant representation at the craft and skilled levels was of little importance (4 per cent in tailoring and shoemaking). Labourers made up 14 per cent of the total employed. Ten years later, the overall situation at Stalybridge had changed little, except for a heavier involvement in tenting and weaving (mainly female occupations), an increase in the number of Irish spinners and self-actor minders (106 out of a total sample of 2,133), and a slight decrease in labouring (from 14 per cent to 12 per cent). By 1861 the Irish at Ashton were concentrated, in large numbers, in tenting, weaving, piecing and to a lesser extent in labouring.

Table 7.2: Occupations of a Section of the Irish in Stalybridge, 1851

Basketmakers	1	Minders	5
Beaters	1	Mixers	1
Blacksmiths	2	Nailmakers	3
Bobbiners	4	Nurses	5
Bricklayers	4	Painters	1
Chairbottomers	1	Pedlars	2
Charwomen	8	Piecers	217
Coalminers	4	Plasterers	2
Doffers	1	Printers	1
Domestic servants	33	Reelers	6
Card room hands	201	Roller carriers	5
Coopers	1	Sawyers	1

Doublers	2	Shoemakers	34
Dressers	6	Spinners (male)	25
Dressmakers	5	Staymakers	7
Foremen	1	Stokers	1
Glaziers	1	Stonemasons	14
Hawkers	5	Strippers	36
Iron turners	2	Tailors	24
Factory — cotton	203	Tenters	148
Grinders	22	Throstle spinners	12
Iron foundry	1	Tin plate workers	2
Labourers	197	Washerwomen	63
Lap tenters	2	Weavers	57
Lodging house keepers	4	Winders	8
		Total = 1,392	

Table 7.3:   Occupations of a Section of the Irish in Stalybridge, 1861

Basket dealers	1	Nailmakers	7
Blacksmiths	1	Nurses	4
Blowing room	25	Overlookers	4
Bobbiners	1	Painters	1
Booksellers	1	Piecers	214
Bricklayers	3	Print workers	1
Card room	181	Provision dealers	1
Carters	6	Reelers	13
Chair bottomers	2	Rope makers	1
Charwomen	14	Shirt makers	1
Coalminers	4	Shoemakers	23
Coopers	1	Silk weavers	2
Cotton factory	364	Spinners and self-actor minders (male)	106
Doffers	3	Spinners (female)	12
Domestic servants	22	Staymakers	1
Doublers	7	Stokers	5
Dressmakers	9	Stonemasons	9
Firemen	1	Strippers	59
Gardeners	1	Tailors	15
Gasmakers	4	Tenters	417
Greengrocers	2	Toy dealers	1
Grinders	72	Travellers	2
Hawkers	2	Umbrella makers	1
Iron moulders	1	Warehouse	1
Joiners	3	Washerwomen	39
Labourers	259	Watchmakers	2
Lap carriers	1	Weavers	137
Machinemen	2	Winders	55
Musicians	1		
		Total = 2,128	

The fact that the Irish entered cotton in great numbers is of extreme significance in that direct competition in the labour market between English and Irish operatives became more acute, and was more keenly resented by sections of the English than in previous decades.[65] For, whilst we have seen that complaints concerning Irish competition were not new, they did assume increased urgency after 1850 and were widely voiced during the riots of the period.

There is, however, far less reason to support the popular view that the Irish presence in cotton resulted in a general lowering of wages in the industry, at least in the 25 years after 1850. Cotton, after all, benefited greatly from the mid-Victorian boom:[66] markets expanded; prices stabilised; the crisis of profitability was largely overcome; and, with the notable exception of the Cotton Famine, the industry did not experience a slump of the magnitude of 1837–42. Stabilisation and expansion made for more regular employment and an improvement in money wages. And, as we have seen earlier, although the latter did not advance considerably in the 1850s (due to price increases), they did so by about 40 per cent between 1864 and 1874.[67]

Despite this increase in wages, the view that the Irish presence had a deleterious effect upon living standards persisted with some considerable force between 1850 and 1870, and obviously requires explanation. It is important to remember in this context that popular attitudes and ideologies are not simply reducible to the economic level: inherited traditions and values do not change simply at the whim of the economy.[68] This general point is significant in that by 1850 the view that Irish competition lowered wages was of some importance, and could not be expected to vanish.[69] Furthermore, such attitudes were not without a material base. Fears of downgrading were reinforced by increased immigration and by the accusations made by operatives in a number of towns that employers sometimes discriminated unfairly in favour of the Irish. Finally (and without suggesting a cause-effect relationship), those sections of cotton in which the Irish congregated were generally poorly paid.[70] Such factors served, along with the propaganda peddled by Orangemen and others, to keep alive unfavourable impressions.

Irish involvement in the periodic attempts to form and consolidate trade unions in cotton in the post-1850 period is difficult to chart with any degree of precision. Many sectors of cotton remained without permanent trade union organisation until the upsurges of the 1870s and 1880s.[71] Irish operatives were probably involved in the growth of weaving and carding trade unionism in the late 1850s and 1860s. Examples of the Irish acting as strike-breakers were certainly rare. In the Preston dispute of 1853 attempts were made by employers to recruit blackleg labour, but, significantly, the majority of immigrant cotton workers seem to have adopted an anti-employer stance, and employers were forced to look across the Irish Sea for labour. On arriving in England some of the potential blacklegs were persuaded to return home by local English and Irish immigrant workers.[72] This brings me to a more general point. In periods of rising industrial militancy (in 1853–4, 1859–61 and 1869) Irish and English cotton operatives generally acted together against the forces of capital.

Industrial unity during periods of heightened class tensions was not, however, accompanied by any significant movement towards integration in terms of patterns of residence. An examination of the census enumerators' books for Stockport between 1841 and 1871, and Ashton and Stalybridge for 1851 and 1861, reveals the physical separation between the two communities. For, although the mass of immigrants were not segregated into large, formal ghettos, the period did witness the accelerated development of distinct Irish neighbourhoods.[73] At Stockport in 1841 Irish quarters were beginning to emerged in the centre of the town around Rock Row, Adlington Square and Jacksons Alley. By 1851 few non-Irish families were to be found in these streets. The streets leading off Middle Hillgate (Crowther Street, Covent Gardens and Cross Street) constituted, by 1851, a further area of heavy Irish concentration. Again, few non-Irish families inhabited this densely-packed neighbourhood. Twenty years later a similar pattern of residence was in evidence.

By 1861 the streets around 'Flag Alley' in Ashton were known locally as 'Little Ireland'. Adelphi Court, Worthington Square, Back Charles Street, Back Portland and Back Cavendish Streets were all areas of dense Irish settlement, and the scene of repeated conflicts in the 1860s. At Stalybridge the Irish settled in four major areas: around the Castle Street mills, particularly on Back Melbourne Street, Back Castle Street and Bennett Street; around the King Street mill in Beardsley's Yard, King Street and Chapel Street; in Leech Street, Cross Leach Street and Back Grosvenor Street; and around Spring Street, Back Cross Street and Pearson's Yard. In all these areas a marked pattern of ethnic clustering was in evidence

The Stockport Riot of 1852: Roman Catholic Chapel of Saints Philip and James, Edgeley

Source: *Illustrated London News*, 10 July, 1852.

between 1851 and 1861, with the vicinity around Back Castle Street the site of heaviest concentration and the scene of frequent disorders in the 1860s.

As noted earlier, the development of Irish quarters was not, however, synonomous with complete ghettoisation. A small minority of the Irish (mainly older folk) were to be found living amidst non-Irish families, and even in the Irish neighbourhoods non-Irish were sometimes not totally excluded. More significantly, perhaps, there were a large number of streets in all three towns which were occupied by both the Irish and non-Irish. This, in fact, was the dominant pattern at mid-century. We would, however, be wrong to interpret this as evidence of assimilation. For on these mixed streets there existed an extremely strong tendency towards ethnic divisions and clustering; and on many occasions the Irish steadily encroached upon streets which had formerly been predominantly English in character. A few examples will serve to illustrate these two trends. At Stalybridge in 1851, Castle Street, while mixed, was characterised by distinct Irish and non-Irish 'ends': the houses from 39 to 19 were for the most part Irish, while the houses below number 19 were English. Bennett Street, while containing some non-Irish families in 1851, had become mainly Irish by 1861. Both these streets experienced considerable tensions at mid-century. On Caroline Street in Stalybridge the Irish, occupying mainly the odd numbers between 15 and 71, were in 1851 effectively sandwiched between the non-Irish who lived at the lower and top ends of the street; by 1861 the Irish had begun to move into the even-numbered houses once occupied by non-Irish families. The tendency towards ethnic clustering operated with equal force at Stockport and Ashton. Most significant was the fact that these 'mixed' streets often experienced some of the worst outbreaks of ethnic conflict during the third quarter of the century.

As we have seen, ethnic separations, in terms of housing patterns, were accompanied by a marked lack of political, religious and cultural integration. The major force in emphasising the separate religious identity of the Irish was, of course, the Catholic Church. For, despite the severe problem of declining church attendance, the urban Catholic parish remained 'the pivot of emigrant community life', and the priest was the central figure in Irish neighbourhoods. Parents sent their children to local Catholic schools whenever possible, and organised their social lives around the clubs and societies set up by the Church.[74] As detailed earlier, in its associations with the 'tyrannical machinations of an alien power', and spiritual intolerance and 'mumbo jumbo', Catholicism constituted a major source of friction between hosts and immigrants. Frequent protestations of loyalty to the monarchy on the part of the priesthood failed to bridge the religious divide.

Furthermore, for many among the population, the majority of the Irish were increasingly seen as a distinct and unwelcome single out-group. Throughout the 1850s and 1860s, and despite the 'improving' efforts of the Church, and the influence of the steady rhythms of factory work, large sections of the immigrants retained their reputation for 'wild and unruly' behaviour. Fights with the police were common, and weekends were often given over to drinking sprees. English families, apart from those living in close proximity to the immigrants, rarely took in Irish lodgers and social mixing was limited. Increasingly valid was the observation made by a Manchester pawnbroker that:

> There are very few Irish with whom the English mix, it is like oil and water: they each keep their own company. Even when they live in the same street or the same house, they do not associate much.[75]

A brief survey of census material for Stalybridge in 1861 suggests that intermarriage was of minor importance, particularly for those families living at the heart of Irish neighbourhoods. Irish and non-Irish, at least in the more mixed areas of Stalybridge and Stockport, sometimes drank at the same pubs but weekend fights were by no means uncommon. And while support for the Liberal Party served to acquaint immigrants with mainstream political life, the growth of Fenianism acted, once again, to resurrect fears of the subversive leanings of the Irish.

To summarise: The roots of mounting tensions after 1850 must be sought within the material effects of Irish immigration. For, although popular beliefs that the Irish lowered wages, acted as strike-breakers and resisted assimilation must be either qualified or corrected, nevertheless, as a result of the vast increase in immigration in the immediate post-Famine period, the potential for conflict rose. Direct competition in the labour market and fears of economic downgrading weighed heavily on the minds of English operatives. The Irish did congregate in their own neighbourhoods and cluster together on the mixed streets. They did remain, for the most part, culturally distinct; and in their Catholicism and nationalism were often viewed as subversive aliens. Such sources of friction were exploited to the full by demagogues like Murphy.

I wish to make three further points in relation to causation. Firstly, tensions and outbreaks of rioting cannot simply be reduced to that overworked and limited concept of 'distress'. From the mid-1840s onwards there was little correlation between immediate 'distress' and instances of rioting. Indeed, apart from the incidents at Oldham, Ashton and Stalybridge in the early 1860s, relations between the two groups appear to have been more harmonious during the depressions of 1847 and 1861–5 than in the relatively prosperous years of 1852 and 1868.

Secondly, an aversion to narrow economic reductionism must not, however, be interpreted as a dismissal of the importance of the economic 'level'. We have repeatedly seen that economic fears (competition in the labour market, etc.) were widespread. Such fears, which were *real* to their holders, constituted the material roots of conflict, and were of crucial significance in informing the consciousness of the rioters.

The material roots of conflict must, therefore, be stressed. But thirdly, I wish, while offering a materialist interpretation of strains and disturbances, to eschew a mechanistic 'base-superstructure' model in which the political and ideological 'levels' are seen simply as passive reflections of the 'base'. I maintain throughout this chapter that consciousness is not totally determined at the economic or any other 'level' and that the 'relative autonomy' of the political and ideological 'levels' must be recognised. These theoretical concerns are of immediate relevance in that outbreaks of rioting and ethnic frictions cannot be seen as resulting soley from economic factors. Religious and political fears were real and significant and cannot be dismissed as masks for the 'real' underlying economic causes. Hence English workers saw the Irish Catholics as a threat not only to their standard of living but also to their settled way of life, their whole pattern of existence. The 'alien' nature of Catholicism (its alleged machinations against 'the traditional liberties of Freeborn Englishmen', etc.) and cultural and political divisions — these were factors of extreme importance in inducing a belligerent attitude towards the Irish. The 'battle tune' adopted by the English rioters, 'Rule Brittania', and the extremely popular cry of 'Murphy, Garibaldi and the Queen', reflected fears of 'alien domination'.

Political Results

I have contended in this book that the decline of class combativity after Chartism must be attributed primarily to economic and social restabilisation. Ethnic conflict operated, against the background of the apparent inevitability of capitalism, to restrict further the potential for class solidarity in Lancashire and Cheshire, and to provide sections of the bourgeoisie with the opportunity to assert their authority, in a fairly direct way, upon workers. For while we must be careful to see the riots not simply as the result of one-sided manipulation from above — ethnic tensions arose out of the real experiences of workers, and many middle-class Liberals and some Conservatives openly condemned mob violence and the excesses of Murphy[76] — nevertheless, sections of the middle-class did make conscious efforts to exploit ethnic animosities and to attach workers to middle-class political and cultural leadership. The most dramatic example of this process was the way in which Conservatives and militant Protestants attempted, with increasing success, to build a mass movement around the issue of 'No Popery'.

We can, in this final section, briefly examine these developments.[77] During the course of the 1860s the Conservative Party's electoral fortunes underwent a remarkable transformation in the cotton districts. Condemned for so long to second-class political citizenship, the party finally came into its own in the elections of 1868 when the Liberal ascendancy in Lancashire was overturned.[78] Between 1832 and 1867 Ashton, Bury, Salford and Manchester had sent no Conservative candidates to parliament; and Oldham and Stockport were solidly Liberal in parliamentary elections from 1852 to 1867.[79] Even in the more auspicious political climate of 1868 many Conservatives were seemingly resigned to permanent second-class political status. At Ashton, where a Conservative workingman was held by local Liberals to be 'the strangest creature imaginable'[80] the Conservatives decided to put up a candidate, 'Tommy' Mellor, only a month or so before election day.

On election day Mellor and many other Conservative candidates were, however, jubilant.[81] While Bury remained solidly Liberal, the Liberal majority at Oldham was reduced to a mere six votes and in 1874 Oldham went Conservative. At Ashton, Salford, Bolton and newly-enfranchised Stalybridge the Conservatives made a clean sweep. Stockport, for so long a Liberal stronghold, returned one Liberal and one Conservative; and Manchester elected one

Conservative and two Liberals. The shift towards the Conservatives continued in 1874 when 26 Conservatives and seven Liberals were elected to parliament from Lancashire.[82]

The 1868 elections were of major significance in that they revealed, to the surprise of many Liberals and Conservatives, the considerable depth of support for Conservatism among workers.[83] At Manchester approximately 7,000 workers voted Tory, and at Ashton, Milner Gibson, the defeated Liberal candidate, claimed that the working-class vote had proved decisive at the election.[84] Sidebottom, the popular millowner and successful Conservative candidate at Stalybridge, claimed that he was not the nominee of 'some half dozen gentlemen in broadcloth . . . but the working people of the district.' Sidebottom had been 'brought out' by some 2,000 workers.[85]

The elections at Ashton and Stalybridge represented the climax of months of intensive worker activity on behalf of the Conservatives: thousands attended Conservative meetings and Liberal gatherings were frequently disrupted. Once Sidebottom's victory was announced, a massive victory procession formed in the streets of Stalybridge and banners were draped from the windows of operatives' houses.[86] Impressive demonstrations of worker loyalty to the Conservative cause continued throughout 1869 and 1870, and Constitutional Associations registered a sharp increase in membership among operatives.[87]

Gains made among cotton operatives by the Conservative Party have traditionally been attributed to five major factors: the influence exerted by Conservative employers upon the political allegiances of their workers and the neighbourhood population; the sympathy with which workers responded to the anti-Manchester School views of Tory Radicals such as Stephens at Stalybridge and Callender at Manchester; the success with which Conservatives seized upon John Bright's opposition to the Ten Hours Bill during the 1868 election; the belief that Conservatives were less dismissive of robust popular culture than the Liberals; and the fact that responsibility for the 1867 Reform Act lay with the Conservative Party.[88] This is not the place to examine the relative merits of such factors.[89] I wish to suggest, however, that any explanation of popular Toryism which fails to take into account the issues of ethnicity and religion is inadequate. The 1868 elections, for example, revolved primarily not around John Bright's attitudes towards factory legislation and trade unionism, but around the question of continued Protestant supremacy in Ireland and the more general theme of Protestantism versus Catholicism. And it was the Conservative Party's ability to make political capital out of the 'No Popery' issue which proved of key importance at the polls.

In order to substantiate this hypothesis, it is first of all necessary to examine the growth of Orangeism and other extreme forms of Protestantism, and the close links which developed between such groups and Conservatives. In the 1850s and particularly the 1860s, the Orange Order and other militant Protestant organisations made significant advances.[90] Extreme Protestants, such as Booth Mason at Ashton and Hugh Stowell at Salford, played a leading role in combating the 'Papal Menace' in the early 1850s and in establishing Protestant Associations and Operative Protestant Associations. At Oldham the Orange Order progressed from being 'little more than a joke' to a position of some importance: by 1855 there were at least eleven lodges in Oldham. In the same year an anti-Catholic Pastoral Aid Society was created, and in 1856 a small fortune was spent on anti-Catholic literature and lectures.[91] At Ashton, Stalybridge, Manchester and Stockport steady progress was made. At Blackburn between 2–3,000 people attended the inaugural meeting of the Orange-inspired Protestant Association.[92] However, despite the Order's ability to spark off religious and ethnic conflict, there is little evidence to suggest that it built up a mass working-class base during the early 1850s. Whilst the Order did win recruits among working people, there is good evidence to suggest that its most active members come from the middle class: publicans, Church of England clergymen, doctors, lawyers and military men constituted the hard core of the movement.[93] This pattern changed markedly during the 1860s. The Order, with its ideological mixture of anti-Republicanism, anti-Catholicism, and its frequent support for trade unionism and factory legislation, made considerable headway in the cotton districts. By 1860 Orange membership at Stockport was 'greatly augmented', and at Oldham the Order established a firm base in the working class.[94] At Stalybridge 500 people, mainly operatives, attended an Orange tea-party in 1863;[95] and in 1866 the *Ashton Standard* claimed that the principles of Orangeism had spread 'with astonishing rapidity' at Stalybridge.[96]

In 1868 the various Protestant groups came into their own. Members of the Order and the Protestant Electoral Union addressed large audiences. In October 800 people attended an Orange meeting in Stalybridge. During the following two years the influence of the Protestant groups remained strong, with some former Chartists adopting the slogan of 'The Queen, Garibaldi and Murphy'.[97] In 1870 hundreds were attracted to Orange functions at Ashton and Stalybridge. And as late as July 1871 more than 100 people, led by an Orangeman, protested against disestablishment.[98]

The secret of extreme Protestantism's successes among working people was twofold. Firstly, some Protestants set themselves up as the champions of the working-class interest against the machinations of the rich and Manchester School manufacturers, and cultivated an intimate and robust political style. Hugh Stowell at Salford supported the Ten Hours Bill, trade unionism and the principle of 'a fair day's wage for a fair day's work,' and criticised a system of poor relief which treated workers as 'felons'.[99] Booth Mason, Deputy Grand Master of the Orange Order, prided himself upon his close contacts with the workers of Ashton and Stalybridge. 'He knew what it was to work,' Mason declared in 1863, 'having been a scavenger under a jenny at seven years of age, and from that time to the present, he had known and mixed among working people more than anyone else in Ashton.'[100] In 1857 and 1865 Mason contested Ashton upon the platform of manhood suffrage, 'No Popery', and support for factory legislation. Unlike many Orangemen, he did not look with disfavour upon political reform:

> He had been brought up with the working classes . . . and was not afraid of them. He called them brethren, and he called them so because the great mass of those present were Orangemen. If they enfranchised the working classes, they would have Church and Queen, and down with dissent.[101]

Other Protestant orators pandered to the economic grievances of workers. During the industrial conflicts of 1860 and 1861, Reverend Verity addressed large gatherings of operatives on the evils of the rich and outlined the benefits of trade unionism.[102] Heffill, during the turbulent year of 1868, painstakingly cultivated a 'proletarian' image by sporting clogs and dismissing Liberal manufacturers as 'haughty, hypocritical and effeminate' snobs.[103] Murphy's speeches were laced with simple, homely images and contained frequent sympathetic references to the economic ills of working people. In

December 1867 he claimed that employers were, 'anxious to put their lectures down', because Orangemen, 'showed up the system of Romanists working for such low wages'.[104] The following month Murphy eulogised the colliers on strike in the Stalybridge area, and promised to raise a subscription to aid their cause.[105] During his election campaign at Manchester he styled himself the 'working-man's candidate' and pledged, if elected, to introduce a bill into parliament to increase the wages of the working class and to outlaw female factory employment. 'Now, Milner Gibson will not do that', cried Murphy, 'Milner Gibson will keep you in the mill . . . and so will John Bright and Gladstone too.'[106] As a result of the activities of men such as Murphy, Heffill, Verity and Mason, Orangeism and extreme Protestantism became identified to some workers with economic and social radicalism. However, we have seen that the second and most important aspect of the ideology of the various groups was their unremitting hostility to Roman Catholicism and Irish Catholic immigrants.

Despite our limited knowledge of the connexions between extreme Protestant organisations and the Conservative Party, there is little doubt that relations were often close in the 1860s. This state of affairs was particularly marked in the case of Orangeism and Conservatism. In southeast Lancashire the Order was almost a branch of the Tory Party; the men who ran the Order were very often the same men who ran the clubs and local Conservative Party Associations.[107] In 1868 many Conservative candidates were either self-proclaimed Orangemen, such as Cawley and Charley at Salford, or, as in the cases of Mellor at Ashton, Sidebottom at Stalybridge and Ambrose and Tipping at Stockport, close sympathisers with Orangeism. Many of the leading Conservatives of the area were to be found at Orange functions between 1868 and 1870. At Stalybridge, Sidebottom's election agent was an Orangeman, and at both Stalybridge and Ashton Orangemen played a central role in mapping out the tactics and strategy of the Conservative candidates. And while some of the Conservative Party elite, particularly in north Lancashire, did dissociate themselves from the 'excesses' of Murphy, nevertheless many Conservatives in south Lancashire did endorse Murphy's sentiments (albeit sometimes in more diluted fashion). They appealed to the ethnic and religious grievances of Murphy's followers and did receive considerable support from them. Hence the Murphyite crowds at Ashton and Stalybridge in 1868 provided staunch backing for Mellor and

Sidebottom, the Conservative candidates. Murphyites continually disrupted Liberal meetings and groaned and hooted outside the homes of prominent Liberals. While Sidebottom and Mellor were portrayed as 'true Protestant heroes', Liberals were branded as crypto-Papists who wished to 'scatter the Established Church of England to the four winds of heaven'.[108] In 1868 some Conservatives raised a subscription to aid the English rioters arrested at Hyde and Stalybridge,[109] and at Salford Cawley and Charley gave full expression to Murphy's anti-Catholicism.

The Conservative Party's campaign at the 1868 election was one of aggressive Protestantism. In the 1850s and 1860s Conservative meetings were often characterised by outraged denunciations of Popery and 'levelling dissent'. And, terrified by Gladstone's proposed disestablishment of the Irish Church, the Conservative Party readily adopted 'No Popery' as its election battle-cry in 1868. One of Sidebottom's placards at Stalybridge reflected the tone of the contests throughout the area.

'THE QUEEN OR THE POPE', the placard began,

> which will you have to reign over you — Will you suffer Mr Gladstone to destroy the supremacy of your sovereign and substitute the supremacy of the POPE? SIDEBOTTOM CALLS to 'English freemen' to assert their rights.[110]

Sidebottom, himself, saw the Irish Church as 'the question of the hour', and constantly reassured his supporters that he was 'opposed to Popery in all its details', and would, 'oppose any measure that would tend to further the interests of the Roman Catholic Church'.[111] Tipping, one of the two Conservative candidates at Stockport, told his audiences that the Catholic Church was, 'a dense, compact body, acting as one man all over the globe'. 'To destroy the Irish Church', he continued, 'would be to drop the flag and lower one's colours as a Protestant power before that aggressive Church in Ireland, and would be perfectly suicidal.'[112] Fears of creeping Catholicism dominated the contests at Ashton, Salford and Manchester. Birley and Hoare, the Conservative candidates at Manchester, articulated a widespread belief among Conservatives that disestablishment in Ireland would be a prelude to disestablishment at home.[113] Elsewhere Conservatives warned that freedom and reason were at stake. 'If we wanted to have religious equality equality with the Church of Rome', declared Cawley at Salford, 'we should have to be content with a Roman Catholic monarch . . . and the people might bid farewell to their liberties.'[114]

All shades of political opinion agreed that religion was both the dominant and decisive factor in the elections. Gladstone, in the opinion of the *Manchester Guardian*, had been 'kicked out of Lancashire for not being a Protestant'.[115] And working-class antipathy towards the Irish Catholics had provided Orangemen and Conservatives with the essential ingredient for victory. 'We may deny it if we like', declared the *Ashton Reporter* in its election post-mortem:

> but the working classes in some districts are not yet sufficiently educated on this Church question. Interested, babbling men have . . . raised the passions and prejudices of our working men to such a pitch that it will take some time to undo the mischief already done.[116]

In truth the visceral politics of Murphyism and Toryism had proved to be more potent than the measured calculations of Liberalism. Workers voted Conservative because they believed Protestant warnings that, 'we were on the verge of Popery, and unless measures were taken to arrest its progress, the Pope of Rome would be King of England'.[117]

This chapter has drawn attention to the powerful forces of ethnic allegiance and ethnic conflict in the post-1850 cotton towns. During the Chartist period class situation and class issues had frequently provided a common rallying point for workers from diverse ethnic groups, but from the late 1840s onwards this was far less the case. Indeed, during the third quarter of the century class and ethnic interests became increasingly incompatible and antagonistic in character. This was especially true of relations between the (largely post-Famine) Irish-Catholic immigrants into the cotton towns and many among their working-class 'hosts'. It has been argued in this chapter that ethnic divisions and conflicts escalated sharply in the cotton districts from the late 1840s onwards, greatly weakened the class unity which had emerged between sections of the Irish and host communities during the 1830s and 1840s, and, as Marx and others observed, constituted a powerful source of fragmentation within the working class. Ethnic animosities greatly reduced the potential for common, class action (especially outside the workplace), contributed to the diminished appeal of independent working-class politics, and attached workers more firmly to the framework of bourgeois politics and bourgeois political control. Moreover, ethnic loyalties and jealousies cut across divisions of skill, income and authority within both the immigrant and host communities (thus casting further doubts upon the validity of the notion of a simple, primary division between labour aristocrats and the rest of the working class); and injected a racial element into the division of the working class into 'respectables' and 'non-respectables' (with the vast majority of the Irish being seen, by many of the hosts, as 'non-respectable'). In sum, although primarily explicable in socio-economic terms, the failure of the working class to act as a 'class for itself' in the mid-Victorian period was, at least in the cotton districts, also heavily influenced by the growing influence of ethnic ties and conflicts in working-class life.

Acknowledgement

The substance of this chapter originally appeared as an article in K. Lunn (ed.), *Hosts, Immigrants and Minorities: Historical Responses to Newcomers in British Society 1870–1914* (Wm. Dawson and Sons 1980). I am grateful to William Dawson for kind permission to reproduce.

Notes

1. See Ch. 4 above, pp. 161–5.
2. For interpretations of ethnicity see A. Cohen (ed.), *Urban Ethnicity* (1974), esp. intro. and Ch. 1; R. Ballard, 'Ethnicity: Theory and Experience', *New Community*, V. (1976), pp. 196–202.
3. I subscribe to E.P. Thompson's view of class. See E.P. Thompson, *The Making of the English Working Class* (Harmondsworth, 1968), esp. the preface; E.P. Thompson, 'Eighteenth-Century English Society: Class Struggle without Class', *Social History*, 3 (1978), pp. 146–50.
4. E.P.'Thompson, *Soc. Hist.* p. 150.
5. For useful studies of the effects of ethnicity upon the working class in America see D. Montgomery, 'The Shuttle and the Cross: Weavers and Artisans in the Kensington Riots of 1844' in P. Stearns and D.J. Walkowitz (eds), *Workers in the Industrial Revolution* (New Brunswick, 1974); D. Brody, *Steelworkers in America: The Nonunion Era* (New York, 1969), esp. V; H. Gutman, *Work, Culture and Society in Industrializing America* (New York, 1977).
6. For the views of contemporaries see L.H. Lees, 'Patterns of Lower Class Life: Irish Slum Communities in Nineteenth Century London' in S. Thernstrom and R. Sennett (eds), *Nineteenth Century Cities* (1969), pp. 359ff.; K. Marx and F. Engels, *On Britain* (Moscow, 1953), pp. 123–7, 506: J.A. Jackson, *The Irish in Britain*

(1963); J.H. Treble, 'The Place of the Irish Catholics in the Social Life of the North of England 1800-1851' (unpublished PhD thesis, Leeds University, 1969). For the most recent survey of the effects of Irish immigration see, M.A.G. O'Tuathaigh, 'The Irish in Nineteenth Century Britain: Problems of Integration', *Trans. Roy. Hist. Soc.*, 31 (1981) pp. 149-73.

    7. K. Marx and F. Engels, op. cit., p. 506.

    8. J.H. Werly, 'The Irish in Manchester 1832-1848', *Irish Historical Studies*, 71 (1973). Werly probably overestimates the extent of ghettoisation among the Irish in the area around Oldham Road.

    9. J.H. Treble, thesis, op. cit., pp. 245-51, 268ff.

    10. E.P. Thompson, *The Making*, op. cit., pp. 469-85; J. Foster, *Class Struggle*, op. cit., Chs 5 and 7.

    11. E.P. Thompson, *The Making*, op. cit., pp. 481ff.

    12. See R.O'Higgins, 'The Irish Influence in the Chartist Movement', *Past and Present* 20 (1961); D. Thompson, 'Ireland and The Irish in English Radicalism' in J. Epstein and D. Thompson (eds), op. cit., pp. 120-51. Barnsley, according to Kaijage (op. cit., p. 516) witnessed high Irish participation in Chartism and constituted a clear case of a place where class consciousness appears to have eclipsed ethnic consciousness.

    13. For these disturbances see *Northern Star*, 15, 22, 29 May; T. Middleton, *Annals of Hyde and District* (Hyde, 1899), pp. 103-4; N. McCord, *The Anti-Corn Law League 1838-1846* (1958) pp. 102-3.

    14. *Northern Star*, 12 June 1841.

    15. *1836 Poor Enquiry (Ireland). Appendix G. Report on the State of the Irish Poor in Great Britain*, pp. 69-70. (Hereafter referred to as *1836 Irish Poor.)*

    16. *1836 Irish Poor*, pp. vii, xxi, 68; K. Marx and F. Engels, *On Britain* op. cit., p. 127; J.A. Jackson, *The Irish in Brit.* pp. 116-17; J.H. Treble, thesis, p. 60. For the attitudes of the Catholic Church towards trade unionism see J.H. Treble, 'The Roman Catholic Church and Trade Unionism, *Northern History*, v (1970), pp. 95-6.

    17. See J.H. Treble, thesis, op. cit., pp. 245-50; *1836 Irish Poor*, pp. 64-7; K. Marx and F. Engels, *On Britain*, p. 157; H.A. Turner, *Trade Union Growth, Structure and Policy*, (Manchester, 1962), p. 48.

    18. J. Foster, *Class Struggle*, op. cit., pp. 8, 244.

    19. *1836 Irish Poor*, pp. 61, 82-4.

    20. E.P. Thompson, *The Making*, op. cit., p. 476. Cotton notes that there exists no evidence of 'any serious conflict between Irish and English workers' in Ashton and Stalybridge during the 1820s and 1830s. N. Cotton, op. cit., p. 23. And Reid comments that, apart from the ethnic conflict of 1841 (which was 'induced by outside influences'), Stockport witnessed no large-scale communal strife until the 1850s. C.A.N. Reid, thesis, op. cit., pp. 309ff.

    21. E.P. Thompson, *The Making*, op. cit., p. 480.

    22. M. Anderson *Family Structure*, op. cit., pp. 156-7; *Manchester Guardian*, 4 July 1849.

    23. *Stockport Advertiser*, 5 September 1850; W.M. Bowman, *England in Ashton-under-Lyne: The History of the Ancient Manor and Parish* (Altrincham, 1960), p. 411.

    24. The most active Protestant organisations were the Orange lodges, the Protestant Reformation Society, and the Operative Protestant Associations. Prominent figures in the Manchester area were Richardson, Bardsley, Consterdine, Doble, Heffill, Touchstone, Stowell and Mason. The leading spokesman in Manchester and Salford was Hugh Stowell at Christ's Church. Stowell was a staunch defender of 'Protestant liberties', a committed enemy of socialism, and president of the Operative Protestant Association. See *Manchester Courier*, 10 November, 15 December 1849, 11 January 1851 for the various organisations. For Stowell see J.B. Marsden, *Memoirs of the Rev. Hugh Stowell* (1868); R.L. Greenall, 'Popular Conservatism in

Salford, 1868–1886', *Northern History*, IX (1974), p. 133. In the Ashton area Booth Mason (brother of the Liberal, Hugh Mason) was the leading Orangeman. For an account of Mason's life see the obituary in *Manchester Guardian*, 11 September 1888.

25. For such Protestant activities see *Manchester Courier*, 9 February 1850; *Manchester Illuminator and General Catholic Record* (Manchester, 1850); *Theological Tracts* (Manchester Central Reference Library). For Protestant propaganda see G. Best, 'Popular Protestantism in Victorian Britain' in R. Robson (ed.), *Ideas and Institutions of Victorian Britain* (1967), Ch. 5; also E.R. Norman, *Anti-Catholicism in Victorian England* (1968), intro.

26. J. Denvir, *The Irish in Britain* (1892), pp. 163–6, book x.

27. *Manchester Guardian*, 6, 16 November, 7 December 1850.

28. *Manchester Courier*, 30 November 1850.

29. *Stockport Advertiser*, 28 November 1850, 20 February, 25 December 1851.

30. *Manchester Guardian*, 7 December 1850.

31. For the Stockport Riots and their aftermath see *Stockport Advertiser*, 2, 9 July 1852; *Manchester Courier*, 3, 10 July 1852; *Manchester Guardian*, 3, 7, 14, 17, 21, 24, 28 July 1852; *Northern Star*, 10 July 1852. For a more detailed treatment see Kirk, thesis, IV.

32. *Manchester Courier*, 3, 10 July 1852; *Stockport Advertiser*, 2 July 1852.

33. *Manchester Guardian*, 7 July 1852.

34. *Stockport Advertiser*, 6 May 1852; *Manchester Guardian*, 14 July 1852.

35. *Manchester Guardian*, 14 July 1852. Kate Tiller notes the central importance of ethnicity and ethnic conflict in Wigan both before and after 1850. Indeed, ethnicity constituted a formidable obstacle to the development of Chartism in Wigan. In 1874 George Roby wrote of the attitudes of the Wigan working class to politics:

> One shouted for the parson, and the other for the priest; one for the church, the other for the chapel; one for the blue; the other for the green, one had its day in March, the other in July, one was Irish, the other English; one was Liberal, therefore the other Tory . . . (working class Tories) have entered the political temple through the Ecclesiastical gate. They are Tories because they are Churchmen and anti-Papists. Their best men belong to the Orange Society, or some of the Church associations. As politicians they are nothing.

K.Tiller, thesis, op. cit., pp. 96, 97, 108.

36. *Manchester Courier*, 16 September, 4 November 1854.

37. *Manchester Courier*, 12, 19 December 1857.

38. J. Foster, *Class Struggle*, pp. 219–20, 243–6; *Manchester Guardian*, 8, 14 July 1856, 16, 23 May 1857. The Lancashire Public Records Office at Preston holds material relating to disturbances at Wigan. See CPR 8. Preston, like Wigan, had a long history of ethnic conflict. See, A. Granath, 'The Irish in Mid-Nineteenth Century Lancashire, 1830–71' (unpublished MA Lancaster University, 1975), p. 59.

39. For the decline in tensions at Stockport see *Stockport Advertiser*, 26 March 1858, 18 October 1861; *Stockport News*, 23 March 1861, 28 June 1862. For the Relief Riots see *Manchester Guardian*, 23 March 1863.

40. *Ashton Reporter*, 15 July 1865.

41. For the growing ties between Irish Catholics and Liberals at Stockport see Robinson, *Catholicism in Edgeley* (Stockport Public Library), p. 62. Vincent notes that Liberal attempts to win the Irish Catholic vote were not a complete success. Catholic politics revolved around 'confession, class and nationality', and only in 1868 did all three issues fully coincide with support for the Liberals. In 1859 and 1865 Garibaldi and the Irish question brought Irish Catholic support to the Tories. As workers, however, Irish Catholic immigrants were generally supporters of Liberalism. J. Vincent, *Formtn of British Lib. Pty*, op. cit., p. 298.

42. W.J. Lowe, 'The Irish in Lancashire' (unpublished PhD thesis, Trinity College, Dublin, 1974), pp. 344–54; Robinson, *Catholicism in Edgeley*.

43. *Ashton Standard*, 15 June 1861; Foster, *Class Struggle* pp. 243ff., *Ashton Reporter*, 15 June 1861.

44. *Ashton Standard*, 21 June 1862; *Ashton Reporter*, 3 May, 14 June 1862.

45. *Oldham Chronicle*, 25 October 1862.

46. For Fenian activity see Denvir, *The Irish in Britain*, book x.

47. The Catholic Church opposed Fenianism for three major reasons. Firstly, the brotherhood was seen as a threat to the dominant position enjoyed by the church within Irish communities. Secondly, the church was hostile to the physical-force methods advocated by the Fenians. And thirdly, for some of the Catholic hierarchy, Fenianism was akin to socialism. The Fenian leadership, while not explicitly anti-Catholic, nevertheless wished to exclude the church from political involvement on the grounds that clergymen had often proved to be incompetent as politicians and that the Catholic Church had been known to act against the interests of Ireland. For a while it seemed that Irish nationalism might ally itself with anti-clericalism. See D.M. McCartney, 'The Church and Fenianism' in M. Harmon (ed.), *Fenians and Fenianism* (Dublin, 1968).

48. *Ben Brierley's Journal*, December 1869.

49. *Manchester City News*, 29 November 1867: *Manchester Courier*, 25 November, 2 December 1867.

50. For reactions to Fenianism see P. Rose, *The Manchester Martyrs* (1970), pp. 68ff. :R. Harrison, *Before the Socialists*, op. cit., pp. 91, 141, 220: N. McCord, 'The Fenians and Public Opinion in Great Britain' in Harmon (ed.), *Fenians*; R. Greenall, *North. Hist.* IX: J. McGill and T. Redmond, *The Story of the Manchester Martyrs* (Manchester, 1963).

51. *Spectator*, 5 October 1867, p. 1108.

52. For an account of Murphy's career see W.L. Arnstein, 'The Murphy Riots: A Victorian Dilemma', *Victorian Studies*, XIX (1975), pp. 51–71. Murphy, born and baptised a Catholic in County Limerick, converted to Protestantism at an early age and the family moved to County Mayo where Murphy's father became the head of a Protestant school. At 18 years of age Murphy became a scripture reader for the Irish Society, an evangelical Protestant organisation. In 1859 Murphy married and temporarily gave up 'missionary' work to run a boot-and-shoe shop in Dublin. In 1862 Murphy sailed to Liverpool and then made his way to London where he eventually became a lecturer for the Protestant Electoral Union. Between 1863 and 1867 Murphy's lectures sparked off riots in several towns.

53. The best sources are local newspapers. See for example, *Ashton Reporter*, 11, 15 January, 1–29 February, 7–28 March, 4, 11 April, 16 May 1868; *Manchester Guardian*, 12, 13, May 1868; E. Taylor, *An Account of Orangeism: A Key to the Late Religious Riots and to the Frantic Opposition to Irish Church Disestablishment* (1868); file CPRI in Prest. Pub. Recds. Office. Full treatment of the events of 1868 in Kirk, thesis, IV.

54. *Ashton Reporter*, 16 May 1868.

55. See, for example, *Ashton Reporter*, 4 July 1868.

56. For the Rochdale Riot see *Manchester Guardian*, 4, 5, 6, 20 March 1868; file CPRS in Prest. Pub. Recds. Office. For Oldham, *Manchester Guardian*, 26 May 1868. For Preston and Blackburn, *Manchester Guardian*, 3, 7 November, 1868; *Ashton Reporter*, 18 July 1868. For Manchester see *Manchester Guardian*, 11, 19 May, 1, 2, 5, 7, 8, 14, 16 September 1868.

57. *Ashton Reporter*, 21 January 1871.

58. W.J. Lowe, thesis, p. 468.

59. See *Ashton Reporter*, 21 March 1868; *Manchester Courier*, 3 December 1867.

60. *Manchester Guardian*, 3 July, 14 August 1852; *Ashton Reporter*, 21 March, 16 May, 15 August 1868; *Manchester Courier*, 14 August 1852.

346   *Class, Ethnicity and Popular Toryism*

61. *Manchester Guardian*, 3 July 1852; *Manchester Courier*, 14 August 1852.

62. *Ashton Reporter*, 21 March, 16 May, 15 August 1868.

63. The population of the municipal borough of Ashton was 30,676 in 1851; Stockport 53,835 in 1851; Stalybridge 35,114 in 1871. Figures and percentages relating to Irish immigration calculated from the Population Census. See *Population Census 1841 Ireland: Report of the Committee Appointed to take the Census of Ireland*, esp. appendix to *The Report; Tables England and Wales 1851* 2, Tables 2,2, pp. 659–64; *Population Census England and Wales 1861*, 2, pp. 655–63; *Population Census England and Wales 1871*, 3, pp. 438–40.

64. *1836 Irish Poor*, pp. v, viii, ix; J. Haslett and W.J. Lowe, 'Household Structure and Overcrowding Among the Lancashire Irish 1851–1871', *Histoire Sociale — Social Hist.*, vol. 10, no. 19 (1977) p. 52.

65. In 1851 there were 17,554 cotton operatives in Stockport (32 per cent of the population); at Stalybridge in 1861, 10,404 (41 per cent; and at Ashton in 1861 10, 856 (31 per cent).

66. E.J. Hobsbawm, *Ind. and Emp.*, Chs 6 and 7; T. Ellison, *The Cotton Trade of Great Britain* (1886).

67. G.H. Wood, *History of Wages in the Cotton Trade* (Manchester, 1910); see above Ch. 3.

68. G. McLennan, *Ideology and Consciousness: Some Problems in Marxist Historiography*, Centre for Contemporary Cultural Studies Occasional Papers (Birmingham, 1976), esp. intro.

69. *1836 Irish Poor*, pp. xxxiii, 49, 61, 67, 70.

70. G.H. Wood, *Hist. of Wages*, pp. 131.

71. H.A. Turner, *Trade Union Struct.*, pp. 114, 124, 141–4, 160–2; see above, Ch. 6.

72. *Manchester Guardian*, 19 October 1853; H. Ashworth, *The Preston Strike* (Manchester, 1854). Dutton and King, op. cit., pp. 178–9.

73. J. Foster, *Class Struggle*, p. 244. According to the *Stockport Advertiser* (9 July 1852), 'the advent of one low Irish family into any locality is generally the signal for the flight of all the English from the neighbourhood'. By way of contrast Smith notes that English and Irish communities in the Deansgate area of Manchester were, in 1851, 'far from rigidly segregated'. In terms of housing, 'the balance of some streets or courts might be heavily weighted on one side or the other but many streets showed an apparently random distribution'. Smith also draws attention to frequent intermarriage between Irish and English people. See J.H. Smith, 'Ten Acres of Deansgate in 1851', *Trans. Lancs. and Ches. Antiqu Soc.* (1980), pp. 43–59. It is perhaps significant that the great majority of Irish in Smith's smaple had been resident in England before the mid-1840s. A study of the 1861 and 1871 census material and other evidence might reveal a very different picture — complete with ethnic clustering and a hardening of relations between post-Famine immigrants and other residents.

74. W.J. Lowe 'The Lancashire Irish and the Catholic Church, 1846–71; The Social Dimension', *Irish Historical Studies*, xx (1976), pp. 129–55.

75. *1836 Irish Poor*, pp. 62, 73.

76. J. Foster, *Class Struggle*, pp. 243–6.

77. For more detailed treatment see Kirk, thesis, V.

78. In 1852 Lancashire had returned 19 Liberals and 7 Conservatives. By 1865 the gap had narrowed somewhat when 15 Liberals and 12 Conservatives were elected. In 1868 the Liberal stranglehold was broken: the balance standing at 22 to 11 in favour of the Conservatives. J. Vincent, *The Formation of the British Liberal Party*, op. cit., p. 27.

79. H.J. Hanham, *Elections and Party Management: Politics in the Time of Disraeli and Gladstone*, op. cit., p. 286.

80. *Ashton Reporter*, 13 January 1866.

81. For the 1868 elections see, J. Vincent, op. cit., p. 27; H.J. Hanham, op. cit., p. 313; Kirk, thesis, op. cit., pp. 347-9.

82. J. Vincent, op. cit., p. 27. In 1879 northwest and southwest Lancashire remained Conservative, but the northeastern and southeastern parts of the country were lost to the Liberals. See M.R. Dunsmare, op. cit., p. 262.

83. During the 1850s and early 1860s many Conservatives often bemoaned their failure to enlist active and widespread popular support and involvement. Within local Liberal Party circles it was widely believed that the great mass of 'respectable' and sober-minded 'artisans' were overwhelmingly of a Liberal persuasion. In 1856 lack of support forced the disbandment of the Tradesmen's and Operative Conservative Association at Stockport. And at Ashton and Dukinfield the Conservatives confessed that before 1868 they had little effective organised popular support. For the weak state of Conservativism see *Stockport Advertiser* 17, 24 October 1856; *Free Lance*, 19 January 1867, pp. 36-7; J. Vincent, op. cit., pp. 147-8; *Ashton Reporter*, 13 January, 12 May 1866.

84. M.R. Dunsmore, op. cit., p. 262.

85. *Ashton Reporter*, 24 October, 21 November 1868.

86. Ibid., 20 February 1969.

87. At Stalybridge, a veritable hotbed of working-class Toryism, the Constitutional Association developed from a modest beginning into an organisation which regularly attracted 1000 people to its various meetings and social functions. Liberal and National Education League meetings were often reduced to a state of chaos by male and female workers who shouted down the lecturers (compulsion was 'un-English'), struck up choruses of 'Britons Never Shall be Slaves' and gave three cheers for 'Mellor, Sidebottom and Murphy'. See *Ashton Reporter*, 19 February, 5 March, 8 October, 19 November 1870. Similar, if often less boisterous, proceedings characterised the political climates of Ashton, Manchester and Stockport. See Ibid., 19 June 1869, 12, 19 February 1870; *Manchester Guardian*, 14 June 1869.

88. For working-class Conservatism see P.F. Clarke, *Lancashire and New Liberalism*, pp. 25-82; J. Vincent, *Formtn. of Britain Lib. Party*, p. 148; P. Joyce, *Hist. Jnl.*, XVIII, and *Work, Society and Politics*, op. cit; W.H. Mills, *Sir Charles Macara Bart — A Study of Modern Lancashire* (Manchester, 1917), pp. 65-7; Hanham, *Elects. and Pty. Mangmt.*, pp. 313ff; *Ashton Reporter*, 15 September, 24 November, 1860, 14, 21 February 1863, 10 February, 22 December 1866, 23 March, 1 June, 14 September 1867, 1 March 1868, 2 April 1870 for the continued political importance of Stephens; Kirk, thesis, V.

89. Some brief qualifications are, however, in order. By no means all Conservatives were sympathetic to the causes of factory legislation and trade unionism and Stephens's social radicalism met with limited approval. The dominant concerns of many Conservatives, both before and after 1867, were the preservation of political and social inequalities. Furthermore, Liberalism had mellowed somewhat. By the 1860s many Liberals had come to accept and even welcome factory legislation, and some had come to terms with trade unionism. See *Ashton Reporter*, 27 January 1866, 1 June, 14 September, 1867, 24 October 1868; *Ashton Standard*, 10 February, 27 April 1866; Kirk, thesis, II and III. For the importance of denominational loyalties and the Irish Church debate in the 1868 elections see J.C. Lowe, 'The Tory Triumph of 1868 in Blackburn and in Lancashire', *Hist. Jnl*, xvi, 4 (1973), pp. 733-48.

90. For a history of Orangeism in the first half of the century see, H. Senior, *Orangeism in Ireland and Britain 1795-1836* (1966). For developments in the post-1850 period see P. Joyce, *Work, Society and Politics*, op. cit., esp. pp. 256-61.

91. J. Foster, op. cit., pp. 219-20.

92. For the progress made by Orangeism in the early 1850s see, *Manchester Courier*, 31 November 1850, 21 May 1851, 5 March, 28 May, 16 July 1853, 19 April 1856.

93. See ibid., 13 August 1853, 7 January 1854; *Stockport Advertiser*, 19 July 1861.

94. J. Foster, op. cit., pp. 119-20.

95. *Ashton Reporter*, 21 November 1863.
96. *Ashton Standard*, 21 July 1866, 26 January 1867.
97. See the letter from 'A True Blue' in ibid., 17 July 1869.
98. For the continued strength of Murphyism in the Ashton area see, ibid., 5, 12 February, 17 December 1870, 21 January, 11 February, 1 July, 9 December 1871.
99. For Stowell's attitudes see, *Manchester Courier*, 6 April, 4 May 1850, 22 March 1851, 12 June 1852; J.B. Marsden, op. cit.
100. *Ashton Reporter*, 4 April 1863.
101. Ibid., 4 February 1865.
102. Ibid., 8, 15 September, 1 December 1860.
103. See for example, ibid., 12 September 1868, 30 January 1869.
104. Ibid., 28 December 1867.
105. Ibid., 25 January 1868; *Manchester Guardian*, 8 February 1868.
106. It is significant that throughout 1868 John Bright's reputed opposition to trade unionism and factory legislation was continually highlighted by Orangemen. See *Manchester Guardian*, 7 September 1868; *Ashton Reporter*, 5 September, 24 October 1868.
107. See P. Joyce, op. cit., pp. 257-8.
108. *Ashton Reporter*, 7 March, 11, 18 April, 7 May, 20 June, 8 November 1868.
109. H.J. Hanham, op. cit., p. 85.
110. *Ashton Reporter*, 5 September 1868.
111. Ibid., 22 August, 17 October 1868.
112. *Stockport Advertiser*, 2 October 1868.
113. *Manchester Guardian*, 31 October, 11 November 1868.
114. Ibid., 4 September, 9 October 1868.
115. Ibid., 16 February 1869.
116. *Ashton Reporter*, 21 November 1868.
117. Ibid., 28 November 1868.

CONCLUSION

This study has hopefully demonstrated that the growth of mid-Victorian stability and the onset of working-class reformism were complex developments which cannot be satisfactorily explained in terms of a single, overriding factor. It has been suggested that both the traditional and more recent emphases upon the key explanatory powers of, respectively, economic improvement and the emergence of a labour aristocracy are by no means convincing. In addition to their inadequate empirical supports, these two explanations have frequently been expressed in terms of a narrow and erroneous framework of economic reductionism in which, 'it is assumed that economic forces have automatic effects in the sphere of ideas, values and political action'.[1]

It is largely in relation to their forceful and convincing critiques of economic reductionism that the works of Gray and Crossick represent such a useful and welcome development in the field of nineteenth-century labour history. Inspired by the criticisms of economic reductionism made by Gramsci, Thompson and others, and whilst fully alive to the (often major) significance of the 'economic', both Gray and Crossick have shown that in the respective contexts of Victorian Edinburgh and mid-Victorian Kentish London the various social levels and practices (economic, political and cultural) did interact in a complex manner, that political and ideological trends could not be reduced to the 'economic', and that the various structures and practices were deserving of careful investigation in their own right. Hence Crossick concluded that economic developments constituted 'a necessary but not a sufficient condition' for the formation of an élite of skilled workers who consciously divorced themselves from the remainder of the working class in Kentish London, and that cultural and other forces played an important role in the growth of this separate group identity.[2] Gray expressed similar sentiments concerning the easing of class conflict:

> The greater economic stability and underlying buoyancy of the mid-Victorian boom was certainly a crucial element; it widened the margin for bargaining between employers and workers, and

349

induced a general atmosphere of social optimism and expansion. But social stability did not follow automatically from economic changes.[3]

The magnitude of my theoretical debt to the Thompsons and Gray and Crossick has hopefully been fully evident throughout the pages of this study. For, whilst I have argued that, unlike Edinburgh and Kentish London, the growth of reformism in the cotton districts was not to be attributed to the emergence of a labour aristocracy, I have, nevertheless, derived great sustenance from the anti-reductionist stance of Gray and Crossick. And I have, of course, come to endorse their conclusion that economic developments were a necessary but insufficient cause of stability and reformism.

Within the specific context of the cotton districts, economic developments failed, as we have seen, adequately to account for the demise of Chartism. Economic and financial gains for the mass of operatives were not greatly in evidence until the late 1850s, and were more limited during the third quarter of the century as a whole than traditionally claimed. Disappointments, even despair, concerning the setbacks of 1848 and the decline of mass interest in Chartism; the increased successes which met some of the other attempts at working-class emancipation; growing concessions from above; and the failure of late Chartism to address itself with forceful and direct relevance to the changed situation of many workers — these were some of the main factors underlying the movement's demise. Furthermore, many of the important influences in the decline of working-class solidarity and class militancy — ethnic conflict, sharpened status divisions, enhanced opportunities for labour's advancement and the like — cannot be explained in purely economic terms. For example, growing ethnic tensions owed as much, if not more, to cultural rather than economic causes; respectability was especially pronounced among, but far from confined to, the more prosperous sections of the working class; and the continued sense of working-class pride arose not only from industrial experiences and struggles but also from within the processes of culture and politics — opposition to the more direct attempts of the middle class to exert control over workers' lives, and continued attachment to the principles of independence, self-respect and control over one's destiny playing a significant role in the sustaining working-class consciousness.

The various points made in the previous paragraph have, of course, constituted much of the subject matter of this study, and do not require further elaboration. Such points have, however, been raised at this juncture in support of the general viewpoint that culture and politics enjoyed a much greater degree of autonomy during the mid-Victorian period than an economic reductionist approach would, either implicitly or explicitly, have us believe. Simultaneously, it must, however, be emphasised that the autonomy enjoyed was relative rather than absolute in character. The 'economic' did get under people's skins, did operate behind their backs, and did exert extremely strong pressures and limits upon their actions, perceptions and modes of thought. In short, opposition to reductionism has been combined in this study with support for a materialist explanation of change at mid-century.

The various ways in which the 'economic' exerted such pressures and limits are perhaps worthy of brief recall. Modest, but nevertheless tangible and perceived material gains for the mass of the operatives during the third quarter as a whole; the substantial advances made by the leadership and many of their institutions; and, in comparison with the second quarter of the century, the more regular employment opportunities of the post-1850 years — these constituted some of the more immediate ways in which the 'economic' made its presence felt. At a deeper, 'structural' level, this study has echoed Hobsbawm's and Stedman Jones's beliefs that a restabilised and dynamic economic system, which offered increased scope for class toleration and manoeuvre, constituted the fundamental fact of life, the basic framework of material existence in which human agency and choice were compelled to operate in a non-reductionist manner. And, given the seemingly permanent character of the system, workers were faced by the stark choice of reform versus revolution: the system could no longer simply be by-passed.

It was thus within this basic material context that political, cultural and ideological choices were to be made, and within which human agency could exert its own pressures upon the whole range of structures and practices. And, given the sociological, political and cultural developments and changes described in this book — the increasingly fragmented character of the working class, concessions from above, the growth of a more privatised version of respectability and the like — it was not accidental that the mid-Victorian working class in the cotton districts did not offer a fundamental threat to the existing system. Rather, piecemeal gradualism, an overall decline in class solidarity and action, and political fragmentation became the distinguishing characteristics of the post-Chartist working class. The movement into reformism did not, however, signal an end to class conflict and the emergence of a smoothly-functioning social order based upon a system of common values. If the system could not be wished away neither could these reformist workers, with their strong sense of independence and class pride and their steadfast determination to secure the recognition and advancement of their own institutions and interests within the capitalist system. The consolidation of bourgeois hegemony was indeed a negotiated and, at times, conflict-ridden process.

Notes

1. R.Q. Gray, *The Aristocracy of Labour in Nineteenth-century Britain*, op. cit. p. 11.
2. Ibid., p. 35.
3. Ibid., p. 57.

SELECT BIBLIOGRAPHY

This select bibliography is organised in the following manner:

I PRIMARY SOURCES

   A. Newspapers and Journals
   B. Manuscript Collections
   C. Government Publications, Miscellaneous Reports and Transactions
   D. Books, Articles and Pamphlets by Contemporaries

II SECONDARY SOURCES

   A. Unpublished Dissertations and Other Manuscripts
   B. Books and Articles

I Primary Sources

A. Newspapers and Journals. Consulted for the following years:

Alliance Weekly News, 1854–70
Ashton Reporter, 1855–75
Ashton Standard, 1860–70
Ben Brierley's Journal, 1869–73
Co-operative News, 1871–1900
Co-operator, 1860–70
Fraser's Magazine, 1860–70
Free Lance, 1867–70
Hyde and Glossop News, 1859
Industrial Partnerships Record, 1867–9
Journal of the Union of Lancashire and Cheshire Institutes, 1867–71
Manchester City News, 1863–7
Manchester Courier, 1849–70
Manchester Examiner and Times, 1848–70
Manchester Guardian, 1848–70
Manchester Illuminator and General Catholic Record, 1850
Northern Star, 1839–41, 1849–51
Notes to the People, 1851–2
Oddfellows Magazine, 1850–70
Oldham Chronicle, 1860–5
Oldham Co-operative Record, 1894
People's Paper, 1852–8
Salford Working Men's College Magazine, 1859–70
Star of Freedom, 1852
Stockport Advertiser, 1848–70
Times The, 1860–70
Working Men's College Magazine, 1859–1873

B. *Manuscript Collections*

Admissions Register, Trafalgar Lodge no. 401 (Oddfellows), 1859–73. Stockport Public Library

All Saints' Mutual Improvement Society, Log Book 1863–97. Manchester Reference Library

Co-operative Movement Collection, University of Pittsburgh

German Street Sunday School Sick and Funeral Society. Minutes, members, subscriptions, doctors' certificates, accounts and correspondence, 1829–1946. Manchester Reference Library

Hulme Operatives' Day School, Lloyd Street and Hamer Street. Log Books, 1865–79. Manchester Reference Library

Marcroft (W.) Collection. Oldham Public Library

Preston Public Records Office. Material concerning ethnic and religious conflict (Files C.P.R. 1, 5 and 8) in the cotton districts

Records of the Amalgamated Association of Operative Cotton Spinners, Great Ancoats Street. Manchester Reference Library

Report on the Records of Saint Paul's Literary and Education Society. Manchester Reference Library

Saint Peter's Mutual Improvement Society. Minutes, 1856–75. Manchester Reference Library

Scrapbook of Edward Brotherton, Hon. Sec. of the Manchester and Salford Education Aid Society. Manchester Reference Library

Smith (J.B.) Collection. Manchester Reference Library

Webbs' (S. and B.) Trade Union Collection, Section A, vols. 34–40. British Library of Political and Economic Science

C. *Government Publications, Miscellaneous Reports and Transactions*

Ashton-under-Lyne Corporation Manual, 1870–8

British Parliamentary Papers. First Report of the Inquiry into the Condition of the Poorer Classes in Ireland. Report on the State of the Irish Poor in Great Britain. Appendix G. 1836, XXXIV

——Report from the Select Committee on Manchester and Salford Education. 1837, XVL

——Report of the Commissioners Appointed to Take the Census of Ireland for the year 1841. XXIV

——Report of the Assistant Poor Law Commissioners into the State of the Population of Stockport. 1842, XXXV

——First Report of the Commissioners for Inquiring into the State of Large Towns and Populous Districts. 1844, XVIIL

——Second Report of the Commissioners for Inquiring into the State of Large Towns and Populous Districts. 1845, XVIIIL

——Accounts and Papers Poor: England and Wales; Ireland; Scotland. February–August, 1849, XLVII

——Reports of Inspectors of Factories, 1850–70

——Census of Great Britain, 1851. Population Tables, vol. 1. Report 1852-3, LXXXV; vol. II, LXXXVI

——Report from the Select Committee on Friendly Societies Bill; with the Proceedings, Minutes of Evidence, Appendix and Index. 1854, VII

——Census of England and Wales, 1861. Tables of the population and houses enumerated in England and Wales, and in the Islands of the British Seas on 8th April, 1861. 1861, L; ibid., Population Tables. Numbers and Distribution of the People. Vol. 1, 1862, LI

——Reports of the Commissioners appointed to inquire into the organisations and rules of trades unions and other associations; with Minutes of Evidence and Appendices. First Report to Fourth Report, 1867, XXXIIL; Fifth to Tenth Report, 1867-68, XXXIXL; Eleventh Report, 1868-9, XXXI

——Census of England and Wales, 1871. Population Tables. Vol. 1 Counties, 1872, LVI; ibid., Part I, 1-Vol. II Registration or Union Counties, 1872, LXVI; ibid., Part II, 1-Vol. III 1873, LXXII; ibid., General Report, 1873, LXXI

——Fourth Report of the Commissioners appointed to inquire into friendly and benefit building societies; with Minutes of Evidence, Appendix and Index. 1874, XXIII

Co-operative Movement. A wealth of reports, journals, etc. in the Co-op Library at Holyoake House, Manchester

Cotton Famine. Fund for the Relief of Distress in the Manufacturing Districts. Central Executive Committee Reports and Returns, 1862-5

Manchester Free Labour Society. First Annual Report, 1870

Manchester Statistical Society. Reports and Transactions, 1850-1900

Medical Officer of Health, Manchester. Reports, 1868-90

National Association for the Promotion of Social Science. Transactions, 1857-70

Oddfellowship. Reports, journals, etc. at Oddfellows House, Manchester

Pendleton Mechanics' Institute. Reports, 1854-70

Salford Working Men's College. Reports, 1859-70

Trials. The Trial of Feargus O'Connor and Fifty Eight Others at Lancaster, 1843

D. Books, Articles and Pamphlets by Contemporaries

Abram, W.A. 'Social Conditions and Political Prospects of the Lancashire Workman', *Fortnightly Review* (October 1868)

Ashworth, H. *The Preston Strike: An Enquiry into it Causes and Consequences* (Manchester, 1854)

Bremner, J.A. 'The Education of the Manual-Labour Class', *Transactions of the National Association for the Promotion of Social Science* (1866)

Brierley, B. *Home Memories and Recollections of a Life* (Manchester, 1887)

——*Failsworth, My Native Village; with Incidents of the Struggles of its Early Reformers* (Oldham, 1895)

Brotherton, E. 'The State of Popular Education and Suggestions for its Advancement', *Transactions of the National Association for the Promotion of Social Science* (1865)

Burton, T. *Royton Industrial Co-operative Society Limited* (Manchester, 1907)

Chadwick, D. 'On Free Libraries and Museums', *Transactions of the National Association for the Promotion of Social Science* (1857)

——'On Working Men's Colleges', *Transactions of the National Association for the Promotion of Social Science* (1859)

——'On the Rate of Wages in Manchester and Salford and the Manufacturing Districts of Lancashire 1839-1859', *Journal of the Royal Statistical Society*, XXIII (March 1860)

Chapman, S.J. *The Lancashire Cotton Industry* (Manchester, 1904)

Clarke, C.A. *The Effects of the Factory System* (London, 1899)

Crimes, T. *Edward Owen Greening. A Maker of Modern Co-operation* (Manchester, 1923)

Denvir, J. *The Irish in Britain* (London, 1892)

Ellison, T. *The Cotton Trade of Great Britain* (London, 1886)

Fairburn, W. *Address of William Fairburn to the Members of the Lyceum, Great Ancoats Street* (Manchester, 1839)

Faucher, L. *Manchester in 1844: its Present Condition and Future Prospects* (Manchester, 1844)

Godwin, J.V. 'Bradford Mechanics Institute', *Transactions of the National Association for the Promotion of Social Science* (1859)

Greening, E.O. 'How Far is it Desirable and Practicable to Extend Partnerships of Industry?', *Transactions of the National Association for the Promotion of Social Science* (1870)

——*Working Men Co-operators* (Manchester, 1914)

Grime, B. *Memory Sketches* (Oldham, 1887)

Heaton, J. *The Late Ernest Jones: his Life and Times* (Manchester, 1869)

Heginbotham, H. *Stockport: Ancient and Modern*, 2 vols. (London, 1882–92)

Hill, S. *Bygone Stalybridge* (Stalybridge, 1907)

Hinchcliffe, J.H. *History of the Stalybridge Good Intent Industrial Co-operative Society Limited 1859–1909* (Manchester, 1909)

The History of the Ashton-under-Lyne Mutual Improvement Society and Bond of Brotherhood (Ashton-under-Lyne, 1858)

Holyoake, G.J. *The History of Co-operation*, 2 vols. (London, 1906)

Ireland. 'Ireland — letters reprinted from the *Morning Post*', Political Tracts, Manchester Reference Library

Jones, B. *Co-operative Production* (New York, 1968; reprint of 1894 edition)

Jones, E.C. 'Labour and Capital: A Lecture Delivered in 1867'. Manchester Reference Library

——'The Politics of the Day: A Lecture Delivered in Edinburgh in September 1868'. Manchester Reference Library

——Newspaper Cuttings Related to the Death and Funeral of Ernest Jones, 1869. Manchester Reference Library

Jones, T. and Rhodes, J.*Jubilee History of the Hyde Equitable Co-operative Society Ltd. 1862–1912* (Manchester, 1912)

Lawton, D. *Village Co-operation. A Jubilee Sketch: Greenfield Co-operative Society Ltd 1856–1906* (Manchester, 1906)

MacDonald, W. *The True Story of Trades' Unions: being a reply to Dr. John Watts, Professor Jevons and others* (Manchester, 1867)

Marcroft, W. *The Inner Circle of Family Life* (Manchester, 1886)

——*The Marcroft Family. A History of Strange Events* (Rochdale, 1889)

Marr, T.R. *Housing Conditions in Manchester and Salford* (Manchester, 1904)

Marsden, J.B. *Memoirs of the Rev. Hugh Stowell* (London, 1868)

Marx, K. and Engels, F. *On Britain* (Moscow, 1953)

Mercer, J.E. 'The Conditions of Life in Angel Meadow', *Transactions of the Manchester Statistical Society* (session 1896–7)

Middleton, T. *Annals of Hyde and District* (Menston 1973; reprint of 1899 edition)

Newbould, T.P. *Pages From a Life of Strife — Being Some Recollections of W.H. Chadwick, the Last of the Manchester Chartists* (London, 1911)

Oats, H.C. 'An Inquiry into the Educational and Other Conditions of a District in Ancoats', *Transactions of the Manchester Statistical Society* (session 1865–6)

Platt, R. 'An Address Delivered at the Presentation Tea Party Given by his Workpeople to Robert Platt Esq., J.P.' (Stalybridge, 1857)

'Protestantism versus Romanism' — a report of three discussions held in Park School, Blackburn 1850'. Theological Tracts. Manchester Reference Library.

Ransome, A. and Royston, W. *Report Upon the Health of Manchester and Salford During the Last Fifteen Years* (Manchester, 1867)

Reach, A.B. *Manchester and the Textile Districts in 1849* (Helmshore, 1972)

Redfern, P. *The Story of the C.W.S. 1863–1913* (Manchester, 1913)

Rowley, C. *Fifty Years of Ancoats* (Manchester, 1899)

——*Fifty Years of Work Without Wages* (London, 1911)

Scott, F. 'The Condition and Occupations of the People of Manchester and Salford', *Transactions of the Manchester Statistical Society* (May 1889)

Taylor, E. 'An Account of Orangeism: A Key to the Late Religious Riots and to the Frantic Opposition to Irish Church Disestablishment, 1868'. Political Tracts. Manchester Reference Library

Taylor, J.C. *The Jubilee History of the Oldham Industrial Co-operative Society Limited 1850–1900* (Manchester, 1900)

Taylor, W. Cooke. *Notes of a Tour in the Manufacturing Districts of Lancashire* (London, 1842)

The Lyceums. A Word for the Factory Operatives of Manchester (Manchester, 1840)

Thompson, J. *History of the Ashton-under-Lyne Working Men's Co-operative Society Ltd. 1857–1907* (Manchester, 1907)

Thresh, J.C. 'An Inquiry into the Excessive Mortality in No. 1 District Ancoats', *Transactions of the Manchester Statistical Society* (1889)

'Trade Societies and Strikes', *Transactions of the National Association for the Promotion of Social Science* (1860)

Walton, C. *History of the Oldham Equitable Co-operative Society Ltd. from 1850 to 1900* (Manchester, 1900)

Watts, J. *The Facts of the Cotton Famine* (London, 1968; reprint of 1866 edition)

Wilson, B. *The Struggles of an old Chartist* (Halifax, 1887)

Wood, G.H. 'Real Wages and the Standard of Comfort Since 1850', *Journal of the Royal Statistical Society*, 72 (1909)

——*The History of Wages in the Cotton Trade during the Past One Hundred Years* (Manchester, 1910)

Wright, T. *Some Habits and Customs of the Working Classes* (London, 1867)

II Secondary Sources

A. Unpublished Dissertations and Other Manuscripts

Bather, L. 'A History of Manchester and Salford Trades Council', unpublished PhD thesis, University of Manchester, 1956

Bradshaw, R.P. 'The Preston Lock-out: a Case Study of a Mid-Nineteenth Century Lancashire Cotton Strike, and its Role in the Development of Trade Union Organisation amongst Textile Workers', unpublished MA thesis, University of Lancaster, 1972

Cotton, N. 'Popular Movements in Ashton-under-Lyne and Stalybridge before 1832', unpublished MLitt, University of Birmingham, 1977

Dunsmore, M.R. 'The Working Classes, the Reform League and the Reform Movement in Lancashire and Yorkshire', unpublished MA thesis, University of Sheffield, 1961

Foster, J. 'Capitalism and Class Consciousness in Earlier Nineteenth Century Oldham', unpublished PhD thesis, University of Cambridge, 1967

Gadian, D.S. 'A Comparative Study of Popular Movements in North-West Industrial Towns 1830–1850', unpublished PhD thesis, University of Lancaster, 1976

Granath, A. 'The Irish in Mid-Nineteenth Century Lancashire 1830–71', unpublished MA thesis, University of Lancaster, 1975

Hall, A. 'Social Control and the Working-Class Challenge in Ashton-under-Lyne 1886–1914', unpublished MA thesis, University of Lancaster, 1975

Hemming, J.P. 'The Mechanics' Institute Movement in the Textile Districts of Lancashire and Yorkshire in the Second Half of the Nineteenth Century', unpublished PhD thesis, University of Leeds, 1974

Kaijage, F.J. 'Labouring Barnsley 1815–1875', unpublished PhD thesis, University of Warwick, 1975

Kirk, N. 'Class and Fragmentation: Some Aspects of Working-Class Life in South-east Lancashire and North-east Cheshire 1850–1870', unpublished PhD thesis, University of Pittsburgh, 1974

Lowe, W.J. 'The Irish in Lancashire', unpublished PhD thesis, Trinity College Dublin, 1974

Reid, C.A.N. 'The Chartist Movement in Stockport', unpublished MA thesis, University of Hull, 1976

Schatz, R.W. 'Co-operative Production and the Ideology of Co-operation in England 1870–95', unpublished paper, University of Pittsburgh, May 1973

Smith, C. 'Stockport in the Age of Reform', unpublished manuscript, Stockport Public Library, 1938

Steele, J.D. 'A Study of the Education of the Working Class in Stockport during the Nineteenth Century', unpublished MA thesis, University of Sheffield, 1968

Tiller, K. 'Working Class Attitudes and Organisation in Three Industrial Towns 1850–75', unpublished PhD thesis, University of Birmingham, 1975

Treble, J.H. 'The Place of the Irish Catholics in the Social Life of the North of England 1800–1851', unpublished PhD thesis, University of Leeds, 1969

Whitaker, P. 'The Growth of Liberal Organisation in Manchester from the 1860s to 1903', unpublished PhD thesis, University of Manchester, 1956

B. Books and Articles

Anderson, M. *Family Structure in Nineteenth Century Lancashire* (Cambridge, 1971)

Arnstein, W.L. 'The Murphy Riots: A Victorian Dilemma', *Victorian Studies*, XIX (1975)

Ashmore, O. 'The Diary of James Garnett of Low Moor Clitheroe 1858–1865' *Transactions of the Historical Society of Lancashire and Cheshire*, vol. 12 (1969)

——*The Industrial Archaeology of Stockport* (Ashton-under-Lyne, 1975)

——and Bolton, T. 'Hugh Mason and the Oxford Mills and Community, Ashton-under-Lyne', *Transactions of the Lancashire and Cheshire Antiquarian Society*, vol. 78 (1975)

Bailey, P. *Leisure and Class in Victorian England. Rational Recreation and the Contest for Control 1830–1885* (1978)

——'Will the real Bill Banks Please Stand Up? Towards a Role Analysis of Mid-Victorian Working-Class Respectability', *Journal of Social History*, 12 (Spring 1979)

Barnsby, G.J. 'The Standard of Living in the Black Country during the Nineteenth Century', *Economic History Review*, 2nd. series, vol. XXIV, no. 2 (1971)

Belchem, J. 'English Working-Class Radicalism and the Irish 1815–1850', *North West Labour History Society Bulletin*, 8 (1982–3)

——'1848: Feargus O'Connor and the Collapse of the Mass Platform', in J. Epstein and D. Thompson (eds.), *The Chartist Experience* (London, 1982)

Bellamy, J.M. and Saville, J. (eds.), *Dictionary of Labour Biography*, vols. 1 and 2 (London, 1972 and 1974)

Best, G. *Mid-Victorian Britain 1851–1875* (London, 1971)

Bowman, W.M. *England in Ashton-under-Lyne* (Altrincham, 1960)

Brigg, M. 'Life in East Lancashire 1856–60: A Newly Discovered Diary of John O'Neil (J. Ward) Weaver of Clitheroe', *Transactions of the Historical Society of Lancashire and Cheshire*, vol. 120 (1968)

Briggs, A. (ed.) *Chartist Studies* (London, 1959)

Burgess, K. *the Origins of British Industrial Relations* (London, 1975)

Chuŗch, R.A. 'Profit Sharing and Labour Relations in England in the Nineteenth Century', *International Review of Social History*, XVI, part I (1971)

——*The Great Victorian Boom* (London, 1975)

Clarke, P.F. *Lancashire and the New Liberalism* (Cambridge, 1971)

Clements, R.V. 'British Trade Unions and Popular Political Economy 1850–1875', *Economic History Review*, 2nd. series, vol. xix, no. 16 (1961)

Crossick, G. 'The Labour Aristocracy and its Values: A study of mid-Victorian Kentish London', *Victorian Studies*, vol. XIX, no. 3 (March 1976)

——*An Artisan Elite in Victorian Society: Kentish London 1840–1880* (London, 1978)

Cunningham, H. *Leisure in the Industrial Revolution c1780–c1880* (London, 1980)
——'The Language of Patriotism', *History Workshop Journal*, 12 (1981)
Dutton, H.I. and King, J.E. *Ten Per Cent and No Surrender: The Preston Strike 1853–1854* (Cambridge, 1981)
——'The Limits of Paternalism: The Cotton Tyrants of North Lancashire 1836–1854', *Social History*, vol. 7, no. 1 (January 1982)
Epstein, J. *The Lion of Freedom* (London, 1982)
——and Thompson, D *The Chartist Experience: Studies in Working-Class Radicalism and Culture 1830–1860* (London, 1982)
Farnie, D.A. *The English Cotton Industry and the World Market 1815–1896* (Oxford, 1979)
Field, J. 'British Historians and the Concept of the Labour Aristocracy', *Radical History Review*, 19 (Winter 1978–9)
Foster, J. *Class Struggle and the Industrial Revolution: Early Industrial Capitalism in Three English Towns* (London, 1974)
——'Some Comments on Class Struggle and the Labour Aristocracy', *Social History*, III (October 1976)
Gadian, D.S. Class Consciousness in Oldham and other North-West Industrial Towns 1830–1850', *Historical Journal*, vol. 21, no. 1 (1978)
Gillespie, F.E. *Labour and Politics in England 1850–1867* (London, 1966)
Goodway, D. *London Chartism 1838–1848* (Cambridge, 1982)
Gray, R.Q. *The Labour Aristocracy in Victorian Edinburgh* (Oxford, 1976)
——*The Aristocracy of Labour in Nineteenth-century Britain c. 1850–1914* (London, 1981)
Greenall, R. 'Popular Conservatism in Salford 1868–1886', *Northern History,* IX (1974)
Hall, S. 'In Defence of Theory', in R. Samuel (ed.), *People's History and Socialist Theory* (London, 1981)
Hanham, H.J. *Elections and Party Management: Politics in the Time of Disraeli and Gladstone* (London, 1959)
Harrison, B. *Drink and the Victorians: The Temperance Question in England 1815–1872* (Pittsburgh, 1971)
——and Hollis, P. 'Chartism, Liberalism and the Life of Robert Lowery', *English Historical Review*, vol. LXXXII (1967)
Harrison, J.F.C. *Learning and Living: A Study in the History of the English Adult Education Movement* (Toronto, 1961)
Harrison, R. *Before the Socialists: Studies in Labour and Politics 1861–1881* (London, 1965)
Harrop, S.A. and Rose, E.A. (eds.), *Victorian Ashton* (Ashton-under-Lyne, 1974)
Henderson, W.O. *The Cotton Famine 1861–1865* (Manchester, 1934)
Henretta, J.A. 'The Study of Social Mobility: Ideological Assumptions and Conceptual Bias', *Labor History*, vol. 18, no. 2 (Spring 1977)
Hinton, J. *Labour and Socialism: A History of the British Labour Movement 1867–1974* (Brighton, 1983)
Hobsbawm, E.J. *Labouring Men* (London, 1964)
——*Industry and Empire* (London, 1969)
——'The Labour Aristocracy: Twenty-five years After', Society for the Study of Labour History Bulletin, no. 40 (Spring 1980)
Hopwood, E. *A History of the Lancashire Cotton Industry and the Amalgamated Weavers' Assoication* (Manchester, 1969)
Hunt, A.J. (ed.), *Class and Class Structure* (London, 1977)
Hunt, E.H. *Regional Wage Variations in Britain 1850–1914* (Oxford, 1973)
Jackson, J.A. *The Irish in Britain* (London, 1963)
Jenkins, M. *The General Strike of 1842* (London, 1980)
Johnson, R. 'Socialist-Humanist History', *History Workshop Journal*, 6 (1978)
——'Really Useful Knowledge: Radical Education and Working-Class Culture

1790–1848', in J. Clarke, C. Critcher and R. Johnson (eds.), *Working Class Culture* (London, 1979)

Jones, D. *Chartism and the Chartists* (London, 1975)

Jones, G. Stedman. 'Class Struggle and the Industrial Revolution', *New Left Review*, 90 (1975)

——'The Language of Chartism', in J. Epstein and D. Thompson (eds.), *The Chartist Experience* (London, 1982)

Joyce, P. 'The Factory Politics of Lancashire in the Later Nineteenth Century', *Historical Journal*, vol. 18, no. 3 (1975)

——*Work Society and Politics* (Brighton, 1980)

Laqueur, T.W. *Religion and Respectability. Sunday Schools and Working-Class Culture 1780–1850* (London, 1976)

Lazonick, W. 'Industrial Relations and Technical Change: The Case of the Self-Acting Mule', *Cambridge Journal of Economics*, 3 (1979)

Liddington, J. and Norris, J. *One Hand Tied Behind Us* (London, 1978)

Lunn, K. (ed.) *Host, Immigrants and Minorities* (Folkestone, 1980)

McCabe, A.T. 'The Standard of Living on Merseyside 1850–1875', in S.P. Bell (ed.), *Victorian Lancashire* (Newton Abbot, 1974)

McLennan, G. *Ideology and Consciousness: Some Problems in Marxist Historiography*, Centre for Contemporary Cultural Studies Occasional Papers (Birmingham, 1976)

Mitchell, B.R. and Deane, P. *Abstract of British Historical Statistics* (Cambridge, 1962)

Montgomery, D. 'Workers' Control of Machine Production in the Nineteenth Century', *Labor History*, vol. 17 (Fall, 1976)

Moorhouse, H.F. 'The Marxist Theory of the Labour Aristocracy', *Social History*, vol. 3 (1978)

Morris, R.J. *Class and Class Consciousness in the Industrial Revolution 1780–1850* (London, 1979)

Musson, A.E. *British Trade Unions 1800–1875* (London, 1972)

——*Trade Union and Social History* (London, 1974)

——'Class Struggle and the Labour Aristocracy 1830–1860', *Social History*, 3 (1976)

O'Higgins, R. 'The Irish Influence in the Chartist Movement', *Past and Present*, no. 20 (1961)

O'Tuathaigh, M.A.G. 'The Irish in Nineteenth Century Britain: Problems of Integration', *Transactions of the Royal Historical Society*, 31 (1981)

Pelling, H. *Popular Politics and Society in Late Victorian Britain* (London, 1968)

Perkin, H. *The Origins of Modern English Society 1780–1880* (London, 1972)

Pollard, S. *History of Labour in Sheffield* (Liverpool, 1959)

——'Nineteenth-Century Cooperation: From Community-Building to Shopkeeping', in A. Briggs and J. Saville (eds.), *Essays in Labour History*, vol. 1 (1960)

Prothero, I.J. 'London Chartism and the Trades', *Economic History Review*, 24 (1971)

Read, D. 'Chartism in Manchester', in A. Briggs (ed.), *Chartist Studies* (London, 1959)

Reid, A. 'Politics and Economics in the Formation of the British Working Class: A Response to H.F. Moorhouse', *Social History*, 3 (1978)

Reid, C. 'Middle-Class Values and Working-Class Culture in Nineteenth-century Sheffield', in S. Pollard and C. Holmes (eds.), *Essays in the Economic and Social History of South Yorkshire* (Barnsley, 1976)

——'Class and Culture', Society for the Study of Labour History Bulletin, no. 34 (Spring 1977)

Reid, D.A. 'The Decline of Saint Monday, 1766–1876', *Past and Present*, 71 (1976)

Reid, T.D.W. and C.A.N. 'The 1842 "Plug Plot" in Stockport', *International Review of Social History',* vol. XXIV (1979)

Roberts, R. *The Classic Slum* (Manchester, 1971)

Rose, E.A. *Methodism in Droylsden 1776–1963* (Droylsden, 1964)

——*Methodism in Ashton-under-lyne 1797–1914* (Ashton-under-Lyne, 1969)

——*Methodism in Dukinfield* (the author?, 1978)

Rose, M.E. 'Rochdale Man and the Stalybridge Riot: The Relief and Control of the Unemployed during the Lancashire Cotton Famine', in A.P. Donajgrodzki (ed.), *Social Control in Nineteenth-Century Britain* (London, 1977)

Saville, J. *Ernest Jones, Chartist* (London, 1952)

Smith, J.H. 'Ten Acres of Deansgate in 1851', *Transactions of the Lancashire and Cheshire Antiquarian Society* (1980)

Sofner, R.'Attitudes and Allegiances in the Unskilled North', *International Review of Social History*, III (1965)

Sykes, R. 'Some Aspects of Working-Class Consciousness in Oldham 1830–1842', *Historical Journal*, 23, I (1980)

——'Early Chartism and Trade Unionism in South-East Lancashire', in J. Epstein and D. Thompson (eds.), *The Chartist Experience* (London, 1982)

Thernstrom, S. 'Working-Class Social Mobility in Industrial America', in P. Stearns and D.J. Walkowitz (eds.), *Workers in the Industrial Revolution* (New Brunswick, 1974)

Tholfsen, T.R. *Working Class Radicalism in Mid-Victorian England* (London, 1976)

Thompson, D. *The Early Chartists* (London, 1971)

——'Women and Nineteenth-Century Radical Politics: A Lost Dimension', in J. Mitchell and A. Oakley (eds.), *The Rights and Wrongs of Women* (London, 1976)

——'Ireland and the Irish in English Radicalism before 1850', in J. Epstein and D. Thompson (eds.), *The Chartist Experience* (London, 1982)

Thompson, E.P. *The Making of the English Working Class* (Harmondsworth, 1968)

——'The Peculiarities of the English' and 'The Poverty of Theory: Or an Orrery of Errors', in E.P. Thompson, *The Poverty of Theory* (London, 1978)

——'The Politics of Theory', in R. Samuel (ed.), *People's History and Socialist Theory* (London, 1981)

Tiller, K. 'Late Chartism', in J. Epstein and D. Thompson (eds.), *The Chartist Experience* (London, 1982)

Turner, H.A. *Trade Union Growth, Structure and Policy* (London, 1962)

Unwin, G. Samuel Oldknow and the Arkwrights: The Industrial Revolution at Stockport and Mellor (Manchester, 1924)

Vincent, J. *The Formation of the British Liberal Party 1857–68* (Harmondsworth, 1972)

Ward, J.T. *Chartism* (London, 1973)

——*The Factory Movement 1830–1855* (London, 1962)

Webbs, S. and B., *The History of Trade Unionism* (New York, 1920)

Werly, J.H. 'The Irish in Manchester 1832–1849', *Irish Historical Studies*, no. 71 (March, 1973)

INDEX

Abram, W.A. 85, 110
Aitken, William 63, 164, 274, 286
Amalgamated Association of Operative Cotton Spinners 280-1
Amalgamated Beamers, Twisters and Drawers Society 291
Amalgamated Committee of Factory Operatives 286
Amalgamated Society of Engineers 137, 268, 274
America, United States of 210, 311
Ancoats, Manchester 105, 109, 114, 190, 230
Anderson, Michael 40-1, 79, 104
Anti-Corn Law League 54, 56, 64
Armitage, Elkanah 185, 245
Arnold, R.A. 122
artisans 39-40; *see also* building trades, shoemakers, tailors, labour aristocracy
Ashton Bond of Brotherhood 212, 223-4
Ashton Brothers of Hyde (cotton manufacturers) 255, 283
Ashton Cardroom Hands Union 273
Ashton Co-operative Society 139, 199, 228
Ashton Operative Joiners Union 274
Ashton Protestant Association 319
Ashton Reform Association 56
Ashton Reporter 165, 183-4, 242-4, 260, 286-7, 292, 323, 341
Ashton Standard 243-4, 275, 293, 337
Ashton-under-Lyne x, 23, 32-3, 38-44, 46-51, 54-9, 63-4, 68-70, 72, 84, 108-10, 114, 116-21, 139, 143, 147, 151, 162-5, 192, 197, 199-200, 202-6, 212, 228, 242-4, 248, 254-60, 263, 269, 273, 282, 284-6, 288-9, 292, 294, 316-18, 320, 322, 325, 327-8, 330, 334-5, 337-9
Ashworth, Samuel 139

Bacup 250-1
Baker, Robert 102
Banks, T. 259, 265, 269, 285

Barnsby, G.J. 79, 104
Barnsley 54-5
Bates, William 140, 144
Belchem, John 59
Bell, William 142
Bintcliffe, Jonathan 257, 260
Birkenhead 316
Birley family of Manchester 38, 185
Birley, Hugh 340
Birmingham 18, 79, 104, 113
Blackburn 10, 33-4, 38-40, 41, 49-50, 124, 192, 211, 246, 249, 256, 265, 287-8, 290, 319, 323, 337
Blackburn Female Reform Society 211
Blackburn Protestant Association 337
Blackburn Standard List (1853) 254-5, 269, 278, 290, 304n59
blacksmiths 134
Blackstone Edge, Yorkshire 68
Bolton 22, 33-4, 38-40, 45, 49-50, 92, 109-10, 200-1, 212-13, 215, 231, 256, 266, 270, 273, 284, 335
Bolton master spinners 289
Bolton Spinners Union 273, 284
Booth, Nathan 227-8
Booth, William 138
Bradford, Yorkshire 54-5, 192, 225
Bray, John Francis 211
Brelsford, Anthony 140
Bridges, J.H. 258-9, 261, 295
Brierley, Ben 197, 210, 214-15, 321
Briggs, Asa x, 65
Bright, Jacob 165
Bright, John 70, 164, 179, 184, 336, 339
Broadbent, J.M. 163
Brotherton, Edward 105, 107, 112, 185
Buchanan, Dr George 124-5
Buckley family of Ashton 54, 297
Buckley, Nathaniel 293
building societies 139
building trades 35, 39-40; and Irish 315, 325; 1869 strike 266-7
Bull, Rev. George Stringer 286
Burnley 23, 34, 38, 192, 250
Burnley Master Spinners and Manu-